THE MALDIVES

G000256672

J. J. ROBINSON

The Maldives

Islamic Republic, Tropical Autocracy

HURST & COMPANY, LONDON

First published in the United Kingdom in 2015 by
C. Hurst & Co. (Publishers) Ltd.,
41 Great Russell Street, London, WC1B 3PL
© J. J. Robinson, 2015
All rights reserved.
Printed in India

Distributed in the United States, Canada and Latin America by
Oxford University Press, 198 Madison Avenue, New York, NY 10016,
United States of America.

The right of J. J. Robinson to be identified as the author of
this publication is asserted by them in accordance with the
Copyright, Designs and Patents Act, 1988.

A Cataloguing-in-Publication data record for this book is available
from the British Library.

978-1-84904-589-6 *paperback*

This book is printed using paper from registered sustainable
and managed sources.

www.hurstpublishers.com

CONTENTS

v

ACKNOWLEDGEMENTS

To the team at *Minivan News*, past and present, and all those whose hard work, heroism and hope for a better Maldives made this book possible.

CAST

A note on Maldivian naming conventions: Maldivians are given Islamic names, mixed with some traditional Maldivian names (such as "Didi"). Rather than defaulting to surname or forename, people usually refer to a person by their most unique identifier: for example, Ahmed Nazeer's friends will call him "Nazeer". To further distinguish themselves, many Maldivians adopt a nickname through which they are known to the wider community—even if this does not appear on formal documents. These can be taken from a business, house, or just made up or given by friends, and are commonly used even in official circles. Nicknames, where noted, are included in quotes. Former President Mohamed Nasheed, for example, is commonly referred to by supporters as "Anni".

Major Characters

Mohamed "Anni" Nasheed First democratically elected president (2008), former political prisoner, toppled in a coup (2012). Affiliated with the Maldivian Democratic Party (MDP).

Maumoon Abdul Gayoom Ruler of the Maldives (1978–2008), Asia's longest serving dictator. Head of the Progressive Party of the Maldives (PPM).

Abdulla Yameen Gayoom's half-brother and President of the Maldives (2013–) Affiliated with the PPM.

Dr. Mohamed Waheed Hassan Manik Nasheed's vice president, later President of the Maldives (2012–2013) following the 2012 coup. Head of the Gaumee Ithihaad Party (GIP).

Gasim Ibrahim business/resort tycoon, member of parliament, media mogul, former member of the Judicial Services Commission (judicial watchdog). Former Finance Minister under Gayoom. Head of the Jumhoree Party (JP).

Fuwad Thowfeek Elections Commissioner (2008–2014).

Aishath Velezinee Member of Judicial Services Commission, whistleblower.

Dunya Maumoon Gayoom's daughter, State Foreign Minister under Dr. Waheed, Foreign Minister under President Yameen.

Umar Naseer former police officer under Gayoom, accused of torture. Energetic political activist, Home Minister under Abdulla Yameen (PPM).

Abdulla Riyaz Police Commissioner under Dr. Waheed.

Mohamed Nazim Instrumental in 2012 coup. Defence Minister under Dr. Waheed. Later arrested under President Yameen and accused of plotting to overthrow the government (again).

Azima Shukoor Gayoom's lawyer, Attorney General under Dr. Waheed (PPM).

Dr. Hassan Saeed former Attorney General under Gayoom, later President Waheed's Special Advisor. Head of the Dhivehi Qaumee Party (DQP).

Dr. Mohamed Jameel Justice Minister under Gayoom. Home Minister under Dr. Waheed, Vice President under Yameen, until falling out of favour in 2015 (DQP).

Sheikh Mohamed Shaheem Ali Saeed State Islamic Minister under Nasheed, Islamic Minister under Dr. Waheed, Yameen. Affiliated with the Adhaalath Party (AP).

Dr. Ahmed Shaheed Foreign Minister under Gayoom, Nasheed. Later, UN Special Rapporteur on Iran.

Judge Abdulla Mohamed Chief Judge of the Criminal Court, arrested by President Nasheed in the lead up to the 2012 coup.

Judge Ali Hameed Supreme Court judge allegedly appearing in multiple sex videos.

Sheikh Imran Abdulla Head of Adhaalath Party, (2013–).

Ahmed Adeeb Tourism Minister under President Yameen, appointed Vice President in July 2015 after constitutional amendment allowing the 33 year-old to take office (PPM).

Minivan News team (assorted)

Note: 'Minivan' means 'independent' in Dhivehi. The publication underwent a rebrand in July 2015 and is now the *Maldives Independent*. Old content remains accessible but is also archived on The Wayback Machine

JJ Robinson British/Australian, editor, (2009–2013).

Ahmed Naish Maldivian, journalist and soul of Minivan (2008–2015).

Neil Merrett Welsh, journalist/marketing/admin/JJ's deputy (2011–2013).

Hawwa Lubna Maldivian journalist (2012–2013), scored a scholarship with University of Lund, Sweden.

Maryam Omidi Iranian-born past editor, JJ's predecessor (2008–2009).

Mariyath "Ehju" Mohamed Maldivian journalist, listed on Reporters Without Borders' list of 'Top 100 Information Heroes'.

Mohamed Naahii Maldivian journalist (2011–2014), studying law (moved to UN).

Ahmed Rilwan Maldivian journalist. Missing, believed kidnapped by fundamentalists in August 2014.

Zaheena Rasheed Maldivian journalist, studied at Middlebury in US. Deputy editor after JJ's departure, later editor from 2015.

Eleanor Johnstone US, intern 2012.

Daniel Bosley UK, intern 2012, later editor after JJ's departure (2014–2015).

Luke Powell UK intern 2013.

Leah Malone US, journalist 2013.

Mazin 'Maani' Rafeeq Maldivian, intern, 2010.

Mohamed "Aeko" Fathith Maldivian, translator, *Minivan News* Dhivehi site.

Ahmed Nazeer Maldivian, journalist, JJ's first hire (2009–2014).

Mohamed "Redey" Naseem Maldivian, Minivan's managing director.

David Hardingham Head of UK-based Friends of Maldives NGO, Minivan's moral support.

Notable political parties

Maldivian Democratic Party (MDP): Party of Mohamed "Anni" Nasheed, the Maldives' first democratically elected president.

Dhivehi Rayithunge Party (DRP): Started by former dictator Maumoon Abdul Gayoom to contest MDP in 2008 election.

Progressive Party of the Maldives (PPM): Gayoom's new party created ahead of 2013 election, following acrimonious split with DRP.

Jumhoree Party (JP): Small party headed by resort tycoon and MP, Gasim Ibrahim.

People's Alliance (PA): Small party of Gayoom's half-brother, Abdulla Yameen, until he joined the PPM and became its presidential candidate.

Dhivehi Qaumee Party (DQP): Small party of President Waheed's advisor, Dr. Hassan Saeed, and Dr. Mohamed Jameel (prior to his joining the PPM).

Adhaalath Party (AP): Small party contesting on religious platform.

Gaumee Itihaad Party (GIP): Small party of Dr. Mohamed Waheed Hassan Manik, who took over the presidency after the 2012 coup.

TIMELINE

1153	Maldives converted from Buddhism to Islam under King Dhovemi Kalaminja.
1558	Portuguese invade, establish garrison and trading post.
1573	Portuguese driven out in revolt led by Muhammad Thakurufaanu Al-Azam.
1887	Maldives becomes a British Protectorate.
1941	British establish airbase on Gan in Addu Atoll.
1959	Southern atolls break away and form United Suvadive Republic.
1962	Suvadive secession violently ended by President Ibrahim Nasir.
1965	Maldives gains full independence from Britain.
1972	First resort opens.
1976	Britain closes Gan airbase.
1978	Maumoon Abdul Gayoom takes over presidency from Ibrahim Nasir.
1988	Coup attempt against President Maumoon Abdul Gayoom, backed by Tamil mercenaries, fails after India intervenes
Sept 2003	Death in custody of Evan Naseem sparks protests, leading to a violent crackdown.
2004	Indian Ocean Tsunami kills 108 people, causes US$400 million in damage
2003–2007	International pressure for greater democratic concessions, especially recognition of opposition and release of political prisoner, Mohamed Nasheed.
Aug 2008	Pressure for reform culminates in new, democratic constitution.
Oct 2008	New opposition movement, led by Mohamed Nasheed's MDP, wins a coalition victory over Gayoom in second round of voting. He leaves office as Asia's longest-serving dictator.

May 2009	Gayoom's party wins parliamentary majority.
Oct 2009	Nasheed gains international climate change profile with underwater cabinet meeting.
Oct 2009	JJ arrives as new editor of Minivan News, replacing Maryam Omidi.
Jun 2010	Cabinet briefly resigns over "scorched earth" tactics of Gayoom-majority parliament.
July 2010	Judicial oversight body reappoints all Gayoom regime's judges, many unqualified and with criminal records, dismissing new constitution's standards as "symbolic".
7 Aug 2010	End of constitutional interim period, and deadline for appointment of judiciary under new code of conduct.
10 Aug 2010	New Supreme Court judges approved by parliament in closed-door horse-trading.
Jan 2011	Whistleblower from judicial oversight body stabbed three times in broad daylight.
23 Dec 2011	Fractured opposition and disgruntled former MDP coalition partners unite at "Defend Islam" rally, one of the Maldives' largest public gatherings ever.
16 Jan 2011	Nasheed's government arrests Chief Criminal Court Judge Abdulla Mohamed, citing corruption.
30 Jan 2012	Nasheed's Vice President, Dr Mohamed Waheed, holds midnight meeting at his house with members of the former regime.
7 Feb 2012	Police and army mutiny, storm the state broadcaster and force Nasheed to resign. Old regime returns to power under Dr Mohamed Waheed as figurehead President.
8 Feb 2012	Police crack down violently on demonstrators in front of international media.
30 Aug 2012	Regime releases Commonwealth-backed report finding no evidence of coup.
27 Nov 2012	Regime evicts Indian infrastructure giant GMR, the Maldives' single largest foreign investor, with a week's notice, after declaring contract void.
Early 2013	Government seeks to sentence Nasheed over 2011 detention of Judge Abdulla, to prevent him contesting 2013 elections.
Feb 2013	Nasheed evades arrest by seeking asylum in Indian embassy.
7 Sept 2013	First round of presidential election contested by business tycoon Gasim Ibrahim, Gayoom's half-brother Abdulla Yameen,

	President Mohamed Waheed, and opposition leader Mohamed Nasheed. Nasheed and Yameen to contest run-off on Sept 28.
23 Sept	Supreme Court overthrows result of first round after Gasim complains, introduces restrictive guidelines for elections.
28 Sept 2013	Police block Elections Commission from conducting second round of voting.
7 Oct 2013	Opposition-aligned Raajje TV studio destroyed in petrol-bombing.
19 Oct 2013	Third attempt at election blocked by Supreme Court, Yameen and Gasim. Security forces block polls, blockade Elections Commission.
9 Nov 2013	Fourth attempt at election. Results mirror annulled first round. Nasheed and Yameen to contest run-off on Nov 16, after end of presidential term.
9 Nov 2013	Supreme Court extends Presidential term.
11 Nov	End of Presidential term. President Waheed stays in power.
14 Nov	Gasim publicly endorses Yameen for President.
15 Nov	President Waheed flees to Singapore on 'state visit'.
16 Nov	Run off polls. Yameen wins with 51 per cent of the vote and becomes next President of the Maldives. Turnout at 92 per cent.
Dec 2013	JJ leaves Maldives, passes Minivan editorship to Daniel Bosley.
Mar 2014	Supreme Court sacks Elections Commissioner.
Jul 2014	Armed Salafi gangs begin kidnapping and interrogating young people in broad daylight.
8 Aug 2014	Minivan News journalist Ahmed Rilwan kidnapped at knife-point outside his home. Still missing one year later.
Feb 2015	Regime arrests former President Nasheed.
Mar 2015	Nasheed found guilty of 'terrorism', sentenced to 13 years imprisonment.

PROLOGUE

"The mind is its own place, and in itself can make a heaven of hell, a hell of heaven."

John Milton

If you want an authentic answer, start the interview with a little flattery. "You're about the only head of state to come out of the Arab Spring—and probably South Asia—without blood on your hands. What's your secret?"

Mohamed "Anni" Nasheed—former political prisoner, global climate change icon, first democratically elected President of the Maldives—stared across the conference table.

"Losing," he grinned.

I was back in the capital Malé, the candy-coloured, 2.2-square-kilometre metropolis jutting out of the Indian Ocean that was my home for four years while I was editor of the country's first and only attempt at a credible national media outlet. That night I slept on the office couch, opposite the desk from which I'd covered riots, coups d'état, murders, floggings, drownings, human trafficking, economic malaise, elections—the fourth estate in a four-year experiment in democracy.

I slept more soundly than I had in months. I'd convinced myself it was a research trip for the book. Perhaps it was also partly an exorcism.

The Maldives is an archipelago of 1,192 islands south of India, populated by 350,000 people of mixed Indian, Sinhalese, Malay, Chinese, Indonesian, Arab, Persian, East African, Portuguese and even French descent. Only 200 of the islands are inhabited by locals, while a further 100 host the upmarket luxury tropical beach resorts most people imagine when they hear the country being mentioned.

PROLOGUE

The Maldives was Buddhist until the twelfth century, when its ruler forcibly converted it to Islam with the help of visiting Arab trader Abul Barakathul Yousuful and a troublesome virgin-devouring sea monster. Throughout its history it was ruled by a succession of kings and sultans, and aside from a brief, ill-fated sixteenth-century attempt by the Portuguese and a stint as a British protectorate from 1887 to 1965, was never colonized. Instead, powerful families in the capital oversaw a cycle of bloody leadership changes. The first reformist president, Amin Didi, introduced educational reforms and promoted women's rights in the 1940s, and was beaten to death in the street after riots by Islamic conservatives. The second attempt at a republic under President Ibrahim Nasir ended in 1978 with him fleeing to Singapore.

The man who replaced him, Maumoon Abdul Gayoom, would become Asia's longest serving dictator, ruling the Maldives for thirty years unmolested—aside from a failed 1988 coup attempt by Tamil Tiger mercenaries.

The introduction of multi-party democracy in 2008 marked the first peaceful transfer of power in the Maldives and was a bellwether for the Arab Spring, a good two years before the first stirrings in Tunisia. The Maldives would also, in technicolour, preempt the problems that emerged afterwards across the region. Indeed, this remote and tiny nation is a testbed for the world's current political, social, economic, religious and environmental maladies, on a scale both observable and solvable. Yet if the all the Western world's good intentions could not sustain democracy and human rights in a country with barely the population of a small European city, what hope for Egypt, Libya, Tunisia, Turkey, Burma?

This book is the story of the Maldivian democratic experiment, told from the privileged vantage point of an observer simultaneously engaged with and detached from the Maldives and its colourful cast of victims, villains and heroes. It is also an account of a small news outlet's attempt to tell that story as it unfolded. As a journalist I sought to be impartial, identify and shelve my own biases and prejudices, give voice to those who had never had one before, hold governments accountable, and explain byzantine political manoeuvring and mundane wickedness factually and respectfully. Now, I cannot shake off the feeling that this traditional and popular understanding of journalism is somehow flawed. After ten years in the profession, it is an uncomfortable feeling.

1

CHAINS AND COCONUTS

"If you are a young, urban couple looking for a week of hedonistic bliss, this is the ideal place. It has that Jade Jagger-lifestyle appeal: no dress code, no formality and virtually no one around to cramp your style. The Ocean Pavilions are the size of a loft, with two bedrooms, a dining room, a fibre-optic illuminated swimming pool, an outdoor Jacuzzi and steps down onto your own patch of reef. Guests in pavilion accommodation get a 24-hour butler service, while the rest of the resort gets a FISH (Fast Island Service Host), which amounts to the same thing. It has the biggest wine cellar of any resort in the Maldives—6000 bottles. £££££"

Condé Nast Traveller[1]

Tourists at more than a hundred upmarket island resorts tucked into their mountainous breakfast buffets. Hundreds of tons of imported bacon, sausages, smoked meats, exotic cheese, tropical fruits and *pain au chocolat* would fuel the gruelling waddle to the beach and a morning crisping under the heavy tropical glare.

On the prison island next door, the future President of the Maldives was being fed a breakfast of broken glass. A twenty-minute boat ride away, his youngest daughter was being born in his absence.

Outside the cells in the prison courtyard, the ants were breakfasting on Mohamed "Redey" Naseem. "I was handcuffed to a coconut tree and the guards poured sugar water on my head. Then they fed me to the ants," he recalled. Redey was serving seven years for refusing to confess to being a drug user, such stubbornness being frowned upon during President Gayoom's rule.

1

The judge, lacking evidence, but reasoning that since Redey had previous drug convictions he must also be guilty of the latest batch of charges, had entrusted him to fourteen years in the care of Maafushi Island prison's imaginative guards.

An unprecedented chain of events would see him set free seven years ahead of schedule. In September 2003 one of his fellow inmates, 19-year-old Evan Naseem, was beaten to death by prison officers. While custodial torture and unexplained disappearance of inmates were prevalent under Gayoom's regime, Evan Naseem's mother took the unusual step of defying the authorities and publicly displaying her son's bruised and battered body in the centre of Republic Square, the largest open area in the capital island of Malé.

A submissive population hitherto willing to ignore dark rumours, subdued by strict Islamic obedience and decades of regime entreaties to "respect our national unity", was finally confronted with inescapable evidence.

The resulting riots led to a cascade of events now familiar to watchers of the Arab Spring, striking the Maldives seven years before a Tunisian fruit seller would fatally set himself aflame. Maafushi's prison guards shot twenty inmates in the 2003 riots, killing three and injuring seventeen, but only succeeded in fanning the dissent now spreading outside the walls. Gayoom's squad of special operations police, dubbed the "Star Force", cracked down violently on the demonstrators, igniting further public animosity and drawing both international media attention and visits from Amnesty International. A world that had heard only about pristine beaches and luxury resorts was introduced to Maldivian politics.

His legacy—and potentially his wife's ability to shop at upmarket London department stores—at stake, Gayoom conceded to democratic reforms. The international community, its foot now firmly wedged in the door, pressured Gayoom to legitimize the opposition Maldivian Democratic Party (MDP) and release its leader from prison.

Nasheed was by now an Amnesty prisoner of conscience. The British government, through the Westminster Foundation, had meanwhile begun helping transform the MDP from a mob of rowdy activists into a political party with its own progressive manifesto.

With a heavily-monitored election looming and a new, relatively liberal constitution in place, Gayoom's ministers sensed change and turned on him. The most ambitious formed their own scattered parties and entered into coalition with the MDP, in a bid to topple their former leader's hastily forged Dhivehi Rayithunge Party (DRP).

The presidential election was held in October 2008. Nasheed's coalition triumphed, and the stunned eighty-something dictator dazedly wandered out of office. He was Asia's longest serving ruler.

Redey was released from jail just in time for the Maldives' first multi-party democratic elections and the fall of Gayoom's government. Despite Redey's newfound freedom to drive his (MDP canary yellow) moped around the capital, in many respects he hadn't left his cell, often drifting into Shawshank-style expositions on fellow inmates and the creative tortures of the guards.

Meanwhile, President Nasheed was riding a wave of international attention and popularity. Young, impulsive and energetic with a boyish charm, the narrative of a jailed and tortured human rights activist overcoming his oppressive captor to succeed him as president—in a bloodless and democratic election no less—endeared him to foreign journalists. Coming ninth in 2010's list of "Hottest Heads of State" didn't hurt.[2]

Nasheed proved himself a master showman. In 2009 he held an underwater cabinet meeting highlighting the country's vulnerability to global warming. The widely publicized revelation that none of the country's 1,192 islands stood more than a metre above sea level put the Maldives on the map for something other than package holidays, and saw Nasheed's international currency soar as an environmental advocate. Wealthy Western governments loved the fact that as the leader of a small and innocuous country not enmeshed in a complex web of corporate and geopolitical interests, Nasheed could take strong and unyielding positions on climate change. Supporting him gave them green-cred-by-proxy with their own voters.

Nasheed saw this and swiftly capitalized, declaring that the Maldives would be carbon neutral by 2020, and excitedly telling at least one reporter that he was saving up money to buy land in Australia for when the Maldives was submerged by melting ice caps.

The play was shrewd. Gayoom and his retreating government had cleaned out the state coffers before their departure, leaving the Maldives in what the World Bank would describe as "the worst economic position of any country undergoing a democratic transition since 1956".[3]

Nasheed needed to fund his extensive promised reforms as well as carry the country's cripplingly bloated and unsustainable civil service, a legacy of Gayoom's desperate last minute efforts to buy votes with government jobs. Sidestepping this financial booby trap left by his predecessor, Nasheed laid on the carbon guilt trip and extended the hat to the West, which was dutifully filled with cash, projects and expertise.

Gayoom was still in the background. He did not make the same mistake of over-confidence in the crucial parliamentary elections in early 2009. Nasheed's MDP, cocky and still buoyed by its presidential win, failed to gain a majority in what turned out to be an orgy of vote-buying and big-money patronage.

The authors of the new constitution, Maldivian and foreign, had anticipated a Gayoom victory in the presidential elections and stripped the executive of its teeth. This power was instead vested in parliament. The MPs who now filled its seats on both sides talked big on democracy, but almost unanimously made little attempt at representation, or even attendance. Supplanting the traditional role of the island chief as local benefactor, the majority simply funnelled their massive salaries—similar in size to those paid to Swedish MPs—into openly bribing their constituents while making a private fortune in behind-the-scenes cash-for-vote bidding wars. One MP, offered a house, rejected it in favour of a silver BMW on the grounds he already had somewhere to live.

Gayoom had previously orchestrated the appointment of the heads of the country's new independent institutions. Now, entrenched in parliament, the old regime launched a systematic and highly successful campaign of sabotage to disrupt and strangle any attempt by the MDP to implement the democratic reforms demanded by the new constitution.

It took the MDP several years to realize it was the only party interested in following the rulebook, and longer still to realize that the constitution's "independent" referees had always been thoroughly compromised by its rival. Faced with the prospect of remaining democratic but ineffectual, the MDP in 2011 traded idealism for pragmatism. Key MPs switched sides in a parliament that degenerated into a mockery of a football transfer market. But critical tax reforms were passed, and some hope for the economy was salvaged. The introduction of a 3.5 per cent Goods and Services Tax (GST) revealed the tourism industry to be worth US$2.5 billion: three times larger than any previous estimates.

Against all odds, by late 2011 the trends were positive. Nasheed had forced through universal healthcare, a pension scheme, welfare for single parents and the elderly, freeing many from implied bondage to the wealthy and corrupt. The economy was still crippled, but financial reforms, international goodwill, investor confidence in the stability of the new democracy and a healthy tourism economy saw all the important graphs pointing upwards.

The MDP had also shed the former government ministers and coalition partners who helped bring it to power, many of whom loudly and publicly protested over not having received the favours, treatment or attention they had been promised or felt they deserved. These slights were taken personally: one Maldivian human rights activist turned on Nasheed after failing to receive a diplomatic passport he insisted he had been promised.

Still, by late 2011 the remnants of the former regime were running low on issues and fragmenting as they turned on each other, becoming more irrelevant with every passing month. Police became adept at quieting the occasional rent-a-mob protest by swiftly pepper-spraying the ringleader, after which the less-than-enthusiastic crowds would quickly dissolve for lack of motivation. The wind was blowing in Nasheed's favour.

Sensing its growing irrelevance, the opposition used the last card it had: Islam. Liberal-minded and British-educated, but president of an Islamic country where freedom of religion was outlawed and the merest sip of liquor a political death sentence, Nasheed had steered clear of religion. The constitution, while largely progressive, had been amended during the drafting committee stage to enshrine a tough-on-sin line popular with those who liked to imagine others drowning in hellfire for the actions they were themselves only too happy to commit every weekend in neighbouring Sri Lanka. As such, every Maldivian was constitutionally required to be Sunni Muslim and all lawmaking "contrary to the tenets of Islam" was banned.

Nasheed, partial to dancing, music, cigarettes and the traditional Maldivian love of a good party, had few populist religious credentials. Gayoom, on the other hand, was a trained Islamic scholar and alumni of Egypt's Al Azhar University, a world centre for Islamic learning. He showed no qualms about using religion as a political weapon.

Xenophobic Islamic nationalism was the last throw of the dice for the old regime, and a risky one, as it gave legitimacy to fundamentalism now out of the bag in a country completely dependent on Western tourism. The tactic worked, uniting the feuding opposition parties and embittered former MDP coalition partners under a single banner for one of the country's largest-ever rallies, the so-called 23 December (2011) protest to "Defend Islam" in the Maldives.

Their demands included the removal of idolatrous "monuments" gifted to the Maldives by other countries in the South Asian Association for Regional Cooperation (SAARC). Somebody knocked the head off the lion statue gifted by Sri Lanka, while the chief offending gift was donated by Pakistan—a country one imagines really should have known better. Theirs was a monument topped by a bust of the country's founder Muhammad Ali Jinnah and embossed with artefacts of its pre-Islamic Indus Valley civilization. The religious grounds

5

for vandalizing the monuments were highly suspect: Nepal's heretical monument, also subsequently smashed, consisted of a small metal sign saying "Nepal".

Another demand was the closure of spas and massage parlours across the country, many of which in the capital Malé were thriving and loosely disguised fronts for prostitution. The closure presumably did not include those venues belonging to local resort tycoons, several of whom were key contributors to the rally, and indeed opposition political figures themselves.

Backed into a corner, Nasheed called the bluff and issued a memo ordering all resorts across the country to close their spas. Almost every resort had "resort and spa" tacked onto the end of its name; politics was finally challenging the tourism industry and threatening its coveted isolation from the rest of the country.

Pockets under threat, the politico tycoons stumbled and prevaricated. Smelling blood, Nasheed approached the Supreme Court and asked it to rule on whether the import and sale of bacon and alcohol to foreign tourists was indeed "contrary to the tenets of Islam"[4] as stipulated in the constitution. The judges were trapped, facing the choice of overturning the constitution or upholding it and obliterating the country's bikini-, liquor- and fornication-based economy. They declined to rule at all.

Nasheed's bluff had worked. He scored his first religious points, and the opposition retired to scheme and lick its wounds. Resort managers nervously awaited the next instalment.

2

"CONTROVERSIAL TRANSFER OF POWER"

"Do I look like someone who would bring about a coup d'etat?"
President Dr. Mohamed Waheed Hassan

It was seven in the morning several months later on 7 February 2012. Redey was by now non-executive managing director of Web News Company, the unassuming corporate front of the Maldives' first and only independent English language news service. This was an unpaid position he occupied by virtue of both his loyalty to the cause of independent media and unquestioning willingness to sign company cheques. Such was his dedication that he would occasionally hold night-long vigils in the office to protect it from arson attacks by local gangs, or disgruntled members of the sales team.

The tall and lanky 50-year-old hadn't slept much that night. He had been at an area of the island capital of Malé known as the artificial beach when a rent-a-mob belonging to Gayoom's opposition party had clashed with an MDP rally. He had watched as police suddenly sided with the old regime and began charging down the narrow streets, beating supporters of Nasheed's ruling party.

Nasheed ordered the police to withdraw. They refused, but broke off from the area as the army's crowd control squad arrived. The rogue police regrouped and headed for Republic Square, via a brief detour to ransack the MDP's headquarters. The security services had begun to mutiny against their commander-in-chief.

Redey's call woke me. For a Maldivian to make a work-related phone call before 11am, let alone breakfast, signaled trouble.

"Something big is happening, JJ."

For a moment I closed my eyes and pondered going back to sleep. The newsroom was just downstairs next to the kitchen, after all, and Gayoom's party had been holding loud and increasingly ineffectual rallies for much of January, protesting against Nasheed's detention of a senior judge.

Chief Criminal Court Judge Abdulla Mohamed was complicit in protecting Gayoom and his cohort from investigation for corruption and human rights abuses during his rule. The judge had also been accused by the government of having links to organized crime—a supposition some reached by studying his track record of arbitrarily releasing obvious felons. He had dodged repeated attempts at disciplinary procedures thanks to his colleagues on the judicial watchdog, and avoided arrest through an increasingly farcical series of manoeuvres that culminated in his taking and hiding the court's warrant stamp in his home every evening. Without a warrant it was illegal for police to arrest him, he reasoned, while any political allies detained could be swiftly freed for "lack of evidence". Trials of loyal thugs and influential drug dealers could likewise be derailed by arbitrarily dismissing state prosecutors for presumed infractions, "contempt of court" being an honorable offence by this point.

Gayoom's new Progressive Party of the Maldives (PPM), the fuchsia-pink offspring of a hostile schism with his original DRP, had spent the better part of a year ineffectually calling for the nightly overthrow of the democratically elected government. This, the PPM declared, was justified due to an assortment of charges against the state which included "consorting with Jews", attempts to "destroy Islam" and judicial interference—notably Nasheed's attempts to arrest and investigate the chief judge.

Much of the media, not to mention the population, was suffering from megaphone fatigue, and just wanted a night's sleep without pick-up trucks with loudspeakers calling for defenders of the nation to emerge from their beds and overthrow the government at 2am every morning.

But that Tuesday, there was something different in the air. I rolled out of bed, grabbed my DSLR camera, stuffed a notebook into the back pocket of my trousers and headed for the square. It was about the earliest I'd been awake in the past two years.

Republic Square is the largest open area in this congested concrete jungle of a city, bordered by the ocean and tourist jetties on the north side, police headquarters on the east, central bank on the west and military base on the south.

An enormous flagpole towers over an empty and decrepit fountain in the centre, providing a thin sliver of shade for the hundreds of indentured Bangladeshi labourers who flocked there on Fridays—their sole reprieve from building the city, sweeping its streets, washing its cars and lugging about its rubbish.

Early on a Tuesday morning the square should have been deserted. Instead, it contained a thousand-strong angry mob of pro-Gayoom demonstrators, paid gang auxiliaries and a great many plain clothed and uniformed police officers.

Several years into the job by this stage, I considered myself a connoisseur of Maldivian political uprisings and thought nothing about wading into furious crowds a full head shorter than me. But two things about this one were striking. Firstly, the team of police who normally oversaw such events and stopped anything getting seriously out of hand were conspicuously absent. Instead, these police were at the centre of the mob, many still in uniform, some busily distributing riot gear to fellow belligerents.

Secondly, the mob had already forced the ranks of military police back into their base behind their portcullis and were now making a decent attempt at storming the gates. The green-uniformed military police were less experienced and less exotically trained than the police special operations squad, most of whom were the remnants of Gayoom's former Star Force—the same officers who made up much of the mutineers' force. The police and military had earlier clashed in the square but the result was indecisive, and an army truck filled with military-grade riot equipment had been abandoned outside the walls and looted by the rioters. The military police arrayed themselves along the walls of their headquarters, peering from the parapets and firing tear gas canisters into the crowd.

This early victory had filled the mob with confidence by the time I arrived. The tear gas was proving ineffective due to the size of the square and the gusty northerly wind, which was blowing it south into the barracks and across the city. The police across the street had distributed their gas masks to the mob trying to break in, and the mood inside the army base was no doubt further sullied by the smouldering canisters now being thrown back over the wall.

I was in the thick of the crowd. The head of the Maldives Journalists Association, Ahmed "Hiriga" Zahir, scuttled past and stopped when he saw me. Hiriga had prospered under Gayoom's propaganda state, training and mentoring a generation of journalists to "respect our national unity". After 2008 he switched jobs to be the figurehead of the new private media establishment and hold the new liberal democracy to account.

"It's not safe for you to be here," he said, a little guiltily.

Hearing this, a paunchy middle-aged man wearing a shirt and tie recognized me and came up to scream in my face. "This government is over. Now you will report what we tell you," he declared.

I became acutely aware of a sense of impunity and impending crisis. With the police mutinying, the army ineffectual and under siege, and a population of 140,000 compressed into a tiny island with no escape, split by bitter political turmoil and a history of torture and arbitrary imprisonment, there was a good chance that the day would end poorly.

The local media was divided on partisan lines, owned and funded at a loss by political oligarchs, and was busily whipping up revolutionary fervour. Aside from myself there were no foreign journalists in Malé and little foreign diplomatic presence, although this was to rapidly change in the days to come. A lack of credible witnesses meant truth was about to become the first casualty. This, I realized, meant the bar to career-making journalism was suddenly very low indeed.

The mob which had been focused on the army base began to show an interest at the incongruous white foreigner in their midst. Luckily a tear gas canister landed at my feet, the smoke driving the curious back even as the contact lens sizzled in my eyes.

I took some photos, and retreated to the outskirts of the square to join the throng of spectators.

"I wouldn't show that today," suggested an older man in the crowd of spectators, pointing at the *Minivan News* press ID card dangling from my neck. *Minivan*, meaning "independent" in Dhivehi, was functionally impartial—as much as I was—but retained a tainted political reputation due to its origins as an MDP outfit.

The police and their gang of auxiliaries had the military penned into the barracks, with President Nasheed also trapped inside. It appeared to be a stalemate, and time to break the story.

It struck me on the way back to the office how normal life was continuing, despite the dramatic events unfolding a few blocks away. There was the odd concession to the chaos as children arrived at schools and teachers waited outside the gate distributing tissues, water and wet wipes to rinse off the tear gas that had spread through the narrow streets of the city, burning tender skin.

Minivan's reporters were trickling into the newsroom as I returned. Several, spooked or distraught, had opted to stay away and not answer phone calls. With most countries lacking a diplomatic presence in the Maldives, nervous embassies and high commissions based in Sri Lanka began bombarding us for details of the emerging crisis. We were incredibly short-handed. Our visiting intern from the US, Eleanor Johnstone, was furious, trapped in the far south of the country on a resort review junket, while my second in charge, a Welshman named Neil Merrett, was hospitalized in the UK with a back injury after an ill-advised attempt at chivalry. I found myself the only foreign reporter on the ground.

Time condensed into a methodical set of priorities. I uploaded my images of the riot as a breaking news story, opened a rolling live news blog[1] to ease the torrent of phone calls and dispatched the available journalists out into the chaos. With nobody in Nasheed's government responding to calls I filed my eyewitness observations, then again tried to call his foreign press secretary, Paul Roberts. Eventually he answered.

"The opposition has been calling for the police and military to mutiny and join the mob in bringing down the country's first democratically elected government," he said.

"You're saying this is a coup?" I asked.

"Yes," he replied softly, and hung up.

Roberts was hiding in a bathroom in the President's Office as the mutineers stormed inside, having retreated behind the building's blast walls after a tear gas canister bounced past him in the street.

"The ministers were in disarray. Nobody knew what to do. My phone was going crazy, with calls from journalists and diplomats hungry for information," Roberts later recalled.

The president's senior security advisors, remembering the 1988 coup attempt that almost ended Gayoom's rule before timely arrival of Indian paratroopers, made panicked calls to New Delhi seeking military intervention.

The government's own military was not proving much help. Shortly before 11am, a stream of sixty or seventy Maldives National Defence Force (MNDF) officers filed out of the barracks and joined the mob, turning on those who had only moments before been their squad mates.

Amateur video footage of the scene inside the barracks showed the diminutive figure of President Nasheed pleading with junior soldiers to take control of the situation before the country fell apart. The troops milled about in apparent confusion—it would later emerge that critical figures in the command chain had failed to turn up despite the red alert, and were outside the barracks in civilian clothes watching events unfold.

Back in the *Minivan* office, we had just obtained footage showing a splinter group of rogue police, army officers and armed demonstrators storming the state broadcaster, the Maldives National Broadcasting Corporation (MNBC). The camera phone footage, shot from the window of the building by a reporter, showed the mob blowing open the gates to the studio's courtyard with some kind of explosive or firearm, before swarming in and seizing control.[2]

"Oh my God, they're opening [the gates], they're opening," yells a man inside, as the mob surges through the gates.

Our star reporter, Hawwa Lubna, arrived to work just in time to be given the story. She called her friends inside the station. "They just stormed into the building and broke the doors and windows to force their way in," said a female journalist. "The first guy who came into the newsroom was a protestor and he ordered us to stop all the work we were doing. He kept on stomping his feet on the ground to frighten us and threatened to 'finish us' if we didn't listen. So we stopped. We were all so scared … There were shouts and cries of girls everywhere. We felt trapped, kidnapped."

The first news anchor the armed mob tried to put on air couldn't speak for trembling. After a second attempt failed, the staff were ordered to patch the broadcast through to VTV. This was a private channel owned by Maldivian politician Gasim Ibrahim, one of the resort oligarchs responsible for backing the "Defend Islam" rallies who had risen from an early head start as Gayoom's errand boy to become one of the country's largest businessmen.

The state broadcaster's managing director Adam Shareef was discovered by the rogue security forces hiding in the lighting room. He was dragged out and presented to Ali Waheed, the brother of Nasheed's vice president, Dr. Mohamed Waheed Hassan Manik.

"He shook my hand and said that he was there to take over MNBC on behalf of Vice President Dr. Waheed," Shareef told Lubna.

The journalists were sent home, while Ali Waheed's team rebadged the station as Television Maldives (TVM)—its former moniker under Gayoom's thirty-year rule—and put on Disney's *Beauty and the Beast*. A photo circulating on Facebook showed the police and military waving batons and Maldivian flags in triumph outside the station, looking like a rowdy crowd of schoolboys posing for a post-match group photo.[3]

Lubna had previously worked at a private media outlet called Sun, owned by another politician and resort oligarch of Gasim's ilk called Ahmed Shiyam. This came with a strong anti-MDP pedigree. After speaking to her distraught friends at MNBC, she rang her journalism mentor and former boss Hiriga from the journalists' association, anticipating outrage. Instead, he expressed delight that MNBC had been liberated, and praised the police for "enforcing the law".

The seizure of the state media raised the stakes and upped the danger. It indicated to us that the day's events were premeditated, rather than a police disciplinary matter that had gotten out of hand. I was aware that *Minivan News* was the main conduit of news on the Maldives to the outside world, and could well be next.

I rang around my expat acquaintances and recruited half a dozen to drop by for tea and to act as human shields. One shield, a British travel writer called Sarah Harvey, was conscripted and sent to the airport to cover a seaplane that had chosen an inopportune moment to crash into a lagoon.

President Nasheed had been inside the military barracks since 5am and was still stuck. Increasingly isolated and uncertain of the loyalty of the military officers around him, he was faced with few options. Negotiation and subjugation of the mob had failed, and the 1953 public lynching of reformist president Amin Didi was no doubt fresh in his mind. Moreover, he had just seen uniformed police reinforcements arriving at the jetty across the square on boats stamped with the Villa Resort logo—Gasim's resort chain. They were carrying rope, he later claimed.

A group of around sixty remaining troops urged him to order the armoury unlocked and to issue them with live ammunition. He declined. We asked him two years later whether he regretted this, and would have done anything differently.

"Oh yeah, we could have shot everyone. It's essentially very simple to suppress a public uprising," he snorted.

"Yes, I could have held on, but that would have been at very huge cost to the country and the people. There would have been a lot of blood."

Nasheed's Fall

The mob outside the military headquarters parted as a disgraced former army colonel, Mohamed Nazim, and a sacked police officer, Abdulla Riyaz, entered the building and gave the president an ultimatum to resign.

In a recording of Nasheed obtained by Australian Special Broadcasting Service (SBS) journalist Mark Davis, the president can be heard pleading for his family to be protected.[4] "You should do that for me under the circumstances. I should settle this with you first, right here, OK?" the president is heard to say.

"Then I'll go to the President's Office and publicly announce that in my view the best thing for this country right now is my resignation. Is that all right? That's what I'll say."

"That was an attempt for me to get out of where I was," Nasheed told Davis later.

Flanked by Nazim and his military officers, the president was frogmarched to his office and ordered to write his resignation letter. The previously retired Colonel Nazim, shortly to be declared defence minister, asked to keep the pen as a souvenir.

The press conference was broadcast to the entire country over the newly renamed TVM, by now under the control of the vice president's brother.

"I resign because I am not a person who wishes to rule with the use of power. I believe that if the government were to remain in power it would require the use force which would harm many citizens. I resign because I believe that if the government continues to stay in power, it is very likely that we may face foreign influences," Nasheed said. "I have always wished the citizens of this country well, now and into the future. I have made this decision and I wish for your prosperity in this life and the life after."

"I was forced to resign," he said later. "I resigned under duress. I was threatened. If I did not resign within a stipulated period it would endanger me and my family's lives. I understood they were going to harm a number of other citizens, party members. They were going to literally sack the town. I felt that I had no other option other than to resign."

The MDP government instantly folded as ministers switched off their phones and went into hiding. Unable to contact anybody in charge, international media outlets turned to *Minivan* to confirm what had happened.

The first was Al Jazeera. Will Jordan, a journalist based at their headquarters in Qatar, had previously worked as editor of *Minivan News* during the 2008 presidential election. He wanted to know if I would go on camera and outline the situation for US$200.

I'm ashamed to say I chickened out. In hindsight I would have gotten away with it, but the uncertainty of the situation and our presumed links to the MDP made me fearful of the spotlight. We had none of the protections of foreign media and many on the regime side already saw us as a target. We had to survive to document the coming days, even if that meant limiting ourselves to feeding information from behind the scenes.

Incongruously, the next call was from Radio Islam South Africa.

"Howz the weather?" asked a thick Afrikaans accent.

The question was so disarming I found myself giving a concise political overview. As I put the phone down I cursed myself for throwing away US$200. Such riches could have bought a lot of tuna for an editor paid a local wage in nonexchangeable Maldivian *rufiya*. Radio New Zealand brought some consolation with a NZ$70 appearance fee.

We were story of the week in India. The story exploded into headline news with the country's raucous cable news channels leaving viewers in no doubt that a coup was taking place, while panels of prominent moustachioed types called for Indian military intervention. Very unusually for the country's loud and argumentative panel programmes everybody seemed to agree, and the new Maldivian regime's attempt to put forth a spokesperson saw him torn apart like a Hindi soap opera villain.

Unlike the BBC, which would politely request your appearance in an upcoming live programme, Indian networks would drop you straight into the broadcast from the first "hello".

"Mr. Robinson, you're live to 1.2 billion people! Tell us what's happening in the Maldives!"

"Don't flush, don't flush," I thought.

Diplomats from around the region booked flights, while a hastily assembled high-level UN delegation ensured that the upmarket US$300 a night Traders Hotel in Malé enjoyed its highest-ever occupancy.

Nasheed's ex-UN, Stanford-educated vice president was sworn into power. Dr. Mohamed Waheed Hassan Manik had proved uncontactable for much of the crisis, and had earlier refused to share with fellow cabinet ministers the details of his secret late-night meetings with opposition leaders in the lead-up to 7 February.

Waheed did appear briefly on Gasim's VTV, declaring that "during this dangerous situation faced by the nation, it is my duty to say a few words. I support the peaceful efforts of a large number of Maldivians trying to protect the Maldivian Constitution and the religion."

In subsequent interviews he insisted he had remained ignorant of events, until being pleasantly surprised by the phone call from the speaker of parliament informing him that he was to be sworn in.

"Do I look like the sort of person who would plan a coup?" he asked foreign journalists, when challenged at a press conference after his swearing in ceremony. He looked like a deer in headlights.

It transpired that Nasheed's wife Laila and Waheed's wife Ilham shared the same beautician. Nasheed would later learn that Ilham had booked to be groomed and pampered for an unidentified special occasion that was supposedly due to take place after 7am, on what would coincidentally be the same day as her husband's sudden coronation.

The biggest clue for anyone watching that this was not a simple presidential resignation was the complete replacement of not just the president, but the entire elected government with pro Gayoom-regime party officials and the dictator's offspring.

The helpful civilians who had coordinated the mutinying security forces during and in the lead-up to Nasheed's resignation, Mohamed Nazim and Abdulla Riyaz, were respectively appointed Defence Minister and Police Commissioner. Gayoom's daughter Dunya Maumoon was made State Foreign Minister. We compiled dozens of these nepotistic arrangements into a helpful excel chart and uploaded it for any diplomats paying attention. Gayoom's side justified the appointments on the grounds that the Maldives is a small country where skills are in short supply. It was fortunate that his family had been educated to the standard required for the burden of leadership.

After stepping down Nasheed was penned into his family's house in Malé, while police raided the presidential residence of Muleaage in search of religious and moral failings with which to convict him. They emerged with dozens of empty liquor bottles packed in a large suitcase that looked remarkably similar to one that had just earlier been wheeled inside. Chief Judge Abdulla Mohamed, released by this stage from his detention on a nearby island, swiftly obliged by finding the warrant stamp and ordering Nasheed's arrest.

Concerned about the deteriorating situation, the British government sent over its High Commissioner from Sri Lanka who held an information session in the Traders Hotel lobby for UK citizens. I attended, chiefly to find out who held the keys to potential evacuation.

High Commissioner John Rankin expressed the British government's alarm over a supposed "list" of foreigners the new regime intended to stop at the airport should they try to escape. It was said to include on it at least two British nationals. Paul Roberts would have a job getting out of the country, I thought. Rankin opened the floor to questions from the assembled expats, who included resort workers, liquor importers, volunteer teachers and assorted spouses.

"If we do get evacuated back to the UK, how does that affect our non-residency status for tax purposes?" asked one gentleman, a retired psychiatrist.

I stayed on in the lobby to meet the first arriving foreign correspondents from nearby Sri Lanka and India. I had just found a secluded table in the corner when a formation of suited diplomats swept past to the scent of Brylcreem. It was Oscar Fernandez-Taranco, the UN's Assistant Secretary-General for Political Affairs and one removed from Ban Ki-Moon. At speed, he looked like an aerodynamic Wall Street banker.

A Russian television crew took me out to Republic Square to re-enact 7 February's events. Given the Maldives' popularity as a Russian tourist destination, they were there to assess potential inconveniences for any visiting oligarchs.

"Russians will feel right at home here," they concluded, departing for the airport.

Large and very American, Bryson Hull was an extremely competent war correspondent who worked as the Reuters bureau chief in Colombo, and had been neck-deep in the Sri Lankan civil war. Long-winded earlier negotiations to enlist me as the Reuters correspondent for the Maldives were hastily accelerated, and I lined up interviews on both sides of the fence, as well as unsuccessfully trying to convince him to attend the airport hotel bar in his flak jacket. Had there been any shooting on the way over, his profile would have made excellent cover.

The orbiting foreign reporters were excellent protection for *Minivan* and its local staff. We made a point of attending both of the new president's press conferences, one to intimidate the local audience and the other a "nothing to see here" spiel for the foreign reporters—many of whom openly laughed at Waheed's responses. His newly-appointed spokesperson, the hawk-like Masood Imad, came up to me afterwards as I was helping myself to the presidential refreshments.

"You shouldn't drink Coke. It's bad for your health," he warned. I suggested that there were plenty of other things going on that could probably be worse for my health.

We learned later from inside sources that some of the mutinying security forces had made a cursory attempt to visit our office, but were unsure of its location and in true Maldivian fashion were distracted by the prospect of coffee and cigarettes before anybody could be bothered to research it.

* * *

Our daily life became a matter of contradiction, a delicate balance. Internationally, confusion and a general lack of information meant that the narrative of what had actually happened on 7 February was up in the air. The cement was still wet. Once it had dried, it would be very difficult to change it. We had to impart the damning facts while ensuring our own survival and continued capacity to function under a government that had shown its willingness to seize media it deemed threatening. I dropped the word "coup" from my language, opting for "controversial transfer of power" and a knowing wink.

I decided that our market niche and credibility, were key to our medium-term survival. The government was desperate for recognition and legitimacy. We were the free media and, for that matter, the news of record. We would hold up the carrot of legitimacy for the government, while letting the facts speak for themselves: a technique known as "handing out rope". They had impunity, the goons and the guns, so we had to leave something on the table so they wouldn't just tip it over in a huff. Should the regime be completely exposed and give up all pretence of legitimacy, then Minivan's foreign staff were likely to be put on the next plane.

We desperately struggled to keep *Minivan News* updated, edited and credible amid the sudden attention and flurries of interviews. The lead-up to the coup was complicated. It involved an illegitimate judiciary, a stabbed whistleblower, byzantine political intrigue and a single mother who smoked. This back story was long-winded but critically important to the country's future, and as the world was soon to discover, had wider implications for the Arab Spring.

From an immediate outsider's perspective, Nasheed had lost control of a chaotic but spontaneous situation, which he had chosen to resolve through resignation and the succession of his vice president. It didn't help that Waheed's own newly-appointed vice president, resort tycoon Waheed Deen, had a history of philanthropically funding many of the pro-democracy civil society organizations which should have been flooding media inboxes with livid press releases. It took almost three weeks for these NGOs to comment on the situation, and then only a bland and cautious statement issued by a pseudonymed alliance of half a dozen. Worse, several supposedly credible local NGOs believed to be supported by Deen were consulted by foreign diplomats desperately trying to make sense of the situation. Behind closed doors they insisted to diplomats that the events of the day were completely legitimate and that there was definitely no need for early elections, proposing instead a "national unity government" in which the MDP would be allowed to participate.

The same language was copied by visiting US Assistant Secretary of State, Robert Blake, immediately after a fact-finding stop with Transparency Maldives.

"A number of good ideas" were being explored to "try and bring former President Mohamed Nasheed's Maldivian Democratic Party into the national unity government," Blake said.

A *Wall Street Journal* reporter in that press conference scoffed.

"He said he didn't resign. Why not just give him his job back?"

Swayed by the new president's Stanford education and the enticement of a potential philosopher king, the Indian government recognized the new regime. The US and others followed its lead. The backroom subterfuge involved in ensuring that these key countries reached and maintained this position would prove a fascinating insight into the shadowy world of international geopolitics and diplomatic fallibility, worthy of any spy movie.

Countries with a more recent history in the Maldives, such as Britain, had less catching up to do and were cautious in their statements. Mostly. One British diplomat, flown in urgently from Colombo, almost addressed the new president as "Baaghee Waheed" on the assumption that it was his first name. The error originated from his earlier meeting with the MDP, who had taken to unconsciously prefixing the new president with the Dhivehi word for "traitor".

It was the President of Timor Leste (East Timor) who stepped up and finally played the role of the little boy in what had become the geopolitical equivalent of *The Emperor's New Clothes*.

Nobel prize winner José Ramos-Horta, himself a former political exile and reluctant politician-turned-president who had visited the Maldives in 2010,[5] condemned the "unsettling silence" of the big powers following the Maldives' "obvious coup d'état".[6]

Ramos-Horta recalled that during his visit, Nasheed had "alerted me to tensions in Maldivian society and the unabated activity of beneficiaries of the old political order directed at toppling the new democratically elected authorities." It was, he said, "now obvious that President Mohamed Nasheed was forced to resign by military elements and the move has the support of former Maldivian dignitaries bent on retaking privileges and political control they enjoyed during the former regime ... It should be of concern to the World that extremist elements abusively invoking Islam were instrumental in stirring up violent demonstrations, religious intolerance and social upheaval as the coup d'état set in motion.

"Therefore, it is all the more strange and unsettling the silence with which big powers and leading democracies respond to the undemocratic developments in the Maldives. It has been a sad day for democracy in the Maldives and beyond," he said.

In the aftermath of Nasheed's resignation, whether out of fear or shock, the MDP all but evaporated from government and the streets. None of its ministers or party officials were answering calls. Paul Roberts and his Maldivian wife managed to flee the country the same evening, thanks to the intervention of the British High Commission. In the absence of any contactable Maldivians, he rang me and asked if I would field media and diplomatic enquiries. The straits were desperate indeed if a 28-year-old expat journalist was to be relied on as a country's sole credible spokesperson, and such a recommendation from the ousted president's press secretary did not bode well for the impartial reputation I had spent years cultivating. Roberts assured me the situation rather spoke for itself.

He wasn't alone in that assessment.

"They're evil. You can see it in their eyes," observed a very senior British diplomat, following a friendly game of football with members of the new regime.

As a foreigner in a tourism-dependent economy I was largely insulated from the general malevolence and intimidation that followed Nasheed's resignation, and could focus on reassuring the local staff who were feeling it keenly. The scariest part was the sense of impunity—the same I had first felt in the square. I had grown up in a country where rule of law and the structures that enforce it were taken for granted. To experience these stabilities and assurances so suddenly stripped away was very frightening. It was suddenly the Wild West, and this was no more evident than when a large group of Islamists took advantage of the political chaos to storm the national museum and pulverise into dust all evidence of the country's pre-Islamic civilization.[7] Despite the abundance of high quality CCTV and open boasting on social media the mob's leaders remained scot free, police complicit in their cultural atrocity.

The Crackdown

The night of 7 February was quiet while much of the country hid indoors, waiting for what was going to happen. There were reports of police and paid gangs, buoyed with confidence, roaming the streets in search of senior MDP figures. Several were severely beaten. Nasheed was silent. A brief statement finally appeared at 10.47pm:

> We strongly condemn the coup d'etat that has been brought against the constitutionally elected government of President Mohamed Nasheed of the Maldives. Last night rogue elements from the Maldives Police Service in conjunction with the supporters of former President Maumoon Abdul Gayoom overthrew the democratically elected government of President Nasheed.

> President Nasheed was taken to the President's Office under the custody of the security forces and subsequently resigned.

> We also condemn the violent attacks carried out against our members by the Maldives Police Service including Member of Parliament and our former chairperson Mariya Didi and other MPs from the party.

> We call upon the international community to assist us in establishing democracy in the Maldives and to protect the officials of the government of President Nasheed. We fear for the safety of President Nasheed and senior members of his government.

This pronouncement was far too late to challenge global diplomatic recognition of the change of government, but it did finally draw attention. The following morning over breakfast in Traders I was compelled to pick up the tab after losing a bet with a foreign journalist over whether the gentleman sitting in the corner wearing shades and a baseball cap worked for an American spy agency.

"What's your name and who do you work for?" said the journalist, striding up to the spy.

"I'm sorry but I'm afraid I can't tell you that sir," he replied in a thick American accent.

The American "analysts"—at least those flown in rather than stationed in nearby embassies—were generally chatty, confident, full of self-importance and couldn't resist advertising their profession. I helped at least one dispose of a liquor bottle he had snuck through customs in a diplomatic bag, not realizing that there was no way to bin the incriminating object without risking arrest and embarrassing the Ambassador's delegation.

The British variety were smoother, but sometimes sprung by the deference of their diplomatic colleagues whose job titles otherwise clearly placed them rungs higher than the visiting "cultural affairs officer".

My second breakfast was with one of the MDP's highrollers who owned a restaurant around the corner. I wanted to find out where they all were. He arrived with Nasheed's former youth and employment minister on the rear of his motorcycle. The minister, Hassan Latheef, looked fearful and agitated, and said little.

"We won't let them get away with this," vowed the highroller.

I pointed out that hiding indoors was hardly movement towards that goal, especially given the large numbers of foreign journalists roaming the streets looking for evidence that Nasheed's government had ever existed.

Perhaps the party would have a large gathering that afternoon, he suggested.

We agreed this might be a good idea before the press got bored and went home, and not for the first time I suddenly became conscious of the journalistic imperative to avoid actively instigating the news.

The MDP held a meeting of its national council that afternoon, with the party-friendly city council loaning it Malé's largest conference hall. The place was packed with thousands of supporters, looking for direction, authority and a communal narrative as to what had actually happened. I notified Bryson, who arrived with the rest of the foreign media pack. This now included an entire film crew from Al Jazeera and a small army of Indian journalists from New Delhi.

"Yes, I was forced to resign at gunpoint," Nasheed told the reporters, over the din of an outraged crowd. "There were guns all around me and they told me they wouldn't hesitate to use them if I didn't resign."

Like many of the MDP's subsequent pronouncements, while metaphorically more or less accurate, the claim was not strictly true. The Indian media loved it, and the extra attention only encouraged further dramatization by Nasheed's party. Allegations of exposed weapons were ridiculed in the government's controversial report on the day, which would cite tourism minister Maryam Zulfa, a witness to Nasheed's resignation, as describing an incriminating "bulge in Riyaz's pants".

Nasheed told reporters that the "powerful networks" of Gayoom loyalists had manipulated events to "strangle" Maldivian democracy—this much was literally true, and had been throughout his presidency.

The party conference ended. The MDP called on people to take to the streets in a protest march and show their anger at Nasheed's ousting. The march began on the opposite side of the city to Republic Square, and by the time it reached the western entrance to the square, almost ten thousand people had joined the column. It was notable that these included women, children, the elderly, and many people who were not necessarily party supporters, but were outraged at the manner in which the government had changed.

"We're just going on a peaceful walk," insisted Mariya Didi, one of the party's senior figures at the front of the march.

The column reached the Central Bank at the edge of the same square in which the government had been toppled the day before. It was met by a line of riot police with shields and tear gas grenades.

As the protesters reached the front of the police lines, a second group of police, mostly consisting of Gayoom's former Star Force, charged the protesters' flank from a side alleyway. Trapped by the line of police in front of them, the water's edge to the north and other protesters behind, the crowd panicked. The police set about spraying, gassing, beating and violently dispersing the protesters in a sordid show of force. The entire scene at ground level was caught on camera by Al Jazeera and much of the foreign media, who expressed surprise at the audacity of the attack. Protesters knocked to the ground were kicked and stomped on by police. Dozens of mobile phone camera recordings taken by civilians from the balconies of nearby buildings showed demonstrators dragged off into alleyways by police and brutally beaten.

"The anger and hate—where did this come from? Has this been inside them all this time?" asked one female protester, who was rescued by some strangers after being blinded by pepper spray and beaten.

Women, children and the elderly in the crowd were beaten indiscriminately. Our journalists were chased—one was knocked to the ground and struck with a police baton. He hobbled home bruised.

"They were beating old women with batons," Ahmed Naish reported.

"It was just like the old days."

We visited the city's hospitals, which had been locked down by police as the wounded were brought in.

One young woman who had gone to hospital with her sister was being treated for a head wound. A gauze wrapped around her head was spotted with blood, and she claimed the wound was still bleeding as she went in for an X-ray.

"The police were just standing there and suddenly we were being beaten with batons and pepper spray was [sprayed] in our face. They threw us to the ground and kept beating us," she said.

She said she, her sister and most of the other women had joined the party's "walk around Male" because they understood it would not be a violent protest.

"It was just supposed to be a peaceful walk. That's why we went, and why there were more women than usual who went. But there was no warning of the attack, no announcements, we were all beaten even after we began retreating. My sister was almost trampled," she said. "I just think it's disgusting that the police could beat so many unarmed women."

Miraculously nobody was killed, although dozens of protesters were hospitalized.[8] One of the worst beaten was Reeko Moosa, an MP and former Maldivian film star who was the MDP's chairman and hated by the Gayoom clan. He was dragged through the police line into the square where riot police beat him and repeatedly stomped on his testicles. He was saved only by the intervention of a military policeman, who escorted him away.

"Inside the hospital, dozens of Mr. Nasheed's supporters are still being treated for injuries, following earlier scuffles in the main square," reported the BBC's Andrew North, who watched the saga unfold. "Among them is Reeko Moosa Maniku, chairman of Mr. Nasheed's Maldives Democratic Party—who was with the former president when the clashes broke out. With a large head bandage and his shirt bloodied, he regained consciousness as we arrived. 'The police said they would kill me,' he told us, 'as they beat me.' Another MP was still unconscious in another ward."

Reeko would require extensive surgery in Sri Lanka and never fully recovered, although the government side dismissed the broken bones as the dramatic antics of a professional actor.

Nasheed and Mariya sought to escape the police violence by hiding in a shop. Camera phone footage showed them being discovered and dragged out. Mariya was reportedly punched in the face while Nasheed suffered head injuries.

While he was detained by police, rumours spread on social media that Nasheed had been killed. Chaos erupted across the country's 200 scattered inhabited islands. Some of these lacked a single police officer, while others had but a few to police populations of up to several thousand. On some islands police were locked in buildings, in others they were rounded up, kicked off the island and set adrift in boats. On many MDP stronghold islands police stations and courthouses were set ablaze. The damage would later be used by the new government as justification for designating the country's first pro-democracy party a "terrorist organization".

A subsequent report by the country's own Human Rights Commission—an assortment of inept and unremarkable regime apologists—justified police violence on the grounds that the police were "inflamed with passion". Many of those involved were promoted, and all received cash bonuses in the form of salary increases, benefits and even houses.

"Fiji and the Maldives' contrasting experiences provide useful tips for coup-plotters everywhere," wrote Nasheed in an acerbic guide to toppling democracies, published in the *Huffington Post* later that year.[9]

"When planning your coup, remember that first impressions count—so don't dress like an obvious coup leader. The man who takes over from the democratically elected leader should not wear military fatigues, as Commodore Frank Bainimarama did in Fiji; instead wear a lounge suit, as former Vice President Waheed Hassan did in the Maldives.

"Secondly, get your messaging right: never, as in Fiji, publicly state you are overthrowing an elected government; instead, as in the Maldives, announce that the President's resignation is a run-of-the-mill and Constitutional transfer of power.

"Finally, have patience: if you follow steps 1 and 2, sooner or later the international community will tire of political upheaval and accept the new, coupled political order, regardless of outward commitments to democracy, human rights and the rule of law."

The international community paid a disproportionate amount of attention to the Maldivian situation given its small size, a fact due largely to Nasheed's high profile stands on human rights and environmental issues. The MDP, however, seemed to expect international supporters of democracy to charge in and restore Nasheed to his rightful post. They were to be disappointed.

"Local solution for a local problem," was the general diplomatic mantra. That meant, speculated one British diplomat, that there were only going to be two winners from the day's events.

"Your CV, and the guy who wholesales teargas."

3

MINIVAN NEWS

"The problem with Minivan editors is that they do not value their paper. They seem to be blissfully unaware that the whole English-speaking world makes up its mind on the Maldives after reading their news."

Anonymous commentator, 23/6/2013

"I can't let you through with that. Look, I'm pressing the button and the belt's not even moving."

My worldly possessions sat on the baggage belt at the check-in counter in Gatwick airport. I'd accepted the job in the Maldives a week earlier, given notice to the magazine in London I'd spent two years working for, then embarked on a week of heavily lubricated goodbye parties. I'd thrown everything into the suitcase the night before when it had seemed as light as a feather, and only barely made it to the airport on time that morning. The girl I'd been seeing had shown pity and driven me to the station, eager to make sure I got on the train.

"This is sad," she observed, as I hauled forty kilos of belongings into the carriage.

I'd spent two years working in London as a staff writer for *Information Age*, a decade-old business technology magazine esteemed in high-level corporate IT circles. I had somehow become an authority on IT security, to the point that I was chairing conferences on the subject in lavish London hotel ballrooms. This was baffling to me as I knew nothing about IT or security, but neither, as I learned, did most of the executives in the audience who were there

27

mainly for the free food. I lived in dread that this conspiracy of ignorance and smoked salmon hors d'oeuvres would be shattered by the raised hand of a genuine software engineer—fortunately these were seldom high enough in corporate pecking orders to be allowed out to any event involving a free lunch.

In many respects it had been the ultimate backpacker's job. Large, monied IT firms would deploy well-funded PR agencies to wine and dine the badly paid tech journalists. In practice, this involved an army of beautiful young women armed with corporate credit cards competing for the blood alcohol level of an assortment of self-entitled, largely male reporters. The more successful of these journalists spent the year roaming the world on trade show junkets, subsisting on rich food, fine wine and foie gras with not a cent spent.

If this ecosystem sounds corrupt or whorish, it really wasn't. You could never really be bought—to be so was to erode one's currency and halt the gravy train. The less you wrote about a company and the snarkier you were, the harder their PRs would try to win you over.

At its best, a sense of conspiracy and esprit de corps developed between journalist and PR, both of whom were usually young and underpaid and trying to scrape by in London. Break the boundary and the corporate credit card would fold naturally into your regular social life, expenses filed neatly away under "hospitality".

It was certainly a different life to my previous job: cub reporter for a family-owned newspaper in the Australian country town of Narrabri. Three years of covering droughts, bushfires, road accidents, cotton farming and the annual horse races of a small population a long way from anywhere was good preparation for reporting from a speck in the Indian Ocean. The *Narrabri Courier* was community journalism at its cradle-to-grave finest, and a splendid way for a young journalist to learn the whole trade rather than pushing buttons on the Nespresso machine for a big city newspaper columnist.

Eventually I got itchy feet and after a brief, accidental and commercially unsuccessful stint as a freelance correspondent during the 2007 saffron uprising in Burma, wound up broke and in London.

Rent took up two-thirds of my staff writer's salary but it was an erratic kind of poverty. One night would be spent gorging on truffles at Claridge's with the CEO of a large IT security company, the next on the couch eating pot noodles with my flatmates.

At some point during the second year I decided I preferred pot noodles with the flatmates. I had seen what the sense of entitlement had done to many of my more established peers, some of whom complained bitterly about the failure of supplicant IT firms to upgrade them to business flights on arduous flights to trade shows in Las Vegas. I saw similar characteristics in myself emerging I did not like. It was time to stir things up a bit.

It was November 2009. Like everybody else I'd never heard of the Maldives beyond its reputation as an overpriced tropical resort paradise. I had to look it up on a map. The first map didn't show it at all.

I'd certainly never heard of *Minivan News*. Why would somebody start what sounded like a small vehicles special interest publication in a country that was 99 per cent water with barely any roads? The discovery that *Minivan* meant "independent" in Dhivehi came later, but would make my future CV no less confusing.

I was interviewed by a panel of former editors who were now working for outlets such as the BBC, Al Jazeera, the *Times* and the FT. They had spearheaded global recognition of the Maldives' pro-democracy movement and substantially contributed to the downfall of Gayoom's thirty-year dictatorship. If I got the job I would effectively become custodian of the news of record for a historic period in Maldivian history and a big chunk of their CVs.

The current editor was Maryam Omidi, a talented Iranian-born journalist who had been working in Malé for eleven months and sounded exhausted. Her taboo-busting coverage of a woman sentenced to flogging for extramarital sex had seen her targeted by fundamentalist groups for apparently "mocking Islam", while her decision to publish a reader's letter on the misery of the Maldivian homosexual experience saw her hounded by local media for "promoting homosexuality". She had contacted the most vicious news station and tried to explain how reader-submitted content did not always reflect editorial line, but was left alone in the station's lobby and secretly filmed while the anchor went on camera and berated her failure to uphold national virtue. She had since taken to getting a taxi to the office for fear of street harassment.

I knew the Maldives had been ruled by Asia's longest serving dictator, Maumoon Abdul Gayoom, until he was overthrown in the country's first multi-party democratic election in 2008. I knew dimly of the man who displaced him: the young, Westernized, progressive President Mohamed Nasheed of the Maldivian Democratic Party. I did not know of the yearning for the stability of dictatorship on behalf of a large chunk of the populace, the political polarization that saw people paint gravestones in the party colours of the deceased, the street-level hostility to "Western" concepts such as human rights and freedoms of thought and religion, the incongruous presentation of the country as both "100 per cent Muslim" and a tourist's hedonistic haven of sun, sand, sex and Smirnoff. Still in London, I had yet to even meet a Maldivian. Information on the country was limited to glowing reviews of resorts and advice to use sunscreen.

Coincidentally, the World Travel Fair was taking place in London and I used my magazine press credentials to wrangle entry. The Maldivian stand in the Excel Centre was a large multi-storey tropical beach hut full of junketeering officials and glossy resort brochures. I introduced myself to Ahmed "Sappe" Moosa, who had edited the virulently and unashamedly tabloid anti-Gayoom website *Dhivehi Observer* before being appointed Science and Technology envoy for the new government. He took me upstairs to a quiet table under some fake palm fronds for my first lesson on Maldivian political pluralism.

"Don't give those bastards any oxygen!" he urged.

The Salisbury Connection

The Maldivian High Commission was in Baker Street. The High Commissioner was unavailable, so I met the Maldives' honorary consul, UK national David Hardingham, at the Sherlock Holmes bar around the corner. The Hardingham family were a fixture in Salisbury, selling fireplaces and kitchenware from a heritage-listed shop in the city centre. Dave was a former school friend of Nasheed, the pair having attended the private Dauntsey's School in Wiltshire. The friendship would be tested years later when Nasheed suddenly arrived on the doorstep of his cottage with the exiled Maldivian opposition party in tow, and asked to crash on the couch.

As a result, Dave now had a Maldivian consulate in his garden shed in the way another person might have a miniature train set. The fireplace shop employed many staff who ran the day-to-day affairs, leaving Dave what he described as "cash poor, time rich". He had taken to actively campaigning for human rights and democracy in the Maldives, and ran a UK-registered NGO called Friends of Maldives (FOM). FOM had shipped a hundred tons of aid to the Maldives following the 2004 tsunami, and in 2009 was helping the Maldives High Commission in the UK to plug the dilapidated education sector by recruiting and sending over volunteer teachers. Dave's efforts had seen him blacklisted by Gayoom's government and labelled variously a Christian missionary and Islamic terrorist, which, noted a leaked US Embassy cable on the matter, would have made for "probably the fastest conversion in history".[1]

"The combined total land mass of Maldives seems hardly large enough to accommodate the elaborate conspiracy theories and counter-theories depicted by the [Maldivian government] and its opponents," noted the same cable, with an audible sigh.

Dave was keen to ensure the continuity of *Minivan News* following Nasheed's election to the presidency. Despite its political conception by the MDP, the publication was regarded by many international diplomatic and human rights outfits as the sole credible information source on an opaque and insular society. Dave would prove to be endlessly supportive in the years to come, proving his understanding of media independence and becoming a stalwart defender of *Minivan News'* independence against the MDP's attempts to manipulate the publication they had founded but no longer controlled.

I woke one morning to find Maryam had offered me the job.

"You're taking it?" asked the girlfriend.

"Yes," I said immediately, suddenly realizing she had gone quiet and wondering if my lack of hesitation had been in some way insensitive. It was a mad and exciting step into the unknown, with no guarantee there was even a job waiting at the other end.

The little research I had been able to do suggested if there was a job, it was going to be extremely hard to do in a small and semi-hostile environment. As for the off hours, Malé was a dry city where drinking a can of beer was considered abuse of a class A drug. Annoyingly, everybody I told about the job assumed I would be lying in a hammock with a laptop sipping piña coladas.

Arrival

Maryam asked if I could be out there in a week. Many would have taken this as a warning, but I was overly keen to appear obliging. I pushed the magazine into letting me run off early. The editor bought me a pint, a book on rising sea levels and a copy of *Islam for Dummies*, and I hastily dismantled my life in London.

At the airport I was made to repack my worldly belongings into a heavy sack I would drag onto the plane as carry-on baggage, like an economy-class Santa Claus. Dave rang to make sure I was boarding the plane, and I wondered if there had been a propensity for other journalists to jump on the next flight home.

The cabin was almost empty. After one final beer, I leaned against the window and dozed off wondering what was to come.

I woke with a start to see the Indian Ocean rushing up to meet the plane. The airstrip was a narrow ribbon of land barely above sea level. Stepping onto the tarmac into the bright sunlight and tropical humidity was bewildering after wintry London. The terminal was scarcely more than a tin shed. I joined the immigration queue with throngs of foreign tourists who were being swiftly waved through.

The officer took one look at my business visa and asked me why I was there. "*Minivan News*!" he exclaimed ambiguously.

I was led aside to wait for half an hour. Immigration had little experience with foreigners working outside the resort industry, and certainly not in fields considered "local", such as media. My visa was a stopgap measure allowing me to work for up to three months while Maryam fought to get me an actual work permit. Eventually I would become the first foreign journalist ever to be issued one.

Security had isolated my bags by the time immigration let me through. Before I could pass through to arrivals they were x-rayed and searched for alcohol, pork and non-Islamic religious artefacts. Unburdened of liquor and sausages, I was met at arrivals by Ahmed Naish, a quiet and exceptionally talented journalist recruited by Maryam. He had attended university overseas but had dropped out, turning inwards and spending years in his room with his books on philosophy—a precious commodity in a country with little culture of reading. He emerged vastly intelligent and introspective, and describing himself as having been educated "by dead white men".

The airport island of Hulhule was a short ten-minute ferry ride from the capital of Malé. The candy-coloured concrete towers took up every spare inch of the island, and from ground level the city looked like a concrete metropolis rising from the ocean. We boarded a *dhoni*—a traditional Maldivian boat design with a boxy wooden hull and curved prow similar to an Egyptian dhow. The tropical water was a tourist cliché for good reason, and the clear turquoise shallows in the harbour faded to deep azure as the boat crossed the channel to the city. However jaded I became, it always looked glorious. I would meet many travel writers in the Maldives struggling to invent new words for the colour blue.

Naish took me to his uncle's guest house on the western side of Majeedee Magu, the main road bisecting the city horizontally. I would stay there a few nights, before moving to his family's flat on the nearby suburban island of Villingili. The intention was for me to move into Maryam's old flat when she left, but this was to fall through. Her two-bedroom apartment was a government housing unit and despite the payment of rent, the President's Office had decreed that the government would distance itself from *Minivan*. This was financially challenging as land was at a premium and private rent was extortionate, with prices approximating those of London. Landlords would often ask for up to a year's rent as a deposit, making the prospect all but financially impossible and requiring many Maldivians to live six to a room. Were it not for the generosity of Naish and his family, I would have been homeless on arrival.

We dropped off the bags and went to find Maryam.

A Candy-coloured City

The city was crowded and overpopulated, narrow streets barely able to accommodate a single vehicle line, let alone the thousands of parked mopeds, and this all ensured that wing mirrors were hot commodities in the city's repair shops. Footpaths only several feet wide had been added to the streets as an afterthought, apparently designed by somebody with either contempt for pedestrians or exceptional balance. The streets had been paved by the Japanese with tessellated bricks of perfect size for hurling at riot police. The gutters were neglected and clogged, with the result that large parts of the city—barely above sea level to begin with—would flood in the lightest of rain showers.

Bicycles were conspicuously absent, despite the city being of perfect size for them. I learned later that to pedal was a sign of poverty. Efforts to equip the police force with several hundred bicycles as a show of environmental leadership fell flat as pedalling made you, in the words of one officer, "scarcely better than a rubbish-carrying Bangladeshi".[2] Proving that no issue was above politics, Gayoom's former Environment Minister and MP of his Dhivehi Rayithunge Party, Abdulla Mausoom, once told me that Nasheed's bicycle initiative proved the country was "going backwards day by day", and that "the Maldives does not have to go back to the stone age to be a carbon neutral country."

Mopeds were the ride of choice, and were reasonably safe since the small size of the city and rampant congestion meant it was rarely possible to reach above twenty kilometres an hour. Most young male Maldivians went into debt to own one as it was considered a prerequisite to getting a girlfriend.

I met Maryam for lunch in the City Garden café, and had the first of a great many plates of tuna fried rice. With the exception of the top end, the majority of Malé's thousands of cafés had an identical menu, several volumes thick and spanning dozens of global cuisines. Most of these would be unavailable, and those that were available would always resemble tuna fried rice. Sometimes this optimistic catering would produce truly unique dishes: I once ordered a "green curry", which arrived as an ordinary curry dyed green with food colouring.

The café scene was an important social fixture in a city in which the vast majority of entertainment was either absent or banned for religious reasons.

It was class-based, with poorer islanders and Bangladeshi labourers frequenting loud tea shops known as *hortas* specializing in 'short eats'—fried and floury fast food treats filled with spicy tuna, as well as more prosaic offerings such as hotdogs and jam sandwiches. The upper end of the spectrum included several superb Thai restaurants, and trendy hangouts such as Seagull Café and Sea House known to serve the occasional green vegetable.

The middle ground consisted of cafés attempting to emulate those of the conventional sense but skipping vital elements: atmosphere, waiters, menu, a chef. You had to learn the specialties of each. Many of these were justly praised: Bolognese pizza was a popular and surprisingly tasty innovation, while the famous lunchboxes from Seera Bites contained your choice of delicious fish, chicken or beef curry, and lurking somewhere inside, a single large thermonuclear chilli.

My favourite dish was *mashuni roshi*. This consisted of tuna (usually tinned), mashed up with onion, chilli, coconut and lime juice, served with *roshi* for breakfast. You would scoop up a wad with the bread and pop it into your mouth. It was an unlikely taste sensation that I greatly missed after I left.

The near-total lack of other entertainment invigorated Malé's café culture. Sitting in cafés and slurping the state-approved stimulant while debating politics was central to the city's society. The ubiquitous Nescafé was despised, with the average young Maldivian spending 200 Maldivian *rufiya* (MVR), about US$13, a day on double espresso shots brewed from imported coffee. Even the most meagre cafés would have a gleaming stainless steel Italian coffee machine, although local preference seemed to be for the coffee to be bitter and burned. Espresso shots were ordered by brand name—a minefield if one did not grasp the politics of bean importation. Lavazza was imported by a Gayoom regime-aligned company, while Illy was brought in by somebody linked to the MDP. I once made the mistake of ordering the former instead of an Illy in an MDP-aligned café, and a hush descended as if I had walked into a Wild West saloon and ordered a white wine spritzer.

A Concrete Box

The *Minivan News* office turned out to be a six by eight-foot, dusty, windowless bunker on the second floor of a concrete box on a street called Alikilegefaanu Magu. Proper pronunciation for the purpose of directing taxis was provided by a helpful Maldivian friend: The *Minivan* office/bunker was sublet by the Maldivian Detainee Network (MDN), which occupied the larger and plusher office next door and had amenities such as a functioning printer. A third room was rented by the South Asian Free Media Association, although I never saw its door open. There may well have been a dusty skeleton hunched over a desk inside.

The only other permanent staff member besides Naish and Maryam was Mariyam Seena, a recent arrival who handled administration and advertising and had worked with Dave to distribute the Friends of Maldives tsunami aid. When I arrived she was being trained by a visiting marketing consultant from the UK, Simon Hawkins, to approach businesses and develop the advertising side of the business into something capable of sustaining it financially. Like Dave, Simon had also attended Dauntsey's School in Wiltshire with Mohamed Nasheed, where he had partnered the future president at tennis.

Simon had worked in media sales for an assortment of large British papers, a cutthroat commission-heavy sector where only the most self-assured and persistent survived. He would snap his fingers while listing benefits in the unconscious manner of a born salesman, and in his darker moments would confess to not being entirely convinced as to the efficacy of print advertising. This had no bearing on his encyclopaedia of techniques for "overcoming objections" of those he was selling it to. He was very good at it.

Sales was a dark art unknown to me, one I had regarded as a necessary but vaguely unsavoury part of running a news outlet. I understood that journalists pursuing the noble cause of truth had to be paid somehow, but had never paid much attention to how the money appeared. I had been reassured prior to departure that I was only to worry about content and let marketing sort out the finances—this utopian optimism was to be short-lived.

The plan was for Maryam Omidi to hang around for a few weeks and help with the handover. She and Naish had spent the past eleven months each writing three stories a day, six days a week in that tiny room without respite or holiday, barely managing to stay afloat month to month. Smoke could be seen wafting from their ears.

Maryam had gone native during her time in the Maldives, ignoring the small expat community in favour of fully immersing herself in the local side in which she was working. I initially followed her example, but so small, insular and isolating were both worlds that I felt it was important for sanity's sake to keep one foot anchored in each. Perspective was scarce on a 2.2 square kilometre island.

I turned down early invitations to hang out with the President's Office crew, many of whom had been *Minivan* journalists before Nasheed took office. The offers quickly dried up, and I found myself impartial, independent and friend-less. I hovered on the fringes of the expat community, an eclectic assortment of resort liquor salesmen, volunteer teachers, well-paid UN employees, marine biologists, Sri Lankan accountants and Filipino call centre girls. Despite being badly treated almost uniformly by their employers, the Filipinos seemed to be the only ones having a consistently good time—a brilliant time if there was a karaoke machine in the vicinity. They were all young, gorgeous, highly extro-verted and much to the disappointment of many, married and very Catholic.

The expats met at the end of the week at the bar in the airport's Hulhule Island Hotel (HIH), a dingy and stale-smelling pit of despair and Sri Lankan Lion beer, part-owned by the state-controlled airport company and fifteen minutes by ferry from Malé. The only thing worse than the ambience was the service. Whenever you approached the bar a dozen surly staff would do their best to wipe glasses and avoid eye contact. Entertainment was restricted to Wrestlemania. A Minivaner did once attempt to dance, but was approached by management and told to sit down "as this is an Islamic country". God's liquor licence apparently didn't extend to the Harlem Shake.

Lion Beer did once bully the place into holding a pub quiz, and invited *Minivan* to host it. HIH management, however, shot this down at the last minute, citing the potential "terrorist threat".

During *Minivan's* leaner months I did on occasion resort to the bar's free popcorn as a substitute for dinner. There was also expat charity. Many of the liquor salespeople followed the Maldives' unstable politics with keen profes-sional interest, and were known to shout rounds in exchange for insight into this impenetrable side of the country.

The Minivan *Talent*

Naish was indispensable: the soul of *Minivan* and among the best journalists I ever worked with. But he was burned out, desperately in need of a break. He committed as long as he could.

I soon found myself alone in that dusty little room, writing as much as I could to keep the publication afloat as I interviewed potential replacements for Naish. The opportunity I'd been given was incredible, but I did feel a little abandoned. Like many writers I arrived a self-doubting perfectionist, masking this with bravado and over-confidence. Was there something wrong with my articles? Was my leadership so uninspiring as to cause the sole remaining staff member to flee? Was I not working hard enough? In the future whenever anyone complained of being overworked I would crow about these days solo-ing the national news of record, like a crotchety old man glorifying old wars. But there was no glory—just a long and confusing slog. I felt like a sucker.

Minivan needed staff, and I needed perspective. But with no culture or history of journalism in the Maldives the media landscape was a shallow pond to draw from. The profession was unglamorous, reporters despised as propagandists. It demanded good English, education, commitment to a cause. Those who fitted these criteria had been snapped up by the President's Office or the newly cashed-up, UN-funded NGO sector. We couldn't compete on status with the first, or financially with the second.

One girl arrived to the interview escorted by her boyfriend, who proceeded to answer all her questions for her while she sat in meek silence. Another promising candidate on paper was so shy that he was unable to even speak, barely managing to nod once or twice. I missed a trick there, as he later gained confidence and grew into a brilliant journalist at the local newspaper, *Haveeru*. A third candidate was a fierce middle-aged woman very senior in the MDP. I wanted to prove our impartiality, and had to delicately decline. She decided it was because she was an older woman, and gave me both barrels.

The candidates trickled in. I had one critical question for all of them: "Why do you want to be a journalist?"

"Because I want a platform for my opinions," was invariably the answer.

Ahmed Nazeer was the only one straight away to jump at the concept of independence. He had worked for a magazine called *Sandhaanu* and was tired of writing to a political agenda. His English initially wasn't as strong as some of the other potentials, but he was a natural journalist and needed the chance. I took him on and he remained one of *Minivan*'s most consistent, loyal and prolific reporters in the four years I was editor. He had superb links with Malé's underworld and was particularly fond of covering crime. He had a talent for blending into walls, and luring incautious politicians into saying outrageously stupid things over the phone. He was our go-to guy for talking to dodgy sheikhs and island chieftain in far flung atolls, who would share with him the sordid details of crime scenes, reveal the sexual histories of underage sexual assault victims and provide their own gossipy "whodunit" theories. We gave his beat a label: Sex, Drugs, Rock & Roll and Islam. He responded by altering his appearance outside office hours.

Nazeer would eventually switch to part time to accommodate a law degree, a decision made after the police (illegally, in his opinion) confiscated his motorcycle.

Naish returned to contribute the odd article, and freed from the daily story grind, mellowed into the Maldives' top parliamentary correspondent. Mazin "Maani" Rafeeq, fresh from university in New Zealand and sporting a thick Kiwi accent, signed up as an intern. Affable, keenly ethical and with a nose for injustice, among other stories he exposed a culture of child abuse at one of the country's largest international schools which indirectly led to exposure of a multimillion dollar human trafficking racket and the Maldives' inclusion on the US State Department's trafficking watch list. He later moved into real estate.

Mohamed Naahii joined *Minivan* in 2011. Slick, charming and well-connected, Naahii was studying law and took naturally to court reporting, ending up far more versed in the legal system than any Maldivian judge—although so corrupt were this lot on his beat that knowledge of the law was hardly a priority for most of them. Naahii moved to work for the UN after the 2013 presidential election.

"Three times the money for a third of the work," he observed.

Hawwa Lubna joined in 2011. She was one of the feistiest and most confrontational journalists in the Maldivian press pack, with a fierce sense of social justice. We poached her from the rabidly anti-Nasheed publication *Sun Online* after its editor found himself embroiled in one too many debilitating sex scandals. Some of the more MDP-inclined staff were initially suspicious of Lubna, while she expressed surprise that I wasn't forcing a political agenda on her. I gave her the space to write whatever she wanted and to work things out herself, and she became our star poster-journalist. She also wore a headscarf, which gave us street cred with members of the public who felt we were morally deficient, irreligious deviants.

She took a hefty pay cut to work for us, but her gamble on *Minivan*'s reputation as a scholarship factory for young reporters paid off. She scored a four-year course in development studies at Lund University courtesy of the Swedish Institute, and at the last update was running the university's South Asian Student Network, had been adopted by the population of Lund and was swiftly heading towards the post of UN Secretary-General. She returned from Sweden to visit during the 2013 elections, pixie-cropped and having lost her headscarf. We were surprised to discover that underneath she looked like a miniature version of Halle Berry.

Zaheena Rasheed had worked for *Minivan* under previous editors before leaving the Maldives for several years to study journalism at Middlebury in the US. Bright, sunny and extroverted with a warm Cheshire-cat grin that could melt icebergs as efficiently as uncooperative sources, Zaheena won fellowship after fellowship and travelled the world's hotspots, becoming something of an expert in non-violent regime change along the way. She returned to *Minivan* in 2013 and took up the post of deputy editor.

Mariyath "Ehju" Mohamed was a 29-year-old single mother who bravely took on controversial and taboo topics such as religion. She exposed the culture of flogging women for extramarital sex, among other religious issues, and found herself stalked, harassed and targeted by fundamentalist groups. "Your sister has hanged herself and we can help you do the same," read one note posted under the door of her house. On occasion she narrowly escaped a man with an iron bar who was waiting for her in the stairwell of her apartment block. In 2014 her bravery saw her listed among Reporters Without Borders' top 100 "Information Heroes".[3]

Mohamed "Aeko" Fathith worked for *Minivan News* as a translator, quietly and diligently transcribing several stories a day into Dhivehi for a small audience of older Maldivian expatriates. *Minivan*'s Dhivehi edition was fiddly, poorly marketed and with only 200–500 extra hits a day, was basically public service broadcasting. Unfortunately it had dedicated readers who complained bitterly whenever service was disrupted. Aeko kept them off my back while needing minimal oversight.

We also had regular contributors who worked on a freelance basis. Aishath "Shazu" wrote many features for us. She sat on the fence and preferred to steer clear of politics, instead covering social issues, arts and entertainment. Her very considered and detailed food reviews earned us the wrath of many restaurant owners.

If Shazu shied away from controversy, Dr. Azra Naseem embraced it. She wrote many anonymous comment articles for *Minivan* before I finally learned her identity. When she revealed herself we offered her a job immediately. She worked full-time for a while, then decided to focus on the PhD she had begun while living abroad in Dublin. She completed it in 2012 and became the country's foremost authority on counter-terrorism, a qualification that made her unemployable in the Maldives as the state was at the time pursuing quite the opposite agenda. She started her own website, DhivehiSitee,[4] tearing into issues and politicians like tissue paper while kindly allowing us to reprint her.

Yaamyn Rasheed applied for a job as a journalist with *Minivan*, but took one look at the salary and became an IT technician at a large telecom company. He was a fantastic writer, one of the country's best, able to present complex issues with common sense sardonic humour, and alongside Dr. Azra, was one of the very few who would challenge religious extremism under his own name. I figured that if we couldn't employ him we could at least publish his writing. He wrote many comment pieces for us and I was often stunned at how his work more succinctly and eloquently mirrored my own impressions of events and issues. Publishing Yaamyn absolved me of writing editorials, which would otherwise have been quite a job hazard.

The New Editor

Aside from the rented room, *Minivan*'s total assets included an ancient, erratic and possessed printer, and a laptop with a broken shift key that demanded the user engage and disengage caps lock for every capital letter. Nazeer would spend four years tediously typing stories in this fashion.

The backend of the *Minivan News* website was a customized content management system that looked dated and had no social media integration or even capacity to show reader comments—in 2009 the web equivalent of a Ford Pinto. The thing ran from a decrepit server under the bed of a mysterious web guy in Singapore, who had to be phoned to give it a kick whenever it chugged to a halt—usually midway through posting an article of great national significance.

I discovered I had arrived halfway through the development process of a new website. Perhaps relying on the web guy's design acumen, Maryam had instructed him to make the new site look the same as the old one, and as a result he had taken a functional and user-friendly Wordpress template and dutifully customized it to the point where complex digital voodoo was required to post content. As the heir to the crisis I took it over and spent long evenings trying to make it coherent. The web guy declared that for whatever reason the old articles could not be automatically transferred to the new platform, and in desperation hired monkeys to manually copy-paste all the old articles into Wordpress, typographic anomalies included, before deciding to just host the old site in its entirety on a new domain. That server subsequently crashed, the backups were nowhere to be found, and so four years of the Maldives' only news of record vanished into the ether. This would prove very hard to explain to the former editors and anybody researching the lead-up to multi-party democracy in the Maldives.

I struggled under the pressure to manage the development process while producing two stories a day, establishing a social media presence, learning about the advertising and meeting local contacts in an attempt to decipher this new and insular society.

I sensed Maryam's displeasure with her new hire. She and Naish had set a high benchmark for quantity and quality of content by focusing on little else.

The site could accommodate six stories a day plus 4–6 shorter NIBs (news in briefs) of 2–3 paragraphs. Putting out anything less felt like a deep existential failure, a debilitating complex I dubbed "Minivan Guilt". The absence of any higher oversight made *Minivan* fully independent, but it made Minivan Guilt worse because at the end of each day there was nobody to say "Good job, here's a biscuit, go home."

The huge pressure to run a respectable and professional national news service in the absence of credible competition did not help this slow-burning sense of inadequacy. Credibility was *Minivan News'* USP not just by intention, but because the rest of the media seemed to have little regard for the concept, following old patterns of intense politicization to the point of having a loose grip on reality. This meant the burden of being the national news of record went unshared; *Minivan*'s monopoly on credibility, international audience and English-language reporting made it the authoritative gateway for what the rest of the world thought of the Maldives, despite it being under-staffed, under-equipped and under-resourced.

This made for high pressure, high stakes reporting. A rushed story on a Thursday night before a visit to the airport hotel bar, a misquote, mistranslation, a failure to properly fact check a story, a hasty subedit; such everyday mistakes were amplified by the credibility of *Minivan*'s voice and made every click of the blue "publish" button both terrible and thrilling. Its successes and failures were its own, and both had real impact.

The site was averaging 1,800–2,000 visitors a day soon after I arrived and installed Google Analytics to monitor the traffic.[5] This increased fifty per cent year on year to around 4,000 by the time I left, a not inconsiderable audience for a news outlet covering a population of just 350,000 people. The occasional story that hit a nerve—usually judicial travesties involving the beating of convicted fornicators—saw huge spikes of up to 40,000 visitors. Many of these came from large mainstream news sites like the BBC, the *Guardian* and the *Huffington Post*. The endorsement of *Minivan News* as a credible primary news source by large and respected media outlets enabled a butterfly effect, giving *Minivan* enormous influence despite its small size.

The spikes in hits were fun and good for our egos, but more important were the regular returning readers who made up two-thirds of the day-to-day audience. These were a 50:50 mix of local and international readers. The foreign demographic reflected the Maldives' core European tourism markets—UK, France, Italy and Germany—but also included many Maldivian students attending regional university hubs such as India, Malaysia and Singapore. The

41

US also ranked highly, which we suspected was more of an oddity of web routing and the preference of many Maldivians to mask their browsing habits with a proxy server.

Minivan's track record of credible reporting made it a key reference for diplomats and non-government bodies such as the Commonwealth and United Nations. It was among the most heavily referenced sources for the UN Human Rights Commission's Universal Periodic Review, a regular assessment of a country's human rights commitment and commitment to the treaties it had signed. We watched fondly as Gayoom's daughter Dunya Maumoon, freshly installed as state foreign minister after the 2012 coup, tried to defend her father's legacy before the UN Human Rights Commission.[6] The panel, appearing surprised and alarmed at the appalling and unanticipated moral bankruptcy in a pristine tourism paradise, plucked forth issue after issue from a ceiling-high pile of *Minivan News* articles: human trafficking and abuse of foreign workers, flogging of women for extramarital sex, failure to criminalize rape, failure to address an institutionalized culture of torture, criminalization of homosexuality, state-sponsored oppression of thought, conscience and religion.

My favourite demographic were the *Minivan* superfans: a largely overseas group consisting of people who had never been to the Maldives and had no intention of ever visiting, but followed *Minivan News* like a kind of serialized soap opera; an Indian Ocean version of *Game of Thrones*.

Credibility as a Market Niche

Domestically the perception of our credibility was more challenging. The "*Minivan*" brand had been founded by Nasheed's Maldivian Democratic Party in 2005 while it was in self-imposed exile in Sri Lanka, before Gayoom had conceded the introduction of multi-party democracy. The outlets included a small newspaper, *Minivan Daily*, overseen by Nasheed's younger brother Nazim Sattar and distributed to the party faithful for a small cover charge. With the registration of the MDP in the Maldives it was eventually moved to Malé and printed on a small offset press brought over for the purpose. The party also launched *Minivan Radio*, with programmes produced in Salisbury and broadcast over shortwave via Radio Miami at €122 for a 59-minute broadcast. The content of both was overtly political, though without the tabloid insanity of Sappe's *Dhivehi Observer*. The early *Minivan* was the country's first serious and organized dissident media, as distinguished from the rabid local blogosphere, with the explicit aim of toppling Gayoom's regime. It attracted the government's ire—the shortwave signal was jammed in Male, but still widely received by many of the islands.

The MDP's approach with *Minivan News*—the online website—was different from the radio and paper. Paul Roberts had been hauled into the cause via a Maldivian woman he had met at university in the UK, and eventually engaged by Nasheed as an advisor. He brought outside perspective and a cooling effect to some of the party's more erratic and impulsive decision-making, and was able to convince it that it was in their interest to encourage credible journalism on the Maldives in the form of a news website. His breakthrough with *Minivan News* was the decision to recruit foreign editors, typically young journalists with some newsroom experience, to produce a high standard of content while protecting them from the MDP's instinct to control, exaggerate and propagandize the message.

It was a fractious relationship. The activist nature of the MDP's roots and the fact that many of its core members had been tortured under Gayoom's regime made trust the organization's primary currency. This encouraged a "with us or against us" mentality that, while frequently indulged, would eventually lead to the party's seriousness being questioned by the diplomatic communities. What the party couldn't control, they ignored.

The challenge *Minivan News* presented attracted a succession of young and talented journalists from the UK: Will Jordan, Judith Evans, Olivia Lang, Ajay Makan among others. While the publication was instigated and supported by the MDP, reports by these journalists on elections, human rights abuses and corruption scandals were functionally independent and widely praised.

A New Democracy

In 2008 Nasheed won the election. *Minivan* was no longer a priority for the MDP, and the newspaper and radio station folded instantly. The *Minivan News* website was by this stage producing the highest quality journalism in the country, but suddenly had the financial rug pulled out from under it. Realizing its importance, the former editors fought to have it legitimized and officially registered under a specially-created local company with non-executive (non-meddling) directors. This, they felt, would free it from political association and give it a chance of thriving or wilting commercially on its own merits in the new democracy, hold Nasheed's government accountable to its pledges and set the standard for Maldivian journalism while training a new generation of local reporters.

The nobility of the goal was not matched by the practicality. Journalists make poor salesmen, the advertising was never properly developed, and the site hobbled along surviving month-to-month on handouts from the odd businessmen or philanthropist—usually an MDP-aligned figure—who could be persuaded that the merits of independent journalism warranted keeping it alive another few weeks. Their interest in doing this waned the more distant the elections became. *Minivan News* had fulfilled its purpose as far as many of its supporters were concerned, and the donations amounted more to palliative care than a real commitment to development.

The upside was that the decision to corporatize *Minivan News* gave it legitimacy, allowed it to seek visas of its own accord, and put it in charge of its own destiny by turning it into a rather unique kind of hereditary small business, passed down from editor to editor. Unfortunately, however balanced and credible the content, in such a politically charged and polarized country it was never going to shake the widespread belief locally that it was an MDP mouthpiece. Popular opinion held that the outlet ran from Nasheed's basement, a belief encouraged by many on the Gayoom side. On one occasion a visiting foreign diplomat who had just met Waheed's 2012 post-coup government, queried our location with her previous appointment then called me to say she had arrived.

"I'm outside Nasheed's house," she said.

Where Gayoom's regime regarded us with suspicion and distrust due to the publication's political origins, many in the MDP considered *Minivan* disloyal if not outright traitorous. The party did value our credibility—at least enough to use our name and logo when they restarted the radio station and paper as party media after the 2012 coup. Several heated phone calls later I decided that the success of *Minivan News* was to be measured in how few friends we had.

Politics affected the enthusiasm of many businesses to advertise with us. Most business owners were strongly politicized and still regarded advertising in local media as a show of political support. Attempts at market education and long discussions about readership figures, audience share and the benefits of attracting more customers would be followed by "So, are you MDP? Will this please Nasheed?"

I encouraged our critics to let the content speak for itself and did my best to make sure concerns about our perceived polarization were unfounded. Many of our local reporters had strong political feelings, and as they were young, urban and educated, often these swayed towards the MDP. I came to see this as less of a liability and more a trait that made them interested and engaged reporters. It was far easier to encourage self-reflection and balanced journalistic process in the politically interested than it was to bully the apathetic into turning up to work.

I emphasized fairness and the importance of the right to respond. No story was published without effort to contact the aggrieved side. However, very often people caught out would refuse to pick up the phone in the mistaken belief that this would kill the story, and then complain bitterly when they came out looking shifty.

"The trouble with sticking your head in the sand is that you leave your ass in the air," observed one commentator.

On the exceptionally rare occasion that this complaint of bias came directly to us, we offered to remove the line "Was not responding to calls at time of press", include their response in an addendum and, if desired, publish their entire response unedited in a fresh article as "comment and opinion". Despite all the grumbling, in four years nobody took us up on either offer. The result of this policy was that our strongest critics accused us of being both biased *and* perfectly fair.

An early example came from Gayoom's spokesperson, Mohamed "Mundhu" Shareef, who had presented a friendly and charming facade following my arrival as I sought to cover the rally events of Gayoom's Dhivehi Rayithunge Party (DRP). Things were rosy, and I was foolishly patting myself on the back for maintaining an amicable working relationship with both sides. Then we wrote an article about Nasheed granting clemency to a writer sentenced to life imprisonment for writing against Gayoom.[7] Ibrahim Moosa Luthfy, responsible for the defunct publication *Sandhaanu*, had evaded his guards and escaped to self-exile in Switzerland after convincing Gayoom's government he needed medical treatment in Sri Lanka.

We sought comment from Gayoom. Mundhu told me that as far as he was concerned Luthfy was "not a person", "a nobody [who will] remain so" and he would not drop his reputation to the same level as Luthfy by commenting on the matter. Furthermore, news outlets reporting on "these kinds of unprofessional people" also risked being categorized as "unprofessional".

"All you achieve in giving this clown space in the media is giving him unwarranted attention and importance. I do not wish to have any such part in such an exercise. Scum will always remain scum," he suggested.

"If you want people to believe that *Minivan* [News] is anything but Anni's mouthpiece, it's advisable to stay clear of such [an] exercise to give cosmetic makeovers to people like Luthfy."

When his remarks appeared in print on the otherwise unextraordinary article, Mundhu insisted they had been for my benefit only and not for publication. A further salvo of threatening text messages followed, before he forever after refused to comment unless issued a formal apology.

"If *Minivan News* is Anni's mouthpiece then Mundhu is Gayoom's poodle. I think the only way *Minivan News* stands to lose credibility is by asking an idiot like Mundhu for an opinion," one reader commented on the story.

We made a point of continuing to call Mundhu at every relevant opportunity.

Stories

Even if we had been the rabid propagandists of our critics' imaginings, bias would have been unnecessary. The stories wrote themselves, with a cast of pantomime villains lining up to appear in print: rotund and greasy corrupt politicians, dodgy baton-happy policemen, shady gold-chain sporting gang leaders, hellfire-and-brimstone religious scholars.

10 January 2012 was a typical front page: a local group of Islamic extremists called for parliament to enact anti-sorcery legislation, five men and a minor were arrested for sodomy on a fishing boat, a seaplane crew member was messily killed in his aircraft's propeller and the government introduced a "gold-digging clause" making it illegal for Maldivians to marry foreigners earning less than US$1,000 a month.

"Some stories here give you a shotgun and a barrel of fish and tell you to go have a good time," observed Eleanor the American intern two days later, the pair of us sipping whisky at a soiree on the helipad of a visiting Indian warship.

Following, and where possible, making sense of the country's byzantine political intrigue was *Minivan*'s core business. It was known for lengthy and often dusty political exposition, and was considered a must-read by local decision makers and businessmen. Maryam Omidi had bravely expanded the remit to social issues, breaking taboos by reporting on floggings and publishing features on abortion. Crime and religion were also key topics, often overlapping with the political coverage—the politician, businessman, religious leader and criminal were more often than not one in the same person.

We covered the economy, business and tourism, which tended to involve drowned tourists, staff strikes, scams by dodgy local tour operators and myriad other dramas that made the industry enthusiastic readers but disinclined to advertise.

We took many of our day-to-day story tips from the Maldivian media, which was highly partisan but generally quick to cover general news and announcements such as parliament's daily antics. Alerted to a story, we would try to call all concerned and tease out the truth, with a healthy dollop of background, context and links to previous articles and source documents.

We were often criticized for our lack of speed, but without the staff to attend every car accident and press conference we could not compete with the likes of *Haveeru*, the country's largest national newspaper which had a print circulation of just 2,000 and a newsroom of twenty journalists. The culture of press conferences was a throwback to autocracy and did not help—ministries and government departments would arbitrarily call media events with scarcely ten minutes notice, refuse to divulge the topic and then keep the reporters waiting for up to several hours. When the dignitary did appear, the press were expected to sit politely and copy down what was said. The content was most often irrelevant and not at all newsworthy, so we picked our events carefully and showed up sporadically for the sake of appearances. Whenever foreign staff attended these, it was disconcerting often to find the other media's cameras pointing at us rather than the speaker up front. This could be deadly.

"My wife saw you on TV last night and wants to know if you want to borrow this?" said Naish's uncle one morning as I was walking down the stairs past his apartment. He was holding an iron.

The rumour mill was often good for a story. Unlike other countries where gossip operated like Chinese Whispers, with facts becoming more garbled with each transmission, the Maldivian rumour mill operated much like Wikipedia. Each person would add their bit to a communal version of the truth which, when fact checked, most often turned out to be perfectly correct.

Our professionalism and quality of writing, something conceded to us by even our strongest critics, meant that we were often approached by whistleblowers with leaked documents—although the noxious nature of Maldivian politics meant motivations had to be carefully assessed. Issue-based reporting was where we really excelled, however; our deep, investigative articles into topics such as abortion, child prostitution and human-trafficking broke taboos and emboldened the rest of the media.

Sometimes our example-setting was subject to misinterpretation by local media. One publication, launching a bold undercover "investigation" of Malé's brothel scene, sent a team of 19-year-old male journalists in for the full treatment. The resulting softcore "analysis" made no mention of the real issues— sex trafficking and social hypocrisy—but was nonetheless hailed as a triumph of Maldivian investigative journalism even as a line of handcuffed Thai women were paraded past eager TV cameras.

Reader Engagement

It took me a long time to confidently excavate our niche and shake off some of the traditions set by former editors. I spent the first year trying to compete with the mainstream local media, much of which was owned by wealthy political figures and had no need to operate as a financially sustainable business. Eventually I realized this was a race to the bottom, and decided we needed to play to our strengths: accuracy, analysis, credibility and gall. I gave up competing on timeliness and took the line that it was better to be slow and correct than fast and wrong, and invented a new category for us in the Maldivian media landscape: "news review". This worked; local readers told us they would go first to *Haveeru* or *Sun Online* to find out if something had happened, and then to us to find out whether this was true, what it meant and to react themselves.

This reaction was a core appeal that drove repeat visitors and gave us huge relevancy. When it launched in November 2009, the new *Minivan News* website introduced the concept of commenting on articles to the Maldives for the first time. Freedom of expression itself had only just been introduced in the 2008 constitution, although it carried the vague caveat "subject to the tenets of Islam". We were its prototype.

Commenting on articles very quickly had four important effects.

Firstly, it provided us security. The kind of people who would read an article, call their mates and show up with placards and handfuls of rocks instead scrolled down and vented their rage and indignation into the "comment here" window. It made for a very effective vent, and also gave us their IP addresses.

Secondly, publishing comments greatly improved perception of our credibility. People who felt strongly about an issue would submit comments below an article, often including an aside such as "You'll never approve this anyway, MDP scum". That we blankly ticked "approve" and published such criticism went some way to convincing everybody else that we were happy to accept it transparently. Direct threats and attacks on our journalists were joyfully published as evidence that we were right on the money.

Not all such commentary made sense.

"Journalists who are working in *Minivan News* know some of the truth, but they dare not reveal the truth as some of them are blinded by the salary and also some are party to this sexual odessey [sic] and they are enjoying it. They love being commented like 'you are hot'. Perverts!" read a 2013 favourite of the team.

Thirdly, the comments made *Minivan News* a benchmark for public opinion and a forum for debate. Such a forum had not previously existed—debate was segregated as groups of people supporting one particular political party or religious line would consume only the heavily partisan media reflecting that line, and then sit around a café table discussing it only with people who had similar views. There were no new inputs and discussion, and, like cheese left too long in the fridge, dialogue tended to rot. *Minivan News* was the only platform where these disparate groups came together.

Boy, was that messy.

We started by copying the UK *Guardian*'s commenting guidelines—clauses such as "no sexual or racial discrimination"—but quickly discovered that this meant sidelining the vast number of readers who genuinely believed rape was acceptable if a woman was showing her ankles, that homosexuals should be put to death or that there was a conspiracy of Jews out to destroy Islam in the Maldives. I reasoned that it was far better that such opinions were aired so others would have the chance to see they existed, and hopefully challenge them. Foreign commentators would often do so, incredulous at the level of hate, insanity and xenophobia behind the scenes of their favourite tropical postcard destination. Many more moderate locals criticized us for publishing these, claiming that we were destroying tourism.

The fourth impact of reader comments was to make running *Minivan News* a 24/7 job. The debate worked only as long as we ensured a high turnover on the moderation and approval of comments, which meant I was glued to my phone from dawn until dusk. Approving comments was the first and last thing I did every day. The slightest delay and people assumed we were censoring them, such was the climate of suspicion and appetite for expression. This could be exhausting, as it was not unusual to get 300–400 comments on a major story—a staggering number for such a small population. Most were not mere one-line reactions but long and thoughtful responses that put comments on news websites in the developed world to shame. At the same time, seemingly innocuous comments had to be carefully read to the end—the really heinous stuff was often slipped into the last sentence, or written in Dhivehi to befuddle the foreign audience (out of shame? I could never tell). The general belief was that we were liable for anything that appeared on the website, and the country's tech-savvy Wahabist groups would scan every line looking for the slightest religious insult or Quranic misquote over which to shut us down. Occasionally they would submit these comments themselves under a different alias, then complain we were blaspheming if we published them, and accuse us of censorship if we didn't. We dubbed this "sock-puppeting" and did what we could to rein it in, along with the practice of reposting entire pages of stock responses on Islamic websites to try and drown out debate. Other than such minor interference to facilitate debate, I made sure all our staff stayed above the "comment here" line.

Comments were a runaway success, and in the absence of any national polling, turned *Minivan News* into a benchmark for public opinion on the issues of the day. Many people told us they didn't read the articles past the headline, but skipped straight to the bottom for the comments. I didn't take this personally—there was no way we could compete with the comments for sheer tabloid shock and entertainment value. Instead I encouraged the team to embrace our role as custodians of public opinion while other media outlets continued to delete anything remotely critical or which didn't fit with the editor's rabid political fervour. Heading *Minivan* was like running a bowling alley—our job was to set up the pins and let the commentariat knock them down. We lifted rocks, shined lights and aired the country's abundant supply of filthy laundry while remaining neutral and detached.

I only appreciated how far we had taken absolute freedom of expression during a conference in Nepal with the UN Special Rapporteur on the subject, Frank La Rue. Invited to present on the Maldives—tellingly, no Maldivian asked was willing to speak publicly on the topic—I took Frank and the other participants outside into the hotel carpark. I asked them to imagine they were in charge of moderating a comments section for a national news publication in a country with no prior history of free speech, and told them to stand by the bus if they would hit publish, or the pot plant if they would censor. I then read out a list of real *Minivan* comments we had published. Besides La Rue, the attendees consisted of the paragons of freedom of speech from around the region: yet the split was 50:50 each time as each sought to reconcile the ugliness of the sentiments expressed with the right for them to be aired. Freedom of expression was far from the liberal concept many imagined.

Money

Financially, *Minivan News* was a shambles. I inherited the company's books, which consisted of a single small Tupperware box stuffed with receipts for pens and notebooks. It came with a couple of chequebooks for accounts at the State Bank of India with unknown signatories. I later managed to move our accounts to the Bank of Maldives and switched all our books to an online software-as-a-service accountancy platform based in New Zealand. For the first time we could tell how much money we didn't have.

Besides rent for the bunker and staff salaries, the main outgoing was renting apartments for the foreign staff. A two-bedroom shoebox in one of the city's shoddily built concrete tower blocks could easily cost upwards of US$1,300 a month—double the monthly salary of a journalist.

Our income, on the other hand, came from two rotating advertising banners and a strip of Google ads. The latter, while paying us in US dollars rather than Maldivian *rufiya*, was a liability as Google scanned the page on which the ad appeared before automatically displaying whatever its code felt was context sensitive. Articles on Islamic matters would attract ads from Christian missionaries, while coverage of floggings for fornication, brothel raids and domestic violence would elicit ads for "Asian beauties". Either was fodder for our opponents to seek us shut down on grounds of breaching public virtue.

The banners were sold on a per contract basis, which committed advertisers to 6–12 months of payments for a rotating fifteen-second slot. We limited each banner to a maximum of six advertisers and rather than randomly selecting a single banner to display on each page refresh, started it at a random point in a cycle. This way we could guarantee to businesses new to online advertising that their ad would display at least three times during the average reader's time-on-page of four minutes.

It was a bit fiddly but the approach worked. During Simon Hawkins' short intervention we picked up both major telecom companies—the two critical clients for anyone in the business of selling ad space. Cunningly he sold space to one for a song, then went to the other and charged double after convincing them they needed to be where their competitors were. Mariyam Seena meanwhile strong-armed several MDP-aligned business owners into somewhat charitable contracts. The new activity on the banners gave us the legitimacy to pitch to foreign blue chip clients such as the airlines, who were genuinely attracted by our cashed-up AA audience of diplomats, businessmen and decision makers. Once we got the first airline on board, others quickly followed to try and keep up with their competitors.

The advertising approach had freed *Minivan News* from relying on sponsors and sporadic handouts, spreading the income stream and making it much more resistant to any attempts at editorial influence. A grumpy advertiser could be replaced with only minor disruption to cashflow, and besides the odd advertiser demanding that we attend their press conferences or publish a dull press release (which we always talked our way out of), there was little attempt to manipulate coverage. Any attempt to get us to publish advertorial was met with the argument that they would not want to see their competitors engaging in this on our site, and that it would damage our credibility with the very audience they were paying a premium to reach. Nobody had a good comeback to this, or else was asleep by the time I finished talking. *Minivan* gave me the most editorial independence I had had in my career to that point and by late 2011, was even making a small profit.

The revenue was still not enough to provide any financial security, let alone permit any expansion. We had to somehow drop our expenditure, especially on rent. Maryam Omidi had moved me to the nearby island of Villingili for the first month I was there. This was a former prison island that had been turned into a resort during the 1970s tourism boom, before later being converted into a spillover "suburb" for Malé. It was a short ferry ride from Malé that made for a gorgeous commute every morning, although Villingili itself was tiny and very isolating. We worked six days a week late into the night, taking only Fridays off (the Islamic weekend), but I found it a very lonely experience. On weekends I sat on a swinging tyre outside the flat draining the books I had brought with me, and gradually found myself drifting into the office to work by myself.

I was looking forward to moving into Maryam's flat in Malé and to a livelier social life, but the plan fell through after she left. After two years of treading water financially at *Minivan*, I decided it was foolish to continue renting separate accommodation. We were paying huge amounts of money for my living arrangements that we couldn't afford, when I was spending all my time in a dark and dingy office and only going to home to sleep. I decided I would drop the flat and live in the office.

This was a financial breakthrough for *Minivan*. By consolidating accommodation and the office we were able to afford a light, pleasant and airy multistorey two-bedroom apartment on the eastern side of the island with a stunning view over the water. I converted the living room into the office, the adjoining kitchen into the canteen, and lived in one of the rooms upstairs. The flight of stairs became my daily commute.

The other room was soon occupied by Neil Merrett, a World War II blitzera war widow reincarnated into the body of a 29-year-old Welshman. Neil had been working for a very successful Maldivian travel interest publication before his employer suffered a paranoid schizophrenic breakdown and sacked all his foreign staff, believing they were conspiring to take over his business. This was a relief to me, as they had been a team of four talented foreign reporters doing a far better job of covering tourism than I was the national news. I was concerned they would turn their sights on *Minivan*'s turf but after hearing about the boss's decline I decided I needn't have worried.

Seena had long since left, and Neil took on the marketing and administration side of the business as well as contributing to the journalism. He was as much infected with Minivan Guilt as I was, which made us not very much fun to invite to parties. When he finished writing he would move to the kitchen and cook for anyone still in the office while I completed the editing. His kindness was somewhat mitigated by his culinary repertoire, which consisted solely of dubious brown stodge he insisted was "Welsh fusion". I would have to hide precious bottles of balsamic vinegar, which he would use liberally as a stew flavouring agent. I walked in on one particularly innovative streak, which involved dicing and stewing entire shawarma kebabs bought from the shop round the corner.

The clash of cultures did have its lighter moments.

"What are these green balls?" Lubna asked, poking at the bowl Neil had placed in front of her in an attempt to broaden her nutritional horizons.

"Peas, Lubna," he explained patiently.

Neil also looked after our janitor, a gentle and kind-hearted Bangladeshi man called Wahid who visited three times a week to vanquish our collective filth. He had once been a cook and, one strange rumour had it, a former professional boxer. Neil fought to protect him from the lethargic callousness of the immigration authorities, managing registration papers on Wahid's behalf. Wahid once fell sick and almost died, after continuing to work despite an undiagnosed ruptured bowel. The public hospital had no interest in patients who couldn't pay, and if you were a Bangladeshi worker your best hope was to bleed out quickly in the lobby. Neil got Wahid admitted for surgery, and lived in the ward for several days after discovering that the nurses were refusing to clean him, feed him or replace his saline drip from the hospital stores. Wahid recovered, and Neil appointed himself HR manager.

The *Minivan* apartment had a third room—really more of a cupboard off the kitchen barely able to fit a small bed, let alone a suitcase. We discovered we could import talented foreign journalism graduates desperate for work experience, stash them in the cupboard and work them six days a week in exchange for a pitiful stipend in nonexchangeable Maldivian *rufiya*.

It was an extremely successful programme. Eleanor Johnstone, detained on arrival over a technicality, remarked on seeing her room that it was smaller than the immigration detention cell. She stayed for six months all the same and was followed by Daniel Bosley, a postman from Cheshire with multiple Masters degrees who had spent two years working internships trying to break into journalism. We would send Luke Powell from Shropshire into the darkest reaches of the country's north for two weeks on an MDP campaign boat crammed with eighty activists and a single toilet. He returned shattered, and moved home to work for the local paper where he met a nice local girl and lived happily ever after. Not all came from journalism backgrounds: Leah Malone's background was in aerospace engineering, but she had a nose for environmental stories and wading through large wordy reports to find nuggets of newsworthy horror that would trigger a torrent of furious callers. The memories were generally fond—Eleanor even returned to help us cover the 2013 election, while Dan returned a year after his internship to succeed me as editor. Key to getting the job was the President's Office press secretary calling him "a little shit" over the phone.

People often asked me whether we were concerned for our safety. If the questioner was pretty it sometimes pleased me to play this up, but in reality the predominance of Western tourism meant attacks on white foreigners were exceedingly unlikely. My real concern was for our local staff, who were much more vulnerable as society considered them property of the local elites. This worsened after the 2012 coup as the government's hold weakened, the security services became more erratic, and a sense of impunity and confidence grew among the country's fundamentalists. Maldivian journalists working for other publications were attacked, an MP was murdered. The stress was high. Mariyath Mohamed, consumed by worry in the lead up to the 2013 election, had a heart attack and collapsed in the street. Doctors from the nearby private hospital zapped her back to life with a defibrillator and she crawled into the office, insisting on working. In August 2014, eight months after the new presidential elections and my departure, the fears proved justified. A *Minivan* journalist, Ahmed Rilwan, was abducted at knifepoint outside his house by a group of fundamentalists and forced into a vehicle. A year later he was still missing, with police showing little interest in seriously investigating the case. At least one suspect absconded to fight in Syria.

In the first few years after I arrived, the greatest challenge to our reporting was far more prosaic: Maldivian phone etiquette. In the vast majority of societies the sound of a ringing phone impels a person to answer. Not so in the Maldives. Neither did people give their name or say "hello" when they did deign to answer, instead triggering an awkward and confusing dance as you tried to establish their identity from the non-committal grunting.

It wasn't a language issue. Most people spoke conversational English, and young people, most of the government and the senior civil service were fully fluent. The vast majority of people simply would not answer the phone unless they had saved the number and had a personal relationship established with the caller. If the conversation was likely to be difficult or something had happened that had the potential to make them look bad, they would simply turn their phones off. This applied twofold to appointed spokespeople.

The flipside was exceptional access. It was normal to ring or SMS cabinet ministers for direct comment, or, as they were all social media junkies, message them on Facebook or Twitter. But generally, if you ever wanted to ring somebody, you had to first spend an afternoon with them drinking coffee and then refresh this procedure every few months. However, unlike civil servants, who spent much of the day on Facebook, we were unable to commit the many hours required to socializing for even the most meagre of stories. I could count on two hands the contacts who answered consistently, and we naturally leaned towards taking their comments more than others. The rest were a lottery, one so unpredictable as to actively determine each day's news agenda.

A second major challenge was grappling with the very tropical work ethic. The foreign staff, living in the office, suffering cabin fever and brought up in a culture of showing up at work on time or being fired, struggled with the Maldives' very different approach. We admittedly did better than many other workplaces, where staff would arrive in the morning to sign in, and then go out for breakfast and not return until the following day. This was indulged by employment legislation: staff were guaranteed thirty days paid holiday, ten days paid "personal leave", six days paid leave to attend circumcision ceremonies and thirty days paid sick leave (taken much the same as a holiday, usually without notice, or if you were lucky, an SMS with a perfunctory reference to "loose motions"). I once calculated that a female employee who became pregnant could take 146 days paid leave off a year under Maldivian employment law—a fatal blow for any small business. It wasn't just us, either—the culture of arbitrary unexplained absence even had a name: *Salaam* (Arabic for "peace"). The CEO of one of the country's largest financial sector employers once privately revealed he had a "Salaam rate" of 15–20 per cent of his staff on any given day.

"On one occasion, a girl took Salaam but happily turned up to Traders in the evening for a drinks party launch," another foreign employer told me. "She thought I was totally in the wrong and a complete bully the next day when I told her off!"

Business-crippling cultural oddities aside, it was extremely demoralizing whenever local staff failed to show, or rolled in at 4pm. There was little you could do in the way of discipline—voluntary unemployment was high, any

Maldivian wanting to work could generally get a job and many young and educated people were supported by their families and had little need to work at all. Kids without 'O' Levels would typically sit around unemployed until a relative arranged an entry level job as a "Director".

The small population meant that there was a very limited talent pool, and we could not motivate through money, as we had so little, or even status. Fancy titles were very popular, but journalism was a widely despised profession of last resort. We could motivate through a cause, but this depended on the whim of the employee and fluctuated on a daily basis.

When staff showed up hours late, this pushed back the editing until late in the evening. We had one day off a week and scarcely any reprieve or chance to take holidays, and so just ended up working constant, back-to-back 16-hour days. It was toxic and bred resentment, but short of doling out shock collars the chaos and inconsistency just had to be adapted to. It wasn't a management issue, just something you had to accept and work around if you were going to function at all.

Still, there were tricks to mitigate the impact. I introduced a sign-in book, pushed the start time to 10am and gave staff a one hour grace period. Anyone who arrived after 11am—that included the foreign staff, although we were just upstairs—simply wouldn't be paid for that day, but were still welcome to come in and write out of guilt. Many staff did, effectively working for free until my guilt got the better of me and they were paid anyway.

Sick days had to be phoned in before 10am, which immunized the system from phoning in sick at midday with an "alarm clock malady". Between this and the liberal use of freelancers, we at least protected *Minivan* from paying for work that wasn't being done.

We managed to appear as a large and well-oiled company to the outside world, an illusion needed in order to inspire confidence among advertisers and sources. A good sign was the sense of ownership that many Maldivian readers seemed to take in us, an ownership that, based on the constant stream of advice, demands and criticism, belied the meagre responses to journalist job ads and which suggested that much of the country were experts at running national news outlets. This was a relief, as I hadn't a clue.

My elevator pitch for *Minivan* referred to weighty higher purposes such as upholding democracy and defending freedom of expression from the sort of people who felt that a "Ministry of Information" was a useful public institution. The actual daily experience was more akin to being a single bench of galley-slaves rowing a leaking boat and trying to escape from pirates while the other oarsmen gathered around yelling "row faster!'

4

RISE OF THE MDP

"Forms of torture and ill-treatment included the use of suspension, lengthy use of stocks, being beaten with fists and bars, kicked, blindfolded, handcuffed, the dislocation of joints and breaking of bones, being forced to roll and squat on sharp coral, being drowned or forced into the sea, being put in a water tank, being burned, having bright lights shone in eyes, being left outside for days while tied or handcuffed to a tree, being covered in sugar water or leaves to attract ants and goats, and in one case, being tied to a crocodile's cage. Many of the testimonies suggest that the only limit to the torture and ill-treatment imposed was the imagination of those whose control they were under."

REDRESS report submitted to UNHRC,
"Addressing the Legacy of Torture and Ill Treatment in the Maldives"

The earnest and vertically-diminutive man walked into the office of Robert Key, MP for the safely Conservative Party seat of Salisbury, Wiltshire, for nearly thirty years.

Mohamed Nasheed made an extraordinary impression.

"You never knew who was going to walk through your office door with what sort of problem," Key told me during an interview in 2011, shortly after he stepped down and yielded the seat to fellow Conservative, John Glenn.[1]

"It might be a regular sort of problem—housing or taxation—but just sometimes there was an issue that really gripped me as really important. This was one of those."

"I saw a young man with great vision and enormous energy and determination, who wanted to change his country. I'd had only one or two similar expe-

57

riences in Salisbury, with other people who had equally great ambitions, interests and determination, but I recognized this particular young man as someone who I could not ignore, indeed who I wished to promote, because I believed he had all the right instincts as a democrat."

Nasheed was very nervous and apprehensive, Key recalled.

"He didn't know if he could trust me. Trust is the big issue in democratic politics, and I think he had one or two rebuffs from other politicians. I took him at face value, and we took it from there. I met him a number of times in Salisbury, and I never ceased to believe in his own vision and his motives, and his motives appeared to me to be all correct. I know nothing about all the party politics of the Maldives, but I do understand a good democrat when I see one."

Nasheed's Maldivian Democratic Party, which included many former political prisoners, had declared its existence in 2001 and sought to register in the Maldives. The application was binned, arrests followed. In the wake of Evan Naseem's death in custody and Gayoom's violent crackdown on the resulting protests, the MDP fled to Sri Lanka and declared itself in exile. Other senior members, including Nasheed, travelled to the UK in late 2003 and sought asylum. This led to the knock on the door of David Hardingham's cottage in Salisbury.

The exiled activists began to establish their credentials in the UK from a small office at the back of Hardingham's house, eventually moving to a room above Milford Street. Leafing through the artefacts of these humble beginnings, I discovered a "Draft Menifesto" and an old chequebook issued to an outfit called the "Maldivian Demorcratic Party".

More successful than its spelling was the party's effort to seek recognition from the British government. Key was approaching retirement but saw in Nasheed an opportunity to elevate democracy abroad.

"I always believed that British politicians had a duty to other Commonwealth countries. And that was why I believed it was more than worthwhile—it was my duty—to assist in this process," he told me.

Key took the MDP's case to ministers in the British government. The reaction was "positive, always open-minded, waiting for the evidence to emerge".

"I think the British government never sought to interfere with political processes, but it did wish to ensure democratic processes were possible in the Maldives. That was why the Westminster Foundation for Democracy—which is an all-party foundation—was willing to supply funds and people to advise."

The involvement of the Foundation, established in 1992 and sponsored by the British Foreign and Commonwealth Office to promote democracy around the world, gave the MDP legitimacy as the Maldives' first opposition party. Its members were now not only motivated, but had access to funds and training.

Gayoom's government, petulant and intolerant of any dissent or criticism, nervously observed the MDP professionalizing itself abroad in Salisbury. By 2005 Gayoom was growing increasingly paranoid about his security, especially after Hardingham and others made a show of attempting to arrest the dictator inside the UN building in Geneva. Gayoom's government hired UK security and private investigation firm Sion Resources to conduct a surveillance operation targeting Hardingham, dubbed "Operation Druid".

Operation Druid employed several "agents" to rifle through Hardingham's financial records, tail him at a music festival and monitor his house. Receipts revealed that this cost the Maldivian government £49,726 (including four parking tickets). Separately, a Maldivian spy was recruited to infiltrate the group of exiled activists holed up in Hardingham's cottage.

Stepping off the train in Salisbury, the spy reported back that the town was home to Britain's largest cathedral. Leaflets subsequently distributed around Malé, alleged that Hardingham and Salisbury Cathedral were planning to blow up the Islamic Centre in Malé and build a "victory church". Mundhu, at the time the government's chief spokesperson, meanwhile circulated "proof" of the plot in a letter purportedly from Hardingham to Nasheed.[2]

"I trust that you and your flock will keep the flame of love that we planted in your hearts burning brightly forever," Mundhu-Hardingham tells Nasheed under the Salisbury Cathedral letterhead,[3] before outlining the plan to blow up the mosque. If a suspicious Maldivian reader still needed to be convinced of the malignant foreign threat to national sovereignty, Mundhu-Hardingham signs off as Nasheed's "Keeper".

A lucky *Minivan* journalist rang Salisbury Cathedral and assumedly asked the old lady who polished the candlesticks whether she was indeed planning a terrorist attack in the Maldives. This conversation sparked a domestic terrorism alert in the UK and led to the MDP receiving police protection from the shire constabulary.

More allegations from the Maldives, this time to the Sri Lankan government, claimed that the exiled *Minivan* was stockpiling weapons for an attempted coup. Following a tip off, the MDP activists writing in the Sri Lankan capital of Colombo were raided by police and their office searched. The officers apparently missed the publication's munitions stockpile and nothing more came of it. The Maldives regime had itself begun to run out of ammunition.

Dr. Ahmed Shaheed served as Gayoom's foreign minister throughout this period. Confident, highly intelligent and astute, he sensed the changing wind and became something of an agent provocateur within the regime, and a key architect of the Maldives' pre-2008 democratic reforms. A pragmatic sort, he also served as foreign minister during Nasheed's government before being vengefully forced out in 2011 by Gayoom's opposition-majority parliament.

By the end of that year the UN had appointed him UN Special Rapporteur on Iran. Before he left, I spoke to him about life inside Gayoom's increasingly erratic pre-2008 government. He was candid about the regime's growing paranoia as the outside pressure for reform grew.[4]

"The [government's] intelligence people got all sorts of reports from all sorts of sources, which any government is obligated to investigate. The range of reports included attempts to assassinate Gayoom, and they came from sometimes official and sometimes unofficial sources," he said.

"I'm not suggesting this applied to Salisbury, but in the summer of 2004, when there was emergency rule here, there were a number of concerns as to who was funding the MDP. The government wanted to know who was behind it, and whether it was a foreign government.

"What these operations did was try to see who was who. And a lot of the operations the government felt were against it came from Salisbury, and I think the government of the day felt justified in engaging a firm to look into what was going on.

"We're talking about people who [the government] had deported from the Maldives for proselytization, people involved in all sort of activities. [The government] felt they needed to check on that, and what came out was a clean bill of health. Nothing untoward was happening, and these people were by and large bone-fide," Dr. Shaheed said.

He conceded that Salisbury Cathedral's "terror plot" was a "mischievous suggestion".

"There were all sorts of allegations about who was behind MDP. Was this a home-grown opposition, was a foreign government behind it? Who was the MDP?

"Part of the concern at the time was that this might have been a religion-based opposition to Gayoom. There was paranoia about [protecting] Islam."

Efforts to marginalize the budding MDP religiously as a threat to Islam and sovereignty, neutralizing it domestically as a political threat, failed to gain traction in 2007. However, the theme would become very important later.

"The various allegations about the MDP were investigated, and it came out clean. It was a bone-fide political party," Dr. Shaheed said.

"Gayoom knew that, and any suggestion that the MDP had links to a cathedral was just utter mischief. It was all rubbish—there was also a picture going around of Gayoom wearing a cross. The allegations were flying left and right, and then somebody got off at a station near Hardingham's residence and saw a cathedral nearby."

Despite crossing the line into Nasheed's government, Dr. Shaheed was for a long time distrusted by the MDP grassroots. During the lead-up to the 2008 election he had continued to field calls from diplomats, journalists and groups such as Amnesty, while the rest of the government switched off their phones. In the process, he became perceived as the face of the Gayoom regime's excesses.

"When I came into the Gayoom regime [in July 2005] it was very unfriendly to human rights. My terms of engagement with Gayoom was that he would pursue and reform certain policies—which happened, ultimately," Dr. Shaheed said.

"We welcomed the first visit of Amnesty International and began working with them, and became much more open and engaged. We opened the doors to all UN Special Rapporteurs.

"We became much more engaged with human rights. I and New Maldives [a group within the regime that pushed for liberal democracy] colleagues of mine were able to impart to Gayoom and his older advisers that we should allow pluralism at home—that we should allow political parties, and give space to the opposition.

"Many of those who are linked to the president himself, through his friends and family, will know that I was an interlocutor between them and Gayoom. Twice I put my job on the line to get Nasheed out of arrest, and said I was going home unless he was released. I also put my job on the line for reporters.

"The controversies around me arose because in Gayoom's time whenever there was a public crisis, all his ministers would turn off their telephones except me. Only mine would ring. So the only voice that was heard was mine, and people associated it with the actual action. For example when people were bashed on the island of Fares-Mathoda in January 2006, only my phone rang. I tried to answer people's concerns and I was the only person quoted, so if you search for the incident all the comments are mine.

"When Hussein Solah was killed and found dead in the lagoon in Malé [in April 2007], all the ministers turned off their phones. It was clearly the Home Minister's charge, but he would not speak to the press. Families were looking for information and I gave all the information I had on the case. Whenever

Nasheed was arrested, I was the only person who would speak to anybody, so my name gets thrown on everything."

* * *

Gayoom's government was only cajoled into recognizing other political parties in mid-2005. In 2008 it accepted a new constitution enshrining multi-party democracy and separation of the executive, judiciary and legislature. It was a neat detail that the process began in Salisbury, home of the Magna Carta—the document that in 1215 established constitutional law in the English-speaking world and imposed the first limits on the power of the monarchy.

The MDP naturally took much of the credit for this. However, other surprising and unexpected forces had been at work.

A PR Coup

Concerned with his image following the 2003 crackdown and state of emergency in the wake of Evan Naseem's death, Gayoom contracted multinational public relations juggernaut Hill+Knowlton to improve his reputation—at a price of US$1.7 million.

The company, one of the two largest PR firms in the world, had represented everybody from the Church of Scientology to *Ladies' Home Journal*, and was no stranger to improving the reputation of governments accused of human rights violations. In late 2003 H+K sent several advisers, including Tim Fallon, a former advisor to Tony Blair, to draw up a preliminary assessment of the government's reputational woes and make recommendations to address them.

The "Issues audit and communications strategy" document, finally leaked in 2012, revealed that Hill+Knowlton had not only recommended but also implemented much of the country's pre-2008 democratic reforms. Rather than simply try and rebrand the dictator, the firm actively drafted new legislation and had Gayoom rubber stamp it in his pet parliament. This ironically made the PR firm about as responsible as the MDP for the human rights and governance reform that paved the way for the country's first democratic election in 2008, and from Gayoom's point of view probably a poor investment.

The surprisingly frank report reads like a human rights dossier. In it, H+K urged Gayoom to allow multi-party democracy, declaring his existing position "untenable, unsustainable and causing significant damage to perceptions of democracy".

"To the external world there is an idealistic consensus that those who are willing to sacrifice liberty for security deserve neither liberty nor security.

Moreover, the process gives the impression of a political elite which feels that it knows best," it stated.

Parliament was considered manifestly corrupt, as particularly on the islands H+K "got the impression that the process of candidates buying votes was commonplace and expected. Indeed, the agency heard some concern that the price of votes was going up and candidates had to spend way more than they did previously to secure the same votes!"

H+K urged "comprehensive reformation of the single candidate Presidential election system, with the adoption of a multi-candidate process", and "a comprehensive reform of the Maldivian constitution to the extent whereby any political party can operate with complete freedom."

H+K's recommendations also included separation of the controversial National Security Service into new police, military and correctional branches, constitutional reform allowing for the introduction of multi-party democracy, support for the Human Rights Commission of the Maldives (HRCM), reform of the Majlis (parliament) and reform of the criminal justice system, including an end to the practice of flogging.

The PR firm's bravest recommendation to Gayoom concerned the introduction of religious freedom. The government's current attitude was "untenable and unsustainable alongside any claim to be in accord with human rights".

"One of the first—and most striking impressions—visitors to the Maldives receive is given to them when filling in the arrivals card. On the back, amongst hard hitting warnings about bringing drugs, spear guns and pornographic materials to the islands, stands further warnings forbidding 'items of idolatry' and 'items contrary to Islam'," H+K observed.

"Notwithstanding the very clear infringement of the Universal Declaration of Human Rights, the situation is manifestly unfair to the citizens of the Maldives who may wish to practice other religions. Indeed, it is worth noting that the Maldives has not always been a Muslim country."

The PR firm urged Gayoom to allow foreign reporters into the country, and prepare itself to face criticism. This was a government that had tolerated no dissent, jailing journalists and even confiscating diaries it deemed controversial. H+K was not only asking Gayoom to endure criticism from foreign journalists, but also allow them to meet people who might say bad things about him.

"In organising the itinerary for such a [press] trip it is important that we enable those attending to get a balanced picture of what is going on and therefore we must be prepared for them to meet with people who are to some extent critical of Government," the consultants suggested.

"This is often quite a difficult step for governments to overcome but unless we do this we believe journalists may feel we are trying to hide the truth from them. We should not expect that a journalist will not ask us difficult questions nor have relations with others who are critical."

The report goes on to list foreign journalists and news agencies to target. *Minivan News* was not among these, but did warrant special mention as a "clandestine newsletter to which many locals do not attach legitimacy".

"[Locals] only recognise as press what is in circulation in the country under registration," suggested the firm, with an optimistic perception of the Maldivian public's respect for Ministry of Information bureaucracy.

H+K's Reform

Gayoom had ruled a rather docile population for almost thirty years with little threat to his regime, barring a coup attempt by Tamil Tiger mercenaries in 1988—foiled though Indian intervention. The outcry following Evan Naseem's death, and the state brutality that followed, showed a leader unused to being on the back foot. The 2013 report he commissioned from H+K to try and stage-manage the crisis was one of the frankest assessments of a Maldivian political situation I read during my four years in the country.

The dictator's willingness to follow the recommendations of a couple of suits from London was surprising, and his political undoing.

"I do not know the motives of Gayoom in hiring Hill+Knowlton," Dr. Shaheed told me.

"When you are in office for thirty years and your ministers and associates make recommendations to you, you don't believe them. But if you have a posh firm from London making recommendations, you tend to believe them. And Gayoom did. But my links with them were on the basis that they would contribute to reform in the Maldives. I agreed to be a liaison person with them, but only if they would work on a governance reform project.

"Their first task was an audit of governance in the country: meeting various stakeholders, gauging public perception and making recommendations on what ought to be done. Their recommendation was that we needed to implement rapid political reforms, including political pluralism.

"Based on that Gayoom engaged them on a longer-term basis. This entailed assisting him with reforms internally, and projecting those reforms externally. It was not purely a PR function and it did entail real policy prescriptions for Gayoom.

"Things that Gayoom did on their recommendation included separating the army from the police, a whole raft of reforms on judicial function, prison reform, constitutional reform—all these things were done at their request."

The only suggestions Gayoom rejected were the dismissal of the brutal Police Chief, Adam Zahir, and the removal of his half-brother Abdulla Yameen from the chairmanship of the State Trading Organization (STO), a body later found by forensic financial auditors to be engaged in the sale of up to US$800 million in oil to the Burmese military junta via a dubious joint venture in Singapore.[5]

Gayoom also rejected H+K's recommendation that freedom of religion be introduced.

"Of course, there's no way any government here can introduce freedom of religion, and H+K's usefulness ended when they recommended Yameen be removed—at that point Gayoom stopped listening to them," said Dr. Shaheed.

Nationalism and Islam had proved too potent a weapon to galvanize support against the MDP, and Gayoom was unwilling to be disarmed of it. Instead he allowed religion to be "weaponized" for political purposes during the drafting of the new constitution, which linked Islam to citizenship—among other provisions including the total ban of pork and alcohol outside resorts. As the penalty for outspoken apostasy was considered to be death—or in practice and at the very least, intense social ostracism—a person born in the Maldives was to have a very proscriptive life forced upon them. The actual provisions were included by the speaker of the new constitutional assembly, none other than Gasim Ibrahim of the Villa Resort empire.

"Despite opposition from a few, I carried out my religious and national duty courageously believing in Allah. By the will of Allah, I was able to succeed," Gasim boasted to a campaign rally in 2013.[6]

He had likewise succeeded at becoming the country's single largest importer of banned haram commodities, with leaked customs records showing in 2011 that his hotels—including the Royal, Paradise, Sun and Holiday Island resorts—imported 121,234.51 litres of beer, 2,048 litres of whiskey, 3,684 litres of vodka and 219.96 kilos of pork sausages.[7]

While generally a success, the plan to introduce Western democracy to the Maldives failed to account for the hypocrisy and protectionism of the country's existing political leadership, and greatly overestimated the public's contempt for such behaviour. And "plan" it was; an Amnesty International source involved in the process privately confessed to me in 2014 that the human rights organization had worked closely with Dr. Shaheed and H+K's Tim

Fallon to bring about concrete democratic reform right under Gayoom's nose. The autocrat believed he was paying for the country's image to be window-dressed with trappings of democracy—instead, H+K sold him the real thing.

Bare Cupboards

"I am proud of my role with God's will in the introduction of a new age of democracy. With much love, thank you for giving me the opportunity to be the leader of this country for the past thirty years."

Stunned by his loss, spotlit by the international community and unable to resist the tide of inevitability, Maumoon Abdul Gayoom stepped down in one of South Asia's rare bloodless transfers of power. The ousted dictator appeared generous in defeat, Nasheed magnanimous in victory. Gayoom should be allowed to live out his days in peace, the new president said. The pair posed for photos, captor and former captive; diplomats and democrats applauded. Malé partied like never before. The mood was euphoric and hopeful, later compared by some to the 2009 election of Barack Obama.

It was a turbulent moment for the old regime, which was not as eager to disappear into the history books as its public platitudes suggested. Rumours emerged later that the then Chief of Defence had rejected a plea from Gayoom to help him cling on to power—a scenario that had no doubt been anticipated by diplomats, and averted by the United States' extensive and sudden "training" of the renamed Maldives National Defence Force (MNDF).

Moreover, Nasheed only won the election in the second round by cobbling together a shaky coalition of vested interests against the dictator. The MDP had not really won the election, Gayoom had lost it. In the first round Nasheed's MDP claimed 24.91 per cent of the vote against 40.34 per cent to Gayoom's Dhivehi Rayithunge Party (DRP). Gayoom had fallen short of the "50 per cent plus one vote" majority needed for a first round victory under the new constitution's hybrid presidential/parliamentary system.

The first round votes had been diluted by ambitious officials in Gayoom's regime who sensed the changing times and saw an opportunity to run them-selves. These were "personality parties", simply representing the interests of a few individuals with little attempt at a manifesto or plan for the country. They included resort tycoon Gasim Ibrahim—at the time Gayoom's finance minis-ter, Gayoom's Attorney General Dr. Hassan Saeed (with Foreign Minister Dr. Shaheed as his running mate), Umar Naseer—a former policeman accused of harsh treatment of inmates, and one of the main brains on the drafting committee of the new constitution, Ibrahim "Ibra" Ismail.

These were all ambitious and important characters who would show up repeatedly in Maldivian politics over the next four years—often with mixed results for the future of democracy. When they first threw their hats into the snake pit during the 2008 election they split the vote: Saeed took 16.6 per cent, Gasim 15.22 per cent, Umar Naseer 13.39 per cent and Ibra just 0.77 per cent.

In the second round, Saeed, Gasim and Ibra sided with the MDP against Gayoom. Nasheed was already in coalition with the Gaumee Ithihaad Party (GIP), the tiny party belonging to his running mate, Dr. Mohamed Waheed Hassan Manik. Dr. Waheed was Stanford-educated, friendly with the Americans and had spent time working in both the education sector and for the UN abroad. He was considered a calm, diplomatic and thoughtful counterbalance to Nasheed's high-energy impulsiveness, though in retrospect would turn out to be more in line with Shakespeare's Macbeth.

The MDP was also already allied with the Adhaalath Party (AP), at the time a group of broadly conservative Islamic scholars to whom he had promised a new Ministry of Islamic Affairs. The MDP hoped Adhaalath would mitigate some of Gayoom's religious attacks and pull in support from conservative voters.

The MDP made promises to Saeed and Gasim in exchange for their support in the second round, including mid-term elections, leadership positions and a share of cabinet portfolios. Some promises were remembered differently by the subsequently embittered.

"Nasheed said to me that I would have a free hand to pick the cabinet and then [he] would straight away sign his resignation dated exactly a week after his inauguration," recalled a still-petulant Dr. Saeed years later in 2014, in a comment piece for newspaper *Haveeru*.[8]

Whatever the eventual consequences, in 2008 this coalition of the desperate succeeded in ousting Gayoom in the second round, with 53.65 per cent to Gayoom's 45.32 per cent. Voter turnout was over 86 per cent.

Parting Gifts

"My prayer is that God give prosperity to the Maldives and show us peaceful and affluent days," said Gayoom in his concession speech.

God's intervention was needed as the coffers had naturally been cleaned out by the time Nasheed's new government transitioned into office.

"The Maldives faces the most challenging macroeconomic situation of all democratic transitions that have occurred since 1956," observed the World

Bank, in its report *Placing the Macro Challenge Facing the Maldives in Context*. "The full level of financial strife may not be fully appreciated."

It apparently had been fully appreciated by Gayoom, who, in a city where many lived six to a room, had an enormous palace containing golden toilets, imported Italianate furniture, a swimming pool and fleet of 55 cars. A short voyage from Malé in the US$9.5-million presidential yacht was the presidential island of Aarah, containing luxury beach villas, a harbour, private cricket pitch and a treehouse for his children.

The palace accounts for 2007–2008 showed that the largesse had been readily extended to family and supporters, with one MP—Ahmed Mahlouf—receiving US$24,000 for a nose job in Singapore.[9] Challenged, he insisted it had been for "a serious surgery."

"It was not theft," he clarified.

Other entries included US$30,698 in plane tickets for a shopping trip to London for the first lady Nasreena and five of her friends, and US$50,000 in cash for a trip to Dubai drawn from the "Theemuge Welfare Fund". Spectacles for Gayoom' son Ghassan set the "welfare fund" back US$2,000, as did Nasreena's spending spree on gold and diamond jewellery. Upmarket hotels were a frequent treat, shared liberally: on one occasion, a family member racked up a US$20,000 bill at the Grand Hyatt in Singapore. On another, the palace had nappies airfreighted to Malé from Britain, earmarked for Gayoom's grandson.

The audit reports, produced by the new Auditor General's office in the first years of the new democracy, were just the tip of the iceberg.

"A lot of the government's money was taken through corrupt [means] and saved in the banks of England, Switzerland, Singapore and Malaysia," declared the new Auditor General, Ibrahim Naeem, at a press conference. His comments were reprinted in a *New York Times* piece on the World Bank's Stolen Asset Recovery Initiative (StAR), headlined "Going after government looters".[10]

Naeem then sent a list of dozens of current and former government ministers to the Prosecutor General, requesting they be prosecuted for failure to declare their assets.

He lasted five days following the announcement. Gayoom's cronies in the opposition majority parliament voted to dismiss him over allegations of corruption, specifically claims that he had bought a tie with a government credit card. The motion to dismiss the Auditor General was put forward by the parliamentary Public Accounts Committee (PAC), chaired by Deputy Speaker and member of the Gayoom-allied People's Alliance (PA), Ahmed

Nazim. It mattered not that Nazim had pressed for the Auditor General's dismissal less than a week after he himself had pleaded not guilty to charges of conspiracy to defraud the former Ministry of Atolls Development.

The auditor's post remained unfilled for the best part of the next few years, both sides apparently having decided that the role was too dangerous.

Economic Sabotage

Nasheed declined the dictator kitsch of the palace at Theemuge, opting instead for the older, smaller and more austere presidential residence of Muleeage from which he would walk the block every day to the President's Office. This decision wasn't universally popular, as many Maldivians felt the street activist should have begun acting predictably "presidential" after being elected.

"I want to see him waving from this gate. Like the Queen does at Buckingham Palace," a passerby told visiting BBC journalist Chris Morris in 2009.[11]

"When we started this administration, the presidency was costing more than US$150 million a year," Nasheed told Morris at the time. "This is something we simply can't afford. We've brought it down to US$4 million. I don't feel the cut, and we can use the rest of the money for old age pensioners, for schools, for housing and very many things we need now."

Nasheed gave Gayoom's tacky and ostentatious palace to the Supreme Court, a decision which five years later could be seen as both fitting and highly ironic. In 2009 Maldivians and members of the foreign press were invited to wander through the building and see for themselves the setting in which the dictator had ruled a country where the average citizen outside Malé earned just $642 a year.

The new government set about trying—without success—to eBay the presidential yacht, while the island of Aarah was used to host events such as the Hay Festival of Literature and Arts held in 2010. Young people, starved of entertainment and forbidden parties, danced in the rain to the sound of visiting French DJ Ravin intermingled with the thump of traditional *bodu beru* drumming. Underneath their feet was the cricket pitch where Gayoom's more obsequious ministers were reportedly compelled to let the autocrat repeatedly score. The Italianate furniture was distributed to government buildings that needed furnishing, disappearing among the plastic tables.

The sudden lack of state assets following the transition would have been less of a challenge for the new democracy if Gayoom hadn't left another problem:

state expenditure. Revenue was receding due to the 2008 economic crisis and the economy's near sole dependence on luxury tourism. With many new democratic institutions to fund and election promises to fulfil, a legacy of bloated expenditure would prove crippling.

In just a few years leading up to the 2008 elections the regime had dramatically expanded its spending on the civil service by handing out jobs as a way to shore up political support. Government jobs were highly desired, as they offered stable employment, a modicum of status and the much sought after pageantry of the office—suits, ties, watercoolers, flatscreen monitors and mobile phone allowances—without the workload, hours or expectations of tourism or the tiny private sector.

Spending on civil servants actually quadrupled between 2003 and 2009, to the point where almost twelve per cent of the working-age population were employed by the government. This was a world record, and it wasn't the only one. Increases to salaries and allowances of government employees between 2006 and 2008 reached 66 per cent, "by far the highest increase in compensation over a three year period to government employees of any country in the world," according to the World Bank.[12]

Nasheed had boasted that the entire country could be run with a laptop and two secretaries. Officials in his government who inherited the mess calculated that only one in every ten civil servants actually did any useful work, and that by and large the entire infrastructure of state was held up by these few individuals. This, one of the Nasheed officials noted, made it impossible to promote talented people as it meant leaving gaping holes in whatever wing of government they were propping up. Instead one's rise through the ranks tended to be based on political connections rather than merit—something hugely dispiriting for the often well-qualified and foreign-educated young professionals in the middle ranks of organizations such as the Central Bank.

The civil service apathy was palpable. An English friend worked for the Environmental Protection Authority (EPA). On arriving she observed proprietary land and resource management software running on every screen on the office, complete with statistics and graphs, and graphical depictions of buildings and agricultural endeavour. It was several months before somebody explained to her it was the Facebook game *Farmville*.

Nasheed's government faced immediate pressure from the International Monetary Fund to balance the books by cutting civil servant expenditure, or else face a slashing of foreign aid and the overseas credit rating. However, an attempt to make cuts was blocked by the Civil Servant Commission (CSC), the body appointed under the new constitution to independently handle the hiring and firing of all government employees, and answerable only to parliament. The CSC was headed by Mohamed Fahmy, one of Gayoom's faithful. Efforts to shake him loose after he was found guilty of sexual misconduct failed when the Supreme Court persistently kept giving him his job back. His stonewalling was only a symptom of a larger problem facing Nasheed, however: Gayoom's majority in parliament.

The results of the presidential election had caught Gayoom by surprise, but he was ready for the parliamentary election months later, in May 2009. The MDP was still celebrating its presidential win and failed to compete with the opposition's epic cross-country vote-buying extravaganza. Islanders who had been ignored by their rulers for decades were suddenly offered cash, fridges, trips abroad, sports equipment, flat screen TVs, jobs and more in exchange for their votes. In some cases they were made to swear on the Quran that they would vote for the candidate who had paid them the bribe, while the more cunning constituents discovered their price could be increased if they staged a bidding war between the two sides. One young Maldivian we employed in marketing boasted to me that he had personally pocketed over MVR10,000 (US$650) after contacting both sides and conducting a bid war, expressing his delight on election day by drawing a smiley face on the ballot paper. Democracy might have arrived, but the country's unique combination of patronage and apathy was not going to budge.

Gayoom's side had thirty years of experience with the Maldivian population, understood well the entrenched system of patronage and were very generous. The MDP had less cash, were still coming to grips with government and retained a naive faith in the population's democratic idealism.

It still wasn't a total slaughter. The MDP took 30.81 per cent of the votes in the 2009 parliamentary election compared to the 24.62 per cent of Gayoom's Dhivehi Rayithunge Party (DRP). However, the majority of Nasheed's supporters were in the country's more densely populated and better-developed islands, particularly the capital Malé and Addu Atoll in the far south, while the DRP's support was spread across the country's many remote and sparsely-populated "rural" islands. This oddity of Maldivian electoral geography meant that the DRP received 28 seats to the MDP's 26, despite the latter receiving vastly more votes. Seven went to the People's Alliance, belonging to Gayoom's half-brother Abdulla Yameen, while a further third of the seats went to ambitious independents. These "unaffiliated" MPs saw an opportunity to make a fortune in what in any other country would be considered an endemic cash-for-votes scandal, but in the Maldives would become common practice. This was so much the case that the phrase "I need cash" would become a Maldivian meme in 2010 after one independent MP was caught stating as much on tape to Gasim, in an effort to derail any attempt at sensible taxation.

Naturally no disciplinary action followed, but the Human Rights Commission of the Maldives (HRCM) did put a press release together stating that it was rude to listen to other people's phone calls. Meanwhile the MP's islander constituents, ashamed of their representative's professed poverty, found a box and had a whip round for him.

Gayoom therefore had a comfortable majority in parliament and was not only free to systematically block all attempts at reform, including minor amendments to correct grammatical errors in bills, but also to control the appointments, sackings and discipline of the country's "independent" institutions. This gave him de facto control over the new organs of state accountability, including the HRCM, the Civil Servant Commission (CSC), the Police Integrity Commission (PIC) and critically, the Judicial Services Commission (JSC). A broad policy of opposing all government bills with no negotiation, and derailing proceedings for months whenever it looked like the MDP might actually pass something, meant that the opposition could blame Nasheed for failing to fulfil his election promises or achieve any meaningful change.

It didn't stop at obstruction. Much of parliament's time was spent voting dismissal motions against Nasheed's cabinet ministers. This reached such a level of absurdity that in June 2010 Nasheed's entire cabinet resigned in protest over the "scorched earth tactics" of the opposition majority parliament.[13] In what was an early precursor of the 2012 coup and a taste of Gayoom's intention to cloak his return to power in the trappings of democratic legitimacy, Nasheed learned of an attempt to bribe six ruling party MPs into crossing the floor and voting for his impeachment. This would have required a two-thirds super-majority of the 77-member chamber, but only the cooperation of half a dozen MDP MPs.

Whenever it was not engaging itself in what other countries would qualify as treason, parliament was busy making the country as cripplingly expensive to run as possible. An attempt to decentralize the Maldives into seven administrative provinces, lowering costs while giving atolls a chance to determine their own priorities, was initially obstructed on the grounds that it had been proposed by the MDP. But then the DRP suddenly reconsidered, amending the bill to include five paid councillors for every island in the country. Unable to defeat the amendments, the MDP walked out of the vote and an unaffordable US$12-million layer of government was added overnight.[14]

Other notable efforts included the disbursement of thousands of dollars in state subsidies to the private media outlets aligned against Nasheed, and insistence that civil servants be given back pay compensating them for Nasheed's short-lived attempt at imposing austerity measures.

It didn't help matters that despite the growing disparity of wealth the size of the national pie had increased to the point where per capita income reached over US$5,000—exceeding the UN's definition of "least developed". From the beginning of 2011 the Maldives formally graduated to "middle income", one of only three countries ever to do so (together with Botswana and Cape Verde).[15] This caused donor aid to dry up, and a plunge in the availability of concessional credit the government was using to sustain its spending.

By early 2011 the IMF was delaying releasing funding to the Maldives due to "significant policy slippages" and the government's "failure to curtail spending".[16] The country was facing financial crisis.

"The origin of the crisis is very clear ... the wage bill for public sector employees grew dramatically in a very short time," the World Bank observed in a report for a donor conference, under the heading "How did the Maldives get here?"[17]

Nasheed was not an economist and expected people around him to get things done with similar verve and enthusiasm. His communication about the economy was subject to his frustration, and he lost friends by reportedly storming out of a crisis meeting with the World Bank. The internationals either didn't understand or didn't care about the political blockade preventing him from cutting expenditure, and had begun to regard him as erratic and impulsive.

The IMF eventually worked it out. A visiting senior official was finally asked off the record if he had observed a systematic effort by parliament to sabotage the country's economy.

"Yes," he answered, and headed for the airport.

The Maldives got some leeway behind the scenes, and India—concerned after the Mumbai terror attacks about the prospect of the Maldives becoming a hotbed of Islamic extremism—began bankrolling the administration by writing a series of cheques for US$50 million.

But this only delayed the problem; the equivalent of fixing a punctured bus tire with a bicycle repair kit. The economy was still broken and the Maldives' approach needed to change fundamentally. Abandoning the possibility of reducing expenditure, Nasheed turned his attention instead to raising income. Almost a million tourists were arriving every year and spending a fortune in foreign currency on luxury hotels—the vanilla rooms at some properties were selling for over US$2,000 a night. But very little of this multi-billion dollar industry seemed to be dribbling into the state coffers. Where was all the money going?

TOURISM, ENVIRONMENT, ECONOMY

"You see yourself as an imperialist and colonial person, who believes they have imperial superiority over us. No one will give you a job outside this country."

Maldivian resort manager, to Welsh *Minivan News* journalist

A salty haze hovered over the surface of the water as the captain of the speedboat carefully picked his way through the maze of treacherous reefs surrounding the island. It was growing dark and a crew member at the front of the small gulf craft was manning a spotlight, calling out a path. The beam made the patch of shallow tropical water it illuminated completely transparent, revealing a seething mass of fish. Marine life, much more active at night than during the day, was attracted by the light.

How we made it to the little island of Olihale that time I do not know. Few boat crews would have attempted reaching the island without full visibility, let alone at night. We were lucky on this occasion in 2011 to have along Salim "Jeffrey" Waheed, the son of Nasheed's vice president. Jeff had encouraged some friends in the military to go on a weekend fishing expedition, dropping our group of a dozen or so Malé escapees on the tiny picnic island on the tip of North Malé Atoll for the weekend.

He had also thoughtfully brought along the vice presidential Cluedo set. Unfortunately, during the trip a passenger's curiosity as to what was inside the box had seen Colonel Mustard, Professor Plum and several murder weapons snatched by the wind and flung into the Indian Ocean. The crippled set would eventually find its new home in the *Minivan News* office. After the coup, Neil

Merrett liked to postulate that perhaps the vice president's descent into Shakespearean madness was brought on by an unrequited need for a round or two of the game. Vice President Waheed was clearly a fan, having used all but a few of the game's clue sheets.

Clear of the reef, Olihale emerged from the mist as the Maldives National Defence Force (MNDF) vessel cleared the reef and motored up to the small jetty. We disembarked. The island was tiny; you could stroll around the edge of the water in under ten minutes. It was also exquisitely beautiful. The lack of over-water development meant that it had a long and uninterrupted stretch of pristine white beach, and a spit of sand at one end that stretched for over a kilometre, slowly growing as shrubs colonized the new land and held it together. It was right on the tip of the atoll, and the north side faced the open ocean. Just a few lights of distant resorts were visible at night—it was completely isolated.

The resort had originally been owned by the Soneva chain and used as a "Robinson Crusoe" picnic and massage day trip destination for well-heeled guests. A few buildings had been constructed: a toilet and shower block, a covered dining area and kitchen, volleyball net, a tiny day room, two bungalows and simple accommodation for the few staff who maintained it. The new owner had ambitions to develop the island, but it was too small to sustain a resort. Stuck in commercial limbo, it was run by a German woman and her husband who lived there as caretakers, charging our entire group just US$300 a night for the run of the place.

Thanks to the former resort affiliation it also had a liquor licence. This meant that expat liquor suppliers could offload their old stock to the island at cost price, collecting it from the bonded warehouse at the airport on the way to the island.

We had learned all our lessons on earlier trips. The first time we grossly overcatered the booze—300 cans of expired Heineken between a dozen people. We had asked everyone to bring food. They obliged, and we ended up with several dozen tubes of Pringles as our only provisions. Luckily the Maldivian boat crew took pity on us and went fishing, returning with a squirming bucket of exotic marine life of varying degrees of edibility and legality.

Sleeping arrangements were DIY. The island had sun loungers and piles of foam cushions, though experience had shown that people tended to sleep where they fell. I would try to make the stagger to the massage hut at the eastern tip of the island, a serene setting away from the migration path of wandering drunks. It also prevented the shock of awakening with a headache under the blazing tropical sun.

These days of sloth, snorkelling and volleyball on Olihale were among the best of my four years in the Maldives. It became a running joke that I would disappear for several hours whenever we made the trip, to catch up on sleep before emerging to join the party. Dozing under a tree, listening to silence broken only by clicking insects and lapping of the water, was an antidote to the mental tangle of Malé. Consumed by *Minivan* guilt and self-inflicted responsibilities, the job had become inseparable from our identities. We lived in the office with colleagues who were our flatmates and our friends. Moments of stillness were as precious as opportunities to blow off steam and relax with a drink without fear of arrest.

Regenerated, I would head to Olihale's fridge, grab a 50-cent beer, and stride into the sea. The clear water was warm as blood. You lost sense of where your body ended and the Indian Ocean began.

People spent thousands of dollars at resorts trying to capture the "Maldivian" experience. Sitting around a barbecue on the pristine white sandy beach under the stars, can of (expired) class-A contraband in hand, listening to a Maldivian friend playing the guitar and singing ancient Dhivehi songs, and you realized the ingredients were really very simple. Fancy hotel rooms and Michelin-star dining obfuscated an already perfect experience.

The Rise of Tourism

Once upon a time making money in the Maldives was as simple as scooping it off the beach. Indian Ocean cowry shells were harvested in the Maldives and used as currency in many parts of the world right up until the twentieth century, useful to traders because natural shells were well-nigh impossible to counterfeit and held their value due to their scarcity. Cowry shells reached as far as China, even influencing the classical Chinese character for money (貝). Visiting Arab traders around 851AD would buy a million of the shells for a single dinar, transporting them to West Africa and reselling them in Nigeria at a thousand to the dinar. By the time the shells reached Uganda, two purchased a woman.[1]

The Maldives' abundance of shells was fortunate as the 1,192 islands had little else in the way of natural resources. The country is 99 per cent water and what little land there is has sandy soil ill-suited to agriculture beyond coconut palms and the occasional small mango, watermelon or plantain plantation. The diet revolved around fish, particularly tuna, and neighbours India and Sri Lanka were relied upon for starchy staples such as rice and daal. Sri Lanka, in particular, was addicted to the dried chips known as "Maldives fish", still a key ingredient in many curries and sambols.

Cowry shell currency faded from use, but scooping money from the sand would return in a more metaphorical sense in the 1970s with the discovery of package beach tourism; "fly and flop", in travel agent jargon.

It did not have an auspicious beginning. A UN-sponsored assessment in the 1960s declared there was no prospect for beach tourism in the Maldives.

"If that seems like the least perspicacious report in tourism history, you could at least see their point," wrote the Maldives' most prolific panama-hatted resort reviewer, Adrian Neville, in a history for *The Daily Telegraph*. "At the time, the Maldives didn't have a bank. Or an airport. Or electricity on the islands. And the only way to get around was by sailing, very slowly, in a traditional dhoni."[2]

The Maldives had been a somewhat ignored British protectorate since 1887, but the Royal Air Force made its presence felt in 1941 by constructing an airbase on the island of Gan in the southernmost atoll of Addu. The presence of the base had positive effects on the population of the southern atoll: income, free healthcare, English tuition, exposure to new ideas and concepts; many of the country's most successful businessmen even today are from Addu. At the same time, the British had shown a general lack of interest towards the rest of the country, and an unwillingness to get involved in the byzantine political conflicts of Malé.

Tourism was ignited not by the British, but an Italian entrepreneur, George Corbin. The story has become somewhat mythologized over its many retellings, but it seems that Corbin encountered a Maldivian in Colombo, Ahmed Naseem (who would later become Nasheed's foreign minister). In 1971 he travelled to Malé via cargo ship with Naseem and an Italian travel photographer, Francesco Bernini.

Corbin discovered a beautiful country hardly touched by the outside world, and excitedly shared his ideas for developing tourism with two young Maldivians: Mohamed Umar "MU" Manik and Champa Hussain Afeef. Returning to Italy, he published articles and eventually a book about the Maldives, and began to generate interest among more intrepid travellers. A year later Corbin would become the first tour operator, chartering an Air Ceylon flight to deliver 22 tourists to the newly-constructed airport next to Malé. They walked straight off the plane without passport checks.

The first meal was a disaster, with the visitors turning their noses up at the spicy curries and biriyani cooked by a restaurant called "Queen of the Night".

MU Manik took up the pots in their stead, trying to work out what his guests would eat. "I was cook, gardener and room boy," he liked to say. "We had to do everything ourselves, and there was nothing in the Maldives then—not even a telephone. We had to use ham radio or Morse code to contact Colombo for supplies."

When they weren't complaining about the Indian Ocean's lack of pasta, the guests stayed in local homes and spent twelve days snorkelling around the reef, taking underwater photos, spear fishing and visiting the surrounding islands. The trip was considered very successful, prompting Corbin to set up as a tour operator in Italy, Agenzia Viaggi Sesto Continente. On the Maldivian side, MU Manik erected thirty coral-stone huts on the nearby island of Vihamanaafushi and stocked up on pasta. Two generators provided electricity powering ceiling fans, and a small restaurant was built catering to sixty guests. This became the first resort: Kurumba (coconut) Village.

The model was wildly successful, and copied by many other Maldivians who were to become the industry's oligarchs. A resort was *the* business to have, and any island within *dhoni*-range of Malé suddenly became hot property.

The early days were heady. Gulf Craft speedboats had yet to take over the country and transport was a particular challenge, with many islands suitable for development but outside the range of what was considered a tolerable sea transfer for tourists. Seaplanes would eventually become a natural fit, after failed experiments with helicopters. Several of the pioneers told me about their attempts to import the first helicopter. The thing was shipped from India to Sri Lanka and reassembled by technicians on the docks of Colombo. The pioneers stood there looking at it wondering how they were going to fly it the 800-odd kilometres to Malé despite the low range of the aircraft. Eventually, they hit on a brilliant idea.

"Refuel it mid-flight! We filled the cockpit with canisters of fuel and leaned outside with a pipe to refill the tank," explained one of the survivors.

So successful were helicopters in the Maldives that the industry is now served only by seaplanes.

MU Manik was the most commercially successful of the early oligarchs chiefly because he was far too busy empire-building to be distracted by self-destructive Maldivian politics. The company he created, Universal Enterprises, was able to recognize the things it was not good at, and solicit outside help. Maldivians could—with a little arm-twisting—run resorts and serve the end product. But nobody really had the background, skills or resources to develop modern luxury hotel tourism. Universal corporatized and engaged the outside world—developers, financiers, hospitality trainers—eventually opening eight resorts in the Maldives and expanding to the Seychelles.

In 1972, a year after Corbin's visit, 1,097 tourists visited the Maldives. The following year, it was 3,790. By 2012 that figure had reached 958,027, a year later over a million.[3]

Tourism and the Environment

Just as those Maldivians who collected and sold shells to early Arab traders must have found the visitors' enthusiasm for such an everyday commodity perplexing, islanders in the 1970s must have looked on in bemusement as the European visitors lay semi-naked on their beaches, growing brown and leathery in the sun. Many South Asian countries, including the Maldives, show a cultural preference for the opposite: pale skin, with darker tint historically a sign of working outdoors and signaling membership of the lower-caste peasantry. The prejudice persists and makes buying soap in the region a hazard for Westerners with pale skin, as every bottle advertises its "whitening" properties.

The disconnect between tourism and the rest of the Maldives was most obvious in attitudes towards the environment. It must have been even more confusing that the visitors wanted to so badly sit around on the island's garbage dump. Maldivian beaches have historically been used as waste sites, even toilets before the very recent introduction of modest plumbing on most islands.[4] Visitors to "local" islands often remarked in surprise and disappointment at the garbage strewn across the sand; the Dhivehi word for beach, *gondu doh*, also translates as rubbish dump. Absurdities abounded: *reethi* means beautiful, so the mid-market Reethi Beach resort in the local language translated as "beautiful dump".

The traditional use of the beaches as waste sites contrasted somewhat with Nasheed's lauded presentation of the Maldives as an environmental icon on the world stage. Most imagined that the country's 200 inhabited islands were no different from the 100 resort islands. I felt this perception vaguely patronising, but could never put my finger on exactly why. Foreigners just *loved* to think of the local islands as pristine tropical isles populated by simple and untroubled fisherfolk, suddenly threatened by a thoughtless and neglectful West grown fat on carbon emissions.

"The Maldives is sinking! See it before it goes!" was 2009's unofficial tourism mantra, echoed by almost every article written about the Maldives over the next four years.

As an editor, this really bugged me. The Maldives is not *sinking*, I would suggest, ducking amid accusations of climate denial. No, the Maldives is not *sinking*. The sea is *rising*.

The foreign media's obsession with the submerging of the Maldives particularly fitted the British media's self-flagellating post-colonial narrative of the "wicked West", and they pursued it with single-minded enthusiasm. In the midst of 2013's election chaos and existential tooth-and-nail fight for the future of freedom and democracy, the BBC rang Zaheena seeking a Maldivian to comment on a new Intergovernmental Panel on Climate Change (IPCC) study.

"They want a brown person to do an ethnic dance of sorrow," she sighed, putting the phone down.

A hoax article[5] about the Maldives being erased from the 2012 edition of the *Times Atlas* as a statement on global warming was widely reported locally as fact.[6] The article, concocted by climate sceptic James Delingpole, cited a fictitious spokesperson from the *Times Atlas* as implying that the Maldives' position on climate change was "a publicity stunt, cooked up by green activist [and Nasheed's climate advisor] Mark Lynas, to blackmail the international community into giving the Maldives more aid money while simultaneously trying to lure green Trustafarians to come and spend £1500 a night in houses on stilts with gold-plated organic recyclable eco-toilets made of rare earth minerals from China."

Gayoom's Progressive Party of the Maldives capitalized, sending out mass text messages proclaiming the article as evidence that Nasheed's climate change advocacy was "erasing the country, erasing religion and erasing the people".[7]

The reality of the environmental issue was complicated. The Maldives' highest point was about one metre above sea level, and the "moderate" predictions of climate scientists had it underwater by 2100. This forecast made for great headlines, but was not without its detractors. Swedish geographer Nils-Axel Mörner disputed the IPCC's 2003 assertion of an annual 2.3-mm sea level rise by pointing to a fifty-year-old tree growing at sea level on the Maldivian island of Vilingili, healthy and unsalted by the supposedly rising ocean. The offending tree was subsequently torn up by a group of visiting Australian climate science students, but was recovered and replanted by Mörner.[8]

Other impacts were of more immediate concern. Rising sea surface temperatures not only drove tuna deeper, impacting the fishing industry, but were causing coral to bleach.[9] When water temperatures rise even slightly, algae leaves the coral polyp and enters the water column, causing the coral to lose its colour and eventually die. The 1998 El Niño event had killed 95 per cent of the Maldives' coral, and a second period of extended temperatures in 2010 killed off reefs that were just beginning to recover. Besides losing a lot of tourist appeal, bleached reefs eventually degrade and no longer protect islands from waves and tidal forces. This contributes to erosion—the country's most visible and destructive climate change impact, as islands were quite literally swallowed by the Indian Ocean.

Nasheed's international grandstanding on climate change was therefore not without justification. However, the problem had not been helped by foolish development. Islands naturally changed shape depending on the time of year and on many the beach would seasonally shift to the other side of the island. Many resorts tried to mitigate this by sandbagging and pumping sand. Any activity, from dredging to building something as innocuous as a jetty, changed the natural flow of the water and led to unpredictable effects such as erosion and flooding.

Resorts were key offenders but they did retain a vested interest in the natural beauty of their islands. Small local islands, on the other hand, would demand the construction of large harbours and the dredging of lagoons to create more land. Some islanders had to live with the consequences of ignorant decisions; the island of Fares-Mathoda, for instance, was developed by joining two islands together with a strip of reclaimed land. Both frequently flooded as a result, not only killing any attempts at agriculture but also salting the water table.

Resorts may have been more concerned with their appearance but this did not protect them from ecological foolishness. The most insane proposal was submitted by a Lithuanian company intent on sculpting an island into the shape of a high-heeled shoe and staffing it entirely with blondes.[10] Another very upmarket "eco" resort was infested with rabbits because one of the owners happened to like cute animals. The creatures were inbred, red-eyed and scabby, and would hop about the guest tables on the beach begging for scraps of food. Suggestions by staff that the bunnies at least be penned were rejected, as "no animal should be caged". Killing the rabbits was a sackable offence, although the odd bunny did encounter the back of a gardener's shovel, the little corpses hidden under the compost heap. Despite these efforts it was a large island and with no natural predators the rabbit population exploded, eating the low-level shoreline vegetation that held the island together. The erosion was, of course, blamed on climate change.

A UN press tour of several islands in November 2010, intended to impress the scale of ecological threat on visiting Danish Ministers for Development and Climate Change, Søren Pind and Lykke Friis, highlighted the gulf between local and foreign perceptions.[11] Among other islands we flew to was Thinadhoo in the far south of the country, which observed the common Maldivian practice of using the beach as a dump.

Friis, who was engaged in negotiating millions of dollars' worth of climate change adaption and mitigation funding from the Danish government, surveyed the plastic bags and rusting fridges with the disappointed expression foreigners display when the Maldives succeed in crushing their fantasies of a pristine agrarian paradise. She slipped her minders and sidled up to ask me whether every local island was similarly neglected by its inhabitants.

Even if the locals didn't seem to mind, the rubbish was still a problem because unlike tourists, alcohol regulation and Sharia law, used nappies did not respect the local island/resort boundary. One resort at the mercy of unfortunate tidal patterns for six months of the year was forced to have staff in boats constantly patrolling the island to intercept rubbish before it made to the beach—and into TripAdvisor.

Many resorts, including this one, took their own responsibilities seriously with composting, incinerators and a recycling programme. Every tourist generates 7.2 kilos of waste daily compared to the 2.8 kilos of a resident in Malé, according to the government's statistics, and this ultimately had to be disposed of in a country without land for landfill. The answer was the national garbage island of Thilafushi, a toxic wasteland much favoured by visiting BBC journalists (Neil remarked that the foreign media's obsession with Thilafushi was the equivalent of a Maldivian visiting a garbage dump in Slough, and then producing a documentary about what a smelly mess the UK was).

Whatever Thilafushi's deficiencies, the real problem was the "out of sight" policy adopted by remote islands. Nobody policed the *dhonis* contracted to collect and ferry waste to the national garbage island of Thilafushi. Fuel was expensive, and the further a resort or local island was from the rubbish island, the greater the incentive to motor out of the atoll and dump the waste at sea.

Cultural acceptance of littering was an issue. Efforts to change the practice of throwing trash on the beach had failed; no amount of foreign aid had been able to change the habits of several thousand years. Several more progressive islands had experimented with bins, but once they filled up nobody seemed very interested in emptying them. We would only hear about it because locals would eventually complain about trash piling up in mountains at bin sites, rather than being spread more equitably across the beach where it could be washed out into the natural dustbin of the ocean.

Large projects to resolve such ecological issues, on the other hand, tended to involve a "memorandum of understanding" signed with a multinational or foreign government. MOU was shorthand for "hold a press conference and then forget about it". We rarely heard of these projects again.

The UN and countless eco-NGOs commissioned hundreds of reports from environmental consultants, typically launched over tea, biscuits and PR at Traders Hotel in Malé. These would then collect dust on a shelf somewhere, the storage of UN reports being the primary function of the Ministry of Environment.

Where the consultancy involved an actual project, those that did follow through had an almost 100 per cent failure rate and were never publicized. "Failure" for the Maldives, anyway—presumably the foreign consultants did quite well.

A rare example of self-reflection on the subject came from the European Commission, which held a press conference in 2010 to announce that ten years and €15 million to establish waste management centres across the Maldives had come to naught.

"The environmental support program was too ambitiously planned and had to be scaled down to solid waste management only. Constructed island waste management systems are, with few exceptions, not operational, and waste management centres are unequipped. Equipment for the island waste management systems, purchased with the project's remaining funding, remains stored in Malé," declared the written assessment with, by contemporary standards for such things, rare and breath-taking honesty.[12]

The rubbish was a male problem, the report suggested, the failings of the waste management project due in part to "insufficient involvement of communities in general, notably the Island Women Development committees".

"Women on the islands are quite well organised and are often the main actors in terms of environmental issues and social and economic life. Many households are managed by women, as men are often working in the tourist resorts, in the fisheries industry, or abroad," the report observed. "However the present local governance structures generally do not sufficiently allow women to play an effective role in the local decision-making process."

The most—and to my recollection perhaps only—successful foreign-authored report in my four years in the Maldives was a document that monetized sharks in terms of tourism value, pricing them substantially higher than their fins were worth to the Chinese soup trade. A shark finning ban was introduced and was widely successful, judging from the number of tourists standing paralyzed in the lagoons post-2011 as they were circled by exploding numbers of curious (and harmless) black and white-tipped reef sharks.

Not all tourist-friendly fauna were as fortunate. Endangered sea turtles were considered a local delicacy, caught and consumed despite bans which were never enforced. Whatever the intention of the bans, in practice they were for show—a publicity tool to make tourists feel less guilty about the plate of air-freighted Norwegian salmon they were about to devour.

Locals were not phased by the restrictions. In September 2012 a marine biologist working in the newly designated UNESCO biosphere reserve in Baa Atoll visited one of the country's fourteen most protected turtle nesting habitats, the uninhabited island of Funadhoo. Sylvia Jagerroos sent us pictures of what she found: the still-smoking remains of an extensive barbecue including scattered pieces of baby lemon shark and the large decapitated head of a pregnant sea turtle.[13]

"My theory is that they saw the green turtle nesting and killed her immediately, while slaughtering and throwing the pieces in the ocean. The baby sharks were attracted to the smell and since they swim in very shallow waters it's a piece of cake to catch them," said Sylvia, weeping down the phone.

Turtle eggs were considered a delicacy—a financial as well as culinary delicacy. A turtle could lay up to 200 eggs, each of which could be sold for around MVR10 (US$0.65). A marine biologist friend working on an upmarket resort explained how word of a nest would quickly spread from local staff to nearby islands. Poachers would then travel to the resort under the cover of darkness to harvest the eggs. In one instance she sat up all night next to a nest, waving her flashlight and yelling to scare off a boatload of poachers who snuck up without lights or engine noise. Thereafter the resort posted security guards to defend the nests—Nepalese, not Maldivian.

The government's Environmental Protection Authority (EPA) was not much use. The same marine biologist recalled accompanying them on a field trip. Breakfast on the boat one morning was delicious: what was it, she asked?

Turtle egg omelette.

It got worse. A Spanish marine biologist who worked at the EPA in 2010 told of sitting at a resort restaurant while several Maldivian EPA staff, barely out of high school, shook down the manager in return for signing off an environmental impact assessment. Their demand? A dozen pizzas and a crate of Red Bull. The Red Bull was taken back to Malé, the pizzas were left uneaten on the table—a show of power.

Much was invested in portraying the Maldives as the epicentre of environmental good intentions. Any suggestion to the contrary attracted a "shoot the messenger" response. In March 2013 we obtained extraordinary leaked photos of a *dhoni* stacked with dozens of sea turtles, images taken and sent to us by one of the hunters.[14] When we asked him why they were killing turtles, his answer was simple: "Very tasty." We ran the story and the horrifying pictures.

In the aftermath a senior official in the Maldives' Marine Research Centre rang up and lambasted me for trying to destroy the tourism industry.

The Tourist Behemoth

Forty years after its inception the tourism industry is the heart, lungs and liver of the Maldivian economy, indirectly responsible for up to seventy per cent of the economy and up to ninety per cent of the country's foreign exchange receipts.

At the same time its relationship with the rest of the Maldives is one-sided and rather exploitative.

Prior to June 2011 state revenue from the industry consisted of import duties, arbitrary rental payments for islands based on one's number of uncles and cousins in the Ministry of Tourism, and a US$8 a night bed tax per guest. This flat tax greatly favoured the development of luxury tourism; a backpacker in a local guest house paid the same amount as a celebrity footballer in a US$6,000-a-night luxury water villa.

The nature of this income also meant it was impossible to determine the actual size of the industry—something the industry itself appeared in no hurry to disclose.

The state's own estimates ranged from somewhere between US$700 million to US$1 billion a year. But its true size would not emerge until June 2011 when Nasheed's government, imbued with its new sense of pragmatism, expensively forced a 3.5 per cent Tourism Goods and Services Tax (T-GST) past the oligarchs in parliament. This was the industry's first per centage tax, and it revealed the true scale of the trough: US$2.5–3 billion. The state had been underestimating the size of its dominant industry by a factor of four.

Nasheed held a press conference to announce this extraordinary discovery, but nobody else seemed particularly surprised or outraged, such was the industry's remoteness from the experience of the average Maldivian.[15] Indeed, many accused the president of fabricating the figure.

"Ahem, why stop at $3 billion? These figures are just like all other figments of President Nasheed's imagination. I have to say, he does have a rich imagination. One wonders whether he lives in the land of the fairies, most of the time," remarked one of the usually commonsensical members of the *Minivan* commentariat, "Ahmed Bin Addu Bin Suvadheeb".

What was obvious was that a small number of individuals—no more than fifty, according to insiders—had been doing exceptionally well for themselves for a very long period of time, with very little of this trickling down to the common man.

Paradise: A Guest's Perspective

The scale and secretiveness of the industry made the resorts exceedingly interesting to me. Until 2011 I had little experience of them beyond the occasional invitation to a fancy party, which typically ended in up in heroic drinking sessions with senior management in which I would learn all about the largesse and depravity of Russian guests. A food and beverage manager told of a Russian businessman who booked two villas, one for himself, one for the two Russian girls he'd flown into the country beforehand. When he arrived, the women took one look at him and decided they couldn't go through with the arrangement. The pair apparently had a pleasant two weeks on the beach while he sulked in his room drinking vodka. On a sourer note, a distressing number of "wives" ended up in hospital.

The Food & Beverage Manager quit soon after, complaining of "having to be nice to too many visiting dictators. Why do we never host Barack Obama?"

Sometimes, if my focus was lured away from *Minivan* by a significant other, I could score an "expat" rate from a sympathetic manager and organize a few days' escape—a luxury paid for with pieces of deputy editor Neil's dwindling sanity.

Visiting a resort as a legitimate guest I knew was an incredible privilege— the resorts are billed as the ultimate luxury honeymoon destinations, and are enormously aspirational to many people; once in a lifetime experiences, within my reach for four years. I write the following with care.

The experience begins thus: you are whisked from the airport in a bumpy speedboat or twin-otter seaplane (invariably flown by a barefooted Canadian pilot), after possibly indulging in hors d'oeuvres, and comfy sofas in an airconditioned resort lounge at the airport. The concrete towers of Malé disappear from the horizon, and the sea becomes dark blue as you cross the deep channels between atolls. Much clucking and clicking as everybody takes photos of the atolls' stunning beauty.

Arriving at the resort jetty, you are escorted to an open-air reception build-ing with a "traditional Maldivian" sandy floor, and checked in by a friendly Filipino. Fancier establishments (US$600+ a night) will skip this step and send you straight to your room, where the Filipino will be waiting with a check-in card and complimentary bottle of Sake.

All Maldivian beaches are not equal—nothing ever came close to Olihale. Despite this, the core postcard appeals of the destination—bright sun, blue sea, white sand—is pretty much universal anywhere in the country except Malé. Your room on the resort really is the most distinguishing factor—simi-lar across the properties only in the apparent lack of anything identifiably Maldivian. Rooms are vastly variable and range from 1970s tiled-floor Club-Med tropicana to hectares of living rooms, bedrooms, kitchenettes, outdoor decks, cavernous bathrooms and private (read: skinny dipping) plunge pools. Upmarket themes include all-natural timber beams, thatch roofs and copper taps, marble pillars, white faux-leather and high concrete walls with separate sleeping arrangements for one's bodyguards/harem. Room varieties range from land-based "garden villas" to the eponymous water villa, reached by a complex network of timber jetties and with an interior highly conducive to romance but distressingly visible to passing Chinese snorkellers. I found it intriguing how appliances which would be relatively mundane in the home—flat screen TVs, Nespresso machines, baths—became objects of intense excite-ment when suspended a metre above sea level in an air conditioned water villa with a pretty view.

Your day is defined by eating. Even the most austere resorts put on enor-mous and lavish buffets (results vary depending on spend) at which you invariably find yourself over-indulging. By day three it is common to hear other couples asking each other "Is it lunch again already?"

Most visitors travel in twos—the single travel journalist on the whirlwind press tour of the resort's facilities is unlikely to get a true sense of the experi-ence, and resorts deliberately keep such visits short (one or two nights) to avoid the creeping sense of loneliness that descends on the reporter sitting alone in his/her sprawling over-water palace, empty bottle of complimentary Sake in hand, contemplating the futility and loneliness of their existence.

With the exception of the mid-market diving resort that compels guests to eat meals with each other, interaction between tourists is rare and often feels like an unwanted interruption. Initially I was taken aback at the lack of animation or smiles on the faces of most guests at Maldivian resorts. I postulated that many, having invested enormous sums of money in relaxation, now felt stressed at the urgency of their need to live up to the expense. Either that, or the wan expressions reflected the guests' discovery that they were trapped for nine days on a hot tropical island where bottles of drinking water cost US$8 a litre. Drink the tap water if you want to spend your honeymoon in the bathroom; otherwise a US$70-a-week bill for drinking water per couple is about standard. Budget a little less if you can accept a degree of dehydration, or surreptitiously fill an empty container when the free stuff is served at breakfast.

On reflection, I feel the money factor may not cover the reaction of guests. I met plenty who operated on a different financial plane to mere mortals, and for whom a US$45 plate of à la carte hummus was genuinely not considered an absurdity.

I extended my hypothesis to include a second observation: even at full occupancy, the majority of resorts feel empty. This, I thought, was probably due to the primary but unspoken form of entertainment: procreation. Those overwater jacuzzis with disco lighting were not for bathing, and the stumbling, blank-eyed stare was as much the sign of a sated libido as a full stomach.

Outside attempts at tanning, pretty much everyone hires snorkelling gear. The Maldives is at its natural best underwater. Much of the coral has been killed and bleached white during a succession of sea temperature rises over the past decade or so, but it remains a habitat for a staggering amount of aquatic fauna. Marine life is staggeringly and reliably abundant, from tiny damsel fish to turtles, reef sharks, manta rays, dolphins and even gigantic spotted whale sharks. Scuba diving circles regard the Maldives as one of the best destinations in the world to see "charismatic megafauna"—the big stuff.

Most resorts offer other stuff to do—watersports, kayaking, sailing, fishing, sunset dolphin cruises—at a price. One weekend after a particularly brutal week at work I escaped to a very nice resort with the resident marine biologist. Staff who mistook me for a genuine guest, rather than a leech, offered us an all-day excursion to Malé. The asking price? US$1,462. Each.

A wave of enthusiasm for "pamper culture" in the 1990s saw almost every resort open some kind of massage and oiling emporium to give wives something to do while their husbands walked up and down the beach trying to get a Blackberry signal. Discovering that Westerners would pay upwards of US$100 for half an hour of kneading, pretty much every property hired a couple of Thai girls with curiously strong hands and bolted "resort and Spa" to the end of the island's name.

Regardless of resort, national stereotypes of guests were hilariously and predictably accurate. Surly German couples would wake at 5.30am and rush out to the beach to reserve sun loungers by draping beach towels over them. Were loungers to run out, some would go to the extreme of constructing makeshift bunkers to secure their tanning spots. These could become something of a trip hazard, and seeking to avoid conflict, managements began fastidiously to number each sun lounger according to room. Use of the wrong lounger was considered a war crime.

The Italians were the Maldives' early adopters in the 1970s and infused it with a very specific flavour, mostly pasta-based. Terrifying in their tiny speedos, Italian tourists eschewed the peaceful lying about in the sun of other European nations and insisted on the employment of resort "animators" to inflict structured activity, games, dancing, quizzes and talent contests upon all guests. Not for nothing would travel agents designate many resorts "Italian only".

The British, on the other hand, wanted alcohol. Beer and cocktails with fruit and little umbrellas. Bottles of cheap pouring booze could be imported by resorts for a few dollars, diluted with copious amounts of fruit juice and a glace cherry, and sold for US$16 (two for one during happy hour, still at a 1,600 per cent mark-up).

Russians took this a step further, making Smirnoff vodka so ubiquitous that it became the preferred black-market tipple of most Maldivians. Resort accountants welcomed Russians with open arms—money seemed to be no object. Privately, managers confessed that the Russians were a mixed blessing given their general abrasiveness towards staff and other guests, and disregard for directions such as "please do not trample the coral" and "kindly refrain from beating the room boy". Japanese and Korean guests, on the other hand, tended to be exceptionally well behaved—but watersports staff complained that you had to watch them lest they surreptitiously pluck and consume delicacies from the reef.

New markets began to emerge after the 2008 credit crunch that affected the Maldives' traditional European clientele. Italy, in particular, shrank to a fraction of its former market share. The growing Indian middle class, nearby and vast in number, occasionally visited the Maldives but were not really drawn to beach tourism and lacked the urge to tan in the manner of their freezing European counterparts. On the other hand, the credit crunch did not seem to affect the small but consistent growth of Middle Eastern tourists. The vast majority of these came from Saudi Arabia, where family members could be reassured that the Maldives was a safely Islamic holiday destination.

China and the Demographic Shift

There was one tourist before whom all other markets shrank: the Chinese. While damage to the Maldives in the 2004 tsunami was small compared to Sri

Lanka, tourists were put off by the perceived vulnerability of the low-lying islands. No sooner had the industry begun to recover than the 2008 credit crunch hit the Maldives' precious European market. Occupancy rates at resorts—usually around 70–80 per cent—began to shrink, and "mid-market" (US$100–300 a night) properties relying on volume were most affected. Low season became particularly brutal for these resorts.

A group of these decided that the enormous and aspirational Chinese middle class was the perfect low-season "filler" with which to stay afloat, and set about persuading the government to lobby Chinese authorities to endorse the Maldives as an official package holiday destination. It did, and the rest was history.

In 2010 China eclipsed the UK as the Maldives' biggest market by volume, and by 2012 was making up almost forty per cent of all traffic through the airport. The vast majority of Chinese booked package tours through local travel agents at home, usually for short stays of four nights—far fewer than the 10–14 days of their European counterparts. Very few came back, too—unlike the 31 per cent of Europeans who were repeat visitors, the return rate for Chinese guests was about five per cent in 2013.

Feelings in the resort industry about the demographic shift were mixed. The Maldives Association of Tourism Industry (MATI), the industry association representing the sector's dinosaurs, warned *Minivan* in 2010 that the surge in Chinese arrivals was "just a passing fad".[16]

"The Chinese can swamp a destination in terms of numbers, but this is not the tourism the Maldives is about. Our product attracts sun seekers—Europeans," MATI's Secretary General, Mohamed "Sim" Ibrahim told me. "The Chinese who come do not come for the sun and the beach—they come because the Maldives is a novelty, a safe destination, and because of their newfound freedom to travel. Resorts are saying there are not many repeat visitors from China."

In this he was right: there were few repeat visitors from China, largely due to resorts' lack of enthusiasm for catering to the rather specific demands of the market. Little effort was put into finding out what these demands were, as language was a major barrier; few resorts had Mandarin-speaking staff, and most Chinese guests had little English.

The Chinese represented the first major demographic shift in the industry's four decades of operation. Modes of thinking were entrenched. The Maldivian resort oligarchs had simply copied each other and become stuck in a 1970s Euro-style Copacabana time-warp. Resistance to change was strong; it was up to the Chinese to enjoy what they were given.

"Chinese tourists are like any Western tourist," MATI's Sim told us.[17] "When the Russians began coming to the Maldives they had some different expectations, but now they are used to what we offer. The Chinese will be the same."

As a result of this thinking, many resorts entered into what could only be described as a cold war with their Chinese guests. One tactic was segregated meal times. Chinese guests would be forced to eat at separate times to other nationalities, when noodles and such would be provided. According to a Chinese friend who worked as a guest services manager at one such resort, this completely missed the point: the Maldives was an aspirational experience for many Chinese tourists, the visit as much a show of status for friends and colleagues back home as somewhere pleasant to go. To discriminate against them was to make the Chinese feel a lower-class of guest, undermining the whole point of the trip and making them very angry indeed.

To be fair to the Maldives, the bullying went both ways. The boom in Chinese tourism had many impacts, including geopolitical. India had always considered itself the regional gorilla and big brother to the Maldives, providing aid and military assistance and generally acting as proxy for US interests. China, however, had been busily establishing what Indian defence and security analysts excitedly called a "string of pearls" around its arch-rival, expanding its influence into Pakistan, Sri Lanka, Nepal and now the Maldives. I often felt that rumours of Chinese government activity in the Maldives were overplayed by the Indian press, precisely because the Chinese didn't need to buy more influence—they already controlled forty per cent of arriving tourists. Besides, nearby Sri Lanka was safely leashed to Beijing—it had a history of national socialism and an appetite for top-level corruption, and its belligerence towards UN criticism of rampant human rights abuses in the closing days of its war with the Tamil Tigers gave it a pariah status in the West which greatly lowered the cost of influencing it. China had invested heavily in Sri Lanka and needed no further control over the Maldives; the flow of tourists could be turned off like a tap.

I never decided whether the surge in Chinese arrivals really was a fad. Everybody in the industry had an opinion on the demographic market shift towards China in the Maldives. But nobody I encountered (besides an American aerospace engineer, George Weinmann, who launched an airline shuttling Chinese package tourists to Male) ever stopped to ask Chinese guests why they had chosen to come to the Maldives. A 300 per cent increase over two years wasn't exactly an accident.[18]

It could be said, however, that they were not flying to the Maldives to be treated like second class citizens.

The simple reason for this was that resorts were not really involved in marketing or analyzing guest trends. A parent company might issue the odd press release or (rarely) a resort would announce something like an apprenticeship or environmental programme, but in general properties indulged a few foreign journalists and stayed silent. Multinational tour operators and travel agents such as Kuoni bulk-booked a resort's rooms, taking on most of the risk and ensuring the flow of guests. The resorts saw their job as providing the end product: boiling the pasta, mixing the drinks, changing the towels. Insurance-heavy components, such as the dive school, were contracted out to third parties on a commission basis.

The government was hardly going to innovate a model that had pulled in dollars for the oligarchs for decades; an attempt in 2011 to capitalize on the climate fame and rebrand from the "The Sunny Side of Life" to "Always Natural" was shouted down.[19] To its credit the government did collect good tourism data and shared it when the numbers looked good. However, to really understand the industry, and how the Maldives sustains its rather contradictory existence, you couldn't stay in the guest area. You needed to go behind the scenes.

Anatomy of an Industry

"Beach Babylon takes you behind the scenes at a five-star tropical island resort. Do all the stories which take place behind the closed doors of the exclusive spa have happy endings? What do the world's richest people expect from room service during their fortnight in paradise? What does the windsurfing instructor do to keep sane after hours? With a cast of millionaires, celebrities, hangers-on and prostitutes, Beach Babylon takes you to a world where extreme luxury is the norm and where excess somehow isn't always enough..."

I never got around to reading Imogen Edwards-Jones's infamous book,[20] which purported to lift the (100 per cent Egyptian cotton) covers on an exclusive but unidentified Maldivian resort. It was widely believed to be One & Only Reethi Rah, a plastic and Plexiglass playground for celebrity footballers, Israeli arms dealers and Russian mafia.

Beach Babylon, published in 2007, was significant in being the only item of scholarship published about the Maldives without the express purpose of attracting tourists since the 1999 *The Maldive Islanders: A Study of the Popular Culture of an Ancient Ocean Kingdom* by Canadian-Spanish scholar Xavier Romero Frías.[21]

93

Before Frías there was the British explorer and Archaeological Commissioner of Ceylon, H. C. P. Bell's *The Maldive Islands* (nineteenth century), French navigator Francois Pyrard's *The Voyage of François Pyrard of Laval to the East Indies, the Maluccas, and Brazil* (seventeenth century),[22] and the Arab adventurer Ibn Battuta's *The Rehla of Ibn Battuta: India, Maldive Islands and Ceylon* (fourteenth century).[23] That was about it. Imogen was in good company.

My understanding of the resorts was accumulated in far less respectable fashion than through the work of these esteemed scholars: drunken nights with resort managers, gossipy friends and staff members, leaked emails and documents, our own salacious stories. Particular credit goes to the friend who worked as a marine biologist at one of the country's most private, upmarket and exclusive resorts, who would regularly sneak me onto the island and let me run loose through the staff areas for days at a time.

Take all the sordid details you can imagine about the backrooms of the hospitality industry—scandal, intrigue, affairs—squeeze them onto a tiny tropical island, and add a generous dollop of feudalism. Stir in Maldivian politics to flavour, bake in the tropical heat, and you're well on the way.

The Business

By the end of 2013 there were 109 resorts in the Maldives, each occupying its own "uninhabited" island and collectively capable of sleeping 23,469 tourists. There were also 163 safari vessels (2,716 beds), 20 city hotels (1,708 beds), and 136 smaller guesthouses (1,918 beds).[24] Four new resorts opened, tourist arrivals increased by 17.4 per cent and the average duration of stay dropped to 6.3 days (largely due to the Chinese market's growth and preference for shorter visits). Average occupancy rate was over 74 per cent.

These figures show that whatever the trend in demographic or travel style, resorts are the big money-spinner. In 2012, 82 per cent of all visitors to the Maldives had a resort booking (safari boats 9 per cent, guesthouses 3 per cent, hotels 6 per cent).

Sound like a good investment? If you want to start a resort, you'll need an island. All land is retained by the government, and must be rented via the Tourism Ministry. This is almost always through a Maldivian partner. In the old days, this person would rent an island on the cheap from a friend or uncle in the ministry—annual leases of US$8 were not unheard of. One of Nasheed's anti-corruption innovations in 2011 was to standardize this rent to the square metre, which greatly annoyed resorts with large islands and few beds.

Notice the system's lack of emphasis on actual resort development. In many cases a Maldivian businessman would rent an island for years, paying little if anything, allowing the lease payments to pile up and accrue a staggering amount of interest and fines and interest on fines. Vicious court battles would be fought should the government seek to reclaim the island from under the mountain of debt. As the businessman involved was usually an MP, politician, minister or senior figure connected to the government, these cases invariably went in their favour, leaving the state coffers short tens of millions of dollars.[25]

Part of the problem was lack of access to capital. During his tenure as Finance Minister, Gasim Ibrahim (remember him?) used his controlling stake of the state-owned Bank of Maldives (BML) to collectively loan himself and several associates almost the entirety of the bank's assets.[26]

"The large exposures that BML held, were in the main, due to members of the board or their relatives," read an audit report finally leaked in 2013.

Gasim's own Villa Group, which owned six resorts among other businesses, had borrowed US$37,601,520 by the end of Gayoom's tenure in late 2008. This sum represented 32.4 per cent of the bank's entire capital, but wasn't even the largest amount. Ahmed "Sun" Shiyam, the MP, media owner and resort tycoon who would later start his own political party in alliance with Gayoom's half-brother Abdulla Yameen, had loans and overdrafts reaching MVR607,345,442 (US$46,879,400).

"This amounted to 40.8 per cent of the Bank's capital as at 31 October 2008," observed the bank's auditors.

What this meant was that the state-controlled bank had no capital left to lend to anybody with an island who wanted to develop it as a resort—or indeed, open even a small corner shop. Your only option for financing was to approach the Malé branch of the State Bank of India, or else beg Gasim, Shiyam or one of the other oligarchs to loan you some of BML's money. The price for this option—in terms, controlling stake and implied subservience—was high. A Maldivian friend's family tried this to just finish the final furnishing of a property they had developed themselves from scratch, and ended up defrauded of the entire resort.

Without local access to capital, the development model was quite simple. It was safer to lease an island and sit on the piles of mounting debt, fighting defensive court battles as needed, until a foreign hotel developer arrived and offered to resolve your financial problems in exchange for your cooperation in securing the island. The chain/brand—be it Hilton, Sheraton, Shangri-La, W, Adaaran, Dusit Thani or dozens of others—would bring in the outside capital, concept, expertise, design, architecture, construction, staff and management. This was a jackpot for the leaseholder, who would get a share of the take and a quiet place to retreat away from the listening walls of Malé.

Despite effectively just being landlords, the majority of leaseholders would announce themselves as "resort owners"—an impression the developers were happy to cultivate to ensure their own continuity. Several large brand name hotel chains were anecdotally reported to pay their leaseholders an additional stipend to not turn up and manage anything on the resort.

The arrangement worked particularly well during the stability that Gayoom's dictatorship provided. Until only recently resorts had an incredible six-year return on investment—one of the best in the hospitality business. Resort investors and developers could proceed with reasonable confidence that the man in charge and his allies would still be there year after year. The resort formula was proven and worked brilliantly. If you kept your head down, kept the Maldivian partners happy and stayed out of politics, you would be printing money within six years.

The result of this model was that the resorts found it in their interest to isolate themselves from the affairs of the rest of the Maldives. Properties would take steps to minimize their involvement in the country as much as possible, such as ignoring the fifty per cent minimum per centage employment of local staff in favour of cheaper and better trained staff from abroad— or by artificially inflating the number with "ghost" jobs. Foreign staff came with less politics, never went on strike, and if there were any issues, they could easily be sent home. On most resorts Maldivian staff would be found predominantly in the boat fleet and housekeeping division, aspects of food and beverage, and sometimes water sports. A few "progressive" resorts hired women from local islands to sweep the beaches or cook for "Maldivian" night at the buffet. Maldivian middle managers existed but were rare, and almost never made it to upper management at resorts not owned and operated by Maldivian businessmen. When this did happen, the management positions tended towards political appointments rather than a meritocracy. At many foreign-owned resorts Maldivians faced hiring discrimination. Get a manager properly drunk, and many would admit that local employment was tolerated as a necessary evil.

It was therefore very possible for a guest to go through their entire holiday without meeting a single Maldivian. In fact, if you did go on honeymoon and happened to see a Maldivian woman, it was time to start buying lottery tickets. In 2011 only eight per cent of tourism employees were female—local and foreign. *Maldivian* women? Three per cent.

This was due to the intense social stigma of working on a resort, impressed upon women by their families. A study on the topic conducted by a pair of Swedish students, "Women in Tourism: Challenges of Including Women in the Maldivian Resort Sector",[27] found resort life perceived as "Western", exposing women to the consumption of pork and alcohol, skimpy clothing and extramarital sexual encounters. Maldivian male employees were presumably exempt from these risks.

"Working in a resort as a woman is perceived as bad, as going the wrong way, as not a good place for a woman to be," one source told the researchers.

A resort manager told the researchers that parents were a major challenge to promoting female employment. "Convincing the parents is difficult. They are very possessive of the girls. The parent's perception is that they will mix with the European culture and do bad things such as drinking alcohol," he explained.

The women interviewed meanwhile complained that if resorts wanted to hire them, they should "become more Muslim".

"Most said they would not work where they could not wear the burqa, although when told that several resorts allow the burqa, they maintained their position," researchers wrote.

Female friends who lived and worked on resorts said the treatment of the female minority by the male majority was oppressive and intimidating. Staff typically lived on the resort, so there was no escape during off hours. One, a guest services agent on a resort with more than 300 staff, said there were only four females on her entire island. If one happened to date another staff member, they became considered "communal property", she explained. Resorts often banned staff fraternization, although it was rare for this to be applied against male members of senior management.

Indian Ocean Fiefdoms

Social, political and physical isolation allowed the resorts to operate like miniature fiefdoms, each with its own laws and community oddities. The general manager was the de facto mayor, responsible not only for running a hospitality business but ensuring the supply of food, electricity, accommodation, fresh water and sewerage. The head of human resources would take on the role of sheriff, and the employee handbook would become the law of the land for fiefdoms of sometimes up to 600 people.

Many of these handbooks imposed a class system on resort employees. This determined what kind of accommodation you could expect, from dormitories right up to live-in villas. Your rank determined whether you ate in the guest restaurant or staff café, and defined whether you were privileged enough to use the guest pool or beach. The branding of this system varied: Shangri La Vilingili in the country's south imposed five tier levels, Soneva Fushi had a large noticeboard with staff photos pinned to "inner" and outer "spheres" like some kind of cabalistic fraternity.

Whatever the conventions, the resort class system at every property in the country broadly broke down into three groups.

The top rank consisted of senior management. These included head chefs, general managers, sommeliers, food and beverage chiefs and so on. Invariably foreign, these staff had most often come out of hotel or hospitality school training and regarded the Maldives as a reputable career boost. As an added bonus, working on an island freed them from food and housing bills for several years while they rented out homes and paid off mortgages. However, hotel school was poor preparation for a job that first and foremost demanded mayoral skill to survive. Certain manager nationalities survived small island politics better than others—Australians, Kiwis, Canadians and British, for some reason.

The second rung consisted of middle management. These were the administrative functionaries who ensured that the resort ticked along—or didn't, when a bit of chaos was in their interest. They included accountants, bar managers, HR staff and the like, many from nearby countries such as Sri Lanka and India, as well as experienced Maldivians who had made resort employment their long-term career choice and moved far from their home islands.

The bottom tier was the proletariat and included the rest of the island: bar staff, waiters, kitchen hands, housekeepers, front desk staff, boat crews, butlers, gardeners (always Bangladeshi), security guards (usually Nepalese), spa girls (usually Thai). Most workers in this tier would live in cramped dorms, were not allowed out of the staff area during off hours, and had stringent rules of behaviour and personal grooming imposed on them such as bans on fraternization or—if they were Maldivian—a ban on entering the vicinity of the staff bar.

Strikes, rebellions and "mini coups" were actually quite common. These almost always sparked over disagreement about service charges, quickly expanding to include gripes about food, accommodation or third class treatment by management, and were most often led by Maldivians on the bottom rung who did not have to worry about the threat of deportation to a country with worse job prospects.

Service charges were a per centage paid by guests on every bill, divided up among staff at the end of each month. At upmarket resorts this was significant.

Staff on a monthly salary of a few hundred dollars, paid in Maldivian *rufiya*, could expect service charge payments of US$500–1,000 a month at some resorts in high season, above and beyond any tips paid to them personally by wealthy guests. Service charges could represent about seventy per cent of the average worker's income.

The most common trigger for mutiny was the discovery that this much-desired foreign currency was not being distributed fairly. The culprit was usually a middle-runger engaged in some creative accountancy, such as the resort's financial controller. The ire of the lower rungs would be aimed at the resort aristocracy, who would be taken completely by surprise, having been reassured by the till-fiddling middle tier that everything was fine.

With nowhere to escape and let off steam, matters could quickly spiral out of control. I heard of least one resort manager who was stabbed, another who arrived back at his bungalow to discover it ransacked and covered in human excrement. Others left after receiving torrents of anonymous SMS death threats—the disgruntled local staffer's preferred method of intimidation. One large resort held the chain's annual general meeting on a newly opened property. Management emerged from the conference room to find all their bicycles had been thrown into the lagoon. Later, all the gas taps were left open in one of the restaurants—the new resort a single cigarette from disaster.

Revolutionary sabotage of a resort fiefdom typically started out as sneaky and vengeful. An English teacher on a resort known for insisting that everyone go barefoot was tasked with looking after a group of six Maldivian schoolgirls on work experience. She had sharp words with the group when they failed to show up for work, and returned to her staff apartment that evening to discover rows of upturned pins methodically planted in her doormat.

Management on most resorts preferred to play down such issues, being especially careful to avoid inciting Maldivians in the middle tier into siding with their countrymen on the lower rungs. This approach facilitated the entrenchment of vested interests in the middle tier, and on older resorts made it extremely difficult to shake loose troublesome middle managers from the protection of friends and relatives. The alternative, however, was disaster. Rather than cooling situations on behalf of senior management the middle tier could instead fan the flames until the conflict escalated and chaos erupted.

Things quickly became eminently newsworthy whenever this happened. Staff at Kurumba in 2010 stormed a guest restaurant, terrifying honeymooners and forcing the parent company Universal to evacuate all tourists to another property.[28] The general manager, a Frenchman, found himself chased around the island by an angry mob. The chaos was only brought to a halt after the government intervened and dumped a boatload of riot police on the island. Nineteen arrests and an empty resort later, Universal purged senior staff and dealt seriously with the grievances of its employees, reviewing pay and service charge procedures and completely renovated staff accommodation blocks. Four years later the property was flourishing under its new Australian management, winning TripAdvisor's top prize for all-inclusive resorts in Asia.

Few resorts resolved situations as deftly. The usual tactic was to go on a sacking binge at the first scent of a strike, and when one inevitably erupted due to all the dismissals, call in police to drag the offenders off the island. Striking staff had little leeway in the matter, while the right to down tools was enshrined in the constitution; in August 2011 the cohort of resort-owning MPs in parliament introduced legislation banning strikes on resort property.

"The working draft looks to have been written as a birthday present for the resort owners, so one-sided it effectively nullifies workers' constitutional right to strike," observed Dr. Jasper Goss from the International Union of Food Workers (IUF), the global trade union federation which represents resort, hotel, food and agriculture workers.[29]

Sabotage was not always intentional or due to staff grievance. Sometimes staff loyalty could be just as lethal. In early 2011 there was a spate of resort robberies, whereby thieves sneaked onto islands ahead of pay day and either stole the resort's safe or threatened staff until they handed over the cash. This happened several times before a group of seven Maldivians donned balaclavas, filled a boat with swords and a harpoon gun and decided to hit Baros Island Resort and Spa after learning that its safe contained US$50,000. Four of the men made it onto the island but were spotted by a member of security who alerted other staff. One was restrained while two swam out to hide in one of the resort's boats. The fourth, 20-year-old Ali Shafiu, also tried to flee but found himself trapped on the resort's jetty and pelted with rocks. One caught him in the head, and he fell unconscious into the water. The mob gathered round and watched him drown. Police dragged the body from the water half an hour later. Ironically, his gang nickname had been "Immortal".

Minivan's crime journalist Ahmed Nazeer was in his element and canvassed the resort's staff for gossip.

"They were not intending to kill him, but after they knew he was dead they rejoiced," a staff member told him. "But later the three staff who led the attack on Shafiu started receiving phone calls and threats that they would be sorry."

After they received these calls, those who claimed have hit Shafiu suddenly claimed to have not even touched him, the source told Nazeer.

I rang the resort's management.

"It was early in the morning and we are still not clear what happened," said a senior manager, expressing concern that *Minivan News'* coverage of the incident had been posted on TripAdvisor "and guests were commenting".[30]

Resorts and the News

General managers were glued to TripAdvisor, terrified of negative feedback. This often translated into an urge to conceal and cover up whenever tragedy struck. Unused to negative publicity, many panicked when contacted by *Minivan News*, clamming up and doing their best to give the impression that a simple guest drowning was nothing short of premeditated murder. The police weren't much better here, being rather unprofessional and displaying a love of drama that sometimes had tragic and unintended consequences abroad.

Forty-two-year-old Sharon Duval from Oxfordshire in the UK was honeymooning on Kuredu Island Resort with her husband in October 2010. She had a few drinks and wandered off. Her body was later found on the beach by another tourist and his children.

The resort stayed silent, but police excitedly told us that Duval had been observed drinking at the resort's bar until late in the evening prior to her death, in the company of another individual.

"There is no sign of physical abuse or injury to the body, and at this point there is no evidence of any suspicious activity. However, we are still taking the investigation very seriously," police told us earnestly.

Details in such cases were scarce and police both vague and inept. Duval's parents told the *Oxford Mail* that they did not know if she died "because of some sort of crime or an accident".[31]

With Maldivian police unable to conduct a post-mortem, the body was shipped back to the UK and found to contain three and a half times the legal driving limit in alcohol. An inquest was held in Oxfordshire, at which it was revealed that Mrs. Duval had suffered severe sunburn and may have attempted to cool herself in the sea, before passing out.[32] The inquest into her death ruled out "any third party involvement" and gave the cause of death as accidental drowning with a contribution of alcohol intoxication.[33]

Spookily, the same resort suffered tragedy the following year, when a quad-bike driven by the son of the resort's major shareholder crashed into a tree and killed the young couple who had been riding on the front. The recently-married British couple from West Yorkshire, Emma and Jonathan Gray, were riding on the quad-bike as passengers when it collided with a tree around 4am on 6 August 2011. The pair had been married for just seven days and had a six-month-old son, Jake.

The driver was identified as 23-year-old Swedish national Filip Eugen Petre, the son of shareholder Lars Petre.[34] Filip was employed by the company as a trainee guest relations officer and appeared to have lost control of the bike in what amounted to a horrible and unfortunate accident. Police charged him with "disobedience to order" and confiscated his passport.

The whole saga was horrific. Emma Gray had been a much-loved local teacher and the couple's death deeply affected their small community, while Filip Petre's life had been also been destroyed. "This accident is by far the most tragic event in my life," wrote his father in a statement to us.[35]

The families of the victims would often contact us for updates as the trial proceedings unfolded over the next several years. The Maldives' handling of the case amounted to no less than psychological torture of all involved, particularly when the possibility of the death penalty arose.[36] The families of the victims were even sent letters asking whether they wanted Petre put to death if he was found guilty.

"It's absolutely horrendous," Jonathan's mother Cath Davies told her local paper, the *Halifax Courier*.[37] "We never expected there to be an outcome like this. It's good they have dealt with it. It's great they have investigated it properly. But I wouldn't want it to be carried out. It's not going to bring Jay and Emma back. It's not going to make us feel any better. It doesn't seem right. I just find it quite abhorrent. It's not like he set out to maliciously hurt or kill them. He never intended it. What happened was a tragic accident and not the result of wilful or malicious intention."

Filip Petre was ultimately acquitted and fled the country in September 2013,[38] even as the state prosecution sought to urgently appeal the decision and put a hold on his passport citing a "serious miscarriage of justice".

Resorts and Politics

Maldivian politics rarely contributed towards stability when problems arose on resorts. Most staff cafeterias had separate tables for MDP supporters and those who supported Gayoom's regime, and it took a shrewd Maldivian middle manager to keep the situation placid.

The politics were much more volatile on resorts owned by Maldivian interests. The majority of Maldivian tourism workers were younger and progressive, tending more towards support of Nasheed and the MDP, while tycoons such as Gasim, Ahmed "Sun" Shiyam and the Champa brothers had established themselves under Gayoom's patronage. With hundreds of votes at stake, resorts like Sun Island, Irufushi and Paradise Island became campaign tools for their owners at election time, and were accused of politically motivated purges. This was an easy thing to do, as many resorts hosted a ballot box for staff on the island.

"I wouldn't call it a tourist resort anymore. It's nothing but a campaign hub," resort worker Ahmed Ikram told us after being among thirty staff fired from one of Gasim's properties, after the first round of the 2013 presidential elections didn't go in his favour.

"We were so afraid of losing our jobs that we had to just agree with whatever political opinions the management voiced. They forced us to do political things to the point where even someone who might have initially supported Gasim would change his mind," said a sacked cashier, Mohamed Ali.

Things seemed even worse on Shiyam's resorts.[39] The tycoon had registered a new party, the Maldivian Development Alliance (MDA), and allied himself with Gayoom's PPM. However, results from Irufushi resort's ballot in the first round of voting showed 59 votes to the MDP against 38 to the PPM. This appeared to make its owner very unhappy.

"The management have ordered all staff to register at the resort for voting. They've also said at staff briefings that all staff must vote for Yameen [PPM], and that no one should dare try implementing a workers' strike," alleged one of those sacked in the aftermath, Mohamed Rishwan.

"One colleague refused to register to vote at the resort, saying he would finish his duty and go to his nearby home island to vote, citing that it was his constitutional right to do so. He was immediately fired. Some of my former colleagues are now saying that they will not dare cast a vote at all," he said.

Another source working at Irufushi spoke of what he described as a repressive atmosphere among resort staff.

"Things are very difficult. I need to hold this job, so don't name me. Shiyam is firing anyone he even suspects of supporting the MDP. Most of us are under what I would say is psychological trauma right now, afraid to speak our minds as there is so much pressure from above. We can't all afford to lose our jobs, but is political affiliation any reason to be legally dismissed from a job?"

"There have been at least five dismissals in the last week, and no one knows who is next. You see, this is our livelihood, how we support families. This is why everyone is bowing down to this repression, even if reluctantly, and attempting to hold our jobs."

"Sun Shiyam has addressed all staff in extremely disrespectful, and even vulgar, terms. Let me quote what he said at a staff briefing: 'You MDP lot are making 'haram' (prohibited under Islam) use of my money as your wages. You are not entitled to any of it. I will make sure I push out every single one of you MDP dogs from my resort. Mark my words.'"

Resorts usually denied all such claims, when they bothered to speak at all. Sometimes you hit the jackpot, however. Neil contacted the General Manager of Irufushi Beach and Spa Resort, Abdulla Thamheed, to get his side of the story.[40] His response explained much and deserves to be reprinted in full.

Before answering questions on the allegations of politically-motivated sackings at the resort, Thamheed requested he be quoted on the record as expressing concerns over "why a white European" was allowed to working at a Maldives-based publication such as *Minivan News*.

"The fact you are a white European doesn't mean you can come to a third world country and break into our privacy," he told *Minivan News*. "You are a white European and a failure in the UK. I have managed many five star resorts and met journalists from newspapers like the *Sunday Times* and the *Daily Telegraph*," he said.

Upon confirming the reporter's nationality as a UK citizen, Thamheed expressed his view that the journalist was a stereotypical reminder of the Maldives' colonial past. Asked to clarify his comment, he accepted that the Maldives itself had not been colonised by the UK.

"You see yourself as an imperialistic and colonial person, who believes they have imperial superiority over us. No one will give you a job outside this country," Thamheed said.

He added that although his comments were "not personal", but questioned *Minivan News*' ethics as a news organisation and said the reporter could not be called a journalist for producing what he believed was "biased, one-sided propaganda".

Thamheed went on to state that as a white European in the Maldives, the *Minivan News* reporter would not have sought to contact someone for a story in their own country during evening time.

"I have met many top journalists from newspapers like the *Sunday Times* and the *Telegraph*. Do you really think this is how journalists are supposed to behave?" he said.

Thamheed requested that his words be remembered by the journalist and quoted directly in this article.

"I don't think you will be able to sleep tonight," he said. "I am very happy I have spoken to you."

Other MP-tycoons, such as one Abdulla Jabir, could not resist gloating about their impunity. Staff at his Alidhoo resort went on strike in July 2011 claiming not to have been paid wages for months.[41]

"It will be arranged sometime today," Jabir told us then. "The payments were delayed because I was not here."

Twelve Alidhoo staff were swiftly sacked. A year and a half later in December 2012, the nascent Tourism Employees Association of the Maldives (TEAM) published allegations that 125 foreign staff at the resort had not been paid for six months, while 85 local employees had not been paid since May.[42] Staff complained that they were trapped, effectively working for free in the hope of one day being paid the arrears.

"If they do not like it, they can leave," Jabir told us.

"[The staff] are not struggling, that's wrong. If they are struggling, they will not stay. They are staying and that means they are not struggling. I am struggling more than them," he added.

Tourism and Contradiction

The Swiss-French couple sit opposite the celebrant, dressed in white and holding a coconut shell. Maldivian staff surround the woven palm frond enclosure like an honour guard. The ceremony will be conducted to "not only Maldivian" but also "Arabic and Islamic" norms, the celebrant explains.

This is, according to the Vilu Reef Beach and Spa Resort website, a place where couples can renew their wedding vows "hand in hand against a golden sunset backdrop" and where their "everlasting love" can be sealed by a "kaleidoscope of romantic hues" that covers the sky during the sunset.

The celebrant picks up his sheathe of papers, and holds his hands over the couples' hands. He begins to speak solemnly in Dhivehi.

"Before buggering a chicken, check if the hole is clean. That is because the people of the countries that you are from are familiar with the taste of the assholes of chicken," he chants. The couple look on, uncomprehending.

"Your marriage is not a valid one. You are not the kind of people who can have a valid marriage. One of you is an infidel. The other, too, is an infidel—and we have reason to believe—an atheist, who does not even believe in an infidel religion," declares the celebrant.

"You fornicate and make a lot of children. You drink and you eat pork. Most of the children that you have are marked with spots and blemishes ... these children that you have are bastards," he intones, with the inflexion of a religious scholar.

"Keep fornicating frequently, and keep spreading hatred among people. The children you will have from this marriage will all be bastard swine. You are swine according to the Constitution.

"Germs of anger and hatred will breed and drip from the tips of your penises," he adds, then begins reciting articles from the employee handbook he is holding.

Miraculously, not one of the Maldivian staff sniggers.

"Aren't they going to suck mouth?" someone asks.

"Make them suck mouth."

The woman is uncomfortable—she adjusts the neckline of her white dress. The crowd escorts the couple to plant a coconut tree.

"I can see her breasts!" declares someone, as the woman leans forward to put the tree in the sand.

"My beard has gone grey watching those things ... I have seen so many of them now that I don't even want to look any more when I see them."

The video clip finished. I looked at Azra. She was quivering with rage.

"Anything in it?" I asked.

The article exploded across the world.[43] It was *Minivan*'s biggest scoop up to that point, and coincided with what by international standards was a quiet news day: 26 October 2010. The Maldives was suddenly a lead story, appearing on the front page of large newspapers across the planet.

Paul Roberts rang from the President's Office.

"You're a bastard," he said. "Also, great story."

The video had been uploaded to YouTube, apparently to be shared among the resort staff. We downloaded the video, added English subtitles, then stuck it back on YouTube to embed in the article. It reached a quarter of a million views in one day.

The story was powerful not only because it spectacularly showcased the civilizational clash between the two sides of the Maldives, but tapped a deep-rooted anxiety of many tourists: the locals might be smiling, but are they saying nasty things about you in a funny language you can't understand? Yes, in fact they were.

It shot down the rather twee idea of the "magical ethnic wedding ceremony", while entertainingly scapegoating victims silly enough to pay US$1,300 for the privilege of being insulted (photos cost an extra US$400).

"Spicing up your marriage with a touch of 'eastern mysticism' is as superficial as adding Tesco curry powder to a dull meal," suggested one commentator in the UK's *Guardian* newspaper.[44] Another suggested that checking for rashes before penetrating a chicken's rectum was "sound advice".

As a luxury honeymoon destination which had successfully hidden its dark side from the world for decades by substituting a cardboard cut-out of a welcoming tropical paradise, the Maldives had further to fall than most. The religious rhetoric, probably intended as mischief rather than genuine funda-mentalist sentiment, was a spectacular own goal for a tourism-dependent country few people knew was Islamic in the first place. In the aftermath I was taught a terrific traditional Dhivehi phrase that truly summarized the saga: *fain erifa* (literally: "to tread on one's own penis").

Since taking office, President Nasheed was used to flattering news being published at international level and the fawning of foreign journalists. The incident that would become known as "swine wedding" was his first major international PR crisis as president. He handled it with grace and dignity—and more than a little cunning.

The first problem was that the resort had the only records of who the couple were and how to contact them—and it wasn't telling. It was owned by Maldivian MP and resort tycoon Ahmed "Sun" Shiyam, who was convinced the debacle was a plot to destroy him for his support of Gayoom. Indeed, some of the 483 comments on the story suggested that Shiyam himself appeared in the footage at 4.50. The tycoon reportedly had to be threatened with the closure of his resort before finally agreeing to hand the information to police.

By the time the government had identified the hapless couple, they were back home in Europe and had all but boarded up the windows. That weekend they were among the most wanted targets by the continent's army of tabloid journalists; the race was on to get to them before the *Daily Mail*. Nasheed ordered staff at the Maldives' small consulate attached to the UN Human Rights Council in Geneva to track the pair down. The Maldivians immedi-ately jumped in a car and arrived at the couple's house in a remote area on the Swiss-French border. They had been just been rung by some very nice journal-ists, the couple said. Should they speak to them?

"No!" was the reply.

Cameras rolling in Malé, President Nasheed picked up the phone and called the couple, apologizing profusely on behalf of the nation and personally inviting them back to the Maldives to have tea with him at his residence.[45]

"He looked like a man who had just got home to his wife at four in the morning wearing his pants inside-out," said one observer.

"Wedding" ceremonies for non-Muslims were already illegal in the Maldives, although resorts offered the same thing under the wet-blanket phrase "renewal of vows". In the aftermath of the swine wedding the Tourism Ministry cracked down on these and introduced regulations forcing them to be conducted in the language of the visitors. The celebrant—actually a food and beverage assistant—was arrested, although the charges were unclear and he was soon released.

Minivan News was naturally blamed for bringing the Maldives into disrepute and damaging the tourism industry. The editor of one publication stood up next to me in a press conference and demanded loudly in Dhivehi that Nasheed order *Minivan* shut down as a menace to society. It was a revelation for me: years of peddling patriotism meant that the media still saw its job protecting society and advancing the cause of the nation and its masters—the opposite of what we were trying to do, which was hold up a mirror to it. No wonder we had so few friends.

"Resort staff in this situation did not intend any disrespect to guests under any circumstance. From their context its just a playful performance both parties enjoyed. No need to dramatise and make journalistic capital out of it."

That was the "Maldivesresortworkers" blogger, an anonymous and articulate tourism worker whose opinion was representative of many Maldivians.

> Minivan is claiming that the messenger has being shot. That minivan is attacked for reporting this issue. But is it not the whole country that is suffering? The damage is already done. Done to whom? To the country, a whole lot of people like us. We have families to feed, parents to care and jobs to attend to. But if the tourists boycott this country then where is the wisdom of the delivered message? Now, to be fair to Minivan, Minivan is actually doing a lot of good journalism, but being the messenger is also a responsibility. The messenger is responsible for delivering a safe message the recipient can read. That's why they screen letters and packages at the post office.

Other commentators took the matter a step further, outright accusing us of treason and of threatening national security. And remember how nationalism and religion are intertwined? *Minivan* was now also responsible for undermining Islam by publishing anything that reflected negatively on the Maldives.

"To be honest, I'm not too surprised. *Minivan News*, whose editors are notoriously secular, have always had a negative view of everything Islamic. In this case, they've proven that they're willing to sell the reputation of this country if it means they can tarnish the image of our religion," read one of the more coherent comments.[46]

"Minivan news is also a hypocrite news which spreads propagandas and lies against Islam," read one of the less so.

* * *

Tourism might have been the Maldives' golden goose, but there was an underlying and increasingly vocal resentment towards it among a growing segment of the population. This voice was actually a legislative threat to tourism, elements of which were technically illegal under Maldivian law.

The legal argument is quite simple: Article 10 (b) states "No law contrary to any tenet of Islam shall be enacted in the Maldives." Without wishing to become embroiled in Islamic theology, the vast majority of interpretations of Islam (including those in the Maldives) not only consider alcohol and pork to be haram (prohibited) to consume, but also extend this prohibition to the sale and supply of haram commodities. Islamic finance generally considers profits obtained through the sale of haram commodities to be tainted, even if these are generated by a mixed business—such as a hotel with a bar.

If a ban on the sale of alcohol is a clear tenet of Islam, then this has direct ramifications for any regulations in the Maldives concerning its supply, such as customs and import procedures. The Maldives has mostly avoided confronting the more sinful aspects of its major industry by designating local islands as "inhabited" and resort islands as "uninhabited", even though upwards of 600 staff may live and work there—more than on many "inhabited" islands. The import and sale of alcohol was already banned on these islands, so the distinction was really just a way of pretending that nothing was happening on resorts, while allowing the tycoons to sell tourists overpriced piña coladas.

Under Gayoom, pork and alcohol could be sold to expatriates under a licensing system similar to that of Dubai or the Arab Emirates. This, however, led to a great deal of "leakage" into the thirsty Maldivian community, encouraging house parties and making Malé a slightly more pleasant place to live. Nasheed's government began phasing this system out in favour of venue licensing, which would have allowed hotels in Malé with over 100 beds to open foreigner-only bars, just like the hideous airport hotel across the channel. The incentive for the change came from Holiday Inn, Malé's new luxury hotel (later rebadged as Traders), which had been promised a liquor licence under Gayoom's regime and opened soon after Nasheed took office.

What happened next was a sign of what was to come. The opposition—then Gayoom's DRP, Gasim's JP and an assortment of minor parties—seized the liquor regulation as a political wedge issue and evidence of Nasheed's "un-Islamic" agenda. This was odd, as the regulations had heavy restrictions and would have made it more difficult to get a drink in Malé. Expats knew what the Holiday Inn was likely to charge, and preferred the system the way it was. But Nasheed was allowing alcohol to be sold on an island with schools and mosques! The MDP's own coalition partner, the Adhaalath Party, which ran the new Islamic Ministry, gathered the Islamic NGOs together, whipped up fervour and arranged mass protests against Nasheed. An expat surfer from the US, Amber, climbed out of the water near Malé's surf break and was surprised to find herself clutching her board amidst one of Malé's largest public gatherings. Somebody gave her a "Maldivians against alcohol" T-shirt, which she would later proudly wear to the airport hotel bar. We learned later that Gasim's signature was on the receipts for much of the 'Save Islam' protest paraphernalia, despite his being one of the country's single largest importers of pork and alcohol.

Nasheed was in an unwinnable situation, caught off-guard by the old regime's ability to whip up a mob to "protect Islam". He backed down and repealed the regulations.

"It was of major concern to him that a large segment of the public are not happy with the new regulations," said his press secretary Mohamed Zuhair at the time, explaining that "a coalition partner" had threatened to "work on bringing down the government" if they were not rescinded.[47]

There was little doubt as to who this was. The problem was that the old licensing system had already been phased out and there was no political currency in restoring it. The only licensing exception were diplomats and UN officials, who were provided for under a clause of the Vienna Convention.

As a result, the black market value for a bottle of Smirnoff vodka went from MVR700 (US$45) to MVR1,200 (US$78) as the system was being phased out, settling on MVR2,000 (US$130) when it was. The same bottle was sold to a resort for about US$6—a mark-up of 2,100 per cent, far greater than heroin and legal on one side of the border. Desperate and with no other access to liquor, Maldivians would pool their funds and pay this price.

I obtained customs import records. The resorts run by the Maldivian tycoons imported substantially more liquor than other resorts with comparable bed counts. By supporting—even funding—the "Save Islam" rallies, they had artificially created a black market for an in-demand commodity they alone were allowed to import. It made sense: Al Capone was one of Prohibition's greatest supporters in 1920s Chicago.

The exorbitant price of black market liquor meant that it was cheaper to fly to Colombo in Sri Lanka for the weekend, often on the pretence of "medical treatment". It was fascinating to watch what happened when the Sri Lankan Airlines hostess wheeled the Lion beer trolley down the aisle on a Friday night: there would be the sound of a "pssst" as a can was opened, and heads would pop up above the seats like meerkats to identify the offender.

I found Maldivians to be natural party animals, even in the absence of alcohol. Fear and extreme prohibition, however, had ensured that there was no culture of social drinking, and when booze was available many would simply drink until they collapsed. Colombo's bars were unofficially demarcated along political lines: the MDP would drink in one set of bars and the

PPM would stick to theirs, thereby avoiding embarrassing incidents with mobile phone cameras.

The Sri Lankans, for their part, liked Maldivian money but were not always welcoming. Many Sri Lankans were religiously sincere Buddhists and regarded the Maldivians as hypocritical and xenophobic problem drinkers. So bad was their reputation in Sri Lanka that many locals refused to lease houses to Maldivians, as friends who tried discovered. Still, renting abroad was a popular middle-class thing to do if you owned land in Malé; with no access to capital, you enlisted a construction company to build a concrete tower and give you several apartments in exchange for the land (usually the penthouse and one or two others). You could then rent these out at extortionate rents to poor islanders who came to Malé to work and needed to live six to a room to afford the privilege. The rental income allowed you to live like a king nearby in Sri Lanka or Trivandrum, India, both of which most agreed was a far nicer environment than Malé. Trivandrum's bars even thoughtfully advertised happy hour specials in Dhivehi.

Tourism and the Grey Economy

The isolation of the resorts from the rest of the Maldives was not only physical and spiritual, but financial as well. The main issue was that resorts conducted all transactions in dollars rather than local *rufiyaa*; indeed, many refused to accept the Maldivian currency. All prices in resorts were printed in US dollars and at the end of your stay, your bill would be tallied in dollars and your credit card charged in dollars. This money would be swiftly squirreled out of the country to an account in a stable financial haven, such as Singapore or India, never entering the Maldivian banking system.

This had substantial ramifications given the economy's dependence on tourism; the industry indirectly responsible for up to seventy per cent of the economy created no demand for the local currency. Moreover, the practice was technically illegal according to central banking legislation, yet these 1987 regulations fitted onto a single page and had never been enforced by the Maldives Monetary Authority (MMA). As a result, the Maldives suffered from a crippling foreign currency shortage.

Officially the government insisted on pegging the *rufiya* to the US dollar at MVR12.85=US$1, which substantially overvalued the *rufiya* making it non-exchangeable. Dollars were scarce. Even local banks refused to transact *rufiya* to other currencies, and black market rates reached as high as MVR20 to the dollar.

In 2011 the government bowed to pressure from the International Monetary Fund and allowed a "managed float" within a twenty per cent bracket, a half measure that saw the value leap immediately to the newly permitted maximum of MVR15.42 to the dollar and stay put. The problem was not one of industry performance—tourism was booming as never before and dollars were pouring into the tills—but of structure. While resorts were allowed to take dollars, the larger economy was hamstringed, and panicked text messages appealing for dollars would fly around whenever somebody was badly hurt and needed urgent treatment abroad.

Not entirely coincidentally, the artificial dollar shortage had the effect of cementing resort oligarchs at the top of the food chain. By controlling access to dollars they controlled access to imports, including food and medicine, as well as travel abroad and access to decent health and tertiary education. Anyone engaged in importing commodities to the Maldives had to find a reliable black market supply of dollars, because while local businesses would happily pay wholesalers in *rufiya*, suppliers abroad certainly wouldn't accept Maldivian currency.

"Our overseas suppliers have to be paid in dollars. How are you meant to run a business in this place? Surely they can't go on like this?" I was told by the new foreign head of one importer in 2010, who had yet to grasp the role of the black market and the unmarked brown paper envelope.[48]

Another importer, representing a Dubai-based resort supply company, complained that while he was expected to pay suppliers in dollars and euros, "the resorts try their best to pay in *rufiya*. Their revenue is acquired in dollars, so they can [sell the dollars] on the open market and pocket the difference. We keep a local *rufiya* account which we use for pay customs payments and incidentals, otherwise the only way to exchange is on the grey market."

"What bothers me is that there are plenty of dollars coming into the country, but the people in control of the economy seem to be hiding it away," he said.

In fact, the government's own State Trading Organization—the primary importer and wholesaler of commodities to shops, hospitals and the general public—depended on sourcing dollars in this fashion.

I became convinced that this was one of the primary methods whereby a small group of Maldivian resort tycoons retained their stranglehold on the country. It was a simple matter for a resort's financial controller to take a large wad of dollars on a banking trip Malé and exchange it for *rufiya* at the black market premium. The difference could be pocketed while staff back at the resort were paid in *rufiya* at the "official" rate of MVR12.85.

This worked well because the market for dollars was enormous: a third of the population were expatriate workers, the vast majority of them Bangladeshi, and on average they remitted US$100 each a month home to their families. Not that they didn't contribute dollars themselves: many had actually been trafficked from Bangladesh after paying "recruitment" agents fees of up to US$4,000 for the privilege of working in the Maldives. Many melted into the underground workforce after arriving to discover there was actually no job, or that the US$400 a month job promised was in fact paying US$70—if it was paid at all—less than the US$120 a month the individual could get working a construction site back in Bangladesh. The urgent need to send money home—and shame of being tricked—meant that very few returned even when presented the opportunity.

I discovered all this during an August 2010 interview with the outgoing Bangladeshi High Commissioner. Unsurprisingly Dr. Selina Mohsin was angry, and of the hour-long interview scarcely twenty minutes was printable.[49] A typical scenario involved a Maldivian paper company paying US$400–700 to a random person in the street for their signature. This would be used to submit plans to the Human Resources Ministry to build a Manchester United-scale stadium or some such project in the middle of Malé, along with a request for (in one case) 1,600 imported workers. The request would be duly stamped and the Bangladesh-side recruit advised, who would then travel to economically depressed villages recruiting workers. Many would sell their land or go into debt to pay the fees demanded, sending their wives back to their families. The recruiter would receive a third of this fee, the Maldivian partner the remainder. The workers would arrive with theoretically legal paperwork and be waved through by immigration, which despite the scale of the problem employed not a single official capable of speaking Bangla. The arriving worker would have a phone number to call that failed to answer, or would be met by somebody shady who would swiftly confiscate their passport. According to Mohsin, forty such victims were turning up to her office daily claiming that this or something similar had happened to them.

We extrapolated the figures and found the industry to be worth an annual US$46 million at a minimum, eclipsing fishing as the second greatest contributor of foreign currency to the Maldives after tourism; Mohsin felt it could be as high as US$200 million. Eventually—by now on the US State Department's Tier 2 watchlist for human trafficking—Nasheed's government was compelled to address the problem, sending the military to take over the human resources counters and immigration desks for a week. They discovered rooms of confiscated passports and an industry worth a reported US$123 million—right in the middle of our estimate.[50] The evidence was hardly necessary; a few minutes in the Human Resources Ministry every day was enough to see the same Maldivians arriving at the counters with sack loads of passports for speedy and unquestioned stamping. The underlying issue was highlighted when I asked Neil to go to the ministry and arrange renewal of his own work permit, a long, tortuous and Kafkaesque process. He approached the counter, and the girl refused to serve him, asking "Where's your owner?"

The absence of a line between "employment" and "ownership" explained rather a lot, particularly the rate at which (non-resort) expat employees left the country almost always on bad terms with their employers. We were lucky in being able to process our own, however Byzantine the procedure.

In late 2011 Nasheed's government finally put a moratorium on accepting Bangladeshi workers, no doubt badly hurting somebody's business. Barely two months later, he was deposed in the coup and business was back to normal.

Financial Disaster

By 2013, all official figures from the government, MMA, World Bank and others indicated that the Maldives was beyond bankrupt and facing imminent financial apocalypse—as it had been for much of the previous decade.

The flow of aid and concessional credit dried up after the UN upgraded the Maldives to "middle income" in 2011, and the ousting of Nasheed in the 2012 coup put an end to the climate change projects that had filled the gap. By 2013 the new government could not get an outside loan for less than 12 per cent interest and had made no attempt to reduce its gross over-expenditure, vast budget deficit or near total dependence on imports (and foreign currency).

Instead, it was handing out huge bonuses to the police and military, funding itself by selling treasury bonds to shadowy figures or simply printing money as needed. In one famous case before I arrived, a counterfeiter was found not guilty as he had been printing fake US dollars—technically it was only illegal to print *rufiya*, and these, frankly, weren't worth the paper they were printed on.

Nobody was more surprised that the country had survived to see 2014 than its IMF representative, Dr. Koshy Mathai, who closely monitored the tumultuous economy as it blundered from one brink of collapse to the next.[51]

"For a long time we've been saying that [foreign currency] reserves at the MMA are very low and that the fiscal deficit is quite difficult and we expect the economy to run into some problems," he remarked in February that year.

"But somehow the economy has shown resilience, a lot of resilience, and we've been surprised—happily surprised but surprised nonetheless.

"The deficit is quite large. Financing is difficult to find. Banks are not that willing to subscribe to treasury bills. We see treasury bill yields rising quite sharply. MMA external financing is difficult to mobilize. We're left then with the MMA printing money in order to finance expenditures [and the state] running up arrears, unpaid bills to domestic suppliers."

The very fact that imports were on the shelves and people had motor scooters, cars and smartphones implied that the undocumented black market was somehow propping up the country's otherwise improbable financial existence.

"The system seems to work. The parallel market somehow is letting the economy work," he observed.

Mathai's hypothesis complemented my conspiracy theory, although he voiced it more politely. Total reliance on the "parallel market" greatly empowered those few in control of it, while creating dependence in the rest of the population. It was the macroeconomic equivalent of drug dealing.

A New Model: Guesthouse Tourism

Nasheed's government sought to disrupt the model by promoting the development of "guesthouse tourism" in the belief this would bring economic benefits directly to small islands, rather than relying on the "trickle down" effect of resort wages and oligarch philanthropy/patronage. He proposed that the level of investment needed for guesthouses—about US$10,000 a bed compared to US$300,000 for a resort—was within the reach of local families and businessmen, sparing them the need to beg the oligarchs for loans.

"Up to today, there are only about fifty people who directly profit from Maldivian resorts," wrote Nasheed.

"According to guesthouse operators, the cost for setting one up is less than what is needed for building a large *dhoni*. It only takes about two to three million *rufiya* to construct a four to five-bedroom house. A great number of businessmen in inhabited islands are capable of providing this level of investment."

Gayoom's government had banned the construction of guesthouses on local islands and focused on promoting the country purely as luxury resort destination. This was partly a bid to get the Maldives off the "hippy trail", and partly to protect islanders from dangerous ideas such as bikinis, bacon, alcohol and other religions. The sentiment was perfectly voiced to AFP in 2013 by the vice president of the Adhaalath Party, Mauroof Hussain.

"Since the Maldives is a Muslim country, we have always supported the idea that the tourism industry should be separate from the inhabited islands," he said.

"If the hippy-type of travellers come, along will come drugs and narcotics which even now our society is suffering from. Things like nudity are not acceptable in a place where people are living. The people complain that they are praying in the mosque and just outside there are tourists in bikinis."

Nasheed's government lifted the ban during its first year in office and 22 properties sprang up. By 2013 there were 171 guesthouses—almost double the number of resorts. The real test case was the island of Maafushi, otherwise known for hosting the Maldives' largest prison, which enthusiastically threw itself into new development and successfully found its way round bans on bikinis and alcohol (a "secure beach" and day trips to nearby resorts, respectively).

Ahmed Naseer, the owner of the White Shell guesthouse on Maafushi, wrote in January 2014 that the island's twenty guesthouses had the previous year achieved a 65 per cent occupancy rate with an average stay of four days.[52]

"With conservative estimates and past revenue records, it is estimated that about US$9.7 million will enter the local Maafushi economy, and the guesthouses will be paying the state—as bed tax and GST—a total of US$1.3 million," he wrote.

Moreover, the success of the local industry had seen the islanders' income per head rise from the UN's average of US$600 for a rural Maldivian to US$4,425 per head—just from tourism.

"The total income per head of Maafushi after adding incomes from other sectors will probably be the highest in the country," wrote Naseer, who presented Maafushi as a case study during the 2012 South Asia Economic Summit held in Islamabad. "It is a perfect example of making economic growth more inclusive, and a case study for inclusive development," he said.

Disrupting the Stranglehold

Dollars earned from guesthouse tourism flowed into Maafushi's economy, freeing it from the dollar shortage and looking very pretty on the UN's development charts. Upscaling the model, however, would require a momentous cultural shift, with the Maldivian equivalent of tearing down the Berlin Wall. Moreover, guest house income was insignificant compared to the vast torrent of foreign currency earned by the resorts which was not even entering the national economy.

In March 2011 Nasheed's government set about trying to resolve the foreign currency crisis and stem the dollars haemorrhaging from the economy. The first step involved undermining the market for remittance dollars by targeting the unchecked immigration exacerbated by labour traffickers and dodgy employment agencies.

Nasheed's second step was to call on the governor of the MMA to enforce the Central Bank's monetary regulation and to force resorts to transact in *rufiya*. He also promised to "put a policeman behind every dollar".[53]

MMA governor Fazeel Najeeb was in the spotlight. The mild-mannered and softly-spoken official was rarely seen, and staff at the Central Bank privately complained that he spent much of his time abroad studying for an unrelated degree. One of these people, having handing me a sizable quantity of leaked documents over coffee in a Malé café, grumbled that Fazeel was constantly on the phone "taking orders" from Gayoom's half-brother Abdulla Yameen—the shrewd Machiavellian mind behind much of the regime's persistence. There seemed to be something in this when Yameen immediately appeared on Gasim's VTV to defend the MMA governor from the government's criticism, insisting that the dollar shortage was not Fazeel's fault. He didn't say whose it was.

Under pressure and with the MDP still in government, the Central Bank made a show of complying and circulated a memo to the resorts. Several printed menus in *rufiya* and held their breath. Fazeel got some attention in parliament, but avoided the chop. No serious action was taken, and the resorts exhaled and cancelled the print orders.

Nasheed had approached the resorts and their role in the currency crisis as an economic problem. However, like many legacies of Gayoom's regime, it was not a problem—at least for those few in control of the foreign currency flows, the system was working perfectly. As such, it was highly resistant, even hostile, to change.

A few months later, Nasheed was forced to resign from office by opposition rioters and mutinying police. Leaked footage filmed inside police headquarters on the day showed Gasim and handful of other resort tycoons among those weeping with joy.[54]

6

RELIGION AND THE "MOSQUERADE"

"In every Maldivian mind there is a sharp struggle between inherited customs and Muslim ideology. Since this conflict remains unresolved, there is a widespread feeling of guilt and frustration at being unable to adjust the ancestral cultural heritage to the Islamic ideological pattern."

Xavier Romero-Frías, anthropologist[1]

———— *Forwarded message* ————

From: ismail mohamed <i.smilemohamed@gmail.com>
To: [Human rights NGO]
Date: 25 June 2010 09:30
Subject: a plea for help

Dear sir,

I'm a 25 year-old Maldivian living in Male'. I have been working as an Air Traffic Controller at Male' International Airport for almost 7 years now.

I started becoming disenchanted with Islam around 5 years ago and am now an atheist. During my transformation, and even now, I am quite the idealist, and when i was confronted about two years back by a couple of my colleagues about my aversion from the daily practices of Islam, i somewhat foolishly admitted my stance on religion.

I had asked them to keep it a secret from the rest of our workforce at ATC, although i now realize i should have known better. It did not take long for everybody at work to find out and since then, i have faced constant harassment in my work environment.

An atheist is not a common feature at all among Maldivians and the word has spread like wildfire since then. It has now come to the point where everyone I know, including my family, have become aware of my lack of belief.

In a society that has always been proud of their religious homogeneity, you can imagine what i am being put through. I have been subjected to numerous consultations with religious scholars and even my closest friends are not allowed to see me.

My company has already begun investigating a complaint regarding me, collecting testimony from fellow workers about my apostasy.

Just 3 days ago, i received two anonymous phone calls threatening violence if i do not start openly practicing Islam.

I am at my wit's end now. I have been trying for sometime to secure employment abroad, but have not yet succeeded.

The only other alternative i can think of is to flee the country to seek asylum elsewhere. I have already written an e-mail to your organization, and am anxiously waiting for a reply. I found your e-mail address on facebook. I am in dire need of assistance and know of no one inside the country who can guide me.

I would have already left the country if i was sure i could meet the required burden of proof in an asylum claim. I would like to know if you would be able to help me in anyway should i travel to the U.K to seek asylum and what my chances are of making a successful claim.

Thank you for your consideration
Ismail Mohamed Didi

* * *

Ismail Mohamed Didi arrived at Malé International Airport's air traffic control tower early on the morning of 13 July 2010. He usually worked the 6am to 8am shift, but that Tuesday had asked his supervisor for the 3am to 5am shift. There were no scheduled air traffic movements between these hours, and only one air traffic controller was rostered to staff the tower. He wanted the quiet time alone.

It was still dark outside and the operations room of the control tower was only dimly lit. He opened the door to the balcony and stepped outside. He lit up a cigarette and discarded his lighter.

The first rays of dawn revealed Ismail Mohamed Didi's limp body dangling from the air traffic control tower. At 5.30am his mother called his mobile phone to remind him to attend *Fajr* (dawn) prayers.

There was no answer.

I spent a long evening working over the follow-up story to Didi's suicide in my head. Our first piece on the morning of Didi's death contained the bare details available: police were investigating the death of a 25-year-old man in a suspected suicide. It was "hard news"—and missed the real story.[2]

After it broke, I received a series of emails Didi had sent to a human rights NGO in the weeks leading up to his death. They revealed someone who after publicly declaring himself an atheist, had been isolated from his friends and family, ostracized by his society and employer, and eventually in fear for his life after a torrent of death threats. He had begged the NGO for help in seeking asylum, but received no reply. A source in the NGO was profoundly upset to hear of his death, and forwarded *Minivan News* the emails.

Reporting suicide is hazardous and difficult. Research shows that almost any reportage sparks copycat attempts, and many outlets adopt a policy of simply not reporting it at all. This has the effect of hiding the extent of the issue. When I worked on the *Narrabri Courier* in Australia we received guidelines for reporting suicides, such as not using language glamourizing or sensationalizing suicide, discussing the method, taking care with phrasing (don't say, "successful" suicide attempt), providing numbers for helpline services, and not publishing suicide notes. Going in the other direction and helping suicide victims make statements of their deaths was not in the pamphlet.

Religion complicated the situation. Suicide is heavily stigmatized in Islamic cultures as a major sin, the act condemning the victim to eternal hellfire, and denying both funeral prayers and sometimes even burial in the community's cemetery. The Maldivian media, where it had reported Didi's death at all, played it down.

There were no suicide prevention helplines in the Maldives to stick at the bottom of Didi's article, as was standard practice in many other countries. There was no senior editor to make and take responsibility for the decision. There wasn't anybody to ask for advice, and most people preferred to believe the problem didn't exist. There wasn't even a single practicing psychologist in the country—mental illness was prevalent but largely unrecognized, and many families considered it shameful. This was part of the problem—conservative parents, traumatized at the prospect of their more liberal-minded offspring literally burning in hell for eternity, instead forced them to attend religious counselling with dubious scholars.

"His family is very humble and religious. His mother tried sending him to religious classes. A couple of months back he said he went to see Sheikh Ilyas, but just argued with him about religion and stormed out," one of Didi's colleagues told me.

This was common practice. Educated, professional and internationalized young Maldivians, many returned after living and studying abroad, would mutely put up with being sent for such counselling out of kindness towards

121

their concerned parents. The consulting "scholar" had often at best received a certificate from some madrassa (Islamic school) in India or Pakistan, and at worst was self-qualified having memorized a few ominous phrases in Arabic. I did wonder what the exchanges were like in these sessions.

"You just sit there and listen politely until you're told to leave," one of *Minivan*'s journalists told me.

I needed to gather information on Didi's case before I made a decision on the story. I tried to ring Didi's scholar, Sheikh Ilyas, famous for his hellfire and brimstone public sermons. He wasn't responding, so I called the Islamic Minister, Dr. Abdul Majeed Abdul Bari. He was a dour and severe man, but one of the more moderate members of the Islamic Adhaalath ("justice") Party which was in coalition with Nasheed's MDP.

Dr. Bari said he was aware that Didi's parents had approached the ministry seeking religious counselling for their son "because of some problems he was facing in his religious beliefs". However, the government, including the Islamic Ministry, had been in turmoil after Nasheed's cabinet resigned en masse in protest against the "scorched earth" politics of the opposition-controlled parliament. The usual scholar hadn't been available.

"I think they met a scholar while they were in our office," Dr. Bari told me.

"I heard he was not a ministry scholar—I don't think it was Sheikh Ilyas this time. I think he saw [Sheikh Hassan] Moosa Fikree."

Fikree was the vice president of a large local religious NGO, Jamiyyathul Salaf. Salaf had been very successful in hoovering up and radicalizing many of the country's dispossessed young people. They had particular success in "reforming" violent gang members, adding religious purpose to existing inclination towards violence. The military had been closely monitoring the group, and at least one government official had expressed concern over their alleged sources of overseas funding.

A picture had begun to emerge. If Didi had argued with Fikree as he apparently had Ilyas, then it was more than possible that some of those in Salaf would have taken it upon themselves to hound him, if not actually attack him once they decided he was an irredeemable apostate. This fitted in with the threats he described in his email.

It was also undeniable that whatever the reporting guidelines on suicide, Didi himself had made a dramatic statement with his death by using the air traffic control tower. The tower directed the jets and seaplanes delivering thousands of tourists to the Maldives every day, most of whom had no idea that the country was even Islamic, never mind the fact that the cocktail they were drinking was as illegal as heroin on the island next door. It was several hours before Didi's body was retrieved. Planeloads of tourists looking out their windows would have seen him hanging, an inauspicious beginning to their honeymoons.

I worried about copycats; I worried I was over-interpreting what may have been the rash and sudden action of a depressed and troubled mind; I worried I was getting involved, fulfilling accusations in the comments that I was imposing my "liberal secular agenda" by challenging a society and culture I had no stake in.

The final factor in the decision to publish the wider story—and Didi's emails—was that I knew of at least a dozen Maldivians in similar straits to Didi: ostracized, isolated, threatened and struggling to survive—psychologically as well as physically—in a small, interlinked society that considered any outward show of free thinking a threat to social order.

The story was published the following day, on 14 July.[3] It was a watershed moment for the Maldives. The story was picked up and raced all over the world. Didi's story appeared everywhere from the BBC to the UN Human Rights Council's press centre. What was truly arresting about the story on *Minivan* were the comments it attracted. Among those on the first page:

"Let him rot in Hell. He has finally got asylum in Hell."

"I'm glad its not a muslim who died this way. Surely all who dies by suicide has no fear of God choosing the shortcut to Hell. May Maldives always be a muslim country and hopefully an islamic country in future."

"Theres nothing to say about this guys acts. WHETHER YOU LIKE IT OR NOT, HES ROTTING IN HELL...THATS THE TRUTH!!"

"MINIVAN NEWS really seems to have something against Islam. The beautiful religion of Islam ... it is soo beautiful ... everything is soo clear. For those people around here who don't support the religion i call them to leave this county and practice your religion somewhere else."

"JJ Robinson is living dangerously! In our home soil he is trying to portray our religion and its believers as wicked and cruel as it can be."

"There is no one else to be blamed for his act other than himself and his atheist friends. And to all Maldivians who desire a religion other than Islam, I say you were brought up within Islamic boundaries and you are only being stubborn."

"I dont know what to say. Even after he is no more in this world, we all seem to be picking on him. Leave him in peace. Thats probably what he wanted. So sad. Stop the comments now minivan."

We did not. At last count, there were 287. The page had been visited a quarter of a million times.

Islamic Identity in the Maldives

The Maldivian government, the constitution and indeed the majority of Maldivians assert the Maldives to be "100 per cent Muslim". The statistic is a keystone of Maldivian nationalism, and vehemently defended in the face of any evidence to the contrary. A 2010 report by Jordan's Royal Islamic Strategic Research Centre and Washington's Pew Research Centre suggested that the Maldives was actually a 99.41 per cent Muslim country,[4] but this didn't seem to impress anyone.

"The world should know the appropriate information about Maldives before publishing documents about Maldives. Everything in the Maldives is conducted in accordance with the constitution," responded the then State Islamic Minister, Sheikh Mohamed Shaheem Ali Saeed.[5]

He was right about the constitution; Article 9 makes being Muslim a condition of citizenship, and is widely interpreted as the source of the "100 per cent" figure.

This actually breaches several international human rights treaties the country has signed, such as Article 18 of the International Covenant on Civil and Political Rights (ICCPR): "Everyone shall have the right to freedom of thought, conscience and religion."[6] The Maldives maintains formal reservations to this article under the treaty's provision for governments to ignore any clauses they find inconvenient. Nonetheless: "We declare that there are no apparent contradictions between human rights and what is there in the Maldives constitution."

That was Home Minister Dr. Mohamed Jameel, appointed in 2012 shortly after Gayoom's old regime toppled Nasheed. He played a central role in that process, having authored the widely-circulated pamphlet, "President Nasheed's devious plot to destroy the Islamic faith of Maldivians".

He was being grilled in Geneva by a UN Human Rights Council panel reviewing the Maldives' commitment to its treaties—part of a regular process called the Universal Periodic Review (UPR). Unusually for an international body examining the Maldives, the panel had done its homework and was not proving susceptible to the regime's diplomatic charm and wriggling doublespeak. The slaughter was being broadcast online, and the *Minivan* crew were glued to the screen.[7]

"The Maldives as a Muslim country clearly stipulates that the rights enshrined in the constitution should be interpreted in a way that do not contradict Islamic Sharia," Dr. Jameel insisted.

The Maldives was, he said, a "homogenous society" that spoke one language, was of "one race and one religion", and therefore there was "no debate in society calling for the removal of the provisions [relating to] language or religion, because of the characteristics of the Maldives as a society."

There was indeed no debate in society, as this was expressly forbidden by Article 27 of the constitution:[8] "Everyone has the right to freedom of thought and the freedom to communicate opinions and expression in a manner that is not contrary to any tenet of Islam."

Fortunately Jameel was rescued from the panel's grilling by the second member of the Maldives' defence counsel, Gayoom's daughter, Dunya Maumoon, who had just been appointed Minister of State for Foreign Affairs.

"Being a Maldivian and being a Muslim have become interlinked and inseparable. There is strong public support for the Maldives being and remaining a 100 per cent Muslim country. Indeed if anything, the introduction of democracy has intensified [this perception]," she explained.

There were no plans to withdraw the reservation, Dunya said.

"This is not dogmatic government policy or preference, but rather a reflection of the deep societal belief that the Maldives always has been and always should be a 100 per cent Muslim nation. Laws, like government, should be based on the will of the people."

But what does the "will of the people" mean for Maldivians like Ismail Mohamed Didi, who declare themselves non-Muslim in a society conditioned to believe that enforced collective harmony overrides an individual's freedom of thought? Were they to lose their citizenship as well as their lives?

The constitution is elusive on the subject. Article 9 defines a "citizen" as anybody who was a citizen at the time the constitution commenced in 2008, their children and any foreigner granted citizenship. It also states that no citizen can be deprived of citizenship, but yet another clause adds that "despite" these provisions, "a non-Muslim may not become a citizen of the Maldives". Presumably if you were a non-Muslim Maldivian before 2008 you would not be considered a citizen. But what if you turned apostate after 2008?

Apart from Didi, only one Maldivian ever tested this publicly.

Naik and Nazim

Dr. Zakir Naik, head of the Islamic cable network Peace TV and ranked the 89th most powerful Indian in 2010 by *The Indian Express*, stood before a packed stadium in Male. He was dressed in a Western-style business suit, topped with a *taqiyah* (Muslim prayer cap).

It was May 2010, and Naik had brought his show to the Maldives on the invitation of a delighted Ministry of Islamic Affairs. Peace TV can be best described as a Salafist version of the Christian televangelism shown on early morning American television. Instead of wish fulfilment or magic water, Naik's gimmick is his question and answer sessions, in which long queues of people ask him questions on Islamic faith and comparative religion. He appears to have a near-eidetic memory, memorizing the holy books of all major faiths in multiple languages, and drawing on jumbles of passages to artfully reassure petitioners of Islam's superiority.

Naik's visit to the Maldives was organized by the Ministry and the preacher was accorded the state honours of a major dignitary. With non-Islamic religious literature banned in the Maldives and bibles the subject of much paranoia, Naik's knowledge of comparative religion was considered by many to be dangerous and exciting. His show attracted a crowd of 11,000 people, one of the largest ever gatherings in the Maldives. The whole thing was caught on film.

Thirty-seven-year-old Mohamed Nazim was one of the Maldivians in line for Naik's Q&A session. When his time came he approached the microphone, arms crossed and nervous, and declares that he is "Maldivian and not a Muslim". He then asks Naik to clarify whether this means that he is to be put to death as an apostate.[9]

"Can you ask the question again?" asks the stunned Maldivian moderator, as a rumble begins to spread through the crowd.

Naik, smiling nervously, suggests that Nazim "should go and ask the government".

"The government tells me the Maldives is 100 per cent Muslim. You say you are non-Muslim. I don't know if they will take away your nationality or not. 100 per cent minus one?"

Nazim pushes him to clarify the penalty for apostasy. Naik deflects the question back to him.

"As far as I know it is death," Nazim responds.

A grin slowly spreads across Naik's face.

"So why don't you go and..."

The crowd becomes visibly more excited. Sensing trouble, Naik tries again to deflect the question back to Nazim, but Nazim brings him back to it.

"The penalty for apostasy is not necessarily death," Naik finally decides. "However any Muslim who converts to non-Muslim, propagates his faith and speaks against Islam, if it is Islamic rule then the person should be put to death."

Naik quickly clarifies that this would only happen in a country where the population follows Islamic law, and not a country where the majority are simply Muslim.

"The Maldives is a Muslim country, not an Islamic state," Naik declares.

The crowd is silent. One person is heard clapping. It is Nazim.

"I don't know of one country in the world which is 100 per cent Islamic," Naik concludes.

That was the last straw. The "100 per cent" statistic was the subject of great nationalistic fervour—he might as well have torn up the flag. To make matters worse, he had executed his humiliation of Maldivian nationalism in front of a respected visiting celebrity.

Nazim stepped away from the microphone and returned to an aisle seat strategically located near the exit.

A Maldivian man wearing Pakistani dress came over and attacked him, all the rage and anger and humiliation channelled into what Nazim would later describe as a limp-wristed swat. But hands-on violence was rare in the Maldives, and Nazim knew he had a problem. He ran towards a group of police seeking protection, who scattered—more afraid of the apostate than of the angry mob behind him. He made his way to the nearby police headquarters and was taken into custody.

"I know what you guys are up to. It will never happen in this country," a policeman told him ominously, as he was booked.

The mob gathered outside, calling for Nazim to be beheaded. He was moved to the prison island of Dhoonidhoo and held for days while he was given religious counselling. The Adhaalath Party accused him of violating the constitution and called on the government to protect it, while the Islamic Foundation of the Maldives called for Nazim to be killed if he failed to repent, "as Islamic law and Maldivian law agree".[10]

On 1 June Nazim appeared on national television and gave *Shahadath*, the Muslim testimony of belief. He apologized for causing "agony for the Maldivian people", and said "major misconceptions I had regarding Islam have been clarified".

"After two days of counselling he said that his misconceptions had been clarified and that he wanted to become a Muslim," explained Deputy Minister for Islamic Affairs Sheikh Mohamed Farooq.

The President of Jamiyyathul Salaf, Sheikh Abdulla Bin Mohamed Ibrahim, told us he was very happy to hear of Nazim's repentance, as the incident had "damaged the good name of the country".

He ominously added that there were "many people trying to introduce other religions to the Maldives underground", and that he would "release the names of these underground people at the appropriate time".

Months later I ran into Nazim at a US State Department function in Malé. I didn't recognize him at first, and when he introduced himself I asked him for his number in the mistaken belief that I didn't have it already. He took my number and dialled my phone. We stood watching the screen as a call from "The Apostate" came through.

To his credit, he chuckled.

"I felt as if I was suffocating. The extremism that was taking hold in the Maldives was increasing so rapidly. I could not travel in any taxi anywhere without having to listen to extremist material," he told us in a follow-up interview, "Revelations of a former apostate".[11]

He had been brought to court the day after his showdown with Naik, where he was formally remanded in custody on Dhoonidhoo. His lawyer told him the Human Rights Commission of the Maldivian (HRCM) would not be able to intervene on his behalf as apostasy "does not fall within their remit", and suggested that his interests would be best served by "living as all other Maldivians do".

"Once a 'born-again Muslim', he had pen and paper and a new cell that was far cleaner than the one he had before. He was also allowed to walk and leave the cell at times," wrote Azra Naseem, who was working for *Minivan* at the time and jumped at the chance to interview him.

The reaction to his declaration of non-belief in Islam, he said, has been mixed—angry and supportive, superficial and profound. He lost 65 friends on Facebook, the social networking site to which almost every computer literate Maldivian subscribes. He did, however, gain 246 new "friends".

His own friends and colleagues, he said, are uneasy talking about it. Very few have actually discussed it with him. He can feel its presence however, unspoken yet potent, in his every social interaction with another person. Among the general public, apart from a few threatening text messages and threats left on his "wall" on Facebook, the reaction has been muted since his public recitation of the *Shahadath*.

He does not regret what he did, he said.

"Somebody had to do it, it needed to be spoken about. The repression of thought, the lack of debate and a lack of a proper public sphere in which such discussion can take place, is dangerous."

One of the two men who publicly expressed their doubts over faith decided to re-embrace Islam and live life as the constitution says a Maldivian should. The other decided life was not worth living.

Buddhism to Islam: A Hostile Takeover

The Maldives' practice of compelling its citizenry to be Muslim while banning other faiths—indeed, banning even the concept of no faith—makes it unique even among strict Islamic countries such as Pakistan and Iran. The constitution states, "No law contrary to any tenet of Islam shall be enacted in the Maldives",[12] and yet the Quran itself declares "There is no compulsion in religion (Quran 2:256)".[13]

Given its isolation and relative cultural homogeneity, the Maldives is a sectarian science experiment, a revealing study in how Islamic trends such as extremist Wahhabism influence a country's cultural, social and political establishment over time, and vice versa. It demonstrates how traditional cultural practices were subsumed and assimilated by imported Arab interpretations, how these interpretations were harnessed for political control, and how this control was lost to growing extremism. Radical Islamic fundamentalism and resort tourism-dependent economy?

My focus in this chapter is not ethnographic scholarship. I am more interested in how Islam affects the lives and politics of the people who live in the Maldives, and how they have adapted to their circumstances to create one of the world's most seemingly contradictory countries.

The path to the present situation does call for some historical context, however, and this is difficult in the Maldives. The state has for decades hidden and obfuscated much of its own history, and the educational curriculum is narrowly nationalistic and suspect in places. Primary source material is limited and considered of little importance where it does exist, or is simply ignored—not just by the government, but by ordinary Maldivians. I found it surprising that people showed so little interest in their own history; Nasheed seemed fascinated by it, but he was one of about a dozen I encountered. Most anthropological and ethnographic studies of the past century are solely in English, conducted by foreigners, such as the archaeologist H. C. P. Bell, the ethnographer Xavier Romero-Frías, the anthropologist Clarence Maloney and the French navigator François Pyrard de Laval who was shipwrecked on the islands in the early seventeenth century.[14] Maldivian tertiary students who attend university abroad overwhelmingly focus on subjects such as economics and business studies, and oral history is disappearing with the current older generation (in much the same manner that traditional local skills such as sailing have been almost totally lost to the diesel engine). The result of all this is that Maldivian history is cloudy and folklorish, officially unacknowledged and mysterious in many places particularly up to and surrounding the country's conversion from Buddhism to Islam in the twelfth century.

The version still taught in Maldivian schools involves the Moroccan scholar Abul Barakat the Berber, who visited the Maldives and noticed that his hosts were weeping. The family explained to him that their virginal daughter had been chosen as that month's offering to the local sea monster, the Rannamari. Abul Barakat volunteered to take the girl's place. The monster appeared and he chanted Quranic verses at it until it went to sleep/fled/was shrunk and put in a bottle and thrown back into the sea. In return for his assistance, the Buddhist King Koimala Siri Mahaabarana Mahaa Radun declared the country Muslim in 1153. If the tale sounds a bit like St. George and the Dragon, then that is because a version of the same tale was itself brought back to Europe from the East by the Crusaders.

A second version of the legend panders to the Maldivian love of a good conspiracy by suggesting that the Rannamari was actually King Koimala himself, who raped and killed the girls offered by the superstitious islanders. Abul Barakat, unimpressed on hearing this, dressed up as that month's virgin (make of that what you will) and, one assumes, gave the king a nasty surprise. The king, justifiably terrified of the public reaction, promised to convert the nation to Islam if Abul Barakat kept his dirty secret. The Moroccan stuck around teaching Islam, and in 1656 his resting place was marked with a tomb: the Medhuziarai, still one of Malé's only tourist attractions.

Official Maldivian history of the kind you'll find in any tourism brochure implies that the conversion to Islam happened overnight on the king's declaration, peacefully setting the nation on the path of good.

"It is still possible to read contemporary articles that claim Maldivian history is 'lost in the mists of time'—a hollow phrase since those mists began to clear 90 years ago," wrote the Australian journalist and curator of Maldives-culture.com, Michael O'Shea, in a 2011 article for *Minivan*, "The inappropriate history of the early Maldives".[15]

H. C. P. Bell, digging in Maldives in the 1920s, discovered ruins of Buddhist temples, some of which appeared to have been deliberately buried in rubble in an apparent attempt to hide them. The Maldivian government refused to recognize Bell's work and only stopped pretending that the ruins did not exist in the 1980s. By then the temples had been destroyed or plundered, while many others had been turned into mosques—still facing the sun, rather than Mecca.

The temples did turn up artefacts suggesting that the conversion was rather more brutal than claimed. Ancient twelfth-century copperplate books, known as *Loamaafaanu* and written in an archaic Dhivehi script resembling medieval Sri Lankan Sinhala, speak of Buddhist monks being brought to Malé and beheaded.

In 1959 a Maldivian expedition on the island of Thoddu unearthed a large, ancient and exquisitely carved Gotama Buddha statue,[16] carefully and deliberately hidden under a temple and surrounded by garlands of flowers and a stone perimeter. With the statue was a piece of hip bone, a coral-stone relic casket, a gold cylinder and some ancient coins. One was identified as a Roman denarius minted in Rome in 90 BC.

The islanders fought with the expedition over the findings and decapitated the statue. The pieces were recovered, brought to the grounds of the presidential residence in Malé and reassembled. Rumours of forbidden "idol worship" and spontaneous Buddhist conversions echoed around the small island. Gayoom's predecessor, Ibrahim Nasir, reportedly refused to even look at the thing.

Six days after it arrived the statue was smashed to powder by unknown vandals. The coins and other artefacts were stolen, and remains of the temple on Thoddu reburied. The head survived, sealed in locked storeroom, and eventually found its way into public display in an extravagant new museum in Malé built for Maldivians by the Chinese government and opened in 2010.

But Maldivian historical revisionism had unfinished business. During the chaos of the 2012 coup as mobs of mutinying police, military and opposition demonstrators occupied themselves with toppling the government, a mob of bearded young men stormed the national museum.[17] Extensive high-definition CCTV footage showed what happened next: the head of the Thoddu Buddha, together with all other traces of pre-Islamic civilization in the Maldives, were smashed into dust.[18]

"This is not like a glass we use at home that can be replaced by buying a new one from a shop. These are originals from our ancestors' time. These cannot be replaced ever again," a museum official told *Minivan* after the incident, declining to give his name for fear of retaliation.

That incident signalled the start of a climate of impunity for fundamentalism in the Maldives. This was despite the abundance of evidence the new government made no serious attempt to bring to justice those responsible for the cultural atrocity. A source involved in the token case told me that the police effectively sabotaged their own investigation by not even including the CCTV footage as evidence in the case sent for prosecution. I pointed out that it was already on YouTube and that I was more than happy to forward the links to the Prosecutor General's office.

"It doesn't work that way," the source sighed.

And so it was that 1,400 years of Buddhist civilization was relegated to an uncomfortable footnote in Maldivian history books, in the manner of the Taliban's destruction of the Bamiyan Buddhas in Afghanistan.

Adapting Religion

The success of religions anywhere in the world has often depended on a population's ability to adapt its tenets to their existing culture. This was true of the Maldives from the time of its conversion right up to the 1970s. Practice of the religion was laid back, much like Sufism, with the emphasis on Islam as part of a shared cultural and spiritual identity. By regional standards women were relatively emancipated for much of Maldivian history: the country had no fewer than four female heads of state. The Maldivian word for queen, *rehendi*, is still used by some resorts to brand their bungalows.

Women did not wear the veil, headscarf or even tops right up until the sixteenth century. The abundance of lithe and topless island beauties was of great distress to the famous Islamic traveller Ibn Battuta, who visited the country in 1341 and found himself appointed a judge. His efforts at reform floundered.

"I strove to put an end to this practice and commanded the women to wear clothes; but could not get it done. I would not let a woman enter my court to make a plaint unless her body were covered; beyond this, however I was unable to do anything," he wrote.[19]

One of the benefits of the geographic isolation of the islands was that cultural imperialism took time to travel—sometimes centuries. One of *Minivan*'s female journalists lamented to me that her grandmother had bounced around her island free-breasted until the age of sixteen but was today insisting that all the girls in the family wore the heavy black niqab.

Maldivian society was even broadly matriarchal; the men would go out fishing every day, while women ran the island's affairs—sometimes rather literally. The Deputy Economic Development Minister in Nasheed's government, Adil Saleem, complained to me that this was one of the major obstacles to development of the fishing industry: Maldivian fishermen were reluctant to do multi-day fishing trips, as they did not trust their wives at home alone for an evening. Rather than following a school of tuna, fishermen returning to check up on their wives would have to find the tuna all over again the following day. There were always other fish in the sea, if not at home.

Fanditha: *Djinn and Tonics*

There are few better examples of traditional Maldivian culture adapting to accommodate Islam than *fanditha*. A mixture of folk medicine, animist spiritism, superstition and Quranic recitation, *fanditha* comes in black and white varieties and is deadly serious to many Maldivians; so deadly in fact, that the state's last execution was for the crime of murder—by black magic. Hakim Didi was tied to a coconut tree and shot in 1953.

Fanditha was still going strong when I was in the Maldives in 2009, although a 1979 law did require persons wishing to practise magic to first "write and seek approval from the Ministry of Health". Black *fanditha* was widely feared even by otherwise liberal and worldly Maldivians, and stories of curses, charms and demonic possessions abounded. The "white" version—healing, curse-lifting, love potions—was not only tolerated but actively promoted by the very people you would think would be fervently against it. In 2011 the Islamic Foundation of the Maldives (IFM) even held a "certificate level" course on incantations, "spiritual healing" and the curing of diseases.[20] The one-month course cost MVR350 (US$23). The class was limited to thirty students, and sold out almost immediately.

"Many people have requested that we teach them this, so we decided to open a course for the public and we are receiving huge support for it," explained the IFM's founder and president, former Guantanamo Bay detainee Ibrahim Fauzee.

"The Prophet's—peace be upon him—Sunnah as well as the Quran reveals many things about the existence of djinns [spirits]. Djinns often cause trouble and disturbances to humans, so we know that they are there. The Quran and the Prophet—peace be upon him—has taught us ways to cure [these disturbances]."

There were certainly no shortage of these. A common incident involved mass-faintings of school students due to cursed trees, often around exam time.[21] Police were often called to islands to investigate, and arrest, alleged sorcerers. White magic practitioners would be called in to conduct exorcisms as required.

The hunt for exotic ingredients made for some splendid stories. As recently as 2014, the popular Sri Lankan singer Amal Perera complained to Sri Lankan police that a rare albino turtle had been stolen from the Kosgoda Sea Turtle Conservation Sanctuary, allegedly for use in a black magic ritual against a Maldivian politician. The asking price for the creature was reported to be US$26,000.[22]

The foreign half of our audience may have been chuckling over the headlines, but we had to take *fanditha* as seriously as our Maldivian readers. Fear over *fanditha* gave it real power to affect small and isolated communities, and some incidents sounded truly terrifying.

"I'm not a believer [in black magic], I never have been, but it's happening. And it's so weird to see happening," a Maldivian friend on the island of Thakandhoo told us in September 2013, after four children on the island aged between nine and fourteen began behaving erratically.

"It just started suddenly. The children began speaking and behaving in a very strange way. Their outbursts happen randomly—any time of day for the girl, but with the boys it happens mostly in the evenings. The girl has been seeing black shadows, acting weird, fainting, complaining of 'frozen' hands and teeth, and saying strange things: 'I'm going to kill you', 'somebody's coming.'"

A squad of *fanditha* men called to the island began reciting *maithiri* (Quranic verses recited to end spiritual possession), before digging up a series of clay tablets buried near the school gate. The girl was admitted to the island's health centre "screaming uncontrollably not to remove the [clay] stones because it would kill her".

The island council held a series of community meetings for the terrified population, instructing them on precautions to take against black magic.

"We were advised to recite the Quran, and for children not to go out after 6pm or to isolated places unsupervised," our Thakandhoo source said.

I was curious as to how Maldivians reconciled belief in *fanditha* with conservative Islam, to the point where scholars actively endorsed the use of Quranic verse in spellcasting by laypeople. To find out more we sought out a *fanditha* "spokesperson", finally settling on Ajnaadh Ali, President and Chief Exorcist of the Spiritual Healers of the Maldives Association. We found his organization on Facebook.

"In Dhivehi, *fanditha* means magic—black or white—but the way it is practised is what makes it good or bad," he explained, following a literal police witch-hunt on Thakandhoo.[23]

"Black magic is when people worship or invoke djinns or devils to cause harm to others. There is a lack of knowledge regarding the religion. Some people who do black magic think it's OK because the Quran is used," Ajnaadh explained.

"Black magic is practised by misusing the Quran, chanting or writing verses and the names of devils or djinns to summon their help. It cannot be done unless someone has some disbelief of Allah. It is also disrespectful of the Quran."

The best way to defend against black magic was to read verses from the last two chapters of the Quran.

"*Ruqyah* is a form of white magic, specifically an Islamic exorcism where Quranic verses are read and prayers recited to heal. *Ruqyah* will neutralize black magic to rid of the evil eye or any other spiritual matter, like djinn possessions or mental illness."

This being the Maldives, black magic was most frequently used for political purposes, bringing new definition to the phrase "casting one's vote".

Some islands, concerned about all the magic being used to influence votes at election time, assembled their own ghost-busting task forces. We sent a correspondent to one of the more supernaturally-troubled constituencies.

"Hassan Shuzeym, 35, is an artist, a caretaker at Guraidhoo's Home for People with Special Needs, and now leader of the drive to undo black magic. Sitting at one of Guraidhoo's newly opened guesthouses, the slim, dark-skinned Shuzeym told us how he organizes a 20-man patrol from dusk til dawn in order to ensure cursed objects are no longer buried at the schools," wrote Zaheena, having made it back to Malé apparently djinn-free.[24]

> A culture of performing black magic to coerce love or for personal gain had always existed on the island, Shuzeym told us over cigarettes and coffee. But black magic to influence votes on a large scale was new, he said.
>
> "This magic is being done to change people's hearts about their votes. But it's only affecting the students who study at the school. We want to minimize the harm caused to people from the black magic."
>
> Shuzeym and his friends dig up objects and perform counter-spells to cancel out their magic.
>
> "In places where it is too dangerous to dig them out, we read surahs [chapters] of the Quran and sprinkle water on the area to cancel out their powers," he said.
>
> When asked how they knew where to look for cursed objects, Shuzeym told us with a mysterious look: "I can only tell you it is not with the help of humans."

Gayoom and the Rise of Islamic Nationalism

Two major events occurred in the 1970s that would shape religion in today's Maldives.

The first was the introduction of tourism, which opened the gates to the outside world and challenged the country's isolation in unexpected ways. The sudden surge of foreign currency introduced the possibilities of the outside world, and the profits at stake in turn attracted foreign interest and investment. But the vast majority of Maldivians, scattered as they were, remained defensive, isolationist and wary of foreign influence. The lack of contact with tourists inhibited the spread of not only wealth, but cultural exposure to foreigners: the geographic nature of the Maldives meant that the "threat" could be easily contained to separate islands, without risk to revenue. This approach also happened to greatly benefit those few at the top of the new industry, who, as discussed in the previous chapter, could tightly control development and choose where and how the fruits of the new industry fell.

The second major event was the arrival of Gayoom to the presidency, displacing the previous president, Ibrahim Nasir, in a single candidate "election" (won with over ninety per cent of the vote). Nasir had modernized the Maldives and sought to prepare it for increasing contact with the outside world. He encouraged the early growth of tourism, ordered the building of the international airport on the island of Hulhule next to Malé, mechanized the fishing industry, introduced an English-based curriculum to government schools, started the first radio and television stations and grew the Maldives into an international shipping powerhouse with sixty cargo ships plying the seas (a combination of managerial negligence and failure to adapt to container ships in the 1980s would sadly all but kill off Maldivian shipping).[25]

Nasir was by no means a saint. In 1962 he had personally led the crushing of a short-lived secessionist rebellion in the south of the country, the Suvadive Republic, by leasing a Sri Lankan gunboat and brutally depopulating the island of Thinadhoo. The population of 4,800 was scattered, and those who were not arrested, raped, tortured or killed in custody were forced to beg for shelter from other islands. The island wasn't resettled until 1966.

"The level of psychological insecurity in Thinadhoo was still palpable in 1997; the house walls, much higher than in other islands, created a garrison atmosphere in the streets," wrote Maldivesculture's Michael O'Shea,[26] after a visit to the scarred island.

Still, when Nasir, facing declining health, stepped down and endorsed Gayoom as his successor, the new president inherited a debt-free country on the cusp of entering the modern world.

Gayoom would rule the country for thirty years, and with scant links to the outside world, an entire generation of Maldivians grew up fundamentally shaped by how he ran the country. Many of his ideas around governance were Arab in flavour and by the time he finished his MA at Al Azhar University in

1966, the potential to harness the power of Islamic nationalism in the Maldives was no doubt beginning to dawn on him. He submitted a successful PhD proposal to the department of Islamic Jurisprudence: *The Theory of the State in Islam.*[27]

It was never completed—at least, in Egypt.

The Man for All Islands

"Cricket-playing schoolboy, student activist, respected teacher, accomplished calligrapher, world statesman: which of these is the real Maumoon Abdul Gayoom?" asks the dust jacket of his sanctioned biography, *A Man for All Islands.*

A good question, and one better answered by a completely different piece of scholarship.

The anthropologist and journalist Elizabeth Colton lived among the Gayoom family for a time in 1976 after encountering him at a UN event, returning after he became president in 1978. She produced a very insightful but little-known thesis[28] documenting the feudalistic scheming of Malé's powerful houses, one of the few copies of which went missing from the University of London's archives before being mysteriously posted under the door of the *Minivan* office.

Colton's work reads like a playbook for Maldivian political skulduggery—not for nothing were margins of the copy I received heavily annotated by some keen young Maldivian scholar. It gives a rare behind the scenes look at Gayoom and the forces that would shape the population over the next thirty years.

Tourism was one of these forces, "controlled by a small group of people, whose chief director was the country's ruler", struggling "to develop and modernise their country, but at the same time remain basically xenophobic and distrustful of the outside".[29]

Her overarching observation of the political elite, however, was the obsession not with Islam, as one might expect in such a strict Muslim country, but with politics.

"The almost exclusive interest of the Maldivian elite is politics ... Politics is all-encompassing—everything is viewed as political, related to competition for power, position and influence with the elite in particular and, thus, within the country inasmuch as the elite control the rest of the country economically and politically. Members of the elite live, breathe, eat, copulate, procreate, think, and even dream, politics. It is the nearly obsessive focus of their lives," she wrote.[30]

But what about Islam?

Gayoom and several other Maldivian students of his generation who attended Al Azhar had not just picked up ideas about political Islam, they had learned Arabic. This not only helped engagement with the wider Islamic world, but allowed them to read and interpret the Quran in its original form, an extraordinarily potent political tool in the Maldives, where the only available Quran was a badly-translated Dhivehi version. Even today schoolchildren still learn by rote, making the sounds in Arabic when reciting prayers but not understanding the language itself.

When Gayoom returned to the Maldives he was by all accounts a popular and respected scholar. Armed with the "true knowledge of Islam", he could "out-Islam" his adversaries: in the land of the blind, the one-eyed man was sultan.

"Controlling what can and cannot be considered true knowledge of Islam, without a doubt, has been the most powerful means by which Islamists' fundamentalist beliefs have triumphed over the Maldivian Islamic faith and identity that evolved over hundreds of years," wrote Dr. Azra Naseem and Mushfique Mohamed, in their excellent review of the process, "The Long Road from Islam to Islamism".[31]

Gayoom was by no means Islamist. Tourism was on the rise and fundamentalism was an inconvenience; indeed, he jailed his more fiery religious adversaries, reportedly shaving beards with chilli sauce. Bars, discos, music and dancing were tolerated in Malé, if not publicized, and still remembered fondly by the more liberal-minded elderly of the city.

"Almost all of the Maldivian population remained oblivious (and a substantial part still does) to ideological changes that rearranged human life—communism, socialism, Marxism, etc. It remained similarly impervious to changes and evolution in Islamic jurisprudence, ideas and thinking," wrote Azra and Mushfique.

"Life, and faith, was simple. All Maldivians accepted themselves as Muslims and adhered faithfully to its core tenets, principles and values without much ado. There appeared no need to declare one's 'Muslimness' ... Religion and politics remained separate."

In Egypt, however, Gayoom had discovered that Islam was a powerful political tool as long as he made sure he held the sole set of keys. When the traditional weapons of dictatorship—secret police, custodial torture, exile—

began to creak in the face of clamour for reform, he "formalised what had been the status quo since his rule began".[32]

The 1997 constitution made the head of state, Gayoom, "the ultimate authority to impart the tenets of Islam".

He had—on paper at least—made himself God.

A Modern Theocracy

Isolation and the intertwining of Islam with national identity has made the majority of Maldivians fearful and defensive towards perceived threats to either. Historically these threats have only occasionally been founded, such as a brief period of Portuguese colonization in 1558–73 which saw the invaders try to introduce Christianity. The Portuguese monopolized trade and established a garrison, before being driven out by Muhammad Thakurufaanu. The occasion is celebrated as National Day, and Thakurufaanu commemorated as a national hero.

Maldivian rulers since have often exploited Islamic nationalism, inventing threats and unifying the population under the banner of "defending Islam" from other religions; Arabic and inclination just made Gayoom the latest and most successful. Centuries of habit, though, has produced the modern paranoia that so surprises many visitors to non-resort islands. Until only recently setting foot on a local island was prohibited without extensive paperwork, but even now foreign visitors are one accusation of "Christian missionary!" away from being swiftly deported without trial and banned from ever re-entering the country.

This sometimes reached absurd levels. In September 2010 an Indian teacher on the island of Foakaidhoo in Shaviyani Atoll had to be rescued after an angry mob of parents tied her up and tried to throw her into the sea for allegedly drawing a crucifix on the chalkboard.[33] A joint investigation by the Parent-Teacher Association and school management found that she had been attempting to teach navigation and the offending cross was a compass symbol marking north, south, east and west.

"[The islanders] refused to accept the facts when their claim that the teacher had drawn a [crucifix] was explained," a senior teacher told local newspaper *Haveeru*.

Another Indian teacher, working in Vaikaradhoo School in Haa Dhaalu Atoll in February 2010, was trying to leave the country but found her passport held hostage by her employers at the Ministry of Education.[34] She announced to her class, her colleagues and the head of the island council that it was time for them to learn about Christianity, and found herself on a free flight home later that day.

These were not isolated incidents. As recently as February 2013 the Islamic Ministry was declaring that "Christians" and "Freemasons" were secretly working to destroy Islam in the Maldives.[35]

"Various Christian organisations and missionaries are strongly involved and active in our society. They are working within us and outside, trying to create doubts on Islam within the hearts of young people," declared Sheikh Shaheem, by this stage the Minister of Islamic Affairs.

Maldivian laws prohibit the public practice or display of other religions, and the immigration card explicitly bans bringing in "Religious materials offensive to Islam" or "Idols for worship". A foreign friend who imported his CD collection from abroad opened the empty case to discover that these apparently included the third studio album by English alternative rock band The Verve, *Urban Hymns*. Customs had helpfully age-rated the rest of his collection with a series of little stickers.

Theoretically items such as bibles, crucifixes and miniature Buddhas could be brought in for "private use", but attracted a mixture of suspicion and curiosity. The greatest fear and public enmity, however, was reserved for "the Jews", who were widely believed to be secretly plotting the downfall of the Maldivian nation. The finest instance of this was the reaction when an Israeli ophthalmologist charity, the unfortunately named "Eyes from Zion", visited in December 2010 to perform free cataract operations.[36]

The Islamic Foundation warned Maldivians not to attend the free clinics, as the Israelis "have become notorious for illegally harvesting organs from non-Jews around the world".[37] "Jews would not provide any form of assistance, unless there is a hidden agenda," the NGO announced in a press statement.

Jamiyyathu Salaf went a step further, urging the government to provide citizens with military training "before Jews take over the country".[38]

Mobs were burning Israeli flags in the middle of Republic Square while Sheikh Shaheem, at that stage State Minister of Islamic Affairs in Nasheed's government, rode around Malé with a megaphone in the back of a pickup truck accompanied by a mob warning the public about the risk of having their eyeballs harvested by the Jews.

Jordan's Royal Islamic Strategic Studies Centre, the same outfit that would calculate the Maldives at 99.41 per cent Muslim a year later, had named Shaheem as one of the world's top 500 Most Influential Muslims in 2010.[39]

I had irregularly met with Shaheem in his office under the Islamic Centre for interviews and chats about Islamic issues. In between two of these meetings I had grown a respectably long and wiry red beard. Shaheem looked up from his desk.

"Hello Brother JJ," he said, without missing a beat.

He was affable and friendly, eager to boast of his travels to Islamic conferences around the world where he had found a niche interpreting trends in Islamic extremism for Western interests. One of these was the US military: he proudly showed me a recent photo taken at some conference in Hawaii, a beaming Shaheem surrounded by rows and rows of medalled generals. I innocently asked if we could publish it. He pulled the photo back, suggesting that this might not be such a good idea as he had recently been knocked off his motorcycle by an angry extremist in Malé.

Neil went to Republic Square to cover the flag-burning over the ophthalmologists. Shaheem was there.

"We made eye contact. He looked a bit sheepish," Neil remarked.

Shaheem resigned his post in Nasheed's government a few days later. Neil rang the president's spokesperson, Mohamed Zuhair—the first person in the Maldives ever to be convicted of a marijuana offence, he would proudly tell anyone listening, before showing them the cigarette burns on his legs from the custodial torture he had endured.

"Put it this way, Mr. Merrett: If I was Sheikh Shaheem, I would have felt my position was no longer tenable," Zuhair said.

The next time the Americans visited I asked them about Shaheem. Yes, they had backed him as a moderate conduit to more extreme Islamic elements. It was clearly a high-wire balancing act for the Sheikh, however, and the US lost interest in him.

"We got the impression he was telling us what we wanted to hear," said the visitor from the US Department of Defense.

Strip him of his camouflage and Shaheem could become deeply unpleasant—and highly newsworthy. One of my side hobbies at *Minivan* was lining up visiting foreign journalists from prestigious news outlets, such as the BBC, the *Economist* and *Wall Street Journal*, to interview ministers and government officials. The latter would be flattered by the attention, greedy for an opportunity to spin and advance themselves. I would then arm the visitors with context, questions, and printed material, and send them in like a journalistic suicide bomber. *Minivan* could report the explosions second-hand, maintaining a veneer of cheerful innocence.

I had thought I was rather good at it. But it was Mariyath Mohamed who arranged the interview between Sheikh Shaheem and Imma Vitelli, an accomplished war correspondent for the Italian edition of *Vanity Fair*.

Shaheem, like Gayoom, maintained his religious authority in Maldivian society by using a great many Arabic words. Unbeknownst to him, Vitelli spoke Arabic fluently. Confused at his sentence, she corrected his grammar. He responded with a torrent of abuse, and a ministry sidekick threatened to have her thrown out of the country.

Translated from the original Italian:

> The Minister of Religious Affairs, a greasy being [named] Mohamed Shaheem Ali Saeed, received me in his office, shook my hand, and boasted that he had memorized the Holy Quran in Lahore and had studied in Cairo and Medina. After half an hour of pleasantries, hypocrisy revealed its true nature: "Why don't Westerners stop going around killing Muslims and teach their women how to cook?"

> We were talking about something else. I was asking the minister to spare the list of wrongs of the West in Palestine, in Iraq and Afghanistan. I wanted to talk about the brutality of the local police. Nothing. The minister suggested that I learn to cook and his assistant, a guy even more sinister, without any connection extolled the virtues of Islam saying that—during the Second World War—polygamy had allowed many widows to find (the same) husband. I left the white building in a trance.[40]

Marriage, Flogging and Fornication

Twenty-six-year-old marketing professional Fathima (not her real name) spoke to *Minivan* journalist Mariyath Mohamed about how she felt forced to marry a man she was unhappy with to avoid the "societal ostracism" of being flogged.

> "I was 22 at the time. Hassan, my boyfriend, was 30. We had been in a relationship for about six months and it wasn't really working out. Hassan was too possessive for comfort, and I was looking for a way out of the relationship. And then, in the middle of all this, I became pregnant," Fathima said.

> "There was no one I could go to with the problem. My parents would have been outraged and I did not, rather I do not, have the courage to take the chance of being found out and flogged; of being banished to some island and losing everything, from my family's acceptance of me to my reputation and this job I love. So, although things were already sour, Hassan and I got married in a rush," she continued.

> Fathima gave birth to a baby girl less than seven months into the marriage. She said the couple had the baby abroad for fear of being found out if they had stayed in the Maldives for the delivery. After a difficult and emotionally abusive marriage,

Fathima filed for divorce a year after the wedding. She does not get any support for the child from the father, and is currently working as a single mother.

"I sometimes wonder if, compared to the hardships I am facing now, it was worth it to spend all my savings on the wedding and the trip abroad for delivery of my child. Hassan was of no help except for the name he lent to my child. I ask myself if it wouldn't have been better to have just faced the shame of flogging back then.

"Who am I kidding? I don't think anyone deserves such degrading treatment. Let's be real. It's something that the authorities ignore until an official complaint is made or someone ends up getting pregnant, but there is hardly anyone in this country who does not have sexual relations prior to, or outside of, marriage. It's the hypocrisy I hate worst of all."

Mariyath's superb 2012 exposé on the culture of flogging in the Maldives[41] saw her stalked, harassed, threatened with death and on several occasions, attacked in the street. It would earn her a place on Reporters Without Borders' Top 100 list of "Information Heroes".[42]

It earned *Minivan* a great deal of hostility. Even writing about the practice was seen as an attack on Maldivian sovereignty. "Minivan news is a threat to islam and maldives. We need to take action against this website urgently," noted one commentator. "Journalism is one thing. But settling political scores at the expense of country's reputation is another. Minivan has crossed the red line with these islamophobic articles," read another.

"We will not rest until these anti-islam foreigners are deported/ made to flee from this country. These people are deliberately aiming to drive maldives into starvation by ruining the tourism industry of the country."

Those were among the first five or six.

Maryam Omidi, the former *Minivan* editor, had previously covered flogging in 2009 after uncovering statistics showing that of the 184 people sentenced to flogging for "fornication" in 2006, 146 were women.[43] It led to protests and calls for her deportation.

She was in good company; in November 2011 the UN High Commissioner for Human Rights, Navi Pillay, visited the Maldives. That year 129 fornication cases were filed, 104 of whom were sentenced. Of these, 93 were female and 10 were children.

During a small and informal press conference I asked Pillay for her thoughts on flogging. She was as surprised as any tourist to learn that women were being routinely beaten by the state for extramarital sex, and said as much. Job done, I sat back and let the real story reveal itself: the outraged Maldivian press pack leapt to attack her for daring to undermine national sovereignty by suggesting that beating women was not a thing. Just who did she think she was?

"[Flogging] constitutes one of the most inhumane and degrading forms of violence against women, and should have no place in the legal framework of a democratic country," Pillay said in her subsequent address to parliament, and called for a moratorium on the practice.

Moments later, protests erupted outside the UN building. People brought their children clutching plastic AK-47s and placards reading "Islam is not a toy", "Ban UN" and "Flog Pillay".[44] The opposition savaged Nasheed for *daring* to allow Pillay to address parliament—something he vainly tried to point out was parliament's prerogative, not the president's.

In his Friday prayer sermon the following day, Islamic Minister Dr. Abdul Majeed Abdul Bari asserted that "no international institution or foreign nation" had the right to challenge the practice of Islam and adherence to its tenets in the Maldives. A mob of opposition-backed religious demonstrators calling itself the Civil Society Coalition accused Nasheed's government of pursuing an agenda to "wipe out the Islamic faith of the Maldivian people" through indoctrination and "plots" to legalize apostasy and allow freedom of religion. A Facebook group was formed calling for Pillay to be "slain and driven out of the country".[45]

This violent and xenophobic Islamist nationalism, twisted into a political weapon by a cynical few, was the Maldives at its most grim. Slavering glee in the Sharia punishment of flogging the vulnerable was the ugly stepchild in the attic, hidden from the outside world. It was going to be difficult to sell the Maldives as a romantic tropical escape to Western tourists while flogging women for extramarital fornication on the island next door. The double standard was liable to cramp enjoyment of one's holiday.

As a foreigner it was easy to forget that the issues we dealt with often were close to home. Mariyath Mohamed's grandmother had been flogged, although halfway through the process she had decided it wasn't for her. She seized the stick from the flogger and started beating him instead, before scampering off into the street. Resistance clearly ran in the family.

"If I ever get flogged I'm going to make sex noises," vowed one female Maldivian journalist. Jokes were a way to mask the gravity of a practice which dragged not just the victim into the square outside Male's justice building, but also their families.

Zaheena's Rasheed's brother had not only been sentenced to flogging but a year of banishment to a remote island, after returning from abroad with his pregnant girlfriend. She wrote a beautiful story about it for her university magazine in the US.

"It was a difficult time. My parents refused to even talk to him because of the shame he had brought on the family," she wrote.[46]

Aiman married his girlfriend, June, but somebody had already reported them to the police and both were convicted. Unlike most men in his situation he confessed, wanting to acknowledge the child as his and spare his wife and child the vicious social stigma of "single" motherhood.

The government's official flogger had died some years previously, and it wasn't until 2009 that the judiciary finally appointed a new one to get through the backlog.

"I accompanied Aiman and June to court. Court officials took them outside the building, and under the shade of a rosewood tree, they made Aiman stand facing the busy street and told him not to cover his face; the sole purpose of the beating was public humiliation. The three court officials stood behind Aiman in a semicircle wearing identical white shirts and black trousers, arms crossed, their eyes hidden behind sunglasses. The brown-shirted man who carried out the beating was portly and balding and carried a short paddle called a *dhurra*," wrote Zaheena, for the *Middlebury Magazine*.

"I broke into loud sobs as the brown-shirted man bent to beat Aiman. I could hear the steady whacks as Aiman trembled in anger, his fists clenched at his side. His body moved forward with every hit. After every thirty lashes, the portly man would straighten up, panting from exertion, droplets of sweat streaming down his face. June went next. Her face was resigned, her eyes old and sad, and she stood straight, shoulders square. Her petite frame rocked back and forth under the beating, and I felt utterly helpless."

* * *

The two worlds of the Maldives finally collided in February 2013. A fifteen-year-old rape victim from the island of Feydhoo in Shaviyani Atoll was found guilty of fornication by the Juvenile Court and sentenced to 100 lashes and eight months under house arrest. The girl had been abused by her stepfather, resulting in a child. The corpse of the infant was buried in the outdoor shower of her home, sparking a murder investigation when it was discovered in June 2012.[47]

The stepfather was charged with child sexual abuse, possession of pornography and premeditated murder, but during the course of the investigation the girl confessed to police that she had been having sex with another man.

Consensual or not, this was still technically child abuse as she was underage. Every step of the justice preyed on her: the police filed charges against her in November the same year. The state prosecutors accepted the case, and successfully convicted her in court. The judge sentenced her. The government (by this stage Nasheed had been overthrown, partly due to the assistance of the religious fundamentalists) prevaricated.

Amnesty International was the first international NGO on the case, having followed the Maldives closely after its adventures in helping to change the government in 2008. The sentence was an "absolute outrage". But the real impact came from Avaaz.org, an online petition website I had casually dismissed as peddling ineffectual feel-good "clicktivism".

After hours of phone calls with them I had to eat my words. They were terrifying. The petition they ran calling for a repeal of the girl's sentence and a moratorium on flogging reached more than two million signatures in just a few weeks—double the number of tourists who visited the country annually. They engaged media outlets across Europe, designed provocative posters for a tourism boycott and threatened to launch a major pan-European advertising campaign should the Maldivian government fail to act.

"Let's put an end to this lunacy by hitting the Maldives government where it hurts: the tourism industry," it declared.

"Tourism is the big earner for the Maldives elite, including government ministers. Let's build a petition to President Waheed this week, then threaten the islands' reputation through hard-hitting ads in travel magazines and online until he steps in to save her and abolish this outrageous law."

President Waheed's government was in a weak position. He had hitherto held to a policy of non-interference—really a way to cover up his lack of any real power. But tourism—and seventy per cent of the economy—was under threat. Tourism heavyweights began calling the country to account.

"No civilized country should get away with such a nightmare system of justice," declared Jürgen Thomas Steinmetz, the publisher of global travel industry news and PR website eTN, announcing it would no longer accept press releases from the Maldivian government.

The defensive belligerence used to undermine Nasheed during the Pillay saga was not going to work this time—the fundamentalists helped throw him out and were now on side with those in power. But the government was going to try.

President Waheed, for his its part, made the right noises.

"This case should never have been presented in the courts and we are working to ensure that cases like this are never brought to the courts again," he said.

"A boycott on tourism will only serve as a setback to the economic opportunities and rights we are all striving to uphold for women, girls and the hardworking Maldivian people in general."

The problem was that he was little more than a figurehead for Gayoom's regime, which certainly wasn't going to listen to him. The Deputy Tourism Minister and Head of the Maldives Marketing and Public Relations Corporation (MMPRC), Mohamed Maleeh Jamaal, declared the campaign a conspiracy by the MDP and "media groups" (I can only imagine he meant us) to "crush the country's tourism" and "cause havoc on the country's economy".

"Looking back, a fourteen-year-old was given the same sentence during former President Nasheed's presidency and nobody seemed to have talked about that. This whole deed is an attempt to defame the country's tourism industry and [damage the] economy," he said.[48]

"People should not be doing anything to damage the industry. In Switzerland, you would not see a campaign designed to damage Swiss chocolate."[49]

Gasim, who was in Avaaz's spotlight as somebody with a proven track record of influencing the judiciary, implied that the case had exposed tourists to the realities of the Maldives and that "more focus should therefore be put on developing the fisheries industry".[50]

The Adhaalath Party meanwhile endorsed the sentence on the grounds that "if such sinful activities are to become this common, the society will break down and we may become deserving of divine wrath".[51]

We did our best to follow the girl at the centre of this desperately horrible storm. She was serving her house arrest sentence in a government orphanage on nearby Vilingili. I did my best to discourage curious foreign reporters from tracking her down for an exploitative weep-and-run story, while Avaaz had sent somebody relevantly qualified to see how she was doing, inspect where she was living, find out what she wanted and see if it there was anything it could do, such as help with an asylum claim. The government denied her access.

We discovered in the meantime that islanders on Feydhoo had been reporting the girl's abuse to police and the government since 2009, but that she had ultimately been left in the custody of her mother and stepfather even after she was found to be pregnant.[52] The island authorities said if she was returned to the island, it was likely the abuse would continue.

In August 2013, the High Court quietly repealed the girl's sentence—the first time I was aware of a Maldivian court doing such a thing.[53] It was a victory and an act of justice, but it was a one-off at enormous international effort and with very little pushing from inside the country or clamour for reform. I worried that the girl had only traded one set of horrors for another.

Short of foreign asylum, anonymity was her best protection and it felt inappropriate to risk this with a "where is she now" follow up. The 2013 presidential elections quickly took over our focus, but from time to time I did find myself hoping that she had been able to make a future for herself.

Sex and Sensibilities

The criminalization of extramarital sex undoubtedly contributes to one of the Maldives' more surprising statistics: the world's highest divorce rate, as established by both the UN and *The Guinness Book of Records*.[54]

Occupying first place and not by a small margin, the Maldives tops the list at 10.97 divorces a year per 1,000 inhabitants, compared to Belarus (4.63) and the United States (4.34) in second and third place respectively. That's more than *double* the runner up.

The reasons are complex—and a fascinating example of a people and culture adapting to suit enforced conservatism.

"It is easy to marry in these islands because of the smallness of the dowries and the pleasures of society which the women offer," observed Ibn Battuta, writing in the fourteenth century.[55] "Most people do not even fix any dowry. When the ships put in, the crew marry; when they intend to leave, they divorce their wives. This is a kind of temporary marriage (*muta*). I have seen nowhere in the world women whose society was more pleasant."

High praise indeed from one of the most travelled explorers of all time. Unlike the rest of South Asia, weddings are not considered a big deal in the Maldives. Circumcision ceremonies, yes—they sometimes go on for days and have specific holiday allowances under Maldivian employment law. But I've been two minutes late to a Maldivian wedding and missed it. The couple stand up, exchange rings and a token dowry of several *rufiya*, the imam gives some wholesome family planning advice and if it's particularly lavish, there might be a tray of hors d'oeuvres to eat on your way out the door.

Just as weddings are considered somewhat arbitrary, so is divorce. While a man gets a three month "probationary period" on marriage and can always divorce his wife simply by saying "I divorce you" three times, a woman has to go through the court system. But there is no social stigma around it for women. I recall one recently married fisherman boasting that his new wife had been married six times; this, he explained with a sly wink, meant she was experienced. That figure was about average for a woman in her forties.

Despite the emphasis on conservative appearance and the vicious social ostracism of anyone caught with their pants down, many Maldivians were surprisingly liberal in their views towards sex—rampantly promiscuous, even. Extramarital sex might have been a crime, but *other people*'s wives and husbands were fair game.

For their part, Maldivian women were absolutely beautiful and somehow completely ageless—a woman who looked like she was in her early twenties could often be as old as forty. The majority had been pressured into wearing the headscarf—a recent innovation—but compensated for this with tight skinny jeans and tops that looked like they had been sprayed on. The effect was somehow more revealing than the Western casual dress that so offended the mullahs. In public, the demeanour was "shy but saucy". I was able to observe this via Dan, who despite (or perhaps because of) a long term relationship seemed to be catnip for Maldivian females. It bordered on the predatory; by the time he had reached the office from the airport ahead of taking up the *Minivan* editor's job, the female immigration staff had already sent him friend requests on Facebook. In another instance we were walking back from a café when a taxi suddenly pulled up beside us. The window rolled down, and a skinny arm with bangles extended, clutching a napkin with a phone number written in lipstick.

Female clothing shops in Malé had shop dummies in the window with outlandishly revealing strips of fabric, cocktail dresses of the kind a teenager might wear to distress her parents. To be fair, a sixteen-year-old girl who bought and actually wore one of these was swiftly taken into custody under the Anti-Social Behaviour Act, but not before she had drawn a large crowd of men concerned for her lax morals.[56]

"The societal norms and values of Maldivian culture were violated," the police spokesman advised us. "Police officers explained to her about how her dress should be as well as called her parents and advised them regarding this."

"She was very, very, very, very naked. Her dress was transparent," he added.

The several female Minivaners in the office eyed the little black number appraisingly. "Slutty and tasteless," they concurred, missing the point.

Malé even had a sex shop, although it was relatively tame by Western standards. Supposedly there were Ann Summers-style parties going round, but naturally these were highly illegal and I was never invited to one. Meanwhile, the owner of "G-Spot", Mohamed Nizam, had endless trouble with the Ministry of Economic Development over his registered business name, which he insisted stood for "girl"—going so far as to scrawl the extra letters on the shop hoarding. The case eventually ended up in the civil court, the state attorney alleging that the name was "inappropriate for viewing by women and children". Nizam defended himself, producing as evidence printouts of articles from the *Times*, BBC, and CNN stating that the G-Spot did not exist,[57] and how could he therefore be found guilty of using the name inappropriately?

"What Nizam has failed to comprehend during all the legal wranglings is that even if he does get permission to continue to trade under said name he will still struggle for custom as most men will almost certainly not be able to locate it," suggested one commentator.

Whether due to prohibition or the heat, sex was on brain in the Maldives. The lack of cognitive dissonance meant as long as the illusion of Islamic conservatism was maintained, as long as the boat wasn't rocked, as long as nothing was stated, written down, admitted or confessed to, *as long as you weren't caught*—ordinary people could be surprisingly accepting. My favourite example was the case of a well-known man who went about his daily business in women's clothing, and for all intents and purposes acted like a woman—and quite a pious one, by all accounts, regularly praying at the mosque with the other women. She was if not accepted, then at least not bothered. However, if she had explicitly and publicly declared herself a transvestite, life would have suddenly become very difficult.

Much hostility was reserved for homosexuality, and very few Maldivians were openly gay—or at least, had admitted to it. One of the few, the blogger Ismail "Hilath" Rasheed, had previously worked as editor of *Haveeru* but since his public declaration had been well-nigh unemployable. We sent him translation work whenever we could, and my motivation to begin with was mercenary. He was one of the few Maldivians to blog under his own name and was the de facto head of the very active Maldivian blogosphere. *Hilath.com* was among the most read websites in the Maldives before the Islamic Ministry finally ordered it blocked, and in my early days at *Minivan* we sourced a good ten per cent of our traffic from his links to our articles.

Having transcended his society's hypocrisy Hilath had a deep understanding of the Maldivian mind-set. Indeed, he needed it to survive, receiving hundreds of death threats and being frequently harassed in the street. His theory was that a lot of the aggression towards him from the fundamentalist set was driven partly by curiosity and sexual repression—a surprising number seemed pulled into his orbit, not sure themselves why. He would monitor the internet searches Maldivian IPs used to reach his blog and regularly publish these: a not inconsiderable number involved the term "Hilath nude".

An openly gay expat friend speculated from the number of propositions he received on a daily basis, particularly from taxi drivers, that the rate of homosexuality in Maldivian society was about thirty per cent. Islands differed in their tolerance. Hilath wrote about one far-flung tiny island with ten openly lesbian couples,[58] while one of our early stories at *Minivan* concerned the arrest of seven men on the island of Maalhos after a tape of their orgy was discovered by local children. Those taken into custody included the island's imam, the mosque caretaker, a second retired imam, a carpenter, a mentally-disabled man and two men who considered themselves "husband and wife".[59]

"I would like to advice the minivannews to stop campaigning against Islam," came the response to the story.

Deprivation led to some very odd behaviour. Four men on the island of Makunudhoo in Haa Dhaalu Atoll aged between 19 and 21 were questioned by police after allegedly gang-raping a goat to death in April 2011.[60]

"The owner of the goat had been getting suspicious that something was wrong because he was finding things such as condoms on his goat farm," the police spokesperson told Nazeer.

"Early one morning when he went to the farm he saw two goats outside the fence and thought it was odd because there was no way a goat could have climbed over it. He found the goat near the beach, it was laid down on a cardboard paper. He observed that it could not walk properly and that its sexual organs were injured."

The goat subsequently died. Closer inspection of the remaining animals revealed five others had been similarly assaulted.

"The owner has noted that he has frequently seen this group of four men near the farm. They have been selecting healthy muscular goats to do this," police advised.

Two months later a famous tea shop in Malé was briefly closed by the food and drug authority after inspectors found a live goat tied up in the toilet.[61] Nothing sinister was insinuated.

Catch Me If You Can

Despite the prevalence of out of wedlock sexual activity, it remained a taboo topic—and was only considered illegal if you were caught, or fell pregnant. For while there was no stigma attached to divorce, there was enormous stigma as regards pregnancy outside marriage. Indeed, this was usually the evidence presented to court that a woman was guilty of fornicating, and the reason why women were disproportionately sentenced to flogging. The men could just shrug.

The UN Population Fund (UNFPA) in 2011 published an entire study into the reproductive behaviour of unmarried Maldivian women, amid growing concerns over the prevalence of risky sexual behaviour, lack of contraception, unwanted pregnancies, abortion and infanticide. It reported that no contraception was used in ninety per cent of sexual activity, and that women were widely expected to deal with the resulting "problems" on their own. Most women went to Sri Lanka for the weekend, or sought abortion medication on the black market. The UNFPA reported that misoprostol was available for MVR3,000–4,000 (US$194–259)—a month's salary in a government office. Poorer families on the islands sent their girls to amateur abortionists who would use everything from kerosene to abdominal trauma. More often the women were so terrified of social censure that they would try to resolve it themselves, even waiting for the term to complete and then disposing of the child.[62]

Mariyam broke the taboo on abortion by writing the Maldives' first article about it,[63] for which *Minivan* was duly blamed for promoting promiscuity and moral decline.

The stories we covered over the next few years were among the bleakest the Maldives had to offer. A particularly horrible two weeks in early 2011 turned up a premature baby thrown into the water at Malé's outdoor swimming area, another hidden inside a Coast Milk tin, another thrown into bushes, strangled with a pair of black panties. The local newspaper, *Haveeru*, carried a picture of another discarded foetus, in a bucket. For some reason they had chosen to mask the foetus's identity with a tiny black strip where the eyes presumably were.

"Look at this!" said Nazeer excitedly, brandishing the photo.

"It looks like a frog," observed Neil.

The Adhaalath Party called for the mothers to be found and sentenced to death, citing Islamic Sharia. Abortion was an issue that should concern all Maldivians, the party declared, and people should be "very afraid" given the "rising popularity of fornication".[64]

Afraid they were. Most often the mothers were caught, quickly confessing under police interrogation. I still remember a series of mugshots police sent us of a pair of teenage girls, barely out of puberty. One had tried to help her friend dispose of a premature infant and had been shopped by somebody on the island. Her frightened face and trembling lip barely made it to the bottom of the police height chart.[65]

Islam and Minivan

Dear Editor,

Whether we accept it or not, like any other country in the world, there are loads of gay people in the Maldives too. Being gay is not something you adopt or acquire, it is who you are and you are born with it. Anyone's son or daughter can be gay or lesbian. They are referred as a taboo and have always been forced to live in the closet. But what we are forgetting here is that we actually deprive a gay person from his rights. His basic right to live, been accepted by the family and society, right to choose his sexual partner and love are all denied.

I think it is time the Maldivian government start thinking about gay rights. Maldivian gays are not going to go anywhere and they are never going to change into straight people. This is who they are and will always remain as gays. And always a new gay person would be born into the Maldives too.

Homosexuality is assuredly no disadvantage, it is nothing to be ashamed of, no vice, no degradation, it cannot be classified as an illness; it is considered to be a variation of the sexual function produced by a certain arrest of sexual development. Many highly respectable individuals of ancient and modern times have been homosexuals, several of the greatest men among them (Plato, Michelangelo, Leonardo da Vinci, Alexander the great etc.). It is a great injustice to persecute homosexuality as a crime, and cruel too.

Modern medical research has clearly proved that homosexuality is not a disease; it cannot be wiped off from a gay person. He or she will remain so in their sexual orientation and it is more genetic in evolution. So how on earth can we penalise someone for his sexual orientation?

If a man and woman have the right to practice their sexual desires freely between them, why can't a gay couple do so? People blame that homosexual acts are against human nature, but what exactly does it mean by human nature? Gays have been here since human evolution, it's just that they haven't been more open before than now. So how can you say it is against human nature. Gays have always been forced to practice their sexuality in discreet, behind doors with fear.

Legally in 2003, Brazil introduced a UN draft resolution titled, "Human Rights and Sexual Orientation", which addresses the topic of equal rights for gays and lesbians. It called upon all states to promote and protect the human rights of all persons regardless of their sexual orientation". Maldives has good record of following all UN resolutions, charters and accords but why is it then the Maldivian government doesn't accept this resolution?

Another barrier hindering the acceptance of homosexuals in Maldives is the religion. Being a 100% Muslim country the Maldives believes that it is going to be against the religion to allow and give the homosexuals their rights. According to the International Lesbian and Gay Association ILGA there are at least seven Muslim countries today which still retain capital punishment for homosexuality.

Maldives has also been found to give severe punishments which include long-term imprisonment and sometimes torture. Not to forget also the shame and belittlement a gay person faces from Maldivian society.

Do not forget there are Muslim countries which HAVE legalised homosexuality. They are Iraq, Jordan, Turkmenistan, Albania, Uzbekistan, Palestine, Indonesia, Armenia, Azerbaijan, Bosnia & Herzegovina, Turkey, Kosovo, Turkish Republic of Cyprus, Chad, Nigeria, Kazakhstan, Kyrgyzstan and Tajikistan.

It is time we need to know the rights of the homosexuals in our country because homosexuality is universal. They are everywhere in this world; rich and poor countries, Muslims, Christians, Jews, Hindus etc, whites and blacks, low and high class societies. They can be doctors, nurses, civil servants, engineers, singers or politicians. Gay Maldivians are also proud to be Muslims and Maldivians and will always remain so. Just Think!

Regards,
Anonymous

My predecessor published the infamous letter on homosexuality the month before I arrived. It was an unlikely watershed moment, the first time the subject had ever been broached in mainstream media, and led to protests, abuse, accusations of "promoting homosexuality". Somebody, possibly a former *Minivan* journalist, publicly revealed that Maryam had once done an internship in the UK at a LGBT publication, *Pink News*. She tried in vain to explain that this was a letter to the editor, not an editorial—but no such concept existed in the Maldives. Media had always been propaganda: it told you what to think. Anything in it reflected the editor's political agenda. Ergo, *Minivan* was now telling everybody to be gay. Break out the rainbow flags.

Maryam had to take taxis to work afterwards. Other media outlets bullied and harassed her. She went to visit the Islamic Ministry to try and explain, and was told to take the letter down. She did.

People asked me if I would have run the letter. I wasn't as brave as Maryam, especially as I had just arrived. This was new territory for me, though in time I would develop an acute sense of how (often surprisingly) far I could push things. The problem for *Minivan* was as much legal as anything else. Homosexuality wasn't expressly illegal under national law but was prohibited under Islamic Sharia, to which national law deferred. Still, once we had the comments up and running—maybe. The initial fury would have been vented on the page, and any follow up rage could be directed to our shiny new disclaimer: "All comment pieces are the sole view of the author and do not reflect the editorial policy of *Minivan News*."

The 'tabloidlizard' part of my journalist brain knew that if they were going to be angry, make them angry on *your news website*. As an afterthought, I added, "If you would like to write an opinion piece, please send proposals to editorial@minivannews.com".

We engaged our opponents, and ran everything we were sent, although few on the extreme conservative side could write as fluently as the more liberal-minded, and the perception of bias persisted. However, in face of threats and accusations of promoting this that and other agenda, I could now give a non-committal shrug and point them to the email address.

I did feel like I got off more lightly than Maryam. Not only did she break the early taboos, but as a woman she may have been seen as an easier target. Somebody did circulate a wanted poster of me in Dhivehi calling for the head of the person "brought to the Maldives by Nasheed's government to destroy Islam in the Maldives", but the intimidating effect was rather let down by the use of the comic sans font and a rather flattering black and white photo of me they'd found on the internet. Somebody else ran around Malé spray painting "JJ Suks" on walls in green, and it became a game to find and post these on my Facebook wall. My true moment of fame came thanks to the underground feminist movement, Rehendhi ("queen"). We had just run a comment piece of theirs, reacting to the Islamic censorship of St. Valentine's Day 2010. This had involved a group of sheikhs going around Malé in the back of a pickup truck ripping down love heart decorations. In retaliation, Rehendhi had bombarded the offending preachers with deliveries of women's underwear. The Adhaalath Party was less than impressed, and predictably went straight for the messenger. *Minivan News* and I were, the party declared, guilty of promoting "lesbianism and national sissyness".[66] We translated and published the statement verbatim and I made sure to add a line on my CV.

Constitutionally, we, like all Maldivians, were permitted "freedom of speech subject to the tenets of Islam". Unfortunately these tenets were interpreted by Sheikh Shaheem's "Religious Unity Act", enacted ostensibly to monopolize the government's control over the preaching of Islam, but also banning media from producing or publicizing programmes, talking about or disseminating audio "that humiliates Allah or his Prophets or the Holy Quran or the Sunnah of the Prophet (Mohamed) or the Islamic faith".[67] The penalty for violating the regulations under the Act was two to five years' imprisonment, banishment or house arrest. Foreigners could expect deportation.

The trouble for *Minivan* was not the content we were writing ourselves: I implemented a policy of 100 per cent attribution, still ingrained in me to the point where voicing an opinion even now engenders a sense of illicit guilt. Rather it was the anonymous comments, and the assumption that since we were moderating them we were responsible for censoring the sentiments expressed. The more fundamentalist readers interpreted "humiliating the Islamic faith" as saying anything they didn't agree with—or anything critical of their own behaviour. I trained moderators to allow discussion of Islamic practice and interpretation in the Maldives, but to be especially wary of anything involving proselytizing or disparaging the Prophet Mohamed. Legally, these were our danger points and the point at which publishing the comments just wasn't worth it.

Our Alamo moment finally came in December 2012, when police showed up at the door with a warrant issued by Chief Judge of the Criminal Court, Abdulla Mohamed. The comment itself was innocuous, which was why we'd let it through. Instead, the commentator had named himself "Maai Allah", literally, "Holy Allah".

"As you know, the Maldives is a 100 per cent Muslim nation and as no human being has been empowered to take for himself the almighty status using the name of Allah, and as this is insulting to the noble name of Holy Allah and undermines noble Islamic principles or tenets, we require information of the person who made this comment for our investigation," the court warrant stated.[68]

My instinctive reaction was to declare that we, as a humble news organization of limited means and resources, were in no position to determine whether God was or was not commenting on our website. The police grinned, but suggested they still needed the IP address of the commentator. This was of some concern, given the climate of impunity and potential for attacks on those deemed irreligious. The problem with refusing was the prospect of having our IT confiscated; we ran everything online in the cloud, but this would have been a serious setback.

I invited the police inside and made them sit in the kitchen writing down their badge numbers while I tried to trace the IP address myself. Luckily it was registered overseas at a UK university and could not be tracked to an individual. There was no harm in handing it over. I informed the university that their network was the subject of a Maldivian police investigation, and we ran a story about the incident.

The Americans saw the article and rang up from Colombo, very concerned. The matter went no further. I was a little disappointed, as I had already lined up a legal defence that would have been a terrific test case for *Minivan*'s impunity in publishing whatever it wished. The assumption all were making was that we were a *Maldivian* news website and therefore subject to Maldivian law. I was ready to contend that as our servers were by this stage based in the US, we were technically an *American* news service that just happened to publish a lot about the Maldives and therefore our content was subject to US law. Was the court about to censure CNN for its coverage of the Maldives' infamous wedding video saga? Yes, we would have probably wound up reporting in exile from Sri Lanka. On the plus side, beer would have been cheaply (and legally) available.

The *critical* trick to ensure *Minivan*'s survival was to not react to the intimidation, to ignore, to not push back, to disarm the aggrieved by soliciting responses, to republish threats as if they were beneath our notice, to let others defend us if they would, and to mire in invented bureaucracy any enforcement action until the offended party gave up and found something better to do. I use the term "critical" because to accept readers as worthy of giving unsolicited criticism, to concede, to even react, was to show vulnerability. This approach might sound a patronising approach to community engagement by *Guardian* standards, but in a place like the Maldives, baring your throat to the wolves only inspired them to greater confidence—and eventually, action.

7

EXTREMISM

SUN, SAND AND SHARIA

"Students, slaves, and servants who are brought up with injustice and tyrannical force are overcome by it. It makes them feel oppressed and causes them to lose their energy. It makes them lazy and induces them to lie and be insincere. That is, their outward behaviour differs from what they are thinking, because they are afraid that they will have to suffer tyrannical treatment if they tell the truth.

Thus, they are taught deceit and trickery ... they fall short of their potentialities and do not reach the limit of their humanity. As a result, they revert to the stage of 'the lowest of the low'.

That is what happened to every nation that fell under the yoke of tyranny and learned through it the meaning of injustice."

Ibn Khaldun, 1377[1]

Ismail "Hilath" Rasheed got out his mobile phone and called for a taxi, but no sound came from his throat.

Instead the Maldivian blogger, journalist and former Amnesty prisoner of conscience, infamous for his willingness to tackle taboo subjects, particularly religious tolerance, felt air escaping from his neck.

"A very bad kind of panic came at that moment. I knew my trachea was cut. I knew it was a deep cut, and not just on the surface of the skin."

Moments before, on the evening of 4 June 2012, Rasheed had turned into the dark alleyway leading to the door of his apartment block to find a man in a yellow shirt waiting for him.

159

"Then I heard someone call me by name from behind, and two more entered the alley. As I was turning the guy in a yellow T-shirt came up beside me, grabbed me from behind, put a mid-size box cutter to my neck and started slashing.

"I put my hand up to try and stop him, but he kept slashing."

Rasheed holds up his hand—besides the jagged slash mark across his neck that almost claimed his life, the blogger lost a digit of his index finger trying to protect himself from the knife.

"That was why they missed a vital artery. I tried to prevent it—they cut the finger to the bone."

Job done, the three men walked "very calmly" out of the alley in separate directions, leaving Rasheed to bleed to death in the alley.

"I got a look at their faces, but it was too dark to identify them," he says. "They all had beards, and they were very young—I would say between 18 and 24. When the man in the yellow shirt was slashing my throat I smelled his breath—it smelled of alcohol."

Acting on instinct, Rasheed held his neck and did not let go.

"I didn't know how bad it was—because it was a box cutter, it was a very clean cut—it wasn't painful. I thought about going upstairs to inform my parents, but I thought I better go straight to hospital rather than go up all the stairs."

Leaving the alleyway, holding his head down to prevent blood loss, Rasheed tried to flag down a passing motorcycle. In the distance, he saw two of his attackers ride away on a motorcycle, while the other walked round the corner.

"I knew it was pointless to go after them as I needed to get to the hospital."

Three motorcycles passed without stopping to help him, even though the front of his shirt and trousers were by now drenched in blood. That was when he tried to call the taxi, only to realise the extent of his injury.

"Even at that moment, a thought came into my mind. All the people who brought change to the world, most of them died for that cause—they didn't live to see the fruits of their effort.

"When this thought came into my mind, survival instinct took over and I felt a rage: 'I am going to survive, I want to live to see the fruits of my work—the fight for human rights."

A young couple walking down the street noticed him—and the girl began screaming. A young man on a motorcycle motorcyclist heard the sound as he came around the corner, and stopped so Rasheed could get on behind him.

"I was still holding my neck, and not talking, and pointed in the direction of the hospital. With my right hand I held onto his shoulder—I was afraid I might faint because of the blood loss and fall off. There was so much blood—there was a pool forming in front of me."

Fighting off unconsciousness, Rasheed stumbled into the lobby of ADK hospital, the young man behind him.

"I was very appreciative but I couldn't talk to thank him," Rasheed says. "Because I couldn't say thank you I just gave him a thumbs up and walked into the hospital. A doctor later said the guy promptly fainted in the doorway."

Still holding his neck, Rasheed walked into the emergency room.

"The people waiting in the lobby started screaming as I went past—I think they were shocked."

A Maldivian girl and a couple of foreign nurses took Rasheed to a bed—"I saw a lot of ADK officials and police officers coming in. The Maldivian girl asked me to show them the injury. I knew I had to show them the extent of the damage so they knew what kind of treatment was needed," he says.

"I lifted my head all the way back. And quickly back down. A doctor told me that a nurse and a police officer fainted."

The foreign nurses quickly inserted a tube into his neck so he could breathe, and pressed bandages to his neck to try and stem the blood loss.

The staff put him on a bed and rushed him to the operating theatre.

"They gave me anaesthetic. It took a while for it to work, but I didn't feel any pain. I could see them opening my neck, putting their hand inside. I knew they were trying to assess the damage and from what they were saying, that my trachea was severed."

The hospital kept Rasheed under anaesthetic for 48 hours—"they didn't want to wake me up," he says.

"My father later told me that I happened to go into the hospital when the new shift was coming in. All the old shift doctors stayed on—there were 6–8 of them. My father said at that moment they told him that I had a less than one per cent chance of survival, but that they would try everything they could."

Rasheed was later told by friends who had gathered outside the operating theatre that while he was undergoing emergency surgery, one of the men who had attacked and hospitalised him during a protest for religious tolerance on December 10—Human Rights Day—came and waited outside the emergency room.

"A relative spotted him and asked him what he was doing there—he said he was there for scans—so the relative asked him why he was waiting in front of emergency. He was the guy who attacked me with a stone on December 10 and fractured my skull, and his excuse was that he was there for a scan."

That was the first of several unsettling incidents to happen while Rasheed was in hospital. Conscious of security concerns, hospital staff forbade access to Rasheed for all apart from his parents.

"While I was under anaesthetic, I was told by a friend of a friend—a gang member—that someone had been sent into the hospital to kill me—to pull the plug. Nobody would have noticed."

"This bearded guy came into the Intensive Care Unit posing as my father. While he was near me a doctor who knew my father just happened to come into the ICU. The doctor was suspicious, and asked him who he was—he said he was my father. The doctor said 'I know Hilath's father, you are not his father,' and called security to have him thrown out. He's on the hospital's CCTV footage."

Four days later, Rasheed woke up on a ventilator, astounding doctors at his miraculous recovery.

"They said they had never seen anyone recover so fast from such an injury," he says.

Rasheed has no doubt in his mind as to the motivation behind his attack—the third in just a few months. The attack was unusual in that most of the wave of recent gang stabbings in the Maldives have involved multiple stab wounds to different parts of the body—targeted throat slashing is new.

In July 2009, Rasheed broke news of a story on his blog concerning an under-age girl allegedly being kept by a family as a "jaariya"—a concubine. Concerns were initially raised when the girl was taken to Indira Gandhi Memorial Hospital (IGMH) and was found to be pregnant.

"Ever since I reported the story on my blog I have received death threats. Things like: 'If we see you on street we will slash your throat', 'we will behead you', 'don't walk in a dark alley,' things like that," says Rasheed.

One of only several Maldivian bloggers to write under his own name, Rasheed courted controversy by continuing to tackle taboo subjects in the Maldives—particularly religious intolerance, and the constitutional provision that all Maldivians were required to be "100 per cent Sunni Muslim". This was at odds, Rasheed argued, with the country's Sufi history and new-found commitment to freedom of expression—which had ironically, he argued, also given a voice to more extreme interpretations of the religion.

The attitude of many to Rasheed's work was summarised in comments made by spokesperson for former President Maumoon Abdul Gayoom and newly-appointed Minister for Human Resources, Mohamed "Mundhu" Shareef, who told AFP following the attempt on the blogger's life that while the new government condemned the attack, "Hilath must have known that he had become a target of a few extremists".

"We are not a secular country. When you talk about religion there will always be a few people who do not agree."[2]

* * *

The night Hilath was attacked, I took those *Minivan* staff who were still in the office out to the restaurant on the second floor of the Traders Hotel. It was foreign, expensive and one of the few corners of Malé that felt safe. I'd just come from the hospital, though it wasn't a very useful visit as the doctors were still operating. I was struck by the large crowd of people who had turned up: well-wishers, closet liberals, those drawn in by the sniff of drama and a darker set, a group of bearded types who looked positively joyous. One of these would later try to turn off his life support.

I sensed that things had changed. No longer could we assume that the threats were all talk, simply to intimidate—previously a fairly safe assumption. The main problem was one of impunity. Despite abundant evidence police had shown no interest in investigating previous religiously motivated attacks, including the vandalism of Buddhist artefacts in the national museum. This suggested at least state complicity, if not sanction—and until we understood how far they were willing to go, this made Malé a dangerous and unpredictable place.

Hilath was exceptionally lucky, surviving despite a one per cent chance of making it through. I went to visit him in hospital once the doctors brought him out of a medically induced coma. He couldn't speak, answering my questions on a pad of writing paper.[3] His attackers had spoken to him before slitting his throat, he wrote: "This is a present from Shaheem, Mutthalib and Imran."

Shaheem was by then Minister of Islamic Affairs under the government that had taken power from Nasheed five months earlier in February, an interim arrangement to pave the return of Gayoom's family. Imran Abdulla was the president of the Adhaalath Party, the political organ of the Islamists that had worked to overthrow the Nasheed government on what looked like a for-hire basis. MP Ibrahim Mutthalib was their de facto MP in parliament, who had a record of submitting bills calling for such things as the abolition of alcohol, the practice of Sharia punishments such as the death penalty and the greater policing of sorcery.

Hilath's attack caused a great deal of muttering among the diplomats in Colombo, especially when the government made no immediate attempt to condemn it. I connected him with Reporters Without Borders, but by then he had decided to flee the country. The Maldives was too dangerous.

Several months after Hilath was attacked, an MP and religious scholar Dr. Afrasheem Ali was found brutally murdered in the stairwell of his apartment building. He had been stabbed four times in the back of the head and a chunk of his skull was missing. Despite being aligned with Gayoom's PPM he was widely considered an Islamic moderate and had taken outspoken and controversial positions on issues such as the permissibility of playing music, and praying next to the deceased. He had been attacked several times in the street since 2007, and immediately prior to his murder had appeared on an Islamic TV programme opposite the Deputy Minister of Islamic Affairs. The government seized the opportunity to blame the MDP for the murder despite the absence of evidence or motivation, and the investigation and trial were ultimately tainted by conspiracy theory and attempts to use the murder politically.[4] One version involved several Sudanese men being brought in to carry out the murder, flown out soon afterwards.

The man ultimately arrested, charged and found guilty was Hussain Humam Ahmed, a violent gang member convicted of other crimes. A confession was read out in court incriminating the family of one of the PPM's most hated MDP MPs, and Human was found guilty and sentenced to death—a penalty traditionally commuted to life imprisonment.[5] Humam afterwards retracted his confession, telling his family that he was coerced into the confession by police.[6] The government moved to set up a lethal injection chamber, preparing for the first state execution since 1953.

The extreme violence of Dr. Afrasheem's death, so soon after the attempted killing of Hilath, deeply shocked Maldivians. People could be aggressively vocal, but physical violence was rare—murder much more so. Even if guilty, Humam was likely a tool; the failure to transparently investigate the circumstances of the death and establish whether the motive was political, religious—or both—greatly increased the level of background fear in Maldivian society. Whether they were involved or not, the sudden clamour for Sharia punishment—stoning, amputation and execution—played right into the hands of the fundamentalists.

Wave of Extremism

The 2004 tsunami devastated many countries in the Indian Ocean region. Indonesia was the worst affected, suffering 130,736 dead and half a million displaced. In Sri Lanka, 35,322 people died, but even more were displaced than in Indonesia: 516,150. Take a train along Sri Lanka's southern coast towards the fort city of Galle, and you can see the legacy of the disaster all along the tracks in the form of graves and ruined buildings.

Despite being in the path of the wave and barely a metre above sea level, the geographic structure of the Maldives spared the country the worst of the disaster. Unlike Sri Lanka, the Maldives does not have a long gradient along the seabed leading to its coastline, which displaces the water and causes a tidal wave. Instead, the Maldives is more like a chain of mesas, the atolls rising steeply from the ocean floor. As result, the tsunami more or less rolled over them. Casualty figures were 82 dead, 26 missing and 15,000 people displaced. A decade later several hundred were still living in emergency housing, but this was largely due to government apathy and the fact that for some the temporary shelters were still an upgrade on their previous accommodation. Islands changed shape, erosion was accelerated, and the salt water contaminated the water table. Agriculture was crippled, although there was not much of this to begin with.

The main effect of the tsunami was fear; tourists shied away for years afterwards. I experienced this myself in April 2012, when an 8.8 earthquake off the coast of Indonesia triggered a tsunami alert for the Indian Ocean. I got a phone call from my friend Mazin Rafeeq, who lived at the top of one of the Malé's concrete towers.

"Did you feel that? All my perfume bottles were shaking," he said, worriedly.

Perfume bottles? The question would have to wait. I hadn't felt anything but quickly confirmed that a quake had occurred that had, according to the Pacific Tsunami Warning Centre, generated a "significant tsunami". It was due to hit Malé within several hours.[7]

Our office faced out to sea; we would receive the wave head on. I felt surprisingly calm. It wasn't like there was anywhere to run to, and Malé already flooded whenever it rained for twenty minutes.

"Don't panic, we're all dead anyway," wasn't a good way to encourage calm in the office. The Maldivians in particular were terrified—they had lived through the last one.

"Look! The water is acting funny!" said one of the journalists, beginning to panic as she pointed at the waves breaking on the rocks outside. The fear felt strangely infectious. We had a clear responsibility to provide accurate information, so I opened a live feed and put everyone to work.

Team distracted, I escaped the newsroom for a few minutes.

"Not to alarm you, but there's been a tsunami warning," I told my parents via Skype.

"Oh," they said.

Nearby resorts rounded up guests and gave them the option of taking a boat out to sea, or evacuating to the highest building on the island. On one resort this was the staff accommodation.

"I was horrified to think what the guests thought of the toilets, they were in terrible condition," said the wife of one resort manager.

The comments on our feed were fascinating. People gave information from all around the region: "We're all good in Mauritius", "Internet problems in Réunion Island", "Sri Lankan people evacuating Galle, Matara, Trincomalee."

The Maldivian comments were revealing.

"God is punishing the MDP. Look what they have done to us now! Hope you are proud, MDP! So sick of you!" read one.

We eventually established that the quake had been caused by a horizontal shift in tectonic plates rather than vertical, which meant there was limited displacement of water and little chance of a tsunami. The appointed hour of doom passed.

"So, about these perfume bottles?" I asked Maani.

* * *

The fear of being swallowed by the ocean in 2012 was palpable. In 2004, when it actually happened, it brought centuries of fear and superstition to the surface. In the absence of science education, many Maldivians believed the wave was God's punishment for their irreligiosity.

"The 2004 tsunami literally put the fear of God into many a Maldivian living in remote islands, which the Islamists exploited as a means of spreading their ideology by depicting it as punishment from God for man's ungodliness," wrote Dr. Azra Naseem in October 2012.[8]

The sentiment was quickly capitalized on by outside NGOs and governments in the Gulf and Saudi Arabia, providing not just aid and reconstruction funding but religious "capacity building". The mosque building and training of imams and scholars abroad had the effect of subtly reinforcing the tsunami as God's punishment for the improper practice of Islam.

The tsunami greatly increased the pace of cultural assimilation Gayoom had begun. He was no extremist himself, but his emphasis on Arab-style Islamic nationalism had undermined Maldivians' confidence in the strength of their own culture and traditional practice of religion, making them especially vulnerable to imported Wahhabism.

"Let no one think that he was ever a moderate. His only expertise is Islamic religion and many of his ministers were appointed on the basis of having studied like him at the religious university of al-Azhar in Cairo," wrote the anthropologist Xavier Romero-Frías in an open letter to the Maldivian people ahead of the 2008 election.[9]

"He cherished the power that his religious halo gave him, for as both head of an Islamic state and religious leader he was invulnerable as long as he was at the forefront of keeping the Maldives as Islamic as possible."

Almost overnight it became accepted that Maldivians needed to travel abroad to learn Islam "properly", and many began accepting free opportunities for "tertiary education" at madrassas in Pakistan and universities in Saudi Arabia. On their return they would return to their islands and set themselves up as "scholars", wielding dubious certificates and a few words of Arabic to gain respect and convince those around them of their superior religiosity.

Gayoom now had competition for the Islam he had empowered and sought to monopolize as a tool of political control—a task that was now impossible across 200 remote and scattered islands.

New freedoms of expression encouraged by the West ahead of the elections in 2008 undermined his ability to crack down on the fundamentalists, and old techniques such as imprisoning jihadists and allegedly shaving their beards were now being frowned upon not just by human rights liberals, but by outside forces bigger and meaner than him.

The First Bombing

In September 2007 a bomb exploded in Sultan Park in central Malé, injuring a group of twelve tourists including eight from China, two from Britain and two from Japan. The device was made from a washing machine motor attached to a gas cylinder,[10] triggered using a mobile phone as the group of foreigners passed by.[11] Nobody was badly hurt, but the incident was widely publicized, exposing the reality of rising Islamism in the country and showing that the tourism industry could not continue to pretend itself isolated from the rest of the country. For the first time, the attack put the Maldives on the international radar for something other than luxury honeymoons, and caused Gayoom's government to panic.

The US State Department, in leaked embassy cables, noted Gayoom's attempt to politicize the bombing and implicate the Friends of Maldives

NGO in Salisbury, declaring that groups calling for the boycott of government-owned resorts must "share some responsibility".

"The wide array of accusations and speculation surrounding the event indicate the degree to which this incident has shocked and alarmed the country. While it is too early to draw firm conclusions, the circumstances strongly suggest that the real target of this attack was Maldives' burgeoning tourism industry," the cable noted.[12]

The search for evidence in the bombing took the government to the island of Himandhoo, in particularly the Dhar-al-khuir mosque which had declared itself independent of the government's line on religious teaching. A force of 200 police and military personnel travelled to the island, only to be confronted on the jetty by a small army of islanders armed with batons and knives and wearing red motorcycle helmets.

In the ensuing skirmish, a policeman was taken captive and another's hand was severed. Shortly afterwards, a video discovered on an Al Qaeda forum was found to contain footage taken inside the Dhar-al-khuir mosque moments before it was raided by police. Leaked US diplomatic security briefings identified three Al Qaeda associates in the Maldives, Yoosuf Izadhy, Easa Ali, and Hasnain Abdullah Hameedh, linking Izadhy to a militant group in Waziristan.

It made for very different reading than the usual Maldivian tourist brochure.

"Izadhy was clandestinely working to recruit others into his organization, specifically seeking individuals who had undergone basic terrorism training in Pakistan. Izadhy planned to create a terrorist group in the Maldives with the assistance of the Waziristan-based group. Izadhy planned to send his members to Waziristan for training. Hameedh was in close contact with a number of individuals who had undergone training in Pakistan, including individuals who were members of Jamaat-ul Muslimeen and completed basic and advanced training by Lashkar-e-Tayyiba (LT) in Pakistan."[13]

The LT was deemed responsible for the 2008 attack on Mumbai, and it was this that made India start to regard the Maldives as its "soft underbelly".

The cable reported that at least two Al-Qaeda-linked operatives were involved in the Sultan Park bombing, "in exchange for travel from the islands after the operation and arranged study at a madrassa in Pakistan".

Further links were identified between a Maldivian national Ahmed Zaki and LT madrassas in the Kashmiri region, and between "Maldivians belonging to a group known as Jama-ah-tul-Muslimeen (JTM) and individuals participating in an anti-American Islamic extremist online forum called Tibyan

Publications. JTM is an extremist group based in the UK that follows an extremist ideology known as Takfiir that actively encourages violent jihad and supports criminality against apostate states."

Three men were arrested and sentenced for the bombing, although others escaped the country, including Mohamed Ameen—a member of the extremist group Jamaat ul Muslimeen—who would be placed on Interpol's "Most Wanted" list.

A few years later, Maldivians began popping up in terrorism hotspots, particularly along the Pakistan-Afghan border. A 30-year-old Maldivian, Ali Jaleel, was involved in the 2009 car bombing of Pakistan's Inter-Services Intelligence (ISI) headquarters that left around 23 people dead and a further 300 injured.

In a video released by Al Qaeda's media outlet, Jaleel, referred to as Mus'ab Sayyid, speaks to the camera surrounded by an assortment of weaponry. "I want my blood to be the bit of the carpet which the Mujahideen have painted from their blood. The red carpet which would take the Umar to its glory," he declares.[14]

Pakistani authorities periodically arrested Maldivians in the wrong place at the wrong time.[15] One of these was Ibrahim Fauzee, who was handed over to the Americans and detained in Guantanamo Bay. Evidence against Fauzee was dubious and circumstantial. According to his file,[16] he was arrested in 2002 while staying at the house of an Al Qaeda facilitator, "the person who sponsored [Fauzee] at the madrassa and whom was allowing the detainee to live in an apartment attached to his home. [The] detainee has traveled extensively in spite of his limited income and has failed to explain adequately the source(s) of the funds he used for travel. Detainee also attended a fundamentalist madrassa, which was administered by the same landlord he was arrested with, that taught extremist Islamic views sympathetic to Al-Qaeda and the Taliban."

He was classed as a "medium threat" to the United States, but was released in 2005 after a tribunal decided he was a non-combatant. Fauzee blamed Gayoom for his arrest and failure to sue for his freedom, and went on to found the Islamic Foundation NGO. The foundation embraced the new freedom of expression under Nasheed's term, loudly campaigning against *Minivan* and anyone else it decided was "un-Islamic". Ironically it would ultimately recognize *Minivan*'s championing of the very freedom of expression it had itself enjoyed, and even became an advertiser. Neil occasionally went over to do voice overs for their radio programme whenever the "voice of the infidel" was called for. They were sad to see him finally leave the Maldives, and even hosted him a goodbye party. He arrived at the party, slightly nervous, to find the whole crew assembled around a cake with solitary candle.

Fauzee saw his hesitation, and urged him to blow it out.

"Don't worry, it won't explode," he promised.

Nasheed's Religious Pluralism

While Gayoom's government had taken a hard line on fundamentalism, Nasheed approached the problem in reverse, seeking to reintegrate and rehabilitate. In August 2010 he ordered the sentences of two of the three convicted 2007 bombers commuted to suspended sentences under the government's Clemency Act.

"They were not the people who were in charge of doing this, they did not having the highest involvement," said Nasheed's spokesman, Mohamed Zuhair.[17] "The government wants to provide an opportunity for everyone to be involved in the society, and the opportunity to rehabilitate and recover."

In February 2010 the government used the Clemency Act to alleviate the sentences of sixteen people convicted following the government's 2007 assault on Himandhoo.

"This government is against all forms of extremism religious or otherwise," said Zuhair, claiming that the government's tolerance and "pluralist" approach towards religious factions had led to a better understanding of the issue rather than driving it underground. "The president has always said that the way to avoid fundamentalism is more democracy," Zuhair said. "People join groups with good intentions."

The reasoning behind the government's beneficence was the realization that the resorts were "soft targets", as well as icons of the same hedonistic Western decadence that so many in the region were fighting to destroy. A resort stood no chance against a Mumbai-style attack, and a single incident was guaranteed to cripple the entire industry. The Maldives barely had the coastguard to monitor its own fishing fleet. Instead, Nasheed's government subtly monitored extremism while trying to stay affably pluralistic. The result was a precariously balanced "neutral territory"—a country allied with the West, but where extremist rhetoric dominated Islamic debate and tourist visas were handed out on arrival to all and sundry.

This made it a natural destination for groups such as the Taliban to meet the Afghan government. Three such conferences were held during 2010, to *Minivan*'s delight:

Afghan parliament member Ubaid Ullah Achackzat, one of the MPs who report-edly visited the Maldives last week, told Al Jazeera the meeting was an effort "to find a third way, a way for the foreigners to leave [Afghanistan], with the possibility of merging the Taliban with the government and the possibility of a cease fire—there are lots of issues."

Seven of the men were reportedly part of an armed opposition group linked to the Taliban and held in high respect by the Taliban's leadership, Achackzat said.

The Al Jazeera report claimed the Taliban selected the Maldives as the venue for the meeting "because it was the only place the fighters felt safe."

"I believe that is a compliment to the Maldivian government and our pluralist poli-cies," said the president's press secretary, Mohamed Zuhair, adding that he did not feel the comment would negatively affect international perception of the Maldives.

"Our government has a policy to include followers of all sects of Islam," he said.

"For years other versions of Islam have been stifled [in the Maldives]. The president has said democracy is the best answer to keep fundamentalists at check."

Assistant controller of Immigration Ibrahim Ashraf expressed a different opinion.

"If this so-called group of Afghans had a link to the Taliban, that is in no way safe for the Maldives," he said.

"If people from internationally recognised groups such as the Taliban or other institutions keep coming to the Maldives, that is quite dangerous."

Zuhair acknowledged that the government had received reports of sightings of "a group of people who look like the Taliban wandering around the streets of Malé."

"Our stance is that the fact people happen to look like the Taliban doesn't mean they should be labelled that way," he said.[18]

While the Maldives pretended it knew nothing about what was going on, Al Jazeera, well informed on the Afghan side, followed the group out on their second visit and filmed it extensively.[19] The Taliban could not have chosen a better venue: Paradise Island Resort and Spa, owned by none other than Maldivian tycoon Gasim Ibrahim, was a gift to headline writers. The bearded *shalwar-kameez*-clad visitors wading through warm tropical water looking confused, while bikini-clad Russian girls threw beach balls to each other in the background. It must have felt like a long trip back to the cave.

Double-edged Swords

Nasheed's pluralistic approach weakened the government's control over Islamic interpretation in the Maldives. In doing so it allowed fundamentalist groups to fully enjoy the freedom of expression introduced by the democratic reforms his party helped enact. The approach assumed that speech in the Maldives was an "open marketplace"—an assumption that was false because freedom of speech was constitutionally "subject to the tenets of Islam". This gave enormous power in any debate to those who seized authority to determine what those tenets were. Under Gayoom, they were government-controlled, determined by him; under Nasheed, the presidency abdicated responsibility for religious matters. This led to a showdown between the Islamic Ministry and the sheikhs and scholars emerging "in the wild", and a theocratic arms-race to portray oneself as the "most Islamic". Liberal debate was effectively neutered, subject to accusations of being anti-Islamic, subjected to threats, intimidation and ostracism, and legally gagged under "threats to religious unity". People may have whispered less in cafés under Nasheed, and given time the situation may have mellowed as the liberals became emboldened, but public debate was one-sided and "secularist" remained a dirty word with which to insult one's opponents. Later in his term Nasheed became bolder, encouraging traditional Maldivian culture and appealing to innate Maldivian nationalism. Government events would begin with Maldivian *bodu beru* drumming, and troupes of girls in Maldivian dress—headscarf-free—would perform traditional dances, seemingly instructed to wriggle their hips seductively in front of the Islamic Minister, Dr. Bari. I would line up my camera and wait for him to steal a glance; he would stubbornly stare off to the side.

Countering the imported Wahhabi narrative and reversing the cultural assimilation by actively promoting traditional Maldivian culture—instead of conceding the floor—was the right approach. Showcasing it in front of foreign visitors and at rallies at public events was intended to inspire national pride, and it showed signs of working, shifting the middle ground towards Nasheed's camp. People could badge themselves Islamic *and* support the MDP.

President Nasheed, always up for a party, would frequently join in at rallies. The Adhaalath Party—then still in coalition with the MDP—called on the Maldivian people to "bow in shame" after Nasheed was filmed dancing while the MDP's parliamentary group leader, "Reeko" Moosa Manik, sang on stage.

"Their behaviour was uncivilised and irresponsible. Heads of nations are supposed to set an example for their people. We don't see presidents of non-Muslim states dancing and performing circus acts in public," the party declared.

"By all accounts Reeko Moosa's singing was pretty awful," admitted a senior government source.

"The Adhaalath Party has new leadership and this may be them trying to flex some muscle and show they are independent," the source said, noting that Nasheed had emphasized the 800-year durability of Islam in the Maldives while handing out certificates to the winners of a Quran recitation competition that very same morning.[20]

Fundamentalist Politics

It was all too late.

The various conservative Islamic factions forming in the country had fought it out, and the more moderate voices forced into obscurity. The saner leaders in the Adhaalath Party were pushed out by a faction led by Sheikh Imran Abdulla and his spokesperson, Sheikh Mohamed Shaheem Ali Saeed. This pair were more shrewd political manipulators than genuine religious authorities, and saw a golden opportunity to generate "king-making" political capital by splitting from the MDP and selling Islamic virtue to the highest bidder.

"Imran runs a lucrative Rent-a-Sheikh business. That is, in exchange for the right sort of political or financial returns, he agrees to bring his religious ideology to bear on whatever issue is causing headaches for his paymasters," explained Dr. Azra Naseem, in a 2012 analysis of the party.[21]

The volume of the party's religious moralizing greatly eclipsed its electoral support: the party only received 0.9 per cent of the votes in the 2009 parliamentary election, not enough to gain a single seat. It increased this to 2.95 per cent (one seat) in 2014 through a door-knocking campaign that threatened with hell those who didn't support it. It was by no means a democratic entity, and was consistent only in its production of entertaining headlines. A media monitoring report produced by the NGO Transparency Maldives established us as broadly impartial (not that anybody else noticed), with one glaring exception: we were apparently 100 per cent biased in favour of the Adhaalath Party, by virtue of printing most of their statements verbatim.[22]

By late 2011 the remnants of Gayoom's regime were desperate. Nasheed was starting to gain mass appeal after introducing pensions, universal healthcare, guesthouse tourism, a university, new taxes and hopes for a functioning economy. The opposition was split by infighting even as Nasheed moved to crack down on a crooked judiciary, the regime's guarantee of impunity against investigations into past corruptions and tortures. The Adhaalath Party held the last card: religion.

In 2012, it would become a catalysing force for the overthrow of Nasheed's government.

8

VELEZINEE, THE JUDICIARY
AND THE SILENT COUP

"What's really alarming though is the constant recourse to an entirely politicised and inept court and then cloaking that in an aura of due process."

US State Department official

Aishath Velezinee sat on the couch in the *Minivan News* office. Her small frame was quivering. She was only in her forties, but a lock of bright silver hair fell across her temple. It was 2010, late July, and the whistleblower had just come forward with a story of extraordinary state-shaking corruption.

She was a member of the Judicial Services Commission (JSC), the independent watchdog body tasked with overseeing the conduct, appointment and discipline of judges. Many such commissions had been created under the new constitution to oversee the organs of state—the Police Integrity Commission (PIC), the Civil Service Commission (CSC), the Human Rights Commission (HRCM)—and to provide a mechanism for people to file complaints. The heads of these commissions had been appointed by Gayoom's administration and rubber-stamp parliament after the introduction of the new constitution in 2008, but before the election the same year. Most, if not still subservient to the master's will, were crippled with the lethargy afflicting all civil employees and did little of consequence.

The JSC was different and, in hindsight, by far the most important. Unlike judicial oversight bodies in other countries, its ten members were made up not of judges but those occupying existing positions across the state, including the speaker of parliament, attorney general, three judges (Supreme Court, High Court, a lawyer, lower civil/criminal court), head of the CSC, two "public" members and members nominated by parliament and the serving president. Velezinee was first appointed to the commission by parliament during the transition period, and afterwards by President Nasheed. This was enough for those who supported the opposition to dismiss her as biased, although she had carefully distanced herself from the MDP and focused with single-minded determination on ensuring that the fledgling democracy received a fair and independent judiciary.

The commission was critical to this enterprise because it was tasked with vetting and appointing judges. The new constitution had separated the power of the state into three branches: the executive, parliament and the judiciary. The first two of these had been elected, yet the judiciary still consisted of all the judges appointed under the Gayoom administration. The constitution allowed them to continue as an interim judiciary for two years after its introduction, when the judiciary would face reappointment. The deadline was August 2010.

The present judges were problematic. Velezinee had used her privileged access to judicial administrative records and discovered that sixty per cent of the 200-odd sitting judges and magistrates had less than grade 7 education; while a quarter had actual criminal records, including sexual misconduct, embezzlement, violence, disruption of public harmony.

"All sorts of things—convictions, not accusations," said Velezinee.

Most had only a "diploma in judging" handed to them by the former Ministry of Justice, which issued instructions to them under Gayoom's administration.

All of this had been noted in Hill+Knowlton's 2003 report, after Gayoom brought the PR firm in to try and improve his image.

H+K called for "fundamental reform" of the criminal justice system, in which it said "there was little to no faith": "Corruption is viewed as embedded, or alternatively justice is seen as being dispensed arbitrarily ... Structurally, there is concern at the signal sent out in having the President as the highest figure within the judiciary and also the executive. Similarly, there is also concern that the President has responsibility for the judicial appointments system and indeed the ages and experience of judges, who are all young and deemed inexperienced."

For the past thirty years the judges had effectively been "handpicked", working as the employees of the government—to the extent that failure to give a particular ruling as required by Gayoom's Ministry of Justice was rewarded with a black mark in the judge's file. These were files that Velezinee had memorized—making her an encyclopaedia of judicial misconduct.

"The only qualification it appears was a willingness to submit to the will of the government at the time—to follow orders," Velezinee said. "We just woke up one day to a new culture. We have always had this culture of subservience, of submissiveness where you are taught to respect your elders—certain people who have been shown to you as the leaders. Then suddenly we adopted this constitution that says everyone is equal.

"Not everyone has the mindset to follow orders and serve in this kind of capacity. I believe it has excluded people with independent thinking, or the necessary legal knowledge—such people would take it as an insult for someone to order them how to decide a case. I would find it an insult if had to go and argue my case before someone who does not understand the law. Why are we content with people who have not completed primary school sitting on the bench and judging us?[1]

"Now the JSC has decided—I believe with the support of parliament—that the same bench will remain for life, retitled as an 'independent judiciary.'"

* * *

Article 285 of the new constitution required parliament to pass a bill—the Judges Act—defining the ethical conduct and educational qualifications of a judge, before the end of the constitutional interim period. The JSC was then required to appoint the new judiciary according to these standards, also before the deadline. It was clear that the majority of the bench were unfit.

Velezinee had sensed the scheming early, during the transition period immediately after the ratification of the constitution and before the 2008 election that would topple Gayoom.

"I found it very hard to believe that people could be that deceptive, so terribly, terribly bad. I couldn't believe it," she told me. "From the first day I was asking about Article 285 because that was the main thing the JSC would do. But they were not willing to discuss it. They kept pushing it back. Three months into the commission I requested a meeting with Nasheed—that was the only time he met me. I explained that Article 285 was not going to happen, that Gayoom's men were in the JSC, and that they had fashioned it after the old Ministry of Justice. They had put in the staff from the old Ministry, and they were running it all again under the name board of the JSC."

In the meantime the JSC, rather than investigating complaints submitted against judges, behaved instead as shield for judicial misconduct.

"My experience, from being part of the complaints committee in the JSC, is that whenever a complaint is received, we have two judges on the complaints committee who will defend the [accused] judge, trashing the complainant, and talk about 'taking action' against these people 'who are picking on judges," she told me in 2010, from the *Minivan* couch.

"Then they will put out a press release: 'Nobody should interfere with work of judges.' Their interpretation is that 'nobody should criticize us. We are above and beyond the law.'"

The JSC began to increasingly break its own laws, releasing annual reports that censored the names of judges who had complaints listed against them and instead revealing the private information of those who had made the complaints. Eventually it abolished its complaints committee altogether. It even went as far as forging documents and adding signatures to official registers to ensure that dubious decisions met quorum.

"Nobody from any civilized country would believe you if you said that judges and MPs were lying. Chief judges, high court judges—you expect office bearers to be working in the interest of citizens and the state. But here we have a judiciary that seems to think the whole country is out to attack them," Velezinee declared.[2]

By revealing what was happening inside the commission and breaking what she described as an "unofficial code of silence", Velezinee became regarded as a threat. The commission tried desperately and unsuccessfully to gag her by inventing new secrecy regulations and scheduling meetings minutes before they started, but were no match for her relentless and obsessive focus.

"For those three years I turned down my professional life, invitations to conferences, I was afraid to leave Malé in case they did something untoward. I never took a day off, I worked weekends, the whole three years was one long working day," she said.

Behind the commission's doors they ignored her—and ordered staff to do the same.

"I had to use my own resources and printed everything at home. They wouldn't give me office space—if I went in they would move the tables and chairs. If I sat in a chair, it would be gone the next day. Staff were warned they could not allow me to sit at a desk or use a computer, otherwise they would get into trouble."

She kept the JSC members terrified and off balance, once attending a meeting in full Islamic dress and making tea and coffee before sitting silently and staring at them. On other occasions, she would be observed pursuing a corrupt judge or commission member down the street, a grown man fleeing from a tiny but furious figure waving a copy of the constitution. Her letter writing was prolific; mountains of evidence and plaintive pleas were thrust at parliament, the President's Office, police, Anti-Corruption Commission—anybody who would listen, and everyone who did not.

Publicly, the commission launched a campaign of personal attacks against "that vulgar Velezinee", targeting her credibility as a "single mother who smokes".

"It's actually a very common attack on all women in public life. With me it was very much a concerted effort. Some of the recordings I got from their meetings revealed they were really scared that I was going out and doing so much more than they as a commission were doing. I think they felt they had to kill my credibility. Judges were going on TV and attacking me rather than challenging what I was saying: I was a liar, doing this and this. Nothing to do with the issues."

The media was scarcely better. Most outlets were Gayoom's old propaganda establishment simply privatized by regime-aligned tourism oligarchs, and were only too happy to help the JSC in dismissing Velezinee as loud and uncouth. She would hold her own press conferences.

"The commission staff were scared to assist me. I would carry the table and chairs and the flag to set it up. The media was in shock. When they got back they would get phone calls from judges and the Supreme Court and the JSC, so they took a step back."

The state-run Maldives National Broadcasting Corporation (MNBC) would send a camera. The cameraman would set it up, and leave.

"I would speak alone to the camera and pretend it was a press conference. I did it many times. Nobody manned the camera. They laughed at me."

As the August deadline for the appointment of the judges approached, Velezinee became increasingly desperate and anxious. Scorned and stonewalled by her local audience, she looked abroad for assistance. The constitution had a back-up provision for the appointment of educated foreign judges, so long as they were Islamic, raising the prospect of an organization such as the Commonwealth bringing in retired judges from somewhere like Malaysia. But she didn't know how to go about requesting this. She approached the United Nations' head office in Malé, at the time headed by British national Andrew Cox.

"I explained to him what was going on and requested he pass into the matter to the International Commission of Jurists (ICJ). He looked at me in a way that made me feel I was mad. I said I understand this may seem like an unbelievable story, but look at it and see what going on."

Velezinee conceded that her obsession and desperation would have readily endorsed Cox's impression that she was mad. Foreigners in bodies such as the UN arrived with little context, and interpreted the Maldives through regular briefings from a very small number of Maldivian Dhivehi-speaking colleagues. Many of those indoctrinated by the former regime were masters at isolating and influencing visiting foreigners by controlling the flow of information. It was easy to be caught off balance as the dictatorship's strongest supporters were often articulate, educated and Westernized. They had benefited from the patronage system, often receiving scholarships abroad, and returned with an implied servitude towards the regime to which they showed extraordinary loyalty. I was able to observe this intriguing brainwashing process first hand, as early on I was frequently on the receiving end. A little context was all that was needed to resist, but in such an isolated, opaque and politically polarized climate this was in short supply. Those who arrived under their own steam and were left to their own devices, such as journalists and volunteer teachers, more or less ended up on the same page after a few weeks. In the ivory towers of the UN building, it wasn't so simple.

For this reason, international attention towards the Maldivian judiciary had focused on "capacity building" within the judiciary and JSC. Foreign consultants and trainers would be flown in at great expense, the "students" in the judiciary would sit there and make all the right noises. If pushed, they would earnestly point to the article of the constitution defining the judiciary as independent. It said so on paper—right there!—what was the problem?

Some of the visitors understood the situation, but there was little they could do. One of the best was Professor Murray Kellam, a former Australian Supreme Court Justice who spent several weeks observing the JSC in action. He was Chief Commissioner of the Tasmanian Anti-Corruption Commission and had extensive experience assisting with the development of legal systems in countries like Burma and Bangladesh. He had also been awarded Officer of the Order of Australia, an award given for distinguished service of a high degree to Australia or humanity at large. Not only was he highly respected, he knew all the tricks.

He had been flown in by the United Nations Development Program (UNDP) based on a recommendation for outside observation by the International Commission of Jurists (ICJ)—whom Velezinee eventually managed to convince to visit.

"To date, JSC decision-making has been perceived as being inappropriately influenced by a polarised political environment. Also troubling is that members of the judiciary have been subject to threats and intimidation as well as improper inducements by both governing and opposition party members," the ICJ's report read, scratching the surface.[3]

A copy of the report had been sent to the JSC, which refused to table it—or even acknowledge that it existed. The UNDP had then brought in Professor Kellam, who gave a splendid lecture, which nobody from the JSC attended, apart from Velezinee.

I arranged an interview with Kellam through his minder in the UNDP. I got no word back, so early on the morning he was due to leave I contacted him directly—naturally, it was the first he'd heard of the request. He agreed to meet me in the lobby of his hotel. He was wearing a Hawaiian shirt, and looked worn, frustrated and keen to be done with the place.

"I think there's a real problem when you've got members of both the executive and the legislative body administering judicial affairs. You have the Speaker, Attorney General and an MP sitting in judgement on their own recommendations. That situation doesn't need describing any further," he said, carefully.[4]

"The process in your Constitution here is that [in the event of] gross misconduct and gross incompetence, the Majlis (parliament) has the job of dismissing them, and that's consistent with other places in the world. But the problem is that the body making the recommendation is also the membership."

I realized that I was dealing with a master bullshit assassin when he observed that while the JSC had given him "full access" to their files, this meant nothing as it was all in Dhivehi.

"The unofficial translation of the Constitution is pretty good, but I have doubts about the accuracy of the translation for the JSC Act. The UNDP assisted, but the [language gap] makes it pretty difficult," he said.

"'Rule of law' does not mean 'rule of judges'. Judges are not free to do as they wish. They are subject to the Constitution and the laws enacted by parliament. It is not their role to make disparaging remarks about parties, witnesses who appear before them, or to send signals to society at large in order to intimidate and undermine other basic freedoms such as freedom of expression. Respect is not gained through coercive use of power. The judiciary earns respect by its performance and its conduct."

There had been, he noted, a requirement for the JSC to undergo training, "but that was removed by the Supreme Court and subsequently by the legislature."

I hadn't realized this—but it was telling and made perfect sense.

The problem, that the UN and others were missing in their idealism, was that the judiciary did not need training or improvement; it was working perfectly for the purposes for which it was created. Unfortunately, as Kellam had subtly pointed out, all the evidence for this was in Dhivehi. Meanwhile, the only person waving it around had been painted as mad.

"I was going around telling this unbelievable story. I said I understand it is hard to believe, but look at the documents, look at the evidence available," acknowledged Velezinee. "You don't have to take my word for it. But nobody did."

She began to question her own sanity.

"I was being attacked and called a mad woman inside the commission. I saw no-one else listening to what was going on. I had to think about it, and started wondering whether I was perceiving things wrong, and questioning my own sanity. I would see fear in the eyes of friends and colleagues when they saw me. I think it was the frenzy I carried. I couldn't talk about anything else—there was no social situation I not bring it up. I was obsessed."

Being of a practical slant, she hunted down a British psychotherapist who had flown in to work on the Maldives' burgeoning drugs crisis.

"I talked and explained my predicament. He said I had got it right, and encouraged me. He said he could give me a sanity certificate in writing."

Countdown to the End

In May 2010 the JSC played its hand.

It voted by five members to two to disregard Article 285 as "symbolic" in favour of reappointing all sitting judges by the end of the interim period.[5]

This was, declared Velezinee, "nothing less than treason to rob the people of an honest judiciary". Without public trust in the judiciary democracy would fail, she predicted, with some prescience.

Parliament had oversight of the independent commissions, including the JSC. The trouble was that not only did Gayoom's opposition have a majority, but the institution also functioned rather like eBay. Several powerful and wealthy members sat in parliament, all opposition figures: Jumhoree Party leader and resort tycoon Gasim Ibrahim, Abdulla Yameen (Gayoom's half-brother), and his henchman in the People's Alliance, Deputy Speaker Ahmed Nazim. Scheduling was controlled by the Speaker, Ahmed Shahid, also an opposition figure.

"There is widespread public perception that certain members of parliament are behind all the serious organized crime going on in this country. This includes serious drug issues, gang violence, stabbings. These are allegations only because they have never come up before a court of law in all this time," observed Velezinee.

"It is a much discussed issue, but it has never come up in the courts. I can see now that perhaps it may be true—otherwise why prevent the formation of an independent judiciary? I don't think they would have confidence that they would get away free."

Her hypothesis was borne out by the behaviour of the courts. Cases involving opposition figures would never be heard, unless one of them had been arrested, in which case the courts would be open even at 3am to declare the detention "unlawful". State prosecutors would be arbitrarily thrown out of courtrooms in major drug cases, and occasionally even banned. Deputy Speaker Nazim was himself embroiled in a well-documented corruption case, facing multiple counts of defrauding the former Ministry of Atolls Development of over US$400,000. A police exhibition of the evidence in 2009 included numerous quotations, agreements, tender documents, receipts, bank statements and forged cheques linked to the scam, as well as the ministry's own audit report. However, he rarely answered court summons, and hearings were simply cancelled. Whenever he did deign to appear, journalists were thrown out of the courtroom and the hearing conducted behind closed doors. Days after the 2012 coup he was cleared of all charges as the "acts were not enough to criminalize".[6]

"When the judicial system defends a suspect more than his own lawyer does ... what else is there to comment about this article?" read the first comment on the story.

Police prosecutors complained during Nasheed's era that it was impossible to secure a conviction in a case involving more than a kilo of heroin. Major drug dealers would be routinely set free due to "insufficient evidence". This often approached absurdity; in one case in 2009, one of the country's top six alleged drug kingpins was arrested after police found tins full of drugs outside his house, and half a million US dollars inside his house. As only one witness claimed the drugs belonged to him—one fewer than demanded by the suddenly invoked Sharia law—the judge ruled there was no proof the drugs belonged to him. Nobody asked where the money had come from.

In another case, the Criminal Court overturned the arrest of two men found loading containers of drugs into the boot of a car. The boxes had been shipped from India, and one of the men's phones had a text message from the Indian supplier that included a code written on one of the boxes. Even by Maldivian judicial standards this was rather incriminating, and the High Court intervened to quash the lower court ruling. The Criminal Court simply ordered their release yet again.[7] The system also worked quite well in reverse because if it looked like a lower court judge was about to develop a conscience, the Supreme Court would intervene and take over the case—which would then never be heard of again.[8] If any laws were needed to make an action legal, it would create or interpret them—and point sternly at the constitution's demand that the (new?) rule of law be respected.

The traditional confession-based judicial system aided and abetted the process. Historically police would lock you away indefinitely and simply beat you until you confessed. This confession would then be presented to the judge, many of whom openly prided themselves on having a "100 per cent conviction rate".

H+K observed in 2003 that police did this even when they had sufficient forensic evidence to convict: "There is the perception that the police make clear to suspects that until they deliver a confession they will be held in prison indefinitely. There are also concerns that the need for a confession is one of the driving forces which leads to torture and or police brutality against prisoners."

As for judicial procedure, the accused "are often not given access to pen and paper and do not have enough time to prepare their case", and "perversely, we also understand that neither are the police required to keep a police diary. It has also been claimed that the accused are not made aware of the full extent of the charges levelled against them (until they are in court) and that often they will not be informed of the date of their trial until the day itself. Anecdotal evidence also exists that prisoners have been in court charged with one offence and then convicted of another."

H+K noted that as a result, ninety per cent of the prison population had confessed to their crime.

In post-2008 Maldives, as long as you didn't confess, had a few friends in politics—and weren't a woman—you could quite literally get away with murder. Those "friends" would, however, ever after hold your strings. And if you had been charged with violent psychopathy, rest assured they would find a use for that.

A 2012 report into the country's gang culture by the Asia Foundation found that politicians and businessmen were paying gangs thousands of dollars to assault rivals, damage property and in some cases have them killed.[9] The relationship was described as "symbiotic", and even included a price list: sabotaging the state broadcaster (US$1,620), setting fire to a bus (US$650), breaking shop windows (US$1,230). The gang leaders who dealt with the politicians earned about US$65,000 a month.

Interviewees told the Asia Foundation that being offered immunity from prosecution was normally part of the deal.

"Sometimes in return for the work we do, we also get to party in their safari boats with girls and alcohol," they added.

* * *

Certified sane and sure of her cause, Velezinee was re-energized. She was among the first Maldivians to seize onto social media, launching her "Article 285 campaign" into cyberspace and becoming easily the country's most prolific tweeter.

The JSC had meanwhile been planning for the oath-taking ceremony to take place in secret all over the country. Days before the August 2010 deadline the lights in the commission were on until the early hours of the morning, as it laboured to print certificates of life reappointment for the entire lower court bench. One night in early August, she received a tip off that the judges had been summoned to a closed-door oath-taking ceremony in the Supreme Court. Calling the media, she stormed into the hall and began berating the room full of judges. The video footage shows them slumped in their seats, refusing to make eye contact, as she marches up and down yelling at them angrily.[10] Other than Velezinee only two members of the JSC were present, both of whom were sitting judges taking the oath. Not a single person in the room backed Velezinee, and she was forcibly evicted and locked outside.[11]

The secret oath-taking ceremony had taken place just days before parliament was due to debate a decision on the Judges Act. That it took place before this passed violated Article 285 and technically made the appointment of the lower courts illegitimate. The ramifications were massive; it could be argued that every verdict thereafter was unconstitutional based on the fraudulent appointment of an entire judiciary.

The President's Office was aghast.

"The outgoing government has made sure it would retain control of institutions like the judiciary," said Nasheed's Press Secretary, Zuhair.

The appointments were "legally questionable and not credible at all to a large section of society—and the whole point of the exercise was to establish credibility."

At the same time the government was timid and paranoid about being accused of interfering with judicial independence. When President Nasheed criticised the JSC in June 2010, the Judges Association was scathing, describing his condemnation of the JSC's actions as "disrespectful towards the honour and dignity of judges" and indicative of the "negative view he holds of the judiciary". He was accused of using the powers of the president to "unduly influence the JSC, and render separation of powers obsolete".[12]

Clueless outsiders in the international community were quick to jump on the same narrative, warning the government off meddling and insisting that parliament was the constitutional authority to deal with situation—one from which most of its members were benefiting.

"So far we have been advised to do everything possible to keep to 'norms and standards'. But that's difficult when of the 197 judges, only 35 have any recognized qualifications. All the others have a local diploma," Zuhair observed.

Gasim's media outlet gleefully aired the reappointments in an effort to highlight Velezinee's conduct unbecoming a woman, but it also had the effect of getting her message out.

"I didn't know it was on TV. I didn't know how people would react. People were very interested, my mother was really proud. My daughter had been panicking that her mother was going mad, but suddenly she started getting phone calls from mothers and fathers of her classmates saying they were very proud of what I was doing. My mother too—and families and friends on the islands. People were impressed."

Horse Trading

The Supreme Court appointments were next. The deadline for the constitutional interim period was 7 August 2010, with parliament required to consider the president's nominations before midnight.

Nasheed had previously received a letter from the interim Supreme Court declaring it had examined the facts of the matter and decided that it was now permanent: there was no reason to nominate.[13] The letter was ignored, and the moment the court's gates shut for the day the military confiscated the keys to the building. Predictably, he was accused of harassing the independence of the judiciary. Parliament called his bluff and closed without considering the appointments, plunging the Maldives into constitutional limbo.

"Parliament has had two years to do these things. It baffles me why they would put the country in this situation—tonight people should be asking who they should blame," Foreign Minister Ahmed Shaheed told *Minivan News*.

The brinksmanship went on for three days. The chaos affected the ruling party a great deal more than the opposition; having democratically overthrown a dictatorship, the MDP was extremely prickly about being labelled one itself, especially by any international onlooker. In the meantime, Gayoom's regime wasn't going to approve any nominations unless it was sure of a controlling majority on the seven-member bench. Rather than stick to its guns, the MDP engaged in backroom horse trading with the opposition. The eventual decision, conducted behind closed doors and passed near unanimously, was hailed as a rare example of cross-party cooperation.

While the government was "not happy with every member of the [Supreme Court] bench, the President decided to bank a win. The mood is not one of jubilation, but of relief," said a source in Nasheed's office at the time.[14]

In reality, and in retrospect, the MDP had lost—as it did on every single occasion it gave into international voices urging "dialogue". It sought compromise on democracy with the uncompromising former dictatorship, and in doing so, sealed its doom.

Broad Daylight

I was in Australia visiting my family for the New Year in 2011 when I heard Velezinee had been stabbed. Two men on a motorcycle had come up behind her and one of them had stabbed her three times in the back on Malé's main tourist strip, in broad daylight, right outside the front door of the Home Minister.

Neil covered the immediate story. She survived, and had just been released from hospital when I got back to Malé. I went to visit her. She had a police bodyguard.

"I thought I had been bumped, I didn't realize I had been stabbed," she said.

"When I looked back I made eye contact with a guy as he was turning around. So I kept walking and then he turned back and stabbed me a second and third time."

"At that point I put my hand up and it was completely soaked in blood, and I realized I had been stabbed. If I had fallen I would have been dead, the second two stabs would have finished me off, as would the first if their aim had been correct. But I'm light and my bag got in the way. I think it was meant to be an assassination attempt or else hit my spine and make me a vegetable for the rest of my life."[15]

"My fear was that I would easily I bleed to death. But I took a deep breath and realized I was alive. As soon as I realized this, the only thing I wanted to do was go and get the blood stopped and get to the Commission because this was the day of the High Court appointments, and I know they wanted me out of the way. I didn't realize how serious the wounds were, I didn't see them until two days later when I went for a dressing change."

Nasheed came to visit her in hospital.

"He came into the room and ruffled my hair three times. He couldn't say anything. I was lying on my front because of the wounds. I squeezed his hand. The interview he gave afterwards was not Anni the president. It was Anni the fighter."

She was calmer than I remembered. It wasn't the bodyguard. I wondered whether she hadn't taken the attempt on her life as a form of validation for her work.

The JSC was due to meet and nominate the High Court appointments the same day that Velezinee was stabbed.

She had been preparing to intervene, and they knew it. Weeks ago, armed with her own sanity certificate, she had proposed a motion without notice "to determine if Supreme Court Justice Adam Mohamed Abdulla, current Chairman of the commission, meets the criteria of possessing a sound mind as required by article 139(c) clause three of the constitution."

She declared the judge was exhibiting "symptoms of a person who has lost his mind" and proposed suspending him from his duties "until a psychiatric evaluation is conducted under state supervision".

Attached to the motion as evidence was a document titled "The Serial Bully", pulled from a UK-based workplace bullying website detailing the symptoms of "sociopaths and psychopaths". These included "self-opinionated, emotionally retarded, deceptive, superior sense of entitlement and untouchability, financially untrustworthy, overbearing belief in their qualities of leadership, spiritually dead although may loudly profess some religious belief or affiliation" and "may pursue a vindictive vendetta against anyone who dares to held them accountable".[16]

"As it is JSC can only discuss and decide what the Chair permits, and that, it has become increasingly evident, is nothing," Velezinee said.

"The interviews were a farce, they handpicked the judges for the court bench. I was ready to delay the appointments. I think they wanted me out of the way so they could get on with it. The meeting was scheduled at 2:30pm, I was stabbed around 10 in the morning."

Velezinee's sole ally on the commission, public-nominated member Sheikh Shuaib Abdul Rahman, had a part time job. The commission knew this, and when it had something dubious it needed to pass it wasted the allotted time and then extended the meeting past the point Shuaib needed to start work.

"I could always predict what would happen next. There were no surprises," Velezinee said.

She announced during one attempt at this process that she had better things to do, such as distribute a large stack of printouts accusing the JSC of misconduct. She gave them a copy. On her way out of the commission, Speaker of Parliament Abdulla Shahid stopped her.

"It is over now, the oath has been taken, it's time to stop this," he told her.

The stabbing temporarily slowed Velezinee down by hospitalizing her, and gave her time to reflect on the toll her objective was taking. Her mother came to visit her, saying she had heard about the stabbing and had called her daughter.

"She was crying, she said. I asked 'Why is she crying?', and then I realized: of course she would be crying."

"I realized something of the human had been lost. I was desperate. I did not feel these things. I feel upset when people said they were scared to lose their jobs, when I had put my whole life at risk. I had lost my fear of death, I did not mind losing my job. I was never going to find work again. I was in real trouble, and I had no resources."

"But I know for a fact that the rule of law has been subverted. I know for a fact that there is corruption at the highest level in parliament. And I know that if I join the majority in keeping silent, I have become the traitor."

The Lead-up to the Silent Coup

After the reappointments, Velezinee switched the focus of her campaign to what she labelled the "Silent Coup"—"an alliance between parliament and the judiciary to subvert the rule of law, derail constitutional democracy and use the courts to bring down the executive".

A fortunate side effect of being stabbed was that it returned to Velezinee the credibility the JSC had tried to take from her. Overt support was rare, but the general public saw her as on their side and people would come and thank her in the street. Meanwhile, whenever a visiting diplomat or journalist expressed interest in the judiciary, I would make sure they went to see Velezinee.

"Give it at least a few hours," I would suggest, making sure the appointment involved a free meal so at least she would be forced to eat. She had fans even abroad—my mother sent her an enormous chocolate frog.

"Is she trying to fatten me up and give me credibility?" Velezinee asked, as I handed the thing over after one of our interviews.

The MDP felt it had lost the judiciary and throughout the latter half of 2011 changed tack, embracing a pragmatism that compromised its idealistic roots. It was very effective, particularly in passing much-needed tax legislation, but such behaviour had no truck with Velezinee. She found herself on the fringes.

Nasheed removed her from the commission, in what we understood was probably a term of some backroom deal with the dictatorship.[17] She didn't mind—her job was done, as far as exposing the JSC was concerned, and he gave her a job as Deputy Home Minister. Suddenly she had a salary and an office, with a desk and a chair no-one kept trying to hide, and time to pursue her campaigning.

The JSC and the opposition did their best to pretend she didn't exist.

Two Men in a Garage

I liked to imagine the Dhivehi Qaumee Party (DQP) as two men in a garage with a fax machine, self-authorized defenders of the constitution molesting a city council over its failure to keep children off a park lawn. Article 49(b) of the amended zoning and land-use regulations demanded the grass be kept child-free. Where were the sergeants with Tasers and pepper spray?

Dr. Hassan Saeed was the leader. In person he came across as effete and articulate, gracious and charming, scholarly and reasonable. He was a lawyer and had been Attorney General during Gayoom's regime. Dr. Mohamed Jameel was the party's deputy. He had headed the Ministry of Justice during Gayoom's time, assuming responsibility for ensuring the judges carried out the wishes and verdicts of the executive. He had also been involved in qualifying the judges, a process achieved by giving them the little scrolls entitled "Diploma in Judging".

Like many minor parties the DQP had achieved the minimum membership to register and therefore to receive state funding from the Elections Commission, although as with the membership of many minor parties, few on this list could remember having joined it. The pair's political output was prolific and belied their size. Once allied with the MDP in its overthrow of Gayoom, the party had quickly broken off its coalition agreement after Nasheed's alleged promises failed to materialize. According to Dr. Saeed, who wrote an anguished editorial for *Haveeru*, these included resigning the day after his oath of office and appointing Saeed as president. The party's torrent of faxed press releases had since focused on interpreting every activity of the MDP as some kind of constitutional misdemeanour.

Eventually it gave up and just started inventing them. The party was one of the instigators of the December 2011 "defend Islam" rally that drew one of the largest crowds in Maldivian history, attracting not just Gayoom's conservative supporters but many MDP members who had strong feelings on the topic. Some participants later expressed regret on realizing that the event's primary motivation was political, rather than religious. It was a rallying call for the scattered and issueless opposition parties, halting the infighting and uniting them under one cause: overthrowing Nasheed's government for being "un-Islamic".

The DQP's job was to work out just how Nasheed's government had been un-Islamic, and reveal this to the public. They did so in a glossy pamphlet, "President Mohamed Nasheed's Devious Plot to Destroy the Islamic Faith of Maldivians".[18]

"Since assuming office Nasheed has been working ceaselessly to weaken the Islamic faith of Maldivians, allow space for other religions, and make irreligious and sinful behaviour common," it began, before comprehensively listing his failings.

They included: supporting Navi Pillay's call for a moratorium on the "divinely revealed" punishment of flogging women for extramarital sex; giving excuses not to hold Zakir Naik's event in the national stadium; dancing at Miss France 2011 at the Coco Palm Resort; dancing in general; failing to jam the commonly pirated Indian satellite television network Airtel and its channel promoting Christianity; consorting with "English priests like David Hardingham"; holding a disco; trying to sell alcohol on inhabited islands; consorting with "Jews"; allowing Israeli flights to land in the Maldives; allowing the MDP chairperson to attend a function in a skirt; accusing the country's Arabic schools of promoting extremism; and allowing his state ministers to "commit many sinful acts naked on the internet"—a reference to the 2011 Facebook blackmailing scandal in which much of the country forwarded naked photos of themselves to a fake profile depicting a pretty blonde girl called "Angelic Sharrown".[19]

The DQP's pamphlet also took umbrage at the banners used for the November South Asian Association for Regional Cooperation (SAARC) event—the first time it had been held in the Maldives. The banners, designed by a Maldivian and prominently displayed at the airport, celebrated South

Asian diversity and included an image of a vaguely shepherd-like figure that might have been a Jesus.

"Christianity is not among either the first, second or third religion of SAARC nations," the DQP advised. "The true purpose of putting up these drawings in Malé and elsewhere across the country is to familiarise, acquaint and slowly bend Maldivians to the portraits, drawings and monuments of other religions."

The party also called for Nasheed to be jailed for allowing other SAARC countries to unveil "idolatrous" monuments, such as a stone lion statue from Sri Lanka. "Under article 4 of the Contraband Act, importing idols to the country is not at all permitted. Such a thing cannot be authorised regardless of whether it is the government. And those who commit this offence or are involved in it can be sentenced to jail for a period of 3 to 8 years," the party recommended, presenting as evidence a photograph of Nasheed and the Sri Lankan president at the statue's unveiling.

The attempt to whip up Islamic nationalist fervour worked. Nasheed's government responded by ordering police to question Dr. Jameel as to the specific nature of the "business with Jews" it was referring to, or face charges of inciting religious hatred.[20]

This triggered a "cat-and-mouse" game that thoroughly demonstrated the former regime's command of the court bench. Every time Dr. Jameel was arrested, day or night, Chief Judge of the Criminal Court Abdulla Mohamed would obligingly open the courtroom and rule his arrest unlawful. Meanwhile, opposition members were doing the embassy rounds in Colombo complaining about Nasheed's persecution of his political opponents. This became radically less successful after *Minivan* translated their pamphlet, a copy of which I later learned was presented to them during a meeting with the Americans. Mumbling something about malicious mistranslation, they scuttled back to Malé.

Judicial Reform: The Arrest of Abdulla Mohamed

Dr. Jameel had been arrested and released half a dozen times before the government fatefully turned its focus towards the bigger problem: Abdulla Mohamed. On 16 January 2012 the military detained the controversial judge.

The laundry list of alleged crimes was long and damning. Nasheed's government accused Judge Abdulla of deliberately holding up cases involving opposition figures, barring media from corruption trials,[21] arbitrarily releasing suspects detained for serious crimes without a single hearing, and maintaining "suspicious ties" with family members of convicts sentenced for dangerous crimes.

The judge also released a murder suspect[22] "in the name of holding ministers accountable", who went on to kill another victim,[23] "twisted and interpreted laws so they could not be enforced against certain politicians" and stood accused of "accepting bribes to release convicts". He was furthermore accused of actively undermining cases against drug trafficking suspects and allowing them the opportunity to "fabricate false evidence after hearings had concluded". Judge Abdulla allegedly "hijacked the whole court" by deciding that he alone could issue search warrants,[24] and arbitrarily suspended court officers.[25] He had, declared Nasheed's Home Minister Hassan Afeef, "taken the entire criminal justice system in his fist".[26]

Many of these complaints had already been sent to the Judicial Services Commission, which had shown no interest in pursuing the matter; it had in fact abolished its complaints committee in 2011.[27] Under pressure, the JSC had in November finally completed a report, the "first time ever that a Maldivian institution has decided against a judge". But Judge Abdulla obtained an injunction from the civil court against its release, and the court dubiously ordered its own watchdog body to drop the matter. The JSC dutifully complied and the report was shelved.

It did raise the spectre of judicial reform, fuelling desperation among the opposition by threatening the legal impunity the former regime had enjoyed even while in opposition. Cases involving past human rights abuses, corruption and organized crime began to grind forward. Gayoom and his half-brother, Abdulla Yameen, left town. Locally, the opposition seized the judge's detention as justification for protests, painting it as executive interference in an "independent" judiciary.

"Under the circumstances—once it was clear that Abdulla Mohamed was an obstruction to justice and a threat to national security, and once it became apparent that neither the Judicial Service Commission nor the Parliament was willing to hold him accountable—the only authority left to take control of the situation was the Head of State," wrote Velezinee in her retrospective book, *The Failed Silent Coup: In Defeat They Reached for the Gun.*[28]

"The judiciary we have today is under the control of a few. This was an end reached by using the Judicial Service Commission as a means. Most members of the Judicial Service Commission betrayed the Constitution, the country, and the people. They broke their oath. There is no room for free and fair hearings. And most judges do not even know how to hold such a hearing."[29]

But the military's detention of the judge did not look good, especially without context, which was available only at *Minivan*. I had quickly recognized the significance of the judge's extrajudicial detention as a late attempt at judicial reform and painstakingly backgrounded our stories with a trail of links to abuses, corruption and misdeeds.[30]

But it was complicated; few people even in the Maldives had command of the backstory, and most were used only to the limited reporting of events by a misshapen and occasionally malicious media establishment. Nasheed was off-balance, used to being an international press darling. On the other hand, locking up judges nicely fitted the stereotype of the power-mad autocrat. It was a simple narrative for the opposition to take advantage of, and for once they seized the initiative and gained traction abroad.

Lacking context, or ignoring it, several figures in Nasheed's government began siding publicly with the demonstrators. One of these was Dhiyana Saeed, the youngest and first female head of SAARC, appointed by Nasheed's government. She became the first SAARC head to resign, and also took first prize for shortest time in the prestigious office.

"[The Chief Judge's detention] is a violation of individual human rights, a violation of the independence of the judiciary, and the violation of the constitution," she declared, several days prior to stepping down.[31] "The government should not take the law into its own hands. This action is very clearly unconstitutional. If you look at the how the government has acted these last three years you can see a trend. The government thinks any means to an ends is alright."[32]

Nasheed's vice president, Dr. Mohamed Waheed Hassan Manik, joined the growing chorus. "Besides all the international legal obligations, the Government of Maldives is bound by the Maldives Constitution 2008 which prohibits arbitrary arrest and forced disappearance. We have just witnessed the first possible violation since the dawn of democracy in our country. I cannot understand why this is not an issue for everyone in this country," he wrote, on his personal blog. "Those of us who have struggled for freedom in this country for over 30 years, are wondering whether we have wasted our efforts. I have expressed my reservations about the way the Government has allowed the disappearance of a citizen, a Chief Judge of the Criminal Court, for the reasons I mention above. I am ashamed and totally devastated by the fact that this is happening in a government in which I am the elected the Vice President."

Nasheed's government, ultra-sensitive to overseas criticism, was on the back foot. The judge himself was fine—the Human Rights Commission visited him and reportedly found him happily fishing. He was asked if he wanted to see his family; he apparently declined, demanding instead to speak to Azima Shukoor. Formerly Gayoom's lawyer, Shukoor had never lost a court case—a feat no doubt due to her brilliant legal mind. The courts and the JSC demanded their judge back; the military continued to refuse on the grounds of national security.

Nasheed's government realized that they had a stalemate on their hands, but underestimated the extent to which the outside world was ignorant of the situation with the Maldivian judiciary and the lead-up to the judge's detention. International opinion swung towards Gayoom's opposition, who were hailing the judge as a hallowed defender of justice, ethics and a shining beacon of judicial independence. Buoyed with confidence, they began an educational email campaign aimed at judicial authorities worldwide. Some answered the call.

Abdulla Mohamed had been "clearly been demonstrating independence as he's supposed to do and the government doesn't like it," said the president of the Australian branch of the International Commission of Jurists (ICJ), John Dowd, in an interview with ABC Radio Australia.[33] None of the government's allegations against the judge warranted his arrest, Dowd argued, "and it's clear that he must be immediately released. This will do serious damage to the Maldives internationally and their tourist industry is a big part of their income and they just can't allow this to go on." The Maldivian judiciary, Dowd declared, was "generally competent".

This was an odd statement, as even Gayoom's own government hadn't thought so. During his stint as Attorney General under Gayoom, Dr. Hassan Saeed of the DQP had raised major concerns about the conduct of the very same judge as early as 2005. In his letter to the dictator he listed allegations against the judge, which included instances of misogyny and throwing out an assault case despite the confession of the accused. Saeed informed Gayoom that the chief judge had also "made two children who were summoned as witnesses against the accused recount the act in the presence of the perpetrator and the rest of the court".[34]

Why then was Saeed at the front of the rallies deifying the judge as a paragon of judicial virtue? When I pressed him on the subject in front of a foreign press conference post-coup, he scuttled backwards.[35]

"As chief legal advisor to the government at that time, I had raised issues with the in-charge of the judiciary at that time. In that constitution the President was the head of the judiciary. So it was my legal and moral obligation to raise that issue with him, which I did. I did not know if it was followed up," he said.

Nasheed's government, which *had* followed it up, was struggling to regain the initiative. They finally began laying out the case and pleading for foreign assistance to reform the judiciary.

The government, declared Nasheed's Foreign Minister Ahmed Naseem, did not want to keep Abdulla Mohamed under arrest, but did not want him sitting on the bench until the charges against him were cleared. "The point here is that we are in a Catch-22 situation—which court do we go to?" he asked.[36]

Existing judges swore themselves in unilaterally without looking into the relevant clauses of the constitution, which says that they have to be sworn in according to the new constitution.

Now, this new constitution strictly stipulates that these judges should have qualification to act as judges. The present judges that we have don't have these qualifications.

There are quite a lot of people whose interests are vested with these judges. That is, there are politicians connected to the former regime, who have many court cases. Now all these court cases are being held by the judge who is under detention at the moment. No cases have been conducted on this and no sentence has been passed. So it's in the interests of the opposition to see that this judge remains as a judge.

What democracy can we have, when we don't have a proper judicial system and we can't dispense justice properly? The democracies of the world should really help us and find ways of sorting this issue out. We have requested UN bodies to help us in this and they've promised to send us some people to sit down with us and work something through.

The government's tactic was sound: appeal for impartial outside assistance, and hold on until it arrived and realized for itself what was happening. Judicial reform—and probably foreign judges—would result. The opposition reached the same conclusion, even as its expensive nightly protests began to run out of steam.

A Commonwealth judicial observation team arrived the morning Nasheed's government was forced from office. There were rumours that the shredders in the JSC were working overtime, disposing of the evidence in Dhivehi that nobody had thought to bother about until Velezinee had found it. Concerned for her safety in the aftermath of the coup, I sent a line-up of suddenly very-interested diplomats her way for a crash course in the Maldivian justice system. Being a clever sort, she had made copies of the evidence and had them hidden away overseas with the help of several cooperative foreigners.

But the damage had been done: with Nasheed's eviction went all hope of judicial reform for the foreseeable future. Yet the new government under his vice president was unstable, an alliance of those united only by their hatred of the man who had stolen their country in 2008. Moreover, the dubious circumstances of their return to power were raising eyebrows among the international community, inspiring caution in the embassy meeting rooms of Colombo when it came to decisions on the provision of much-needed technical and monetary assistance. Maintaining the illusion of calm for the sake of the tourism industry, especially the jittery Chinese market, was also paramount. "Misplacing" Nasheed at sea wasn't an option, given the widespread destruction the day after the coup.

The returned dictatorship was therefore limited in its ability to act directly against Nasheed, at least without giving the game away. I understood from the more sympathetic diplomats that this was the "red line" as far as they were concerned.

The path put forward by the diplomatic community—early elections—was an unfavourable prospect for the dictatorship. Nasheed's sympathy vote had skyrocketed after the police crackdown on 8 February. Many who may have disagreed with his policies and enthusiasm for speedy reform, particularly the older and more conservative generation, were disgusted at the manner in which the government had changed. Fence-sitters and dispossessed former supporters had been reinvigorated as party activists; an early election was firmly in Nasheed's interest.

The dictatorship needed a way to pursue its agenda without jeopardizing the veneer of democratic legitimacy it had put up by installing Nasheed's vice president as a puppet ruler until the scheduled 2013 vote. The "independent" judiciary was the perfect agent, and would more than prove its value in the months to come.

Revenge, Courts and Kangaroos

Following President Nasheed's resignation, Chief Judge of the Criminal Court Abdulla Mohamed was swiftly released from detention on the island of Girifushi. He returned to a hero's welcome in Malé. Among his first acts of freedom was to issue a warrant for Nasheed's arrest, charges unspecified.

This was problematic for President Waheed's new government, which was already dealing with a surge of awkward questions from arriving diplomats regarding its legitimacy. President Waheed had been offering emphatic reassurances of a "national unity government" in which Nasheed would presumably participate. The Criminal Court's eagerness to put the former president behind bars barely a day after he was compelled to resign somewhat threatened the conciliatory mask.[37]

The urgent need for legitimacy prevailed, and the government caved in to diplomatic pressure. Police did not act upon the warrant.

As the new government fought diplomatic spot fires, the MDP regained the initiative and took control of the narrative, particularly in the international press. Barely any foreign media favoured the government's view that the power transition was natural and proper. Locally, the MDP's protests were energetic and almost constant, with bigger events on the weekends regularly attracting up to 10,000 people. The clamour for early elections grew and diplomatic opinion, which had initially given President Waheed the benefit of the doubt, began to swing towards elections—the sooner the better.

Returning a democratic mandate to the MDP in a free and fair election was out of the question for the dictatorship. Nasheed, politically martyred, had become a cult figure. This characteristic made the party resistant to attempts to split it by appealing to the more ambitious senior leaders, who showed remarkable loyalty by Maldivian political standards. But it was also weakness, as it meant that the party had no alternative leadership. If it was going to be forced to submit to elections, there was no way that the dictatorship would allow Nasheed to contest them. The question was how to do this under the nose of the suddenly very attentive international community—while ensuring the executive's hands stayed clean. Actually jailing Nasheed wasn't necessary; they only needed to have him found guilty of criminal charges to constitutionally disqualify him from contesting the election. But what charges?

In July 2012, six months after Nasheed's ousting, the Prosecutor General filed charges against the former president and several figures in the military, accusing them of violating Article 81 of the Maldivian Penal Code. This stated that the detention of a government employee who had not been found guilty of a crime was illegal. If found guilty, the sentence would be jail or banishment to a remote island for three years, or a fine of MVR3,000 (US$193.50).[38]

The DQP's Dr. Jameel, who by this point had been appointed Minister of Home Affairs, declared the case a "historic criminal trial" and the "first step towards the national healing process".

Pressed for a response, President Waheed's new spokesperson, Abbas Adil Riza, told us the president would "not interfere with the independent Prosecutor General's decisions".

The international community watched these pronouncements with furrowed brow. Concerns were raised about the conflict of interest in holding the trial in the Criminal Court—the same court whose Chief Judge the defendants were accused of improperly detaining. The JSC devised a solution: hold the trial in the Hulhumale Magistrate Court. To further ensure impartiality, it went the extra step of appointing three judges to hear Nasheed's trial.

Hulhumale is a large island next to Malé, consisting mostly of reclaimed land and connected to the airport island of Hulhule by a narrow spit. Together with Vilingili it is constitutionally considered a "suburb" of the capital rather than a separate island under separate administration. There was no mention in the Judicial Act about Hulhumale requiring its own court, and certainly no mention or legislation empowering the JSC to open new courtrooms or appointing judges to cases of their choosing. Such concerns were rarely an obstacle for the JSC; the local understanding was that the court had originally been opened to ensure a job for the wife of one of the JSC members.

There was also the matter of Gasim Ibrahim, who sat on the JSC as parliament's representative and yet was himself a declared candidate in the 2013 elections. The conflict of interest in having one presidential candidate appoint the judges in the trial of a rival candidate did not appear to bother the JSC, despite its own thorough (and leaked) documentation of his lobbying efforts.[39] The tycoon's response to such allegations, via his spokesperson, was to suggest that such reports were a slanderous attempt by the MDP to tarnish his "good name", for fear of his electoral popularity.

The MDP eventually made the matter of the court's legitimacy the basis of its legal strategy—insofar as such a thing was possible in the Maldivian justice system. Appeals were made to the High Court. Parliament declared the Hulhumale Court illegitimate. The Supreme Court intervened and insisted it was legitimate, despite having no constitutional authority to overrule the legislature. Any dissent was met with accusations of contempt of court.

None of this impressed legal observers from the UK Bar Association's human rights committee, who arrived in time to watch the whole courtroom debacle unfold. "[The Bar Association] is concerned that a primary motivation behind the present trial is a desire by those in power to exclude Mr Nasheed from standing in the 2013 elections, and notes international opinion that this would not be a positive outcome for the Maldives," the British legal observers concluded.[40]

The dictatorship's plan was unravelling and the situation was getting desperate. The worse the Maldivian courts behaved, the more difficult it was for Nasheed's anti-democratic adversaries to hide the strings over the courtroom. Hearings tended to coincidentally coincide with major MDP campaign events, and the judiciary was quick to summon the police to enforce Nasheed's attendance. The Deputy Speaker of Parliament Ahmed Nazim might have been able to fail to show at dozens of his corruption trial hearings, but when Nasheed was summoned hundreds of officers dressed in balaclavas would storm his house in Malé and drag the former president off the island for pre-trial detention.[41]

The government positioned itself at a distance, emphasizing the "independence" of the judicial process and insisting that the courts be respected. The MDP wavered, unwilling to acknowledge the court's legitimacy by complying with the increasingly erratic and malevolent rulings and summons, but under pressure from outside to "follow the rules" and allow the process to play itself out.

Tensions really spiked on 14 February 2013 when Nasheed, learning of another arrest warrant issued by the court in a bid to stop him making an official visit to India, slipped his minders and sought refuge in the Indian High Commission, claiming to be in fear for his life.

India, by now under no illusions about the nature of the new government it had prematurely endorsed as legitimate a year previously, welcomed the deposed president to what was, under the Vienna Convention, Indian territory.

This spontaneous diplomatic couchsurfing was a shrewd and brilliant move on Nasheed's part. The international media rushed to focus on the Maldives just as the government, in its fury, let its mask slip. Perhaps forgetting the matter was still under trial, the various parties accused India of "assisting a criminal to escape from justice". Gayoom's PPM labelled him a "coward", while President Waheed's office pretended that nothing had happened. "I wouldn't call it an arrest warrant. It's a court order for police to summon him to court," insisted Waheed's spokesperson, Masood Imad.[42] "I'm not a policeman but presumably they will ask him to come with them, and if he does not they will put him in a police vehicle. The actual strategy is a police function. I hope they don't do anything excessive," he added.

Our fly on the wall in the riot police canteen said that the occupants were upset and afraid because the Home Ministry had angrily ordered them to storm the High Commission and extract the ex-presidential fugitive. The building's defences were unclear. The orders were rejected, more out of fear of Indian retaliation than respect for the Vienna Convention. It sounded pretty close, though.

Nasheed remained inside the High Commission for eleven days, allowing the tantrums of the government and the courts to assuage any remaining doubts among foreign observers that the strategy was to convict and bar him from contesting the elections. It worked: the brinksmanship united the international community, and committed them to pressuring the Maldivian government to allow for elections which Nasheed would be allowed to contest. "Free", "fair" and "inclusive" were the agreed unilateral buzzwords.

"We urge that the Presidential elections scheduled for September 7, 2013 be free, fair, credible, transparent and inclusive. The integrity of and public confidence in the Maldivian electoral process must be maintained. Accordingly, we note that all parties participating in these elections should be able to put forward the candidate of their choice," declared the Americans.[43]

"It is necessary that the Presidential nominees of recognised political parties be free to participate in the elections without any hindrance," said India.

The UK "stressed the importance of all parties being able to participate in elections with the candidate of their choice".

Even UN Secretary General Ban Ki-Moon waded in, urging "all political actors to exercise restraint, renew their commitment to the constitution and work toward creating conducive conditions for fair, peaceful and inclusive elections".

No more mention was made of respect for "judicial process". The game was all but up.

Velezinee's Vindication

The judiciary had long been an object of fear and apprehension in Maldivian society. It was somewhere you ended up when Gayoom decided he wanted rid of you. Because of the many family connections and general Maldivian disdain towards violence, political adversaries tended to be banished rather than executed. This punishment—in 2011 still the number one sentence for cheque fraud—removed the accused from the Malé's centre of political power without cost to the state or deep schisms caused by execution. A common pattern under Gayoom's rule was for the banished to be given amnesty after several years and invited back, even given a government job, on the understanding that one's loyalty was now assured. The psychological manipulation was subtle and brilliant. It was not uncommon to meet people who had lost everything to Gayoom—jobs, property, position, reputation—but who years after their "redemption" had nothing but good things to say about the man.

It was debatable as to whether banishment was worse that prison, trapped on a remote island, forced to beg a living from an unfamiliar population often resentful of the new mouth to feed and of being treated like a dumping ground for "criminals".

"When communities refused to care for exiles, some exiles spent weeks on the beach, starving, unable to find work or a family to take them in," wrote Zaheena, in her emotive and magnificent article for *Middlebury Magazine* on her brother Aiman's sentencing.[44]

Velezinee had exposed the inner workings of the judiciary, revealing the men, motivations and processes behind its cruel banalities in much the same manner as one might lift the curtain on *The Wizard of Oz*. For this she had been tormented, stabbed, ignored and ostracised by the very people whose interests she was supposedly protecting. It wasn't until Nasheed was facing political censure from the same judiciary he had first attempted to negotiate with, and then belatedly reform, that the MDP began to see her as anything other than a loud inconvenience.

But the outside was finally taking notice. The Maldives was a small country highly sensitive to international opinion and one on which diplomats, frustrated with the complex agendas of their various countries, were realising they could safely take moral positions.

It was early 2013. The diplomatic community that had been caught off guard by the coup a year ago had finally caught up, particularly the European Commission and the UK. The US, surprisingly willing to take a smile and a handshake at at face value, would take another three months: "What are the Americans up to?" the other diplomats would frequently wonder at the time. Cross-embassy diplomatic huddles on the Maldives became common over in Colombo, notes were compared and meetings shared. Context was kryptonite for the government's charismatic and substanceless diplomats, who increasingly returned home disbelieved and disappointed.

Surprisingly given its track record so far, it was the UN system that finally put the handshakes away and called a spade a spade. The UN Special Rapporteur on the Independence of Judges and Lawyers, Gabriela Knaul, a former judge from Brazil, landed in Malé in February 2013 and comprehensively tore through the Maldivian judiciary in eight days.

"It is indeed difficult to understand why one former President is being tried for an act he took outside of his prerogative, while another has not had to answer for any of the alleged human rights violations documented over the years," she wrote, in her final report to the UN Human Rights Council.[45]

The JSC had created the Hulhumale Magistrate Court to try Nasheed, and appointed the three-member panel of judges overseeing the case. The JSC's head Adam Mohamed, also a Supreme Court judge, had cast the deciding vote in a Supreme Court ruling on the court's legitimacy. During the press conference with the rest of the media we asked Knaul directly about the legality of the Nasheed trial. "It seems to me that the set-up, the appointment of judges to the case, has been set up in an arbitrary manner outside the parameters laid out in the laws," she replied.

It was the first time a senior international official had publicly criticized the judiciary. And she was just warming up.

"I have heard from numerous sources that the current composition of the Judicial Services Commission, the body in charge of the appointment, transfer, and removal of judges, is inadequate and politicised. Because of this politicisation the Commission has been subjected to all sorts of external influence and consequently has been unable to function properly," she wrote in her report, a thorough documentation of a "deeply concerning" judicial system in crisis.[46]

This remark, from effectively the world's highest source on judicial independence, was a public vindication for Velezinee. She had been right all along—and, finally, here was the best acknowledgement she could have hoped for.

It was one of the most satisfying articles I've written. I remember ringing her excitedly. She was prosaic; she felt elated, but saddened it had come so late.

In the wake of Knaul's report the government was literally speechless. Several months later, in June, it released a limp and belligerent statement blaming the corruption and politicization of the judiciary on the "residual challenges of democratic consolidation".[47] It went on to accuse her of undermining national sovereignty: "Engagement between national governments and international actors should not undermine national jurisdiction and the court system of any country, especially relating to ongoing cases."[48]

Fortunately for the government, Gasim was on hand to delicately handle the crisis diplomacy. "[Gabriela Knaul] claimed that the judges were not appointed transparently, I am sure that is an outright lie. She is lying, she did not even check any document at all nor did she listen to anybody. She is repeating something that was spoon-fed to her by someone else. I am someone who sits in JSC. She claimed there were no regulations or mechanism there. That is a big joke," the tycoon declared.[49]

The JSC had been "ruined" by none other than Velezinee, he pouted.

"At first, the JSC were not able to carry out its duties because of a person called Aishath Velezinee who was appointed to the commission by [President] Nasheed. She destroyed the whole place. The damage she inflicted on the JSC was so severe that we had to do so much work to bring the place back to order," Gasim explained. "A person called Gabriela came and met us. She told us there are lots of issues that need to be corrected within the judiciary. Judiciaries in all countries should be reformed. Which country has a judiciary that does not need to be reformed?"

Sensing the changing winds, Knaul's report inspired another member of the JSC, Sheikh Shuaib Abdul Rahman, to blow the whistle. The JSC was politicized, he told parliament, and trying expressly "to eliminate Nasheed and the MDP from the elections".[50] The chair of the commission, Supreme Court Judge Adam Mohamed, had abused his post and powers by "using the commission as a political tool".

"Gasim even went to the point of asking the UN Special Rapporteur Knaul when she held a meeting with us to state in her report that it was MDP who torched the courts [during the post-coup riots of 8 February 2012]. I heard him say exactly that," Sheikh Rahman said.

"The politics of the majority control the commission, hence the rule of law, due process and due diligence do not exist in the JSC. The commission has no amount of respect for constitutional principles. The Hulhumale' Magistrate Court is actually abolished automatically with the concept of judicial districts coming into effect upon the ratification of Judicature Act on 10 August 2010. And yet, they continue to run the court."

The election date was around the corner. With the internationals now armed with Knaul's report I knew the Hulhumale Court stunt was done for and that the government would be unable to resist pressure to actually hold elections in September 2013. The lead-up to these was an enjoyable sequence, for the next chapter.

Velezinee's gift for prescience was unfortunately not affected by her vindication.

"We are now in the midst of some very strong political battles," she told us, days after Knaul departed. "I, for one, suspect that the current judiciary may abuse its powers to orchestrate political plots planned to interfere in the independence and fairness of the approaching presidential elections, and use the Supreme Court to issue rulings in favour of a particular side."

Aftermath

It was mid-2014. We were sitting in a small beachside café on Vilingili, watching children play in the sand as the glass and concrete towers of Malé shimmered in the distance.

"I was convinced in the belief that Nasheed was for democracy and I was not going to let it go. I was convinced that where Nasheed lagged it was because he did not have the parliamentary support. I created opportunity for him where I could—I knew his own MPs were not going to totally back him on the constitutional road to judicial reform," Velezinee recalled, sipping from her coffee cup.

The lock of silver in her black hair was gone. Still tiny and stick-thin, she looked much healthier and was quick to smile. She had spent months living in Sri Lanka trying to decompress. The break was semi-enforced, as she was considered both wildly popular and all-but unemployable in the Maldives.

"People praise my honesty, but that honesty scares them," she sighed.

"The MDP are not comfortable and they marginalize me. I find my life has been made very difficult. I have no access to work. People are reluctant to give me contracts, let alone full time work. People are afraid to hire anyone the government is not favouring, especially when the MDP is not favouring me either, as it puts me in a very difficult position."

She had been offered work in Sri Lanka with one of the embassies, but this would have entailed the impossible—giving up speaking on the Maldives. Velezinee was by now the Maldives' most respected and prolific tweeter, and it was not a throne she was about to abdicate.

"What we have done in the last five years is expose the truth of the country, and revealed the extent that the state and the system has failed in the preceding thirty years—the democracy experiment, if you want to call it that," she said.

"It is a mixed feeling. On the one hand the judiciary has absolutely no credibility, and the people are quite aware of the courts and their politics. No-one is under any impression that justice is being delivered from the courts. I have succeeded in what I tried to prove—that the judiciary is not what is promised in the constitution."

"Right now we are at the point where we need to discuss democracy, because with the adoption of the 2008 constitution we really did not make much headway in consolidating democracy at all. We think we are living in a democracy but realistically, we are not, and that constitution is a cover."

I asked if she remembered our first meeting, when she landed on the *Minivan*'s couch in 2010 ahead of the reappointments, shaking like a twig in a strong wind. It seemed an epoch ago.

"I have memory gaps. Personally all this has been terrible. It has cost me years of my life," she said.

"I cried for two weeks in Colombo. I spent the first six months sitting alone. I had gone with the plan to write but had to work on myself. I would panic in the supermarket, trying to buy the simplest things. I felt happy going to the bank—little things people take for granted made me happy. I started doing gardening. I realized mothers take time off for their daughters' A-level exams, but I was... in this."

She waved in the general direction of Malé.

"I haven't had the opportunity to talk to her about this. We've become a bit distant. She's been away since last year. I went with her on a holiday last year; she's not much of a talker. I realized I had neglected her.

"I cannot imagine how it must have been for her. She would do the cooking when she was around, looking after me. I wasn't there. I was only for the JSC. It was all I was doing. I had to learn.

"Only now am I learning to live."

9

PRESIDENT WAHEED AND THE ART OF 'LEGITIMANCY'

> *"Glamis thou art, and Cawdor, and shalt be*
> *What thou art promised. Yet do I fear thy nature,*
> *It is too full o' th' milk of human kindness*
> *To catch the nearest way: thou wouldst be great;*
> *Art not without ambition, but without*
> *The illness should attend it."*

Lady Macbeth

The recently-inaugurated President Dr. Mohamed Waheed Hassan Manik took the podium. The former vice president was headlining his first public rally since controversially assuming office on 7 February 2012, after the mutinying security forces compelled President Nasheed to resign.

Waheed was calm and softly spoken, educated at Stanford in the US and the first Maldivian to both receive a PhD and appear on state television. He had worked for UNICEF, briefly heading the organization's office in Afghanistan, and was widely regarded as a respected educator. He took a liberal view on religion, particularly regarding the rights of women, and had often expressed belief in the confluence of Islam, human rights and democracy. He had three children with his wife Ilham Hussein, all US citizens and educated abroad. His son, Jeffrey Salim Waheed, was among the few people to openly challenge the conduct of the Maldivian judiciary, calling for reform and publicly criticizing it in comment pieces published under his own name on *Minivan*.

Nasheed, on the other hand, had developed a reputation in diplomatic circles for being brash and energetic, quick to show frustration and on occasion to simply storm out of meetings. Like many in the MDP he seemed to operate on a policy of "with me, against me, or get out of my way". Diplomats perceived Waheed to be a mellow counterbalance to what they regarded as Nasheed's erratic impulsiveness. When Waheed assumed power many of them breathed a sigh of relief. Amid the uncertainty and instability he shook their hands, said all the right things, promised a "unity" caretaker government and early elections. He was reasonable and unambitious—a force for stability. Here was someone the diplomats could finally work with.

Waheed was joined on the podium by the leaders of the former opposition, cramming themselves onto the platform behind him. Several appeared to be giggling.

"Be courageous. This is no longer the age of colonialism. Today no foreign country can influence the Maldives. Today we will maintain our sovereignty with bravery," yelled Waheed to the assembled crowd, gesticulating angrily. "Be courageous. We will not back down an inch. Today, the change [in power] in the Maldives is what Allah has willed. This did not happen because of one or two people coming out into the streets. Nobody had been waiting for this. Nobody even saw this day. This change came because Allah willed to protect Islam and decent Maldivian norms. Be courageous. Today you are all mujaheddin."

The foreign diplomats put down *Minivan's* translation of his speech[1] and went for lunch together in Colombo. Waheed had only been in power a few weeks. What was going on?

Waheed's Party: GIP

Dr Waheed's Gaumee Itthihaad Party (GIP) entered into coalition with the MDP ahead of the 2008 election that ousted Gayoom. GIP was tiny and never attracted more than several thousand members, but it did have a core of respected technocrats such as Dr. Mustafa Lutfi, who would become Education Minister and later the first chancellor of the newly inaugurated Maldives National University. It was the only party besides the MDP that attempted a manifesto, but it lacked membership and grassroots appeal and had difficulty distinguishing its generally progressive agenda from the MDP.

Education

When Nasheed won the election, Dr. Waheed became vice president and GIP was awarded the education, fisheries and economic development portfolios in cabinet. GIP's ministers were by all accounts effective, particularly Dr. Lutfi, who led ambitious attempts at education reform and made lifting the poor standard of teaching a priority. Former president Ibrahim Nasir had made English the teaching language as a way to ensure that Maldivians had access to jobs in the burgeoning tourism industry. While this ensured basic fluency (and made life much easier for foreign reporters at *Minivan News*), the majority of teachers were imported from India and Sri Lanka where the standard of English speaking varied greatly. This became particularly challenging in high school, and there was little standardized testing until the Cambridge GSCE "O" levels. The annual pass rate for these in 2008 was just 27 per cent, resulting in 5,000–6,000 16-year-olds pumped out onto the streets every year with no functional high school qualification.

Options for these young people were limited: there were no apprenticeships or tradecrafts, and the majority of skilled and unskilled labour was already performed by imported foreign workers for a pittance. Moreover, the minimum legal age of employment was 18; most young adults were all but unemployable after two years in the wilderness. Mass unemployment among youth was compounded by family support and patronage structures that discouraged participation in the entry-level private-sector workforce; many middle-class young people of property-owning parents were funded by their parents' high rental incomes in Malé, and as a result had very high expectations of the workplace—many employers found it hard to generate interest in roles short of "Managing Director".

Tackling this problem by refurbishing education and opening young people to opportunities was one of the MDP's major pledges, driving its election to office. Lutfi's mega-reforms of the sector saw the pass rate steadily climb to 37 per cent in 2011 and 46 per cent in 2012, even after the coup that toppled Nasheed's government.

The reforms also included an attempt to make Islam and Dhivehi optional subjects at A-level (senior high school). The existing practice of forcing these subjects on students as part of a nationalistic agenda limited their ability to take other subjects, and was an obstacle to young Maldivians becoming the "world citizens"[2] Lufti envisioned. It meant that almost no Maldivian student pursued science because these compulsory subjects bloated their five-subject schedules before they could take the prerequisite biology, mathematics, chemistry and physics they needed

Lufti's efforts to modernize senior high school were naturally seized on by the political opposition and the Adhaalath Party, portrayed as an assault on national identity and evidence of the government's supposed irreligiousness. Gayoom's opposition-led parliament ultimately passed a vote to dismiss him, after the helpless MDP parliamentarians walked out of the building in disgust.

It was a shrewd electoral manoeuvre on behalf of the dictator, as the young, educated and informed tended to overwhelmingly vote against him. More sinisterly, it was also a move driven by market forces. Educational failure, a shortage of appealing jobs and the near total lack of entertainment had resulted in staggering levels of boredom and idleness among Maldivian young people. This purposelessness made it easy to capture young people in a cycle of drug abuse.

Drugs

The most common street drug was hash oil, closely followed by brown sugar heroin; the latter could be ordered by phone and delivered to your door faster than a pizza. It had flooded the streets since the 1980s, brought in from Afghanistan via Pakistan and Trivandrum, India, either smuggled in luggage or dropped overboard from large shipping vessels surrounding the island city.

Like everything else in the Maldives, drugs were political; older reformed addicts at the drug rehabilitation centres in Malé would readily name politicians sitting in parliament as the country's early pioneers of the heroin trade.

This much was acknowledged even on the side of the former dictatorship. Umar Naseer, a brutish former policeman under Gayoom who later became a rabble-rousing politician devoted to Nasheed's downfall (and eventually Home Minister) himself made such claims. Naseer had contested the PPM primaries seeking to become its presidential candidate over Gayoom's half-brother Abdulla Yameen, backed by many of the authentically anti-Nasheed crowd.

Unsurprisingly, Naseer lost this attempt to inconvenience the succession. Following the vote, he alleged major discrepancies including the influencing of voters, vote buying and intimidation of his supporters—when they were even allowed to vote.

"We even witnessed that those who are heavily involved in drug trafficking were present at the polling station wearing Yameen's campaign caps. Not only did they exert undue influence, they travelled to islands with stashes of black money and attempted to turn the votes. In fact they even did turn some votes. We came out knowing that the referee, the linesman and even the match commissioner along with his 11 players were playing on [Yameen's] side."[3]

Whatever the connections, the drug issue was clearly heavily intertwined with politics. Nasheed's new government gave vice president Dr. Waheed the task of unravelling the problem. Between this critical job and Dr. Lutfi's reform of the education sector, Dr. Waheed's GIP had an opportunity to give young Maldivians their first fighting chance in decades. Unfortunately for them—and the MDP—his ambitions proved rather more far-reaching.

Act I: The Thane of Cawdor

The first inkling of Waheed's disaffection with Nasheed's new government emerged in April 2010, not even two years into its term.

"I don't feel I am able to contribute, that consultation is not there. The people of the Maldives didn't elect me to sleep for five years. I believe I am part of the leadership of this country and it is necessary for me to be involved," he told *Minivan News* during an interview in April 2010. "The way we function in [this] government is not too different to what it used to be. It's still one man running the show."[4]

Nasheed's high-energy boisterousness and willingness to trample vested interests did lend a certain "my way or the highway" flavour to government, but comparison to the former dictatorship? Torture had ceased, the country was awash with new freedoms and potential. The world had taken notice of the Maldives, and thrust it into the spotlight as both an icon of modern Islamic democracy and a symbol in the fight against climate change.

Dr. Waheed's comment was, in retrospect, something of an early warning. *Minivan* interviewed him after he had, in his capacity as vice president, appeared on opposition-aligned resort tycoon Gasim Ibrahim's television station to complain that Nasheed was not listening to him. To the activist MDP and its finely tuned blend of "with us or against us" politics, the vice president's denunciation of his boss on the *Hot Seat* programme of the rabidly anti-government VTV was outright betrayal.

The effect was predictable. Cabinet meetings turned frosty, Waheed found himself consulted less. As his isolation increased, staff in the President's Office began treating him with ridicule. An insider recalled the moment the Maldivian team made the final of the South Asian Football Federation Championship.

"Get the captain on the phone," ordered the vice president, as the raucous noise of cheering staffers died down. Someone dialled and handed him the phone.

"This is Waheed," the VP declared.

"Who?" asked the captain.

The staffers sniggered, as Waheed fumbled to explain he was the vice president.

The little humiliations were many, but the greatest blow came with the MDP's decision to sever its coalition agreement with GIP, sacking the party's ministers. Caught between the two sides, Dr. Lufti abandoned GIP and joined the MDP out of a pragmatic desire to continue with the education reforms he had started. GIP no longer had a reason to exist, and Dr. Waheed found himself truly sidelined. He could only watch as Nasheed travelled the world, collecting awards and having his praises sung in the international press.

"Will you be running for the presidency in 2013?" we asked Waheed in a follow up interview in 2010.[5]

"I have no idea where this is coming from," he said, pleased. "There are lots of political pundits in Maldives, there's no shortage of them now. It must be coming from them. No, I have not made that decision. I think it's a little early. But if that's how the political formulations work in the country, and if that's the best way I can serve, then why not?"

Act II: The Three Witches

Gayoom's opposition watched Dr. Waheed's growing disaffection with keen interest. His mother was from the southern atoll of Thinadhoo and had been tortured during the regime, but Waheed himself had spent most of his time outside the country at his various UN postings. This fact had been exploited in some of Gayoom's 2008 campaign material, a crudely offensive cartoon "Waheed Come and Waheed Go", set to the tune of the Rednex's 1995 one-hit wonder, "Cotton Eye Joe".[6]

Having neutralized Waheed as a political obstacle and distracted by their many political battles of 2011, the MDP left him to his own devices. He had a house, a title, an office and a single secretary, and was wheeled out at events such as long-winded UN meetings and school prize-givings. In return, he stayed quiet.

But when Nasheed ordered the military to detain the Chief Judge of the Criminal Court, Dr. Waheed made his move.

"Besides all the international legal obligations, the Government of Maldives is bound by the Maldives Constitution 2008 which prohibits arbitrary arrest and forced disappearance. We have just witnessed the first possible violation since the dawn of democracy in our country. I cannot understand why this is not an issue for everyone in this country," he wrote on his website, in a blog post titled "Freedom from fear: are we about to lose it?"[7]

"Those of us who have struggled for freedom in this country for over 30 years, are wondering whether we have wasted our efforts. I am ashamed and totally devastated by the fact that this is happening in a government in which I am the elected the Vice President."

The MDP government had thus far displayed remarkable unity and loyalty to Nasheed, resisting the opposition's attempts to split the party and sow discord. Waheed's reaction to the detention of Judge Abdulla was the chink in the armour Gayoom's clan needed.

Late at night on 30 January 2012, exactly a week prior to the toppling of the government, Waheed met privately with three key members of the opposition at his private residence. These were president of the Adhaalath Party Sheikh Imran, Umar Naseer (at the time vice president of Gayoom's PPM), and vice president of Gayoom's former Dhivehi Rayyithunge Party, Ibrahim "Mavota" Shareef.

The relationship between the ruling and opposition party was fractious. Many in Nasheed's government had been imprisoned and tortured under Gayoom's regime, while Gayoom's side resented the "theft" of their government by a man they had jailed as a "petty criminal". Despite the urging of many MDP members, Nasheed had pledged himself "magnanimous in victory" and left Gayoom to his own devices.

By the time Waheed's secret meeting took place, the two sides were not talking to one another; whenever the MDP tried to compromise, as with the appointment of the Supreme Court judges, the party tended to come off second best.

As Waheed had spent much of his life outside the country (and unlike his mother, had largely escaped torment at Gayoom's hands) this gave him an air of impartiality he used to occasionally hold meetings with Gayoom's opposition, playing himself up as a mediator. The MDP proletariat regarded such "unsanctioned" exposure to the opposition as deeply suspicious, particularly since these meetings tended to take place at his residence in the early hours of the morning.

"He has an office," a President's Office official remarked to me, after one early morning escapade.

Waheed may have wished for the 30 January meeting to remain discreet, but it was the nature of Malé's small size and saturated politics that any such fraternization was quickly spotted. The opposition cared less for secrecy than Waheed did: immediately following the 30 January meeting, the three emerged and called a press conference, announcing their decision "to pledge allegiance to Mohamed Waheed Hassan Manik".[8] "We have asked the vice president to save this nation," Shareef declared to reporters. "I would like to call upon the security forces [to accept that] since the vice president is elected by Maldivians, and should the president be incapacitated to perform his legal duties, the vice president must assume the duties of the president. [And so] we have decided that he has to start performing these duties."

Umar Naseer was later asked by Australian SBS reporter Mark Davis as to whether the public call to mutiny had been privately accompanied by other inducements.

"There were," he confessed. "We called on the army and police and said that if a person was fired from his position because of their refusal to follow an unlawful order, the opposition would take care of them."

Responsibility for defining which orders were "unlawful" and which were not natural fell to the former regime, providing a convenient euphemism for the mutiny a week later that would terminate Nasheed's government.

Alarm bells rang for me after Waheed's meeting. The MDP government saw in him a foppish and ineffectual boor they had sidelined for the handing out of children's swimming certificates. We knew that he was taken very seriously by the international community, partially because of his UN background, but also due to his diplomatic air that gave him credibility with the majority of visiting officials not in possession of Maldivian context. Given the impenetrability of the Maldives, this was the case with most of them.

Waheed would later give evidence at an inquiry into the events of 7 February, an affair arranged by his new government with the blessing of the Commonwealth. "It was Adhaalath Party President Imran who called and requested the [30 January] meeting," Waheed said, according to a transcript of his meeting with the inquiry panel.[9]

"A few days passed, and he called me again. I think it was the night of 30 January. They would come to meet me after the protests ended for the night ... When they came, there were about 12–15 of them. There were some leaders, leaders of protests too. This included Imran, Umar Naseer ... I can't recall their names right now ... they came.

"If there is a change in leadership, given how the protests are going, are you ready to take on the responsibilities of the government?" they responded.

"There is no need for a question like that. If, for any reason, the president steps aside, I should take his place. That's my legal responsibility", I told them.

"Say you had to carry out the responsibility. What would you do then?" one of them, I don't know who, asked me.

"I am a member of a small party. This government came to power in a coalition," I responded. If I were to take on the responsibility, I said, "I will work with everyone."

"If that's how you stand, we are with you," they responded.

"We have a pact now," one of them said to me as they left.

That was how the meeting went.

There was a cabinet meeting the next morning. The moment I walked in, before I was able to say a word, Sheikh Hussein Rasheed jumped up.

"That was some meeting last night! I will not sit at the same table with someone who's been in such a meeting!" Sheikh Hussein Rasheed walked out.

Other Ministers wanted to know what I had discussed at the meeting. I got a little upset.

"None of your business. I don't have to answer to Ministers," I said. I was really very displeased with them.

"I don't have to tell you anything," I said. "It's not that I am going to keep it from you, it's just that there's no need for such questioning."

The questions came mostly from people like Shifa, Zulfa, Hassan Latheef. The rest had none to ask.

I told them what I have just told you, what happened [at the meeting], what we talked about.

They began asking more questions. The President [Nasheed] interrupted.

"The vice president has explained what happened. That's the end of it," he said.

Nasheed claimed to have phoned Waheed during the coup. Waheed denied this, playing himself up as a passive observer.

"President Nasheed didn't call me. He made no attempt to discuss things with me. And, given our relationship at the time, I didn't want to take the initiative and get involved in things he hadn't invited me to. He hadn't called me, so I didn't know how things were going," he told the inquiry.

It wasn't as if those involved had signed, stamped and sealed a written masterplan.

The Written Masterplan

The written masterplan landed on the desk of *Minivan News* in late August 2013, a month before the scheduled presidential election. Its arrival followed a week of scuttling intrigue, blackmail and betrayal involving a series of leaked videos of a Colombo hotel room and starring a naked woman and a robust gentleman who very much resembled Supreme Court Justice Ali Hameed.[10] She was not his wife.

The former Deputy CEO of the Maldives Ports Authority, Ahmed Faiz, was widely believed to be an individual familiar with the video's circulation. Faiz was known up until that point to be affiliated with President Waheed's GIP, taking on the messier tasks of running a Maldivian political party. He performed the role with cartoonishly villainous incompetence, thoroughly demonstrated in a steady stream of leaked audio recordings arriving in the *Minivan News* inbox.[11] One of these, recorded in a crowded coffee shop, involved Faiz attempting to enlist gang members to go around loudly menacing people in MDP-leaning cafés.

"Not necessarily going out into the streets with huge knives and attacking people, okay?" he explains. "What I want is, for example, when key people are in a certain place ... for example, four or five of these people might be in a coffee-shop. You go in there, do you understand? You go and barge in right into the middle, and say, no need to be discreet at all, just say it out loud openly, 'Hey you [expletive] dogs, this country is being destroyed because of you [expletive]. Don't even think you can do what you please with this country.' You know what I'm saying. Start off in this manner, and then say 'We support this government. We will keep protecting this government as long as there is even a single drop of blood left in us.' You should also go on motorcycle rides. What you will do is go around on your motorcycles one night, all around Malé, yelling things like 'Ganjabo' [pothead] and finish it up in about half an hour. Small things like this need to be done."

Ganjabo, meaning marijuana addict, was a common term used by Gayoom's side to portray Nasheed as a degenerate druggie. In exchange for the gang's services Faiz promised jobs, cash and other corrupt incentives, as well as promises to get their people out jail "with a single phone call".

Faiz openly acknowledged the tape when we rang him about it. His only concern was that it was five months old, and therefore dated. Allegiances had already shifted.

Police eventually arrested him not for corruption, but in connection with leaking the video featuring the allegedly fornicating judge. Waheed distanced himself from his henchman, leaving Faiz to rot in a cell with a sense of aggrieved abandonment. The MDP came to his "rescue", its lawyers by this time adept at following people through the Maldivian prison system.

Freed, Faiz switched sides and joined the party. A day later the "coup agreement" surfaced.[12]

"As the current President of the Maldives, Mohamed Nasheed of G. Keneryge, has disrespected Islam as well as the country's laws and regulations, declared blatantly anti-Islamic sentiments, obstructed the enforcement of Islamic hadd [punishments] in the Maldives, carried out laadheenee [irreligious or secular] actions, illegally arrested politicians, committed many acts that undermine the dignity of the country's courts, and since the fraternal political groups have determined that he is unfit to remain as President of the Maldives, this agreement is made among the fraternal political groups to remove him completely from Maldivian politics and do what is required to completely erase the Christian-influenced Maldivian Democratic Party (MDP) from the Maldivian political arena," read the introduction.

Dated 29 December 2011—less than a week after the "Defend Islam" rally on the 23rd that united the fractious opposition parties—the agreement featured the signatures and seals of the Progressive Party of Maldives (PPM), the Adhaalath Party (AP), Dhivehi Qaumee Party (DQP), Jumhoree Party (JP), Dhivehi Rayithunge Party (DRP), People's Alliance (PA) and the Civil Alliance (a rent-a-mob group of "Islamic" NGOs that usually rallied on the whims of the PPM).

Signatures on the document appeared to include those of Umar Naseer, Sheikh Shaheem Ali Saeed, leader of the DQP Dr. Hassan Saeed, leader of the JP Gasim Ibrahim, DRP leader Ahmed Thasmeen Ali, and Deputy Speaker of Parliament Ahmed Nazim on behalf of the PA, Yameen's holding party prior to the formation of the PPM.

Reading like a playbook for the 2012 coup, it proposed an "Islamic symposium" on 24 February that would escalate into civil disobedience and protest by the security services. Nasheed's bodyguards would escort him off Malé for his "security", while the Supreme Court, via Gayoom's lawyer Azima Shukoor, would arrange to have him found incapable of continuing in the presidency. Opposition-aligned media would work to escalate the situation, while the military's unwillingness to resort to lethal force could be counted on to ensure their eventual laying down of arms and joining the protest.

"It is believed that under the circumstances, with the situation brought to this [state], the military will have no other option and will accept the proposal. If they do not accept, the defence minister will do it forcefully," the plan stated.

Dr. Waheed would be sworn into the presidency and immediately dissolve cabinet. Retired Colonel Mohamed Nazim would be appointed Chief of Defence Force; dismissed Assistant Commissioner of Police Abdulla Riyaz installed as Police Commissioner. Umar Naseer would become Home Minister.

Nasheed was to be criminalized and the MDP delegitimized. In the interim the regime would back the then president of the party Dr. Ibrahim Didi, described in the document as politically weak and easily manipulated. The MDP's chairperson, MP "Reeko" Moosa Manik, could remain in his position as he was deemed susceptible to blackmail and threats against his business interests.

The project included a budget.

"It has been calculated and agreed that a total of 43 (forty-three) million rufiya [US$2.8 million] will have to be spent to complete the matters stated in this agreement and to fulfil the demands of the persons who will provide assistance. The funding will be secured through the political parties involved in this agreement and supportive businessmen. PA parliamentary group leader Ahmed Nazim will be tasked with collecting the funds and spending it in accordance with the agreement. And 20% per cent (8.4 million rufiyaa) has been handed over to Nazim by the Jumhooree Party on 26 December 2011."

The document was impossible to fully authenticate; the parties involved either refuted it or refused to comment. The seals appeared genuine, and the plan consistent with actual events if not dates. If the document was real the plan had apparently been expedited by circumstances but was otherwise broadly executed as written, making 7 February substantially more planned than advertised.

The *Minivan News* team was at first sceptical over the authenticity of the document; writing, sealing and signing what appeared to be evidence of treason seemed intellectually short-sighted even by the standards of contemporary Maldivian politics. But on reflection it made perfect sense: the opposition parties had been at each other's throats, and the creation of a mutually-incriminating document was a way to guarantee enough cohesion to bring about the change in government. We ran the story with appropriate caveats and invited readers to evaluate the source material for themselves.

Act III: 'Legitimancy'

As the dust settled on the events of 7 February, a battle of an altogether different kind was just beginning. To the outside Nasheed appeared to have resigned amid political turmoil and his vice president hastily sworn in by the speaker of parliament. It was not until 10.47pm, after Dr. Waheed's swearing in, that the MDP issued a statement condemning the change of government as a coup.

If the party expected the international community to condemn the day's events and hold off legitimizing the new government, they were to be disappointed. Standard procedure among democratic nations was to issue a statement welcoming new leaders and acknowledging legitimate transfers of power, usually as a reflexive formality. In cases where the transfer is disputed, the decision by other nations to recognize or refute a new government can have immense political impact locally. In the case of the Maldives, Western powers looked to India as the regional authority and as one of the few countries with a permanent diplomatic presence in Malé.

This put the Indian High Commissioner Dnyaneshwar M. Mulay in a powerful position—a fact not lost on the rioting opposition, which would have been very conscious of India's military intervention during the 1988 coup attempt.

Sure enough, Gayoom's half-brother Abdulla Yameen was with Mulay as the events of 7 February unfolded. Mulay, an intellectual and softly-spoken poet, had enjoyed a fairly uncontroversial posting in Malé, hosting Republic Day celebrations and generally sidestepping local politics. Nonetheless, while the rest of the opposition leaders were celebrating Nasheed's resignation in police headquarters, Yameen was with Mulay.

Senior figures in Nasheed's government, including former Chief of Defence Ameen Faisal, would subsequently accuse Mulay of failing to pass critical information to Indian authorities as the chaotic events unfolded. "I believe that proper information was not passed on to Indian authorities," Faisal alleged. "I was surprised that instead of contacting us, the government [of the Maldives], Mulay was having a discussion with opposition party leaders like Yameen in the Indian High Commission, when the coup was happening. In a situation like this, why call the opposition and not establish contact with the government? Before this happened, I never suspected [any conspiracy]. We were very close," he told India's *Open* magazine.[13]

"I maintained a close relationship with Mulay. I called him three or four times while the coup was underway. I could not contact President Nasheed. At that point, he was inside the army headquarters and his phone was jammed.

I spoke to Foreign Minister Ahmed Naseem, instead, for his advice on seeking Indian intervention to control the situation. He told me that President Nasheed did not want any military intervention as it was an 'internal matter'," Faisal recalled.

"Later, Naseem called me to request some assistance from India. As the national security advisor, I called up Mulay and sought Indian assistance ... He asked me to ask the foreign minister to send a note. I told Mulay that this was no time to be sending notes or love letters."

India's Ministry of External Affairs acknowledged that concerns about Mulay's conduct had been raised by the ousted government, but expressed full confidence in their diplomat.

Mulay declined to comment on the specific allegations when we raised the issue with him, "as my government has already responded", but did describe them as "completely baseless, a flight of fancy".

We rang Yameen. He confessed he had met with Mulay on the morning of 7 February. "It was Mulay who SMSed me and asked me to come and discuss the national crisis," he said. "Mulay asked me to get a checklist of demands [from the protesters] and try to see if there could be a three-day respite."

Asked why he believed Mulay had contacted him, Yameen said he believed it was "because PPM was the largest opposition party [at the time]."

Whatever Yameen's influence, in the face of confused signals from the ousted government Mulay's approach appeared to have been to stabilize the situation and buy time.

A Waheed presidency was also not a bad option from his position. Mulay had periodically hosted gatherings of what he termed his group of "wise men", Maldivian "intellectuals" who would sit around in the High Commissioner's residence (liquor-licensed under the Vienna Convention governing sovereign territory) discussing poetry and the challenges of Islamic radicalism. Waheed, ex-UN and Stanford-educated, was one of the stars of his prestigious stable. This I learned during a dinner he hosted for all senior Maldivian editors prior to his departure in 2013, at which he berated the press establishment for its extreme politicization and indulgence of Islamic radicalism.

There were, Mulay declared to the assembled editors, two outcomes for the Maldives: one was Pakistan.

He went around the circle in the manner of a lecturing school-master. Did the journalists want to live in a Pakistan? Challenged individually, they shook their heads sulkily, in the manner of misbehaving children dragged into the principal's office. Unwilling to take on the authority figure, they stared at the ground and shuffled their feet guiltily. He reached the only woman in the room, a head-scarfed lady working for the state broadcaster. Would she want to bring up her children in the kind of country the media seemed bent on creating?

"I don't feel comfortable answering that question because of the other people in this room," she said, quietly.

Mulay reached *Minivan News*. We were, he declared, the only news worth reading. The circle glared at me with the murderous stare children reserve for the teacher's pet.

The lecture resumed. Mulay sounded personally aggrieved that Waheed— one of *his* wise men—had apparently been transformed on assuming the presidency, indulging Islamic radicals and promoting nationalistic xenophobia. Indian workers, including doctors, were being mistreated, robbed and having their passports withheld by the government, which did nothing.

All this hinted at a potential error of judgement by India on 7 February. Waheed was apparently not the person Mulay had believed him to be when the Indians acknowledged his new government.

The Americans appeared to have outsourced approval of the new government to India, but as more information flowed in over subsequent days they seemed to backtrack. "President Waheed informed us that the security situation in the Maldives is now under control and generally peaceful. He expressed his strong commitment to a peaceful transition of power, the preservation of democracy going forward," said State Department Spokeswoman Victoria Nuland during the daily press briefing on 7 February.[14]

Assistant Secretary Robert Blake, himself a former ambassador to Sri Lanka and the Maldives, had added the country to his South Asian itinerary, she said.

The next day journalists asked her about Nasheed's allegations that the change of power was a coup.

"Well, our view as of yesterday—and I don't think that that has changed— obviously, we'll collect more information going forward—was that this was handled constitutionally," Nuland said.[15]

By 9 February, footage of the new government violently cracking down on protesters was all over international cable news networks. "We have been concerned about the fact that it doesn't appear to have been as peaceful in subsequent days as it was initially," said Nuland.[16] Blake would, she explained, "encourage [a] national unity conversation".

"So does the US consider the new government a legitimate government of the Maldives?" asked a reporter.

"We do," replied Nuland.

An asterisk subsequently appeared beside this comment in the official transcript. "The United States will work with the new Government of the Maldives but believes that the circumstances surrounding the transfer of power must be clarified, and suggests all parties agree to an independent mechanism to do so," it read.

"I got myself in a place yesterday that was not borne out by the facts," Nuland told the press gallery during the following day's news briefing. "We do not have a clear view of the facts at the moment."

By the time the facts did emerge, the new government had entrenched itself and appointed much of Gayoom's extended family to the cabinet: his daughter, Dunya Maumoon, was made State Minister of Foreign Affairs, while his lawyer, Azima Shukoor, became Attorney General. Gayoom's son, Gassan Maumoon, was appointed Minister of State for Human Resources. Sheikh Mohamed Didi, head of the Civil Alliance group responsible for organizing the 23 December rally "to defend Islam", was appointed State Minister for Islamic Affairs, while Mohamed Hussein Shareef, Gayoom's spokesperson "Mundhu", became Youth Minister.[17]

These names were very familiar to Maldivians, and an obvious indication of who was back in charge. We put together a handy spreadsheet for the benefit of the foreigners.

Dr. Waheed had claimed that his "national unity" government would also be a new government. But with every appointment it was becoming increasingly obvious, perhaps even to the odd foreign diplomat, that this was very much an old government.

The First Interview

What was Waheed's role in all this? Was he an unwilling puppet? What sort of hold did they have on him? Who was really running the show? Such questions began to trickle in from the sharper diplomats. Visiting journalists— even the normally fractious Indian media—were unanimous in condemning the coup, dismissing Waheed as a puppet at best, dictator at worst.

Waheed's own advisors were quite open about this. Dr. Hassan Saeed of the DQP, appointed the new president's "Special Advisor" after his arrival in the presidency, confided to a group of Maldivian students that his boss was "politically the weakest person in the Maldives" with "a lot of legitimacy issues". This was not anecdotal; one of them recorded him and posted the audio on Maldivian social media.[18]

"There was no major role for President Waheed in the previous government. Very many days [spent] bored in the office," Dr. Saeed explained. "I wouldn't just sit. Honestly. When an educated man like [Waheed] whiles the day away being like this, going on the Internet ... [chuckles are heard. A voice says: 'on Facebook'. More chuckles]. Really it is sad. This is how Waheed was. What happens when this job comes all of a sudden?"

We rang the new president's spokesperson for comment, the looming and rather avian Masood Imad. The president's team had spoken to Saeed, Imad explained, who insisted he "had been played" and the recording "taken out of context".[19]

The most surreal moment was Waheed's first major press conference with foreign media, just over a week after his arrival in office. Compared to the diplomats, the visiting journalists were under little illusion as to the nature of the power transition. The Indian media in particular were, perhaps for the first time, united in earnest condemnation of the "coup regime".

Holding a meet-the-media session was risky. His earlier "Do I look like a dictator?" comment had foreign headline writers rubbing their hands with glee. The need to go ahead with it belied the urgent pressure on the government to convince the world of its democratic legitimacy.

The interview[20] was to be held in Waheed's house (he had opted to remain in the vice presidential residence on Hileaage). There was some official reticence about me attending this event; I was considered "local media" and thus full of difficult, context-enriched questions best confined to the safety of a Dhivehi-speaking audience.

I found an uncrumpled shirt, had Reuters write me a letter stating that I was working for them,and walked past security into Waheed's living room. Dr Hassan Saeed was there, as well as a mysterious Malaysian gentleman who spoke over the top of Waheed whenever the questions became too difficult.

I went up to the man afterwards and asked him his name.

"Just a friend passing through," he replied.

Exactly who the "friend" was or why he was "passing through" remained a mystery, although he would later show up in Sri Lanka representing the Maldivian government, ruling out early elections and insisting that Nasheed's resignation was "voluntary". Subsequent research revealed him to be Dr. Ananda Kumarasiri, a thirty-year career diplomat with the Malaysian Foreign Service and author of a Buddhist book, *Siddhartha: Prince of Peace*.[21]

"[Nasheed's] own doings led to his voluntary resignation, including the arrest of a Judge of the Criminal Court and other atrocious acts which turned the public wrath against him," Dr. Kumarasiri alleged to his Sri Lankan audience.[22] "There was no duress whatsoever on him, he wrote the resignation letter in his own handwriting and handed it over in front of the TV and the public."

The Maldives, he alleged was in severe financial straits as a result of Nasheed's mismanagement, "and cannot even think about snap polls."

Several foreign governments were extremely interested in Dr. Kumarasiri's presence during Waheed's press conference. We speculated that he was a friend of the Gayoom clan shipped in to make sure Waheed didn't snap in front of the foreign press. They had reason to worry. Mark Davis from SBS Australia, showing no sign of the deference shown to the president by the selected Indian press pack, steamrolled him.

It was a pleasure to watch Davis at work. He opened with a personal challenge, asking Waheed to comment on his brother Naushad Waheed Hassan's resignation as deputy of the UK High Commission, and his call for Waheed to follow.[23] "I say this to my brother—you are my brother and I will always love you. Do not rob our people of our right to choose our government," Naushad had declared in London a few days earlier. "Do not be party to this police brutality that is ongoing in the country. Do not join with the people of the autocratic ruler [former] President Gayoom. Do the right thing—resign and hold fresh elections. Let the people of the Maldives decide."

"I didn't appoint my brother to the High Commission, he was appointed by the former president," Waheed told Davis. "I know where his loyalty is."

The hot issue was the prospect of early elections to restore democratic legitimacy. This was a shrewd demand by the MDP, a "moving forward" step that banked on the likelihood of storming the polls via a sympathy vote instead of simply calling for Nasheed's reinstatement. Waheed's, Gayoom's and indeed US Assistant Secretary of State Robert Blake's position was that the Maldives was not ready for an election, the latter having apparently been convinced of this after consultation with certain "independent" civil society groups.

"I believe the conditions have to be right. We have to have a calm atmosphere, we have to address some of the deep rifts that we have in the political situation in the country, and then move towards free and fair elections," President Waheed insisted. Nasheed had resigned, he was vice president, and the Speaker of Parliament had invited him to be president.

"You are an educated man who has been deeply involved in the United Nations, you know that that when a general puts a gun to your head, even metaphorically, that is not a resignation. Do you not accept that?" asked Davis.

"I do not accept that," replied Waheed.

He was about to continue, when Dr. Kumarasiri jumped in.

"If I may interject, from the video tapes, I do not see how my colleague has got this impression that there was a coup," said the voice from the corner. "If there was a coup then [it would show] from the tapes ... from the evidence."

That evidence—of Nasheed offering to resign in exchange for his family being protected—would appear in Davis' piece.

"He publicly announced his resignation in front of television," emphasized Waheed. "He could have said something, indicated that he was under duress—but he didn't. And then I get a call from the Speaker telling me that he is expecting to receive resignation from the president. And as soon as he received that resignation he told me to come and I was sworn in by the Chief Justice ... As far as I'm concerned the whole process was legal, and I maintain the legitimacy of this government."

"Does it concern you that people in this country are terrified of you and the people around you? Does it concern you that dozens of people, whom you were colleagues with, were brutally beaten?" asked Davis, unrelenting.

"People are terrified because some people are propagating violence. We have seen so many police buildings burned down," Waheed said.

"Those were buildings, not people," Davis returned.

Waheed insisted on the need for "political divisions to be resolved" before holding elections. "We can't live under the threat of violence and conflict. We are ready to engage and move forward. This country is too small for violence and confrontation," he said.

"All the violence on the streets of the capital has been by police and their supporters—now your allies. They were the violent ones," observed Davis.

"That is a matter of opinion," said Waheed.

"No it's not. Would you dispute that?" said Davis.

"You know there was one instance where you saw police violence on camera. But there have been demonstrations in this country for one month," Waheed replied.

"From the opposition," noted Davis.

I explored the theme, asking whether given the baton-happy scenes of 8 February, Waheed felt he had control of the police and military.

"I have full control over them. I am not shy to take responsibility. Including for the law enforcement agencies," he declared.

Waheed emphatically emphasized his role as an innocent and ignorant bystander in the affairs of 7 February. I was curious as to the response of the assembled journalists on learning of his secret late January meeting with opposition leaders.

"You have maintained that the events of the 7th were not planned. However, on the early morning of January 31 you met opposition leaders in this house, who subsequently gave a press conference in which they pledged allegiance to you, called on you to take over the government, and called on the police and military to follow your orders. Based on that press conference, which was widely reported in local media at the time, do you still maintain that the events of the 7th were spontaneous?" I asked.

Reporters looked up from their notebooks, eyes glinting.

"I said it was a spontaneous change as nobody really expected that events would turn out that way," Waheed said. "You're right, I met them, and they asked me whether in the eventuality that there was a change, would I be ready. Because I have very much been in the background here—not involved in most of the policy making and so on .... But it is my constitutional responsibility to step in. All I said was 'this is the purpose I was sworn in for', and that as vice president I was ready for such a situation. That was it—nobody expected things to turn out this way. Who expected the police to come out and demonstrate? It was totally bizarre."

"That means certain political parties had anticipated a possible change that might come," said another journalist, smelling blood.

"I don't know that it was so much anticipation as their wish that there would be a change of government," Waheed rallied.

I asked Waheed about Umar Naseer's remark to a mob of at least a thousand several days earlier that he had personally warned Nasheed that there would be bloodshed unless he stepped down.[24]

"Given comments such as this coming from other former opposition parties, do you still maintain that there was no intimidation in the resignation of Mohamed Nasheed?"

"Umar Naseer should explain himself," Waheed said. "I cannot explain for him. He is not known to be someone who is particularly careful with what he says. You know him better. Whatever he said in the political rally—and I have heard people have said that he said these things—you should really ask him. He is around in Malé."

I asked Waheed if it was true that the MDP had been given a three-day ultimatum to participate in what he was badging his "national unity government", as per a statement on the president's office website.

"No ultimatum has been given to anyone. I can assure you. We will continue to remain open to discussion and dialogue, forever," he said.

An Indian journalist caught on.

"You have informed that the MDP should join a national government by February 20," said the reporter.

"No we haven't, I deny that. I am not aware of it. If somebody has, then somebody else is doing this," said Waheed, in perhaps his most insightful comment of the afternoon.

"On the president's website there is a statement that says 'inform us by Feb 20 if you want to join the national unity government,'" said the journalist, reading from his phone.

"No, that is not true. I have certainly not signed anything to that effect, and until now I have not even heard about it," Waheed said, growing flustered.

"But it is on the website."

"Anything can be on the website. I am categorically denying that there is an ultimatum to MDP. There is no ultimatum. I continue to remain wanting to engage with them, and I will continue to the last day," he said.

I noticed Dr. Saeed attempting to blend into the shadows in the corner of the room. I asked him to confirm his identity for the benefit of those present—Gayoom's former Attorney General—and then asked him to confirm that he had in 2007 indeed been the first person to outline the laundry-list of abuse allegations against the judge so controversially detained by Nasheed's government.

"In that constitution the president was the head of the judiciary. So it was my legal and moral obligation to raise that issue with him, which I did," said Saeed. "I did not know if it was followed up."

I refrained from pointing out that it had been, seven years later, resulting in the present situation.

The pleasant afternoon concluded with Waheed promising a full inquiry into the events of 7 February.

Answering Awkward Questions

The 8 February crackdown, Waheed's unsettling interview, the Gayoom-era cabinet appointments and the Criminal Court's arrest warrant for Nasheed—not to mention a growing quantity of witness testimony and video footage—were creating some awkward questions for Waheed.

By late February, foreign governments which had ignored the Maldives after 2008's victory for democracy and reflexively acknowledged the new government in the interest of stability—the diplomatic equivalent of "we'll fix it in post"—were catching up and beginning to ask these questions.

Chief among these groups was the Commonwealth. As a former British protectorate, the Maldives was a member and the serving foreign minister therefore sat on the Commonwealth Ministerial Action Group (CMAG)—the organization's human rights and democracy watchdog body. It flexed its muscle, and the Maldives was suspended from CMAG on 23 February, the first step towards throwing it out of the Commonwealth. President Waheed and former President Nasheed were ordered "to commence an immediate dialogue, without preconditions, [and] to agree on a date for early elections, which should take place within this calendar year".[25]

The threat was sincere; Fiji had been thrown out in 2009, after its military government failed to hold promised elections. This estranged it from the Western aid community, and impacted adversely on tourism and foreign investment. Neil even wrote up the case study for the benefit of our government readers.[26]

The European Union had also taken a dim view of February's events and joined the Commonwealth in calling for early presidential elections.

"[The Commission] is of the view that the legitimacy and legality of the transfer of presidential power in the Maldives should be determined by an impartial, independent investigation as agreed by all parties in the Maldives," said Catherine Ashton, High Representative of the European Union for Foreign Affairs and Security Policy and Vice President of the Commission.[27]

I later learned from an EU official that Dr. Hassan Saeed had sent Ashton a letter critical of the EU's position, worded in such a way to ensure her keen and continuing interest in Maldivian democracy.

The international community greeted the announcement of Waheed's inquiry into the legitimacy of his presidency with cautious enthusiasm. CMAG voiced what many others were thinking. "There should be international participation in any investigative mechanism, as may be mutually agreed by political parties in Maldives,"[28] read the group's 22 February statement.

The head of Waheed's hastily assembled three-member inquiry panel—Gayoom's former Defence Minister Ismail Shafeeu—held a press conference in April 2012. "Due to the nature and importance of this issue, I do not believe we can wait for assistance from the UN system or Commonwealth system or wait for a consultant to arrive," he suggested.[29]

The panel had been busily interviewing police and military officers in closed door hearings, while courteously offering the MDP the opportunity to participate. Suspicious of the distinctly regime-flavoured panel composition, the MDP had stayed away. "The people we are accusing of overthrowing the government in a coup d'état can't be the same as the people investigating it," said the MDP's spokesman, MP Hamid Abdul Ghafoor.

"Ask Civil Society"

The international community looked to the country's civil society organizations for loud opinion leadership on the matter—after all, outsiders had no idea as to the backstories of the panel appointments. The MDP, as the international community's former pro-democracy darling, was given a sympathetic ear but was also regarded as somewhat prone to exaggeration. A third opinion was sought, and it was expected that local human rights and pro-democracy NGOs would be foaming at the mouth after February's events. Yet they had stayed silent, failing to publicly comment on the coup until almost a month after it took place, and then only in a limply worded, committee-drafted group press statement widely ignored by local media. More than one diplomat privately expressed surprise at their ineffectualness; noise from local civil society organizations was needed to justify foreign statements and interventions.

The root of this apparent apathy was best summarized by a very senior UN staffer during Nasheed's era: civil society was "the new middle class profession of choice". "We give them funding and they rent an office, buy computers and go on training trips to exotic places abroad," he complained. "Then they come and ask us for more money next year."

When asked to justify their impact, the NGOs would point to having "raised awareness". In practice this involved sending a press release to *Minivan News* every six months, followed by a torrent of abuse and accusations of heartlessly "ignoring the issue" if we failed to publish it. The story was needed in the annual report to convince the donor of the organization's worthiness of further funding. As *Minivan* could barely afford rent, let alone computers (staff used their own), I felt secure in my bitterness over this.

Challenged on the subject, the NGOs would attribute their silence to fears of appearing politicized. This had some grounding: Nasheed had arrived in office on the back of issues such as "human rights" and "democracy", which under the twisted rules of Maldivian politics meant that any group espousing these themes would be seen as sympathetic to the MDP by association. With few exceptions this proved a convenient excuse to take UN money and do nothing, a sentiment which would also later fuel the "Colourless" movement—a group actively and counterintuitively devoted to apathy as a political statement.

A press release from the "Third Voice" coalition of NGOs finally appeared in late April condemning the composition of Waheed's commission. They were, they said, "deeply concerned by the recent political polarizations in society".[30]

I had the distinct suspicion they had been coached. This rare sign of life came on the tail of a strongly-worded statement from CMAG. "The Commission of National Inquiry (CNI), established to assess the events leading to the transfer of power on 7 February 2012, is not independent or impartial, and has failed to gain sufficient support in Maldives," it declared.[31]

It came with an ultimatum.

"Should the composition and terms of reference of the [CNI] not be amended within four weeks in a manner that is generally acceptable and enhances its credibility, CMAG [will] be compelled to consider further and stronger measures."

"Bullied" by CMAG

The government threw a tantrum, threatening to leave the Commonwealth and warning of "civil war" should early elections be held. "We have to build a peaceful and secure atmosphere. We have to strengthen our institutions so that they are independent. Otherwise, I have no doubt that if we hold elections, the political situation of the country will deteriorate further," declared the State Minister of Foreign Affairs, Dunya Maumoon—Gayoom's daughter.[32] "[The Maldives] is already quite divided. If there is an election, and if some people do not accept the election results, I cannot say there won't be a civil war. I do not want to see such a thing happen."

The new vice president, resort tycoon Waheed Deen, warned that outside interference in the Maldives' domestic affairs would be seen as an "attack on our independence and national sovereignty". Gayoom called for a "rethink" of the Maldives' membership in the Commonwealth,[33] while President Waheed accused it of "intimidating" and "punishing us".[34] For exactly what was unspecified.

CMAG's criticism was clearly a sensitive issue for the government. But the inflamed response revealed a need for the legitimacy that an endorsement from the outside world offered. My primary concern after 7 February was that they would dispense with charade and resort to the force and violence their impunity afforded them.

Fortunately the government remained susceptible to diplomacy. The Commonwealth appointed its former Secretary General, Sir Don McKinnon, as Special Envoy to the Maldives, and tasked him with bringing about a legitimate inquiry. He brokered the inclusion of an independent "co-chair"—a foreign judge—and the inclusion of an MDP nominee.

As a parting shot, the dissolved panel released their work in what the MDP claimed was an attempt to preempt the work of the legitimate commission.[35]

Azra Naseem published a translation of the document on her DhivehiSitee website,[36] noting that the first page contained a disclaimer advising that the released document was "not a report of findings" but a timeline "with omissions" released in the interest of "public opinion". It contained a compelling blend of fact and one-liners: "[The state broadcaster] was not providing sufficient information to the public, so Adhaalath Party's Sheikh Imran Abdulla arrived at MNBC One to rectify the situation," read one of the 282 points. The channel's senior executives, apparently concerned about "potential attacks from a public dissatisfied with lack of proper information", decided to broadcast "a clean feed" from Gasim's Villa TV.

The Commonwealth's Commission

The government imposed a stringent set of criteria on Nasheed's nominee to the new, now Commonwealth-backed inquiry commission. These included the requirement that the nominee be somebody "of integrity with high ethical, moral and professional standards with at least an undergraduate degree from a recognised university" and who had not been politically active for the previous two years. Many were rejected, until finally with much additional prodding from the Commonwealth, the government accepted a former school principal to represent the MDP, Ahmed "Gahaa" Saeed.

All three previous members of the former commission were retained—the new criteria apparently not applying to them—and a retired Singaporean judge, Govinda Pannir Selvam, was chosen as co-chair.

This was ominous. The Gayoom clan's roots ran deep in Singapore, the business links were many and Selvam was considered by several Singaporean bloggers 37 to be a tough and wily operator in the Singapore Supreme Court, where he issued many defamation verdicts to silence political opponents of President Lee Kuan Yew.

"Lee's principal tool for repression is using the courts to sue for defamation of character, bankrupt the opponent, disqualify him from politics and jail him if necessary. In fact such misuse of the law courts is so rampant and systematic so much so that there is not one opposition politician who has not been victimised this way," wrote Singaporean blogger and lawyer Gopalan Nair, now living in California.[38]

At *Minivan* we wondered about the negotiation and concession that had led McKinnon to endorse this idea. Then we saw the inclusion of two new foreign advisors: a retired Court of Appeal judge from New Zealand, Sir Bruce Robertson, and a Canadian, UN Legal Advisor Professor John Packer. Perhaps there was some hope of a credible report?

Months of interviewing took place, including investigation into the police abuses of 8 February, and we grew cautiously optimistic that the findings would include some reflection of reality. The reasons for confidence grew as, with just days to go before the report's release, Gayoom gave an interview to local press expressing "frustration" with "foreign influence" in the commission. He would not, he declared, accept any conclusion that found the 7 February power transfer to be a "coup".[39]

President Waheed meanwhile appeared on the BBC, during a visit to the UK to partake in the Queen's Diamond Jubilee celebrations. "If [the commission] find out that I had a role in bringing about a coup, then I would definitely resign," he told the British broadcaster. "But if I have no role—if somebody else has done it—it doesn't mean I have to resign, according to the law of the Maldives."[40]

The consequences of his resignation and early elections would be far worse than his remaining in power, he explained. "We have to consider the political situation. We have other political parties—big political parties—who are not ready for an election. I have to exercise my judgement—as leader of the country—to make sure we don't get into a worse political turmoil."

Calling early elections would be "reckless"[41] as this would require him to resign and hand power to the Speaker of Parliament, Abdulla Shahid, "who got elected with just 2,000 votes" in the 2009 parliamentary election. Waheed neglected to mention that his own Gaumee Ithihaad Party (GIP) had received 518 votes in the same poll.

The 31 July deadline for the release of the Commission's report was fast approaching. There was the sense of an impending watershed moment, a chance to acknowledge what had happened and correct the democratic derailment. The anticipation was palpable. Adhaalath Party president Sheikh Imran Abdulla promised that the ruling parties would assist security forces in maintaining peace and order, whatever the outcome.[42]

Waheed extended the deadline by a month, to 30 August. There were, the Commission said, hundreds more people coming forward with testimony.

With just days to go, Waheed and Gayoom announced that they would respect the result.

The Report

That should have been a warning. On the evening of 29 August, Nasheed's representative suddenly resigned from the Commission, denouncing its credibility and alleging that the final report excluded testimony from key witnesses as well as crucial photo, audio and video evidence. Protests erupted in Malé almost immediately.[43]

Waheed unveiled the report the next day.[44] Nasheed did not resign under duress, there was no coup, nor even a police mutiny.[45] This last part was especially surprising, given the amount of photographic and video evidence suggesting the contrary.

The tone of the document itself was striking—bitter and aggrieved, defensive to the point of irascibility. It read much like one of Hassan Saeed's letters, containing a weighty treatise on Nasheed's failure to honour unspecified "coalition agreements". He really was very unpopular, urged the report, and brought the events of 7 February upon himself. It was up to him to convincingly prove that the events were illegitimate. "Until the time of his resignation, President Nasheed possessed of many powers under the Constitution that he could have utilised including the lawful use of force. He chose not to," the report read. "That decision may be classified as praiseworthy, but he cannot now contend that because he made those choices, that he was 'forced' into resigning because of what others were doing around him."

Civilians Mohamed Nazim and Abdulla Riyaz, who would subsequently be appointed Defence Minister and Police Commissioner, had innocently arrived at Republic Square to see what the fuss was about, and took command of the security forces as they "felt it was their moral obligation and public duty to intervene".

The timeline released by the original three-member panel was endorsed as it faced "virtually no challenge of substance".

Many witnesses demonstrated "heavy commitment to their positions", but "on occasion their recollections were simply wrong. It is unhelpful to call this 'lying' but it must be allowed for as conclusions are sought."

Some even had the temerity to give names and "naively suggest that if the Commission trolled through scores of bank accounts, telephone records, SMS logs and intelligence reports, all would be revealed."

It did not, as the named individuals were trusted implicitly.

"Aslam, while appearing before the Commission, read about an SMS attributed to Mr Saleem, the Permanent Secretary of the Ministry of Environment. The SMS spoke of a distribution of MVR2.4 million (US$155,640) to the 'mutinying' policemen. The Commission summoned Mr Saleem. He debunked the message effortlessly, claiming that he did not recall sending such a message."

The actions of the police meanwhile were "an internal matter subject to disciplinary proceedings", as the Maldives Police Act 2008 "does not contain the offence of mutiny by police". Besides, "the Constitution does not call for loyalty of anyone to the President. It calls for the loyalty to the Constitution."

Comments from the foreign observers were included in an appendix, not released as part of the original report and later removed from the government's website (but still available on the Internet Archive).[46]

"Four of the five members acted at all times with independence and integrity while carrying out the important task for the future of the nation," read the appendix, signed by Packer and Robertson. "The evidence as it unfolded described a national obsession with street demonstrating at an alarming level. Some would want to call [this] an example of the rights of freedom of expression and assembly," they argued. "In reality it is rather more bully-boy tactics involving actual and threatened intimidation by a violent mob. This perpetual behaviour is sapping public life and hindering the Maldives' development as a modern democracy."

The Commission stories were, agreed Neil, among the more depressing of our years at *Minivan*. I wrote them myself to spare the others.

Aftermath and Autopsy

The release of the report was welcomed, if somewhat awkwardly, by the Commonwealth and international community. Calls for early elections were dropped, as were foreign challenges to Waheed's legitimacy. Locally, bits and pieces of the Commission's process began to leak to the public. Nasheed's representative, Ahmed Saeed, revealed a letter he had sent to the Commonwealth on 26 August outlining the concerns that would subsequently prompt his resignation. The Commission, he said, had withheld evidence, crucial witnesses failed to cooperate, the panel failed to examine certain witnesses while others were intimidated and obstructed, failed to review testimonies and evidence, and was subject to manipulation by the government-appointed secretariat.[47]

No officer from the Special Operations branch of the police force—the core of the mutinying security forces had been interviewed, Saeed claimed. "The [Commission] has not been able to 'summon' any of the alleged 'perpetrators' or 'culprits'," he wrote.

Many witnesses who did appear before the panel seemed to have been "coached" and simply gave standard responses such as "no", "I don't know", or "I can't remember", despite—as in the case of Umar Naseer—having previously having made loud and provocative statements. The commission took all this at face value; the original three members of the Commission (Dr. Ibrahim Yasir, Dr. Ali Fawaz Shareef and chairman Ismail Shafeeu) showed a lack of interest in witnesses, "rarely posing questions".

Critical evidence such as CCTV footage from police headquarters and the President's Office was never provided, or had crucial hours of footage missing. After "much stonewalling", Saeed said he was told that the footage was simply not available.

The MDP commissioned a point-by-point analysis of the report by a team of Sri Lankan legal experts,[48] including two Sri Lankan Supreme Court attorneys—Anita Perera and Senany Dayaratne—and the former Sri Lankan Attorney General Shibly Aziz.[49] Their criticisms of the Commission included, among many others, a failure to account for Umar Naseer's public statements taking credit for the government's overthrow, no examination of Waheed's meeting with the opposition on 30 January, no mention of opposition leaders joining protesters, no inclusion of an account by Nasheed's wife despite the basis of coercion adopted by the Commission including threats to Nasheed's family, no analysis as to why Nazim had appointed acting heads of the police and military prior to Nasheed's resignation, and dismissal of testimony from key witnesses such as the Chief of Defence, Deputy Police Commissioner, and the military's Malé Area Commander. The tone throughout presented Nasheed as the accused and implied "he got what he deserved", suggesting that the report was "tainted with manifest bias".

Aishath Velezinee went a step further, pointing out that the Commission's report dwelt heavily on the supposed "unlawfulness" of Nasheed's arrest of Chief Criminal Judge Abdulla Mohamed, a pretext based on the false premise that he was actually a constitutionally appointed judge in the first place.[50]

Nasheed held a press conference in a Malé hotel following the release of the Commission's report. He seemed exasperated, but was still grinning. The Commission had, he said, effectively set a legal precedent under Maldivian law for the overthrow of an elected government through police or mob action.

This, he said, left the Maldives "in a very awkward, and in many ways, very comical" situation, "where toppling the government by brute force is taken to be a reasonable course of action. All you have to do find is a narrative for that course of action."[51]

"I see the report as a document that tries to map a way forward. The Commission was of the view that reinstating my 2008 government would be so messy that it would be best to move forward with another election. So the report has tried so hard to come out with this view through a proper narrative. You will have read the narrative and will understand that at times it is comical, but still, it is a narrative.

"My message to the international community is when you recommend issues, situations, solutions programmes and projects to other societies and people, it is so very important to understand the detailed intricacies of the local conditions."

Bubble Theory

What became of the foreign observers? Their involvement remained, for me, the enduring mystery of the Commission's act of "legitimacy". I doubted the bribery speculation of more cynical Maldivian colleagues. I felt I understood how the former regime manipulated Maldivians: a combination of carrot—monopolizing and dispensing opportunities and gifts to the favoured—and stick—censure and criminalization through a tightly controlled judicial system. Families were large and interconnected, and threats and intimidation could be passed through the network: rarely would a victim be directly confronted, instead "advice" would be offered by a mutual source. Freedom from this manipulation was one of the rationales for having a foreigner as *Minivan* editor. Left to their own devices, foreign teachers, journalists and other expats living in Malé all tended to arrive at the same conclusion after a month or so in the country.

But Gayoom's regime had been remarkably successful at propagating the image of the Maldives as an apolitical tropical island paradise, so successful, that few visitors even realized that they were honeymooning in one of the world's strictest Islamic countries. Image control was something Gayoom and his senior ministers were remarkably good at, and the government's visitors during his era often dwelt on the charm and courteousness of their hosts. The facade only began to crack after 2005 with the torrent of headlines involving human rights abuses and political upheaval, many picked up from *Minivan*.

Well-informed visitors were much harder to manipulate, but the more clueless left themselves wide open to a very effective technique we witnessed at first hand: "Bubble Theory". This involved delicately restricting the visitor's access to information and counter sources, while simultaneously maintaining a charm and hospitality offensive. Alternative sources that the "victim" might stumble upon and query, particularly *Minivan*, would be gently disparaged as politically biased: "Oh, well they have their perspective." Supporting sources would be energetically endorsed. Crucially, translation and interpretation of material in Dhivehi would be controlled and monitored, often by a third party 'administrative assistant' reporting back to the higher authority.

The result was that a diplomatically sensitive arrival with little background on the Maldives would find themselves in a bubble of very limited information and in a trust relationship with people controlling their access to information without their knowledge. Some would venture out into Malé, arranging their own appointments, but if voiced this was typically discouraged on the pretext of "safety". Ideally the "victim" would be located off Malé, perhaps on a nearby resort, thereby isolating them from chance encounters with locals. Interestingly, British and EU diplomats were required to stay in Malé, often at greater expense, due to the "Daily Mail" factor of being caught at work in a swimming costume. The Americans had no such qualms, and would block-book beach bungalows.

Minivan's *Evil Twin*

We were able to watch the entire process unfold with the arrival of the *Maldivian Daily* online publication. Following their CMAG scare, senior figures in Waheed's government began to question the quality of their media coverage. The Commonwealth and others were known to read *Minivan* extensively, and the legitimacy of the government had been a tough sell to us due to our habit of extensively backgrounding stories. At some point they decided that they needed their own *Minivan*—but what did we have that was allowing us to so lead astray the outside world? Dr. Hassan Saeed and the DQP had tried earlier to mimic us with the launch of *Maldives Today*, which inconsistently pumped out embittered and badly-written anti-Nasheed propaganda, before eventually settling on republishing edited *Minivan* articles with the disclaimer: "revised for correction of facts and ethical journalism".

With *Maldivian Daily* they hit on what they felt was the missing ingredient: foreigners. A pair of young British journalists—male and female—were duly recruited on the pretext of starting an independent media publication. The project was believed to be backed by the vice president, Waheed Deen, with the oversight of Dr. Saeed. The journalists' handler was a Maldivian from the Chamber of Commerce.

We first noticed the new journalists reporting on Twitter. The substance of their work seemed to correspond to what President's Office spokesperson Masood Imad thought about any given issue. Dan—at this stage *Minivan*'s intern—ran into the male reporter during a game of football, and later went for a coffee with the new arrivals. They told us they had been advised that we were political agents operating from the basement of former President Nasheed, and to avoid us at all costs lest we lead them astray.

Conversation steered to less controversial territory. The worst thing to do to a bubble is suddenly pop it, playing to the fears planted by the victim's handler. Better to show a hint of the world outside and let reality slowly dawn.

I was astonished at how persistent and effective the bubble was. The female journalist worked it out first. She had been seen meeting *Minivan*, asked some awkward questions and was booked on a flight home the following day for reasons involving "safety". We met for drinks in the airport hotel bar before her departure, and learned all about the process that had led them there.

She had only arrived recently, quitting her job in the UK. The male journalist had spent four months building the website. Both had answered job advertisements in the UK press (another British journalist, Luke Powell, saw this ad, did his research and contacted *Minivan* to see whether it was us. I read the ad and felt vindicated, thinking that the MDP had finally relinquished the *Minivan* brand and was trying to establish a newer, sympathetic media outlet. Wishful thinking. Luke didn't get a job at *Maldivian Daily*—but he did get an internship at *Minivan*).

The *Maldivian Daily* crew had been issued with a team of young "friends" on arrival, tasked with interpreting the Maldives for them in English. Roaming outside their apartment in Malé was discouraged; it was "too dangerous". To compensate, they had the run of the vice president's resort at the weekends. After several months of quoting Masood Imad, the male journalist had asked his minders whether they should be contacting the MDP for comment.

"You're not ready to speak to the MDP," he was told.

The carefully manicured image of the MDP as a mob of loud and thuggish criminals was endorsed by the Maldivian Twittersphere's discovery of the pair. They were caught completely unawares by the furious torrent of abuse from MDP sympathizers.

It was unsettling to witness the indoctrination process working so well. The male journalist reached the point where he was actively emailing British MPs, informing them that they had got the Maldives all wrong. Nasheed had by now been arrested by dozens of masked police ahead of his show trial in the Hulhumale Magistrate Court.

"I have spoken to the President's Office today who assured me that Nasheed is receiving the best treatment possible and that they want to make sure people know nobody is above the law," the journalist informed the MP. "I'm not sure if you know this also but the reason Nasheed fell from power was because he had failed to deliver most of the promises he made when elected and the people protested en masse against him. Yes the army and police were also involved but it's their country too.

"I'm not writing this as an angry letter or anything like that it just frustrates us incredibly when we read and see support for Nasheed who is willing to take power at any cost and the government doesn't get to give their side of the story which in journalism is a necessity.

"Both myself and my staff have all received threats from MDP supporters to the point where one of my staff is now having to leave the country because she feels so threatened."

The MP wrote back, gently advising him not to be "naive", and to "think carefully about the ethics you are choosing to work under".

The male journalist's phone rang while we were talking in the pub. It was their handler. Where are you, he wanted to know? Who are you with?

"Please, I have to live here. I have a wife and child," the voice begged.

The journalist put the phone down. He appeared shaken. It dawned on me that whoever had been tasked with following the pair was probably Maldivian, and therefore had phoned in after being blocked from entering the airport bar.

The male reporter was also put on a plane back to the UK soon afterwards. He was told he was to continue writing as the publication's "UK correspondent", and to expect a cheque in the mail. We checked back with him several months later after noticing the site had not been updated. The website was "down for maintenance", he explained. The admin, on the other hand, told us he had been ordered to pull his access.

Bubbled?

I never found out whether the behaviour of the Commonwealth observers Packer and Robertson was a result of being similarly "bubbled". Certainly the hallmarks were there: they were safely isolated on a resort, their meetings and movements around Malé choreographed by the government-appointed Commission secretariat. Their inability to understand Dhivehi would have forced them to rely on interpreters—again, provided by the government. The panel, administration and government would have been extremely pleasant and courteous towards them; in contrast, their experience of the MDP would have been a succession of aggrieved and plaintive characters appearing as if defendants in a court trial. The MDP often didn't help itself in such cases—many Maldivians had a tendency to emphasize a point through exaggeration: rough handling by police could quickly become "torture", a bad habit that sabotaged their credibility in the eyes of many Western observers. But it did not change the reality that police were engaged in a campaign of mistreatment and abuse of the opposition they had overthrown.

Most alarmingly for observers affiliated with rights-based organizations such as the UN and Commonwealth, Packer and Robertson in their statement seemed to equate freedom of assembly with "bully-boy tactics involving actual and threatened intimidation by a violent mob".

The problem was the protesting, in other words, not the actions that led to people gathering on the street. Moreover, the vast majority of Maldivian protests were self-evidently peaceful, especially by regional standards, with casualties limited to the occasional shop window and those sensitive to megaphones.

No, the most disturbing thing about this sentiment expressed by Packer and Robertson was that it was near word-for-word that expressed by Gayoom and his entourage.

Act IV: Waheed's Rule

The success of his Commission of National Inquiry report gave President Waheed legitimacy and a honeymoon from international pestering. But the foreign ministers of CMAG were not entirely convinced. Respecting the Commonwealth's backing of the report they lifted the Maldives' suspension, but kept it on their agenda as a "matter of interest". The Canadian Foreign Minister John Baird personally challenged Waheed over the government's ongoing persecution and criminalization of the MDP.[52]

"President Waheed offered no substantial defence of these questions, which is a telling response in itself," Baird declared, describing "the declining state of democratic values in the Maldives" as "alarming and deeply troubling".[53] Portentously, he also flagged concerns about the independence of the judiciary ahead of calling for open elections. "Canada with others fought to keep Maldives on the Commonwealth Ministerial Action Group agenda, and we are glad it remains there. We will continue to focus on anti-democratic activities in the Maldives, especially in terms of police brutality, and intimidation of opposition parliamentarians."

The Baroness and the Bill

CMAG's belligerence, despite their win, irritated the Maldivian government. It went on the attack, and for £75,000 in state funds purchased the services of an unlikely ally: Baroness Patricia Scotland, former Attorney General of the UK, Labour cabinet minister and member of the House of Lords.

Minivan News obtained the terms of reference for the Baroness's employment.[54] "The specific output expected from the assignment is a detailed legal opinion on whether the Maldives was unfairly placed on the CMAG agenda and whether this continuation of being on the agenda is unfair," the document read. "In particular, the consultant will assess whether the CMAG had acted in contravention of its own mandate and powers and had demonstrated bias in their actions." As part of the deal, Baroness Scotland was to come to the Maldives "and meet all relevant stakeholders" including the MDP.

"We were not even aware of this woman; she never approached us," MDP spokesperson Ghafoor told us. "Now we hear she was in the Maldives, probably staying in a fancy resort with somebody interesting likely footing the bill. It is very disturbing that a member of the House of Lords from an 800-year-old democracy would come to a little banana republic to stir up trouble in league with the plotters of a coup d'état."[55]

Baroness Scotland issued a statement to the *Daily Mail*,[56] informing the paper that the advice she was giving the Maldivian government was "confidential and legally privileged".

The 2012 audit report of the Attorney General's office was not privileged,[57] and showed Baroness Scotland had been paid a further £50,000 in addition to her £75,000 fee, "for further advisory and drafting work". The audit report noted that the payment of this "bonus" violated article 96(c) of the constitution, the Public Finance Act, and public finance regulations.

Such transgressions were academic, as Waheed's government was past caring about such controversies. Who was going to prosecute them? The Attorney General's office? The judiciary?

Public Relations

Gayoom's employment of Hill+Knowlton prior to the 2008 election showed the regime's predilection for lavish consultancies and attempts at image control. While privately pursuing CMAG through Baroness Scotland, Waheed's government, concerned about the impact 7 February and protest headlines were having on tourism, engaged the US public relations firm Ruder Finn at a fee of £93,000 per month (according to *PR Week*).[58]

Minivan obtained the "request for proposals" document issued by the government's tourism promotion office. The successful PR firm would be required to target stakeholders in the UK, USA, Commonwealth countries, "all relevant EU institutions", academic institutions and NGOs, "arrange 1:1 meetings with influential and open minded potential champions", and "arrange briefings to build links at various levels with the UK, US, Commonwealth and major European governments". The agency was to "feed in academic arguments to those identified", and "determine champions who are willing to speak publicly on Maldives", in a bid to "Rally an alliance of support for the Maldives".[59]

It was an odd arrangement. Behind the scenes, the Maldivian government was quietly appeasing the extremists who had help it come to power; its first actions in power included the release[60] of 2007 Sultan Park bombing suspect Mohamed Ameen, reportedly a member of the Jama'athul Muslimeen group responsible for the 2009 bombing attack on Pakistan's Inter-Services Intelligence agency in 2009. Ruder Finn was meanwhile embroiled in controversy over its distribution of the incendiary anti-Islam film *Fitna*, produced by Dutch ultra-nationalist politician Geert Wilders. The PR firm also represented Israeli airline El Al, which MPs of the Maldives government coalition had only a week prior to signing the contract voted to ban from landing in the Maldives.[61]

Six months—and presumably £558,000—later, the arrangement appeared to stall awkwardly.[62] *Minivan* contacted Ruder Finn's "Senior Vice President and Ethics Officer", Emmanuel Tchividjian. "We do not comment publicly on contracts that we have with our clients," said the PR man.

A Ruder Finn insider familiar with the Maldives account, through a mutual contact, said that the PR agency had decided to drop the Maldives as a client. This meant that the company responsible for the original Philip Morris "Smoking is good for you" campaign had fired the Maldives because the firm was concerned it was making the company look bad.

Economic Collapse

The payments to these consultants may well have bounced. By May 2012 the economy's upward trend had reversed and the Maldives was rapidly heading towards bankruptcy. Foreign aid not already affected by the Maldives' graduation to middle-income status dropped off almost entirely due to the sudden political uncertainty. Climate change adaptation and mitigation aid, particularly Scandinavian, was very much tied to Nasheed and ceased almost immediately. Dramatic news headlines and travel advisories issued by foreign governments had badly hurt tourism arrivals. Tourism land rental payments from resorts—one of the government's main earners—plummeted by 25 per cent in the second quarter,[63] resort tycoon Gasim having insisted that one of President Waheed's first acts in office be the "re-interpretation" of the MDP's island lease reforms.[64]

With revenue declining the government appealed to Saudi Arabia and China for soft loans, but turning polite assurances of support into actual cheques had proved difficult. Extravagant overseas borrowing at commercial rates had seen the cost of foreign credit rise dramatically, leading the government to print money to fund its expenditure.

The income situation was dire, but more problematic was the enormous and superfluous expenditure the new regime had used its parliamentary majority to introduce, bogging down Nasheed's government in an effort to prevent it meeting the many demands of the new constitution.

A delegation from the International Monetary Fund (IMF) arrived in April, two months after the coup, and warned that if the new government did not reduce its expenditure, it would run out of foreign currency reserves and mire the country in poverty. "These may be politically difficult measures, but the consequences of not reducing the budget deficit are likely to be even more difficult," warned the head of the IMF delegation, Jonathan Dunn.[65]

Several months into his tenure Waheed had increased the budget deficit to 27 per cent of GDP, a 175 per cent increase on earlier forecasts. He was shoring up support: the security forces were given an abundance of promotions and paid several years of allowances in lump sums, while the engorged ranks of the civil service were paid back all salary cuts implemented under Nasheed's austerity measures. A team of US economic advisors sent in to help stabilize matters privately confessed astonishment at having to explain "basic economic terms" to Waheed's Finance Minister, Abdulla Jihad.

The situation worsened. By October, the government had given up paying its electricity bills and was found to owe more than US$10 million to the state-owned electric company.[66] A flustered Jihad publicly declared that the state would be unable to pay salaries in the final quarter of 2012 without an immediate US$25million loan promised by the Indian government.[67]

President Waheed had a different take. "The Maldivian economy is fine. Don't listen to whatever people say. We don't have to [worry] about the Maldivian economy being in a slump," he declared.

Faced with impending economic apocalypse, the government responded calmly and rationally by suddenly evicting the Maldives' single largest foreign investor.

The Airport Deal

The Indian infrastructure giant GMR, in consortium with Malaysia Airports Holdings Berhad (MAHB), won a contract in June 2010 under Nasheed's government to refurbish, upgrade and manage Malé's international airport.[68] One of India's largest companies, GMR had an infrastructure portfolio of highways, power plants and airports, most significantly the newly-opened Delhi Terminal 3.

The 25-year agreement with the Maldives involved the construction of a shiny new terminal by 2014 to replace the existing structure, which could charitably be described as a tin shed. The GMR-MAHB investment would eventually run to US$511 million—the single largest foreign investment in the Maldives. In return, the government would receive concession fees on fuel and airport revenue.

The existing state body responsible for running the decidedly third-world airport was the Maldives Airports Company Limited (MACL). MACL had no capital for investment or much interest in anything other than overseeing a small arrangement of dubious airport duty free concessions. It paid the government US$5.05 million in 2009, an amount which under GMR was expected to rise to US$87.05 million in 2015.

I first learned of the airport upgrade on the day the winners were announced. The bid had hardly been conducted in secret, but had been pushed through by Nasheed's government at alarming speed in an attempt to keep the opposition off balance. Elements believed to have interests involving the supply of aviation fuel were liable to use their parliamentary position to sabotage any arrangement that threatened this.

Attempting to preempt allegations of corruption, Nasheed's government invited the World Bank's International Finance Corporation (IFC) to run the bidding process.[69] This attracted several groups: GMR-MAHB, a Turkish-

244

French consortium TAV-ADPM, and the European Zurich Airport-GVK. Each bid was accorded a score (Net Present Value, or NPV) according to how it met the government's priorities. The big scoring priorities were upfront cash and share of fuel revenue; MACL had never made much money from the airport itself—hence the tin shed.

The Europeans misjudged this, offering an upfront US$27 million and sizeable 27 per cent chunk of airport revenue, scoring a meagre 266.94. The Turkish-French consortium did much better, scoring 454.04 with a 29.5 per cent share of non-fuel revenues, 16.5 per cent share of fuel and US$7 million upfront.

GMR analyzed the bidding priorities.[70] They offered just 10 per cent of airport revenue, but promised US$78 million upfront and a 27 per cent share of fuel sales. The head of the Turkish consortium, Gusiloo Betkin, grumbled to the newspaper *Haveeru* that 27 per cent was an impossible margin: "We are a party that provides services to 170 million passengers annually in 39 airports. We also have experience in fuel trade," he declared.[71]

GMR scored 495.18, winning the bid by banking on fuel as a loss leader with the knowledge that MACL was woefully underestimating the value of airport revenue; as one of the world's premier luxury resort destinations, the average spend of a passenger passing through theMaldives' airport was potentially extremely high. The Gucci, Prada and Rolex concessions would make a killing.

The first sign of trouble came when several members of the MACL board refused to sign the concession agreement. A swift reshuffle saw it take place the following day, and work began almost immediately.

GMR was foremost a project management company, its skill primarily invested in wielding a large army of subcontractors. This arrangement worked well, as any transactional difficulties could be similarly outsourced to these subcontractors, allowing the parent company to remain clean and ignorant. All the same, many Maldivians broadly believed the airport bidding process to be have been an odd one and would wink conspiratorially when asked their opinion, but were unable to point at any specific instance of impropriety.

Airport privatization meant that the Maldives would lose control of its airspace, declared Umar Naseer. This, he explained, meant that Israeli aircraft would refuel in the Maldives on their way to bomb Arab countries.[72]

Naseer's grasp of geography notwithstanding, the opposition was able to turn the airport into a wedge issue, playing particularly to nationalism and fears of foreign ownership. When GMR eventually plucked up the courage to ask the owner of the Alpha MVKB duty free concession to vacate, Ibrahim Shafeeq refused. He was ultimately evicted after months of court battles,[73] and immediately launched a public campaign demanding "GMR Go Home". A large orange helium balloon with this message was flown over Malé, quickly becoming a rallying flag for Adhaalath-driven protests fueled by xenophobic anti-Indian sentiment. Hassan's Saeed's DQP provided the literature: a 24-page book entitled *Handing the Airport to GMR: The Beginning of Slavery*.[74]

Minivan translated it. Amongst the nationalistic protectionism was advice to be cautious of Indians, who were "particularly devious people".[75]

The opposition's campaign to sabotage the airport redevelopment finally bore fruit. In late 2011, just a few months before the coup, GMR attempted to introduce an airport development tax on departing passengers as part of its financing of the new terminal. This was stipulated in the concession agreement signed a year earlier and was thus hardly a surprise, but Hassan Saeed's DQP—heavily invested in the anti-GMR campaign—saw an opportunity. His party filed a case in the civil court, which dutifully ruled that this fee was a tax and therefore could not be imposed without the consent of the—opposition controlled—parliament.[76]

Nasheed's government, preoccupied with the fallout of the 23 December protest, backed the concession agreement it had signed and vowed to appeal the DQP's case. MACL wrote GMR a letter authorizing it to deduct the charge from the revenues due to the government pending the outcome of an appeal, a stopgap measure. Saeed and friends celebrated, the coup happened and everyone forgot about GMR.

"GMR Go Home"

GMR appeared sanguine in the wake of the coup. During his visit to India in May 2012 President Waheed reportedly assured the Indian Prime Minister Manmohan Singh that the government would honour its commitments.

In the first quarter of 2012, GMR deducted the airport charge from the revenue due to the government, paying it US$525,355 rather than the US$8.7 million it had been expecting. MACL's letter entitled GMR to do this as a stopgap measure, pending the government's appeal of Hassan Saeed's civil court case blocking the charge. In the second quarter the development charge eclipsed revenue from the airport, which had declined in the fallout from the coup. GMR presented MACL with a bill for US$1.5 million, and in the third quarter, a second bill for US$2.2 million.

Hassan Saeed was incandescent, and wrote a furious letter to the Indian prime minister. We obtained it.[77] "The net result of this is that the Maldivian government now has to pay GMR for running the airport. On this basis it is likely that the Maldivian government will end up paying about MVR8 billion [US$519 million] to GMR for the duration of the contract," Saeed wrote.

Not only was the government hemorrhaging millions of dollars in potential revenue, it was stuck paying for the development of the airport as a direct result of the court case Saeed's own party had filed.

Saeed was hardly self-reflective. "GMR and India bashing" were becoming "popular politics", he warned Prime Minister Singh. As a result, "the Maldives is becoming fertile ground for nationalistic and extremist politicians ... I want to warn you now that there is a real danger that the current situation could create the opportunity for these extremist politicians to be elected to prominent positions, including the Presidency and Parliament on an anti-GMR and anti-India platform ... That would not be in the interests of either the Maldives or India. You are well aware of the growing religious extremism in our country."

This was a remarkable reversal of the DQP's former position on religious matters, given its prominent role not only in fomenting that very same extremism ahead of the 23 December "Defend Islam" rally, but also in its public urgings that the airport project be abandoned due to the "devious" nature of the Indian people.

GMR sought a compromise that would bring the government to its senses—while allowing it to save face. The company's CEO, GM Rao, wrote a letter to President Waheed proposing that Maldivian nationals be exempt from paying the development charge.[78] This could have been spun as a win over the company, as it meant that Maldivians would get a free airport funded entirely by wealthy tourists.

If Rao expected his proposal to be considered sensibly amid the government's increasingly unhinged brinksmanship, he was to be disappointed. His letter was ignored.

Meanwhile, rallies organized by the Adhaalath Party on the streets of Malé were whipping up nationalistic fervor and demanding forcible seizure of the airport.

Over at the Indian High Commission, Mulay was unimpressed. He voiced his concern to the government. In response President Waheed's spokesperson Abbas Adil Riza publicly reprimanded him, standing up at one of the televised rallies and accusing the High Commissioner of threatening the government and taking bribes. Mulay was, declared Riza, "a traitor and enemy of the Maldives and the Maldivian people".[79]

The Indian press had a field day. We rang Riza for a follow-up the next day, anticipating remorse and supplication. "The comments were my personal opinion and I still stand by them," he declared.[80]

GMR had by now been ordered to cease construction of the new terminal, which was 25 per cent complete. The company had complied, and the steel foundations started to rust in the salty air.

I chanced across GMR's head of airports in the airport hotel bar one evening. Would the government really terminate the concession agreement, he wondered? The contract had a clear termination clause requiring compensation, but the country was broke.

I suggested that the government would simply declare the contract invalid from the outset, and claim that the termination clause did not apply.

That was impossible, the GMR man replied, with a businessman's unshakable faith in the sanctity of his piece of paper.

On 27 November, President Waheed's government gave GMR a seven-day ultimatum to leave the country.[81] "The agreement states that GMR should be given a 30-day notice but the government believes that since the contract is void, it need not be followed," said Waheed's Attorney General, Azima Shukoor.

The contract was, she explained, "void ab initio": invalid from the outset.

GMR described the move as "unilateral and completely irrational", and filed for an injunction in the Singaporean court of arbitration. The company was initially successful in obtaining a stay order on its eviction, even though the government vowed that it would disregard the court ruling despite the high court injunction.[82]

The government would, pledged Defence Minister Nazim, "continue the airport takeover. Insha Allah from next Saturday onwards MACL will be running the airport."[83]

Preparing for the worst, GMR evacuated non-essential staff from the country. All the same it appeared stunned when, a day before the company's scheduled eviction, the government won its appeal in the Supreme Court of Singapore. "The Maldives government has the power to do what it wants, including expropriating the airport," ruled Singapore's Chief Justice Sundaresh Menon.

The verdict effectively legalized the sovereign eviction of foreign investors regardless of contractual termination clauses or pending arbitration proceedings. It was, claimed one GMR insider, "completely unexpected. The lawyers are still in shock."

A day later GMR left town and the army assumed control of the airport.[84]

The Indian government weighed in. "The investment by GMR represents the single largest foreign direct investment in the history of Maldives. The decision to terminate the contract with GMR without due consultation with the company or efforts at arbitration provided for under the agreement sends a very negative signal to foreign investors and the international community," announced the Indian Ministry of External Affairs.

It was a unique achievement: the Maldives had succeeded in inspiring widespread sympathy for a multinational mega-corporation.

"It is our pin and we have every right to pull it out of this grenade," summarized "Peasant", one of the *Minivan* team's favourite commentators.

GMR retreated to lick its wounds, and stock price. It went back to the arbitration courts in Singapore, filing a claim for compensation and assembling a team of high-profile lawyers headed by the former Chief Justice of the UK, Lord Nicholas Addison Phillips. The damages sought? US$1.4 billion, an amount eclipsing the Maldives' annual state budget.[85]

This was enough to pause even Waheed's administration. The state's foreign currency reserves had dwindled to scarcely US$300 million, and the country was now facing the prospect of being sovereign defaulted for several generations. "GMR Maldives" was a real possibility.

The government hastily moved to transfer MACL's assets into a new state-owned company, Malé International Airport Limited (MIAL), and sought outside bids for development of the airport. The move did not fool the Singaporean judicial system, or the international governing body for airports, Airports Council International (ACI), which warned its members to stay well away from the Maldives.[86]

Eighteen months later, in June 2014, GMR would win its arbitration case. MACL and the Government of the Maldives were found jointly liable. As a sweetener, the government was ordered to immediately pay US$4 million in costs while the court settled down to decide the extent of the Maldives' bankruptcy.[87]

Condoms, Roosters and Black Magic

In the months after the coup the MDP settled into an area in the southeast of the city known as Raalhugandu. The area became bedecked with yellow flags, walls were painted with colours and the party's frangipani flowers, and a permanent campsite sprang up to accommodate visitors from the islands. The area took on a decidedly festive atmosphere and every week the party hosted rallies. Police kept their distance, taunted by chants of "*laari laari* yes sir, yes sir" (a *laari* being the smallest unit of Maldivian currency). Groups of protesters occasionally sallied forth from the campsite, to be inevitably blocked by lines of police. The protesters would fling money at them contemptuously, occasionally stuffing a police motorcycle with wads of cash. The message was clear but counter-productive: the taunting hardly convinced the rank and file to change sides.

The government found the MDP's protests enormously irritating, which may indeed have been the point. India was hosting "All Party Talks" mediated by the UN over on the vice president's resort island, and resolving the matter of "public disturbance" was a key priority for the governing parties. "Disruption of peace and harmony was not something that just fell out of the sky. At least a third of the country are upset about the rights that have been taken away from them," said the deposed Tourism Minister Mariyam Zulfa.[88]

The international community, which had made the assumption of mutual goodwill and emphasized the use of the word "dialogue", threw itself into these talks with a naivety not shared by the participants.

It was a play for time that became increasingly obvious, perhaps even to the UN mediator Pierre-Yves Monette, surrounded by his phalanx of friendly translators. The parties in the ruling coalition eventually presented the MDP with an impressive list of thirty demands to "resolve the problem of public disturbance". These included: "Not hold rallies on the street", "Not hang swings that obstruct pavements", "Stop the use of sexual and erotic tools" and my favourite, "All political parties to stop practicing black magic and sorcery". After months of expensive consultancies and business-class tickets to Malé, the talks process was quietly abandoned.

The government was constrained in what it could do about the protest camps, because the unashamedly MDP-inclined city council issued every official permit the party requested. It hit on a workaround: to have the Ministry of Housing and Environment repossess the land from the council and declare the MDP's occupation illegal.[89] Large numbers of police and military were sent in to disperse the camp and tear down the tents and structures.[90] The flowers were painted over with grey paint. A day later the area was deserted, save for a small garrison of police left to move along those who attempted to return.

The council leased the MDP a smaller area nearby, Usfasgandu, the only other open area in the city apart from Republic Square, where the government had, learning from its own example, banned protesting on grounds of national security.

The MDP painted Usfasgandu yellow and erected a stage, as well as several cages containing crows and a disconnected telephone, and began referring to the birds as the *baagees* ("traitors"). This annoyed the government no end; Gayoom's clan were acutely suspicious of *fanditha* magic, and black crows smelt of witchery.

The government repeated the process of reclaiming the area through the Housing Ministry, and approached the courts for a warrant to dismantle the area. One was duly issued, stating as reasons "suspected criminal activity", "damage to public property" and "suspected black magic performed in the area". Under the section marked "evidence", the warrant alleged that people in the Usfasgandu area had verbally abused police officers, damaged a police vehicle and thrown "a cursed rooster" at passing military officers.[91]

I attended the execution of the warrant. Lines of police held back angry MDP crowds while dozens of police officers put on the pageantry of a forensic search. Cigarette butts were carefully retrieved. A crumpled MDP membership form was found containing a suspicious brown substance. Inside a shed, I watched as a very serious gloved policeman reached into the rafters and retrieved a small box of Moods ultrathin contraceptives. Police also discovered paraphernalia for the committing of sorcery, although distinguishing this from the debris and empty paint tins was beyond my magical expertise.

I saw the mayor of Malé's city council, Ali "Maizaan" Manik, standing mournfully next to the cage of crows, and asked for comment. "I'm too angry to talk right now," he said.

I approached the police barricades. A group of young men were pushed forward by the crowd. "These are PPM! Not ours!" yelled a woman in the front row. Sure enough, one of the men leapt the barricades and was dragged off by police, to be released around the corner. The now "disorderly" crowd was dispersed.

A visibly upset protester expressed frustration at what he described as "a police state". "We just want somewhere to peacefully protest," he said. "They are just going to plant something, like drugs or explosives, so they can blame us. What can we do? We are helpless."

Lights Out

There was an unexpected casualty in the wake of 7 February, one with potential ramifications beyond island politics. Beginning with his underwater cabinet meeting and pledge to make the Maldives carbon neutral by 2020, Nasheed had set the country on a path of strident environmental advocacy. As explored in earlier chapters, the eco-rhetoric was not always matched by domestic achievement, but it did get attention—and funding. The climate change movement found in Nasheed a passionate and outspoken advocate able to command public sentiment and with access to world leaders. These in turn saw in the president the possibility of pleasing their environmental con-stituencies locally. Nasheed had fame and political will, but lacked the edu-cated and experienced people to execute his environmental agenda locally. Developed countries faced the opposite problem: an abundance of talent, but a lack of political will to commit to significant change. Nasheed's energy attracted these people into his orbit, typically pro bono, motivated by the opportunity to do something ambitious and meaningful—from literature festivals to ecotourism. Nasheed's Maldives was a sandbox for bright ideas.

One of these people was Mike Mason. A former mining engineer from the UK, Mason was an early pioneer in carbon trading and a successful entrepre-neur. A meeting with Nasheed saw him appointed, unpaid, to the specially created office of renewable energy. His task, with the help of a single secretary, was to make the Maldives not just carbon neutral, but energy self-sufficient. The Maldives was completely dependent on imported oil for transportation, food distribution and electricity, to the extent that it was spending over a quarter of its annual GDP on fuel. The economy is extremely vulnerable to extraneous oil price shocks.

As an engineer, Mason realized that he was short on data. He analyzed the options for renewables: wind was too erratic, ocean currents too seasonal, and only a few sites had tidal ranges suitable for tidal generation. Ocean geother-mal, where deep water pipes create energy via heat exchange, had potential, but was new, small-scale and expensive. Solar was the most obvious, and cer-tainly the most consistent. Shivering Europeans did not flock to the Maldives for the snow.

The vast majority of Maldivian islands were powered by diesel generators, a majority the result of island politicking and far larger than needed. These generators could only be turned on or off, and were thus extraordinarily inef-ficient. Mason found some operating at US$0.70 per kilowatt hour (kWh), compared to US$0.28 per kWh in Malé, which was already very expensive. In comparison, electricity in the UK hovered around US$0.15 per kWh—a fifth the price of many Maldivian islands.

Mason's research showed that solar photovoltaic (PV) cells could supply power directly to Maldivian consumers at US$0.23 per kWh during the day, but only at US$0.44 per kWh from batteries at night. A biomass generator could supply power to Malé at US$0.16 per kWh.

He concluded that the most realistic and commercially viable renewable option was to run ninety per cent of the country on solar, supplemented by small-scale wind power, while a 24-megawatt biomass plant would power the Malé region forty per cent cheaper than the existing diesel setup.

"With renewables, on day one you buy twenty years of electricity," Mason said. The challenge was attracting this capital investment in the first place, the cost of which, in the Maldives, was "stupidly high".

Mason's innovation was to approach the international donor community not for solar project funding, but investor risk insurance and sovereign guarantees through the World Bank and Asia Development Bank that dramatically reduced risk for foreign investors and lowered the cost of capital to between six and seven per cent—in line with building a power plant in Germany.

It worked.

Mason attracted US$200 million of risk-mitigated renewable energy investment almost immediately, with further investment of US$2–3 billion pledged over time.

The World Bank team working on the project were ecstatic, reportedly describing it as one of the most "exciting and transformative" projects of its kind in any country. For all the madcap rhetoric, a carbon-neutral Maldives was not only possible, but economically feasible—even optimal. The Scaling-Up Renewable Energy Program (SREP) was drafted and due to be signed into existence—on the morning of 7 February.[92] Investors who had been queuing up quickly made their excuses and headed for the door.

"The whole point of the plan was to take out the instability. The thing about a coup is that it takes that model and turns it upside down," Mason said, tendering his resignation and booking a plane ticket home.

The SREP tragedy did have a tiny silver lining—a speck of insight into Waheed's mind. Mason had worked closely with Waheed when he was vice president, and considered him a friend. Hearing of Mason's resignation, the new president emailed Mason urging him to continue with the SREP project and to remain as energy advisor.

"I don't think Dr. Waheed is a bad man—actually I like him a lot personally," Mason wrote in an email to an official in the Trade Ministry obtained by *Minivan News*. "However, he has done nothing to assure me that this is really a democratic process. Rather, my intelligence tells me this is a Gayoom inspired coup with Dr. Waheed as an unfortunate puppet." If the new government sought political accommodation with the MDP, made "a concerted attempt to remove the corrupt judiciary" and ceased police brutality "so that people can walk the streets freely as in any other civilised country", "then I will be back on side in the blink of an eye", Mason said. "I have given the best part of my life to this over the last 18 months, but I fear I have a set of democratic and moral principles that override other considerations."

President Waheed responded on March 23: "It would be nice if you listened to something other than Nasheed's propaganda. He is free to go anywhere he wants and say whatever he wants," Waheed wrote. "Have you ever thought that Nasheed could have made a stupid mistake under the influence of whatever he was on and blown everything away? I thought you had more intelligence than to think that I am someone's puppet and Maldives is another dictatorship," said the president.

Mason considered this, but decided the promises of "business-as-usual" were hollow and unsupported by actual events. "That is not believable in an atmosphere in which [airport developer] GMR is being attacked as an investor in infrastructure; the legal system is, frankly, corrupt so contracts cannot be relied upon; the politics are (in the most charitable possible interpretation) a major risk factor; and the President has no parliamentary party of consequence. I also doubt that the SREP sub-committee will approve funding the plan as they too will see through the plan to the problems (or at least they should if they are any good)," he wrote. "If things clear up, and faith in democracy and the rule of law is restored then a second go at this would be worthwhile—but meantime I am sceptical."

Besides, the very premise of the plan—mitigating investor risk—had been scuttled by the political upheaval. "Even if I did work with Waheed, I couldn't deliver the plan now [because of falling] investor confidence. They have destroyed US$2–3 billion worth of investment and condemned the country to an unstable economic future based upon diesel," Mason told us.

Later that year he wrote back to Waheed. "Until the last few days I still held out hope that the Maldives would recover some of its sanity but what I see unfolding is madness. It will, I fear, become a failed Islamic state unless you are very careful. Yet only 10 months ago this was a country with everything going for it!"

Act V: Undone

It was 26 July, a little over a month before the constitutional deadline for presidential elections. The UN Special Rapporteur's report on the state of the Maldivian judiciary had vindicated Velezinee, the government had exposed itself as erratic and irrational by evicting GMR, and its single-minded efforts to imprison Nasheed had finally unified international pressure behind the mantra of "free, fair and inclusive" elections.

Even the Americans, having finally caught up on affairs in the Maldives three months after the rest of the diplomatic corps, were now openly criticizing the competency of the judiciary. A mysterious curly-haired American woman had appeared as President Waheed's campaign consultant—to help him win or commit him to the polls, nobody knew.

26 July was also Independence Day, an opportunity for national agenda-setting speeches. Former president and former vice president laid out their separate visions for the country.

We ran the speeches side by side.

The Maldives relied on tourism and hospitality. It could not, said Nasheed, "afford to be an inward looking, and xenophobic country".[93] "We need to be outward looking and cosmopolitan. And yet the coup government turns deeper inwards and shuns the wider world," he declared. "We were a beacon of hope. We are no longer a leading voice in the climate change debate. We are less concerned about widespread human rights abuse in Syria and Egypt. We have once again become just another member state.

"It is high time that this insular mentality is dropped, and that we reapply for our old job of being a responsible international citizen."

Whatever your feelings about the Commission of National Inquiry and the events of 7 February, "what was clear to all even then, was that this was not how a democratically elected government in any country should be changed."

And what has become increasingly clear over time, is that the coup has reversed many political and developmental gains that the country had made during our three years of democracy.

We thought democracy and human rights were here to stay simply because we had free elections and a new constitution. We were wrong. No country in the world has a perfect democracy. It takes constant effort. For that, we need strong institutions, an independent judiciary, good laws, and an active and vigilant civil society. And we need the assistance of our partners to build these essential blocks of our country.

The flame of liberty and hope that once burned brightly has quickly dimmed to nothing more than a few embers. On September 7 we once again have the opportunity to rekindle this flame by having an elected government with a legitimate mandate from the people.

We need your assistance to ensure that these elections are free and fair, and that there will be a peaceful transfer of power once again to whomever emerges successful at the polls.

We urge you to be vigilant and welcome your engagement during this crucial time, as we in the Maldives, once again, find ourselves at the crossroads of history.

Meanwhile President Waheed, confessing that he was "brimming with nationalistic pride", opened his own address by awarding Gayoom the highest award of the Maldivian state, the Nishaan Ghazeege Izzaitheri Verikamuge Izzai.[94] The former dictator was, Waheed declared, a "national treasure".

This move surprised even the most jaded cynics at *Minivan*. Scarcely a month earlier Waheed had given a speech to a rather hostile audience on his mother's island of Thinadhoo. He had empathized with the islanders, telling them that his visit to the island was "bittersweet" as his mother had been subjected to torture and inhumane treatment following her mild criticism of Gayoom's regime.[95]

"As you would all know, back then the political environment was such that criticizing the government was a big crime. My mother while watching the TV said that Gayoom had lied," Waheed recalled. "The poor lady was dragged to court, people gathered around her on the streets and pulled her hair, spat on her and committed other derogatory acts."

One month later he was standing before an assembly of local dignitaries and foreign diplomats, in the national museum vandalized by the very fundamentalists his government had failed to prosecute. "The government decided to give this award to President Gayoom in recognition of his invaluable contributions to the betterment of this country, and to accord him the status that he truly deserves," Waheed declared. "I thank him for his service to this country. I wish you, Mr. President, good health and happiness."

The diplomats looked at each other. The atmosphere, I was later told, was rather awkward.

Waheed narrated his heroic efforts to stabilize the country amid the national turmoil of 2012, sparked by his predecessor's decision to "hold hostage" a Maldivian citizen: Judge Abdulla. "It was the period in which the independence and sovereignty of the country was challenged most profoundly. External forces infiltrated into our domestic affairs to the extent that such forces started dictating what should be taught in our schools. The government had become so weak that the leader of this country could be easily forced to sign agreements that directly affected the sovereignty of the country. Foreigners were deciding when our Constitution should be amended and when elections should be held," Waheed declared.

Our economy may be dependent on catering to tourists from around the world. But our independence should not be the price we pay to meet these needs.

Today, a country does not have to be invaded, or occupied for it to lose its independence and sovereignty. A country might not enjoy independence and sovereignty even though it might still be a full member of the UN. We should be mindful of situations like this. Independence is something that needs to be safeguarded from within and from outside.

In today's world, attacks on countries are not limited to guns and swords. We must be vigilant to attacks in various manners, and from outside and within the country. We must be aware of the efforts being made by certain factions to dominate our economy. We must be vigilant of the efforts being made to destroy our religious unity.

We must be attentive to the efforts being made to damage the tourism sector of the Maldives. We should know the people responsible for these campaigns, and what they have to gain from these efforts. Whether it is trying to dominate our economy, or to destroy our religious unity, we must be concerned about their intentions.

Encroaching on other people's rights is not freedom. Inviting outside forces into our domestic issues is not freedom either. This is not something that any Maldivian should be allowed to do. Nor should any foreigner be allowed to do that on our land.

The English version was somewhat abridged for the benefit of the diplomatic community. But I suspected that they—perhaps even the Americans—were finally beginning to re-evaluate Stanford's cosmopolitan philosopher-king. I hoped dearly for another round of leaked cables.

It was difficult to decipher what was happening with Waheed. Publicly and privately he adamantly denied he was a puppet, his faith in his autonomy absolute. Money, blackmail—these did not gel with my sense of the man. Yet he had clearly hitched his cart to Gayoom—if voluntarily, then all the more extraordinarily given the family history. Was his bitterness towards Nasheed so intense that he would instead back a man responsible for torturing his own mother? Earlier I had wondered whether he would resign, triggering early elections and giving him the chance to portray himself as the heroic saviour of Maldivian democracy. Did he really genuinely think he could win the upcoming polls? The huge posters of his face going up around the city suggested he was set on riding this thing out to the bitter and inevitably humiliating end. Had the Americans convinced him of their support? What of the influence of his wife Ilham, who had become infamous for appearing at the forefront of every state event? Was it a case of "Out damned spot"?

Whatever sense of matters I had, it was wrong. Things were about to become much, much weirder as the election date approached.

Spies, Lies and Scandal

"In line with longstanding practice we never comment on intelligence matters," said the spokeswoman for the Government Communications Headquarters (GCHQ), the British communications spy agency.

The leaked document had to be a hoax. Emailing the spies for confirmation was pointless, of course, but needed to be done for the sake of the article.

At the same time the photographed documents,[96] both marked "TOP SECRET STRAP 1", conformed to the format of similar documents leaked by Edward Snowden during the NSA/GCHQ scandal. I carefully considered the balance of probability. Domestically produced forgeries targeting the Maldivian audience tended to be short on extraneous detail so as to maximize the quantity of one-sided content. This transcript was different, so absurd and bizarre that there was a solid chance of it being genuine. I decided to take the same approach as with the coup agreement, publishing a disclaimer that the documents were impossible to authenticate.

The document referred to the "Maldives June 2013 crisis", and summarizes an apparently tapped 230-minute phone conversation "consisting of direct telephone link to client residence Z4 in California (two locations), United States of America. Parties present included daughter Mrs Widhadh Goodrich and son-in-law Mr Jeremy Goodrich."

Mr Goodrich proposes concession to Adalath party in terms of allowing more Sharia law in addition to proposed punishments

Mr Goodrich suggests temporary martial law enforced from Aug 2013 to end of Dec 2013

Mr Goodrich advises the president on a number of campaign strategies, including addition of alien workers as temporary wards for voting purposes

Mr Goodrich advises on smear campaign against President Mohamed Nasheed and PPM party candidate Mr Yameen A Gayoom

Mrs Goodrich [Waheed's daughter] suggest using social networks with marketing firm Rooster to "astroturf" a new "massive grassroot" support structure aimed at "winning hearts" of Maldivian citizens

Mr Goodrich suggests such efforts have failed previously and suggests exercising executive power

Mrs Goodrich and Mr Goodrich discuss pros and cons of both systems and come to conclusion on a hybrid system—as need arise

Dr Waheed states other coalition partners might be leaving, including DQP Party Leader Dr Hassan Saeed

Mr Goodrich asks if concessions could be given to DQP

Mrs Goodrich informs that DQP is not a long term risk and could be seen as collateral.

Dr Waheed states Adalath might join either PPM or JP

Mr Goodrich clarifies Adalath strength and suggests launching campaign to weaken leadership

Various discussion of proposed temporary martial law followed, ending with funding discussion followed by 'NRTR' discussions.

The document also referred to an "embedded" source in the Maldives, whose identity is blacked out: "Malunet continues to furnish with highly detailed, high-value, sensitive reports on target and power structure and variances in a timely manner."

A "key focus has been on [the] President's immediate power distribution and structure". It highlights as of secondary concern a "flow of funds" to Norway via Italy. "Funds transferred via IC/42 were intercepted at control point in Italy and further in Norway. A sum of USD 2,500,000.00 was noted in metadata. Later deposited into CHASE Bank, California, with IF: 4201840–22 and IC: 401-CHASE," the document stated.

We tracked Waheed's son-in-law down on Facebook, wishing to discuss further his apparent recommendations for the declaration of martial law in the Maldives.[97]

He failed to respond.

Fortunately he had published his own mini-biography on his Twitter profile, so we were able to introduce him to *Minivan* readers. Not only was Goodrich a former senior executive at search giant Yahoo, he was also a "bestselling self-published author and digital mercenary" who is "passionately interested in a better tomorrow" and works "at the junction of social good and business profit".

He was also very active on professional networking website LinkedIn, citing as his career highlights "winning and or being nominated for prestigious marketing awards at large companies, being quoted in the *Wall Street Journal* on behalf of a startup I co-founded and being able to semi-retire to the tropics, travel and reflect on my career for more than a year."

The leak of the GCHQ document closely followed, as predicted by Waheed in his alleged conversation with Goodrich, the abandonment of the president's "Forward with the Nation" coalition by both the Adhaalath Party and Dr. Hassan Saeed's DQP.

Saeed issued a public statement accusing the president of failing to take advice from coalition partners in favour of "family members and expatriates".[98]

Exit Stage Left

The election saga unfolded. Waheed's government behaved very oddly during its final days in office. Cabinet ministers were each awarded bonuses of three months' salary in lump sums, 35 convicted criminals were granted clemency and agreements were signed to hand over the regional airport of Kaadehdhoo to Gasim Ibrahim's Villa Air company. The government signatory was the Transport Minister Ibrahim Ameen, a senior member of Gasim's own party.[99]

The outgoing Finance Minister finally confirmed that the government had been paying US$10 million in installments to the forensic accountancy firm Grant Thornton.[100] The company had been commissioned under Nasheed's government to investigate an estimated US$800 million in black market oil shipped to the Burmese military junta between 2002 and 2008 by the Maldives' State Trading Organization (STO) while it was headed by Gayoom's half-brother and presidential candidate, Abdulla Yameen. We had challenged Yameen about this when the Grant Thornton report leaked in 2011.[101] Yameen claimed the shipping was a legitimate business activity, denied personal knowledge of any impropriety but confirmed he had used the STO's accounts to send money to his children in Singapore: "I have all the receipts."

The agreement with Grant Thornton signed by Nasheed's government was such that the forensics firm would investigate the trail of funds pro bono, in return receiving a per centage of any money recovered. The termination clause, intended to discourage future governments from making a political deal with the scandal's architects, was US$10 million.

Five per cent

President Waheed decisively lost the election with 5.13 per cent of the popular vote—the lowest per centage of any incumbent president in any election, in any country, ever.

The Supreme Court meanwhile struck down the first round of polls, plunging the Maldives into constitutional and democratic crisis.

An hour before his presidential term was due to expire, Waheed announced he was extending his tenure to 16 November. The Supreme Court endorsed this, despite the constitution clearly handing the presidency to the Speaker of Parliament, Abdulla Shahid—by now an MDP MP.

"Many Maldivians, international organizations and countries are pressuring me to resign and temporarily hand over the government to the People's Majlis Speaker. On the other hand, even more citizens want me to stay on, to continue with administration of the country, to carry out my duty," Waheed declared, somewhat disingenuously we felt given his electoral performance.[102]

The international response was livid, if one and a half years too late. Waheed's decision was, said the Commonwealth's Sir Don McKinnon, "regrettably not unexpected despite the best efforts of the Commonwealth and the United Nations to encourage the President to stay within the constitution".

CMAG immediately put the Maldives back on its formal agenda. "Let CMAG decide whatever they will," responded the president.[103]

Two days before the run-off election was due to be held, he left the country on a US$34,047 state visit to Singapore.[104] The Finance Ministry confirmed that he had initially requested a budget of US$84,306, but that the full amount was not approved due to "procedural matters".

Waheed, for his part, claimed to be making a "personal trip regarding medical treatment" for First Lady Ilham Hussain.

The country was left leaderless. Contacted abroad by Maldivian media Waheed declined to give a tentative date of return, saying instead that he would "need to consider the situation back in the Maldives first".

When the second round of polls were finally held, he publicly endorsed Gayoom's PPM.[105]

Less than a year later, Waheed was lecturing on liberal democratic transitions at the National University of Singapore, after being appointed Distinguished Visiting Fellow by the Lee Kuan Yew School of Public Policy. "It is clear the road to democracy is rough and painful," he declared during a public lecture in August 2014.[106] "Presidents have to learn not to overstep the limits of the constitution."

10

ELECTION

"Democracy is the theory that the common people know what they want, and deserve to get it good and hard."

H. L. Mencken

The Pizza Hut in Colombo was garish and noisy, filled with the sound of children's birthday parties. The air smelt slick, like an oil spill. Brush your finger through the air, and it came back greasy.

The man who had chosen the venue for the interview was sitting opposite me, sipping a coffee. He seemed an unlikely hero. Stocky, double-chinned and wearing glasses, he spoke softly with a mild speech impediment. He had the air of a harried mid-level bureaucrat. There were few signs that this was the man who had assumed responsibility for the integrity of Maldivian democracy, despite knowing the inevitability of the outcome. But if you looked closely, they were there: the iron stare, the calm self-assuredness, the quiet confidence suggesting that sometimes it was right to fight, even if loss was predetermined. Confirmation of his character was sitting in the chair next to him: an intelligent and very beautiful wife. She said hello before excusing herself to go shopping.

Fuwad Thowfeek, Elections Commissioner of the Maldives and one of the few people who managed to rise above the polarization of national politics, championed free and fair elections in the face of the old dictatorship that sought to subvert them, and in doing so became a symbol of hope for the future of Maldivian democracy.

Six months after the September vote, he was unemployed and in exile.

263

The End Run

The Elections Commission formally accepted Nasheed's candidacy on 18 July 2013. This was the culmination of months of speculation over whether the courts would allow him to contest. It was a triumph of pressure diplomacy and a substantial victory for Maldivian democracy.

The MDP was elated. This was the end run.

"Today we submitted the election forms and begin the task of restoring democracy to our country," declared Nasheed, praising Maldivians' resilience.[1] "It has been a slippery slope but we have come a long way. Despite all the barriers and hurdles that were put in our way, we never gave up. We are confident of winning this election in the first round with a handsome majority."

The sudden silence of the courts made the *Minivan* team very suspicious. We felt it was unlikely that Gayoom's faction would risk allowing a fair poll without a contingency plan. Somebody asked Nasheed if he was worried about election rigging. He did not discount the possibility, but was otherwise optimistic.

"The election will be free and fair after the voter list is properly finalized and [if] observers, monitors and agents are able to participate. When the tide has turned it becomes very difficult for anyone to swim against it."

Three other parties announced their intention to contest the watershed election. Gayoom's Progressive Party of the Maldives (PPM) put forward Abdulla Yameen, the former dictator's half-brother. Gasim Ibrahim's Jumhoree Party (JP) fielded Gasim Ibrahim. President Waheed's Gaumee Ithihaad Party (GIP) gathered all the minor parties into his "Forward with the Nation" coalition, including Hassan Saeed's Dhivehi Qaumee Party (DQP), the Adhaalath Party (AP) and the largely forgotten and irrelevant remnants of Gayoom's abandoned Dhivehi Rayithunge Party (DRP). Waheed chose the DRP's leader, Ahmed Thasmeen Ali, as his running mate. Vice presidential ambitions thwarted, the AP and DQP quickly abandoned Waheed and searched for another wagon.

Dr. Saeed and Mohamed Jameel of the DQP, so long united as brothers in their ambition to see Nasheed jailed, suffered an acrimonious divorce when the latter was invited to become Yameen's running mate.

Nasheed named as his running mate Dr. Mustafa Luthy—the former education minister who had been so attacked for successfully daring to reform the education system. Gasim's running mate was, for all intents and purposes, Gasim.

With the candidates locked in, international election observers began to flood into Malé. There was a sense the election had gained momentum—*something* had to happen on 7 September.

Election Fever

If politics were the Maldives' national sport, a presidential election was the Super Bowl. A carnival atmosphere spread across the country in the weeks leading up to the vote. Posters coated every inch of wall, coloured flags criss-crossed every street. Pick-up trucks equipped with loudspeakers circled Malé playing pre-recorded speeches and party songs for what seemed like 24 hours a day. The MDP, blessed with many young creative types, pumped out popular musical hits interlaced with Nasheed's exuberant speeches. These were very catchy, and could sometimes be heard drifting from the campaign centres of opposing parties.

"*Eh Burun*!" ("one round") became both the MDP mantra and a popular form of greeting. The party needed "fifty per cent plus one" of votes cast to avoid a run-off, and was confident of achieving this despite polling just 25 per cent in the first round of the 2008 election.

The party's manifesto stressed jobs, education and social welfare. Unusually for a political document, policymakers budgeted their promises against revenue to show that the pledges were possible.[2]

The PPM message was eclectic. Pink signage on a wall adjacent to Malé's main road read: "Hope is the dream of a waking man. Yameen for hope. For economy. There are so many men who can figure costs and few who can measure value." The manifesto was not budgeted but heavily emphasized youth issues. It promised 94,000 jobs, the creation of a "youth city" on Hulhumale and a theme park.[3]

The PPM focus was telling. The politically apathetic tended to be younger, and data from the Elections Commission showed a fifteen per cent rise in the number of eligible voters compared to the 2008 election: 31,000 new voters. The MDP's liberal and progressive ideals appealed to the younger set, so it made sense for the PPM to target this demographic.

The MDP, and often Nasheed himself, had meanwhile spent months door-knocking all over the country seeking vote pledges. The party optimistically claimed to have secured 125,000 pledges: 61 per cent of the electorate.

The international election experts arriving in the country thought a first round MDP win very unlikely in a vote featuring four candidates. I was less sceptical; political lines moved fast in the Maldives. All things being fair, I tipped a 55 per cent MDP win. More than half of the population was concentrated in the top two most populated islands: Malé and Addu. These populations had almost unanimously voted MDP in the recent local council elections. Fifty per cent plus was certainly achievable.

I tipped 20–25 per cent PPM, 10–15 per cent Gasim and 5–10 per cent to Waheed. The foreign experts shook their heads at this last prediction—such a poor result for an incumbent defied the political science textbooks. Besides, he was Stanford-educated.

We did agree that the MDP's challenge was not so much beating Yameen, but beating voter apathy—particularly among young people, many of whom were not around to experience the regime's excesses.

The MDP was certainly trying. Armies of volunteers were mobilized across the country, gathering in rented headquarters to help register voters and sew yellow flags. These shops and huts quickly became social hubs, occupied day and night. The other parties copied this, the PPM having particular success in luring young people with the promise of football and high definition projectors.

Nasheed was in his element. Foreign media found him hard to pin down, but eventually managed to get him to agree to a series of quick one-on-one interviews. When the journalists arrived he was busy signing a mountainous stack of letters typed on yellow paper, one to each of the country's 239,593 voters. "He insisted on signing each one personally," sighed a party official.

It was my turn to interview him.

"Our whole campaign has been very personal," Nasheed, looking up across the stack of paper as his pen continued to fly across the pages, his secretary removing each as it was signed. "I'm trying to reach out to the normal Maldives person. I've met them, I've touched them, I've visited their homes, and finally I want to write them a letter. When I'm signing them, I'm looking at the homes. I know who I am signing it to. I like that. I don't think a printed version is appropriate."

I asked him what would happen if he lost.

"There is no doubt. Not even entertaining that thought,"[4] he replied.

His sharpest retort was directed at the international community. They should, he said, "not be so naive or short-sighted."

"Please don't fund coups. Please don't encourage forceful change of government. What we saw was a lot of evidence that the UN was busy at it. Instability comes because outsiders side with one faction or another. Just don't do that," he suggested.

I knew the MDP was deeply suspicious of the local UN office's apparent silence in the wake of 7 February, but this was the first time I'd heard them voice the accusation publicly.

"What do you mean when you say the UN was 'busy at it'?" I asked.

"The [now reassigned] UN Resident Coordinator's safety address in case of an issue on 7 February was the vice president's residence. I was shocked to learn that," Nasheed alleged. "I felt the UN specifically wanted to recognize the new regime instead of conducting a proper investigation. They dragged the investigation out until they could cover it up. From the evidence we saw afterwards, especially from the government accountability committee in parliament, it is obvious it was a coup, and it is obvious that anyone should have seen it as a coup.

"We should have gone for an early election instantly. We should not legitimize any forceful transfer of power. Right now the situation is that everyone believes 'winner takes all'."

This sentiment was correct, and however carnivalesque the campaign preparations, there was a tangible atmosphere of fear and finality among many people in Malé. The election was a zero-sum game for both sides.

Transparency Maldives anticipated this in a pre-election assessment produced for the diplomats that would become the playbook for the election. The election would unfold "against a context of uncertainty, crises of political legitimacy and unprecedented levels of political polarisation," it predicted.

"The latter is characterised by mistrust, categorical negative framing of one another and by the lack of self-accountability of institutions, politicians and their parties for their role in the existing political crises. The electoral background is therefore discouraging."[5]

Buy-election

Vote buying was widely acknowledged among Maldivians as endemic; it was the primary method of influencing elections in the Maldives. There had been little attempt during previous elections to investigate the real extent of the practice. When Dan and Zaheena covered a by-election on the island of Kaashidhoo in April 2012 and uncovered an orgy of unabashed bribery, the most telling responses were from those curious as to why it even warranted a story.[6] In the wake of the piece, Transparency set out to study the issue.

"A crisis of confidence in candidates' sincerity to deliver on their electoral promises could be one of the main reasons why many people take offers," the NGO wondered. "Almost all the participants in the discussions thought the candidates would not bother about them or their community post-elections, or after winning the elections. 'They would not even answer their phones' was a common retort."

Vote buying was overt, the amounts surprisingly high. The two candidates in the Kaashidhoo election spent almost half a million dollars on a constituency of just 2,231 people—approximately US$230 per voter. "In Fuvahmulah, we were told, one candidate did not even have to campaign, but visited the island a week or so before the election and just distributed cash to his constituency," Transparency reported.

Bribes could be in cash, but more often came in the form of "gifts"—whatever you were in particular need of. Shopkeepers would receive refrigerators; bored youth, sports equipment, alcohol, TVs; the sick, medical treatment abroad. Transparency claimed that addicted young people were offered drugs or even ongoing discounts from their dealer.

Criminalization of vote buying simply discouraged reporting. Far more practical, I thought, to encourage people to milk the candidates for whatever they could get and reassure them that their real vote was confidential. Secret voting was vote buying's real vulnerability, a flaw recognized by the candidates who would demand proof via mobile phone, or even insist that the recipient swear on a Quran.

The twisted play to honesty worked rather well. A *Minivan* staff member, having caught a Gasim campaign boat back to his home island to vote, rang up distraught. He'd had a crisis of conscience and at the last minute had voted MDP. Now how was he going to get back to Malé?

"Take Gasim's boat," I suggested.

The same journalist had joked to his friends about voting for Waheed. His island ended up recording a single vote for the incumbent. He never lived it down.

You didn't need to take bribes to benefit from the largesse of election season. Plenty of paid work was available; someone had to put up the flags and spray paint the slogans.

Mariyath Mohamed ventured out to interview the various campaign teams.[7] "We're doing this for democracy. We don't want any money or incentives for this," said a 26-year-old accountant, spraying dot pictures of Nasheed on a wall. "The thing is, if we don't get involved and try to guarantee a better life for ourselves, why would anyone else bother?"

A team of surly PPM street decorators were less forthcoming. "Our leadership refuses to speak to you, and that means we have nothing to say to you either."

Others were more mercenary. Mariyath found one busy handing out flyers advertising Waheed. "It doesn't matter which candidate's campaigning I am doing, it's not even like these ugly flags and photos will make a difference for any party," he told her. "I sometimes even go with the Jumhooree Party guys. Point is, this is an excellent time to make some money on the side and I'm going to make the best use of it. But then, I know who I'm voting for and no one's got any business asking me who it is."

Gasim's JP offered the best paid gigs in town; putting up a single piece of JP party graffiti paid US$650. "When we finish putting up the strings of flags across a street, we need to ring a number that the party has given us. Then a party official will turn up with a file which has information on when and where the teams are active. They will put a tick confirming the job is done and pay us in cash on the spot. We get about MVR3,000 (US$195) a night on average," another team explained. "Some teams wait a while after the official has left and then cut down the recently hung flags, thereby allowing some other team to earn from the same street a few days later. It's probably not right, but well, the politicians spend like crazy when elections near, and so us lucky folks earn like crazy."

Cursed Coconuts

The Maldives' *fanditha* magicians also made a killing at election time. Election magic was a distinctly Maldivian school of sorcery. With the 2013 elections a zero-sum game for the major parties, every possible edge was sought.

The first coconut was discovered near a Guraidhoo island polling station on 4 September, several days before the election. It was found by a group of school students, who took it to their principal. He dutifully called the police, who in turn summoned a *ruqyah*—a white magic practitioner.

We contacted our sources on the island to learn more.[8]

"The four-inch coconut had a *Sura* [Quranic verse] written in Arabic," we were informed. "It was not really *fanditha* [black magic] on the coconut. If it was *fanditha*, there would have been Arabic letters and numbers written, not a *Sura*."

The theory was that the candidate chosen by the first person in line standing over the buried coconut would influence the rest of the island's voters. The case echoed an earlier incident in July in which parents of students at Guraidhoo Island School refused to allow it be used as a polling station due to concerns over a local witch.[9] Fuwad Thowfeek soothed the situation by offering public assurances that the Elections Commissioner would take full responsibility for any black magic that occurred.

Nonetheless if the September coconut was a warning, it was effective. "Now police are patrolling the school at night, so magicians can't practise real black magic at the school," said our source.

Despite the vigilance of the Guraidhoo authorities, however, the threat was not confined to one island. Fights between MDP and PPM supporters erupted on the island of Fuvahmulah in the country's far south after an ominous-looking coconut was discovered with Arabic writing and suspicious symbols.[10] We contacted Ajnaadh Ali, president and chief exorcist of the organization Spiritual Healers of the Maldives, to learn more.

Spells cast to influence voting were "spells of separation", he explained. "It's the same idea as a love spell. It can either bring people together or split them apart. The black magic will attack them mentally, by demanding the individual think a certain way even if they would normally know something is bad. It makes them blind in the mind." Coconuts were useful mediums for curses because, like eggs, they were "life structures".

The coconut saga was picked up by the international media,[11] making the day of many a "Strange but True" columnist. For all the sniggering Westerners, the globalization of the story had a serious and beneficial side effect: it greatly increased international attention on the actual election.

The Voter Register

Thowfeek's team were meanwhile working day and night to clean up the voter registry. In such a small country every vote was important, and making sure every eligible person had the opportunity to do so had been the commission's priority for the preceding months. The government's voter register, maintained by the Department of National Registration that issued ID cards, was poorly maintained and filled with errors. This manifested itself in previous elections as the problem of "zombie voters": those who were registered as deceased and yet inconveniently showed up in the flesh to vote, and voters who were genuinely dead but managed to rise from the grave on election day.

The original list was in a terrible state when Thowfeek was first appointed part of the interim Elections Commission in 2008. "At the time the voters list was very poor—there were so many duplicates and omissions," he told me, months later.

Was the state of the register deliberate?

"It was very badly managed. A lot of people wanted to take advantage of it. For example, if their parents lived on two different islands, a person was often registered on both the mother's and father's island. Sometimes if they were living somewhere else, they would be registered to a house in Malé. This allowed for multiple voting," he explained. "We knew some people might use this to their advantage, and since 2008 we worked to make the voter registry perfect."

"I thought everybody—Gayoom supporters, Nasheed supporters—would be happy I was doing this. I thought [corruption of the list] was not deliberate, done only for the advantage of individuals. But now I am very doubtful. Because of what happened, it looks like these things were done deliberately."

The register system linked every voter to a particular ballot box. In the lead-up to the poll, voters were encouraged to confirm their box either online or over the phone. By default, people were registered to vote on their home islands, and many used the holiday—and the free political party transport—as an opportunity to visit their families. Voters not on their home islands, such as those working on resorts or in Malé, were allowed to "re-register" to vote at another ballot box.

The commission was preparing to deploy 470 ballot boxes to accommodate 239,593 eligible voters across local islands and overseas missions in countries with a substantial Maldivian diaspora, such as Sri Lanka, Singapore and the UK. Each box was accompanied by the number of ballot papers for voters registered to that box. Some resorts hosted ballot boxes, although many managers refused out of a furtive desire to keep politics off their islands.

Police involvement in the elections was controversial, given their role in toppling the last democratically elected government. They were tasked with securing the polling stations, but excluded from the voting areas. Actual counting would be conducted locally at each polling station after the close of voting, observed by accredited observers from Transparency Maldives, international agencies and the various political parties. The boxes would be sealed and transported by police to the Elections commission's headquarters in Malé for a second counting and verification. This avoided issues with potential tampering during transport and provided speedier announcement of the preliminary results.

Running so many ballot boxes over a geographically disparate country was labour intensive and logistically difficult, but with the exception of the Malé boxes the relatively small number of ballots in each made discrepancies easier to identify and chase down.

Election security was aided by one factor: a lack of credible polling since the last election, large egos and the lure of legitimacy meant that all four candidates were convinced they were going to win. It wasn't worth the risk of undermining one's own chance of democratic legitimacy through vote fraud, at least in the first round.

International observers were also abundant. The Western embassies and High Commissions in neighbouring Sri Lanka sent teams, while the Commonwealth sent a large group headed by the former Prime Minister of Malta, Lawrence Gonzi. India, now vocally committed to the Maldivian democratic process after the GMR saga, sent a team of former chief elections commissioners.

There was a sense of a grand finale in the air during that first week of September 2013. The government had dropped its resistance to inclusive polls due to a combination of international pressure and perhaps genuine curiosity as to the outcome. All the pieces were in place for the restoration of democratic legitimacy. *Minivan* had used its spotlight to help ensure that it was Maldivians who decided who this would be. Our job now was to step back, to watch, report. The final choice—and responsibility—was theirs. It felt liberating, and exhilarating, to watch it the process unfold.

This attitude flooded the office, and the crew were excited and energized. *Minivan* had wind in its sails like never before, and perhaps for the first time, what felt like a full complement of crew. The gang was back together: Hawwa Lubna, who was studying in Lund on a Swedish Institute scholarship, returned to help us cover the election, likewise our former intern, Eleanor Johnstone. Another intern, Daniel Bosley, had also returned to take over the editorship after I left. We were arguably one of the credible institutions in a country facing elections where credibility was a crisis commodity. People were listening to us. We had a responsibility to be a steady hand on the wheel.

The Vote

The 7 September election day surprised everyone by being orderly, peaceful and unfolding almost exactly as planned. Voter turnout was an extraordinary 88.44 per cent, with 211,890 people casting their ballots. Observers praised the conduct of the polls and unanimously declared it credible.[12]

"The success in the first round is an achievement which any of the mature democracies would have been proud of. This was a transparent and fair election," said the Indian delegation's head, JM Lyngdoh. The observers particularly lauded the voter registry as "accurate and robust". "Fears expressed by some political parties regarding possible large numbers of deceased voters and voters registered in the wrong geographic area seem to be unfounded, based on the low incidence of election day complaints," declared the Commonwealth delegation.

Fuwad Thowfeek had managed to refine the voter register to near 100 per cent accuracy, a feat several of the observers privately confessed was unparalleled in most modern democracies. "Surprisingly few people complained after that first round. Hardly anybody. One or two people in entire country came to us and said their names were missing," Thowfeek said. "We verified these, found clerical errors, rectified the problems and allowed them to vote."

The Elections Commission counted throughout the night. By 4.30am the provisional results were confirmed: Mohamed Nasheed had come first with a clear majority of 45.45 per cent of the votes (95,224), painting almost every atoll yellow but falling shy of the 50 per cent needed to avert a run-off vote. President Waheed received a record-breaking 5.13 per cent of the vote (10,750).

Gasim Ibrahim was truly devastated. He received 24.07 per cent of the vote (50,422), much higher than expected, but still less than a per centage point behind Abdulla Yameen's 25.35 per cent (53,099). He was out of the race.

The small margin between Yameen and Gasim greatly increased tension over the result. Transparency Maldives, which fielded the largest domestic observation team, had ruled out that any of the minor incidents during the day would have "material impact on the outcome of the election".

However, the outcome was a bitter pill for the Jumhoree Party. A group of Gasim's supporters began to gather outside the Elections commission's counting headquarters in the early hours of the morning. Many took to Twitter to toss around spurious accusations of corruption, enthusiastically retweeted by a deeply suspicious electorate. The Maldivian media's inaccuracy in reporting the election was not particularly helpful; bigger outlets like *Haveeru* used their own data to call results rather waiting for the Elections Commission to release official counts. This was fed into very pretty web widgets that for large chunks of the evening showed more votes than voters in a number of electorates. This was less an issue of vote fraud and more an indication of sloppy reporting, but was held up as evidence of misconduct. The problems were quietly fixed with no corrections or explanation, leading to further allegations of conspiracy. Gasim and his supporters were unable to digest their result, and their claims were circulated by many Maldivians who should have known better. We noted these problems on our live blog but reported the results ourselves very conservatively, holding back on calling the election until the Elections Commission confirmed the figures in the early hours of 8 September. If you're going to be last, be right.

Gasim was convinced he should have received 70,000 votes. How he knew he was owed these was unknown, but in the aftermath of the first round he behaved like a man robbed of services paid for, but not delivered. Accompanied for some reason by the Adhaalath Party, he launched a series of strident "Rigged Vote!" rallies, and his television station took to displaying images of Thowfeek upside down. "What is certain is that it is not 50,000 votes that we got. I believe the result should have been more than 70,000 votes," Gasim declared in one of his many speeches on the topic.[13] "Those are people who joined us and supported us. These people are sobbing in all corners of the country, shedding tears of pain and crying: 'This is not the reality, so many crimes have been committed. We will never forgive, never forgive, this major crime committed by the Elections Commission.'"

The Jumhoree Party filed a case against the Commission with the Supreme Court, alleging fraud. The constitution actually identified the High Court as the arena for election-related disputes, but the judiciary had long proven itself above such technicalities.

The more spurious the JP's case grew, the more erratic Gasim's speeches became. "We saw people, dressed in a particular colour, closing up the vote boxes with shaking hands. Yes, I am telling you about Laamu Atoll. A person monitoring near one of our vote boxes there told me s/he saw a person wearing a yellow shirt closing a box. We are leading. We are leading. When you minus that 90,000 votes [received by MDP], we are the leaders. Yes, when you subtract 20,000 from those 90,000, I believe it is us who are in the lead. We know it is our vote that was changed. I am telling you what I believe. I am telling you what I believe. Maldivians, have courage. I am ready to make any sacrifice with my body and my money to bring you Maldivians a happy and prosperous life. We will not give in to anyone. This talk of me hospitalized for a heart attack—these are all blatant lies to dishearten you. This talk of me endorsing this person or endorsing that person. We will endorse when we have to endorse. But today we don't have to endorse. There is nobody we will endorse. God willing, it is others who will have to endorse us. We don't have to endorse anyone. We are not in such a position yet. God willing, it will be Gasim Ibrahim who will be the President of the Maldives."

Judicial Interference

The new Indian High Commissioner to the Maldives, Rajeev Shahare, invited me to dinner at his residence on 23 September with a small assortment of Maldivian and visiting Indian journalists. Whisky was promised and much appreciated.

Gasim's lawyer—none other than Dr. Hassan Saeed—had built a case largely on vague speculation from anonymized witnesses and allegations of deceased voters. The Commission presented these "deceased" voters to the courtroom—very much alive—and argued that even if the evidence presented by the JP was factual, it would still not be sufficient to alter the outcome of the first round.[14]

The Supreme Court judges responded not by dismissing the case but by barring the Elections commission's lawyer, former Attorney General Husnu Suood, from the courtroom on unspecified charges of "contempt".[15]

The constitution required the run-off election to be held within 21 days of the first round: 28 September. President Waheed's term was meanwhile due to expire on 11 November, whereupon the newly elected head of state was supposed to take over. Waheed had declared his endorsement of PPM's Yameen in the second round but had otherwise been very quiet in the wake of his resounding defeat. However, he did express concern about the "very serious allegations regarding the election", urging that these be resolved "by the respective legal and judicial venues".[16]

Over dinner, Shahare wanted to know our thoughts on what the court was up to. It felt like a tipping point; but just how far was the judiciary willing to go?

While we were talking, the Indian defence attaché received a phone call. He put the phone down and made the announcement: the Supreme Court had issued an injunction indefinitely delaying the election.[17] The journalists rushed off to file their stories. Dinner was muted, the air thick with disappointment.

The court's announcement triggered global condemnation, and foreign governments began to issue travel warnings to their citizens. President Waheed lashed out at "irresponsible statements by foreign governments and international organizations" which he declared were "not be helpful in consolidating democracy in the country ... Our statutory institutions, including the judiciary, have shown that they are capable of making sound and impartial decisions on some of the most complex issues of national importance."

This last pronouncement was a surprise to those who had read the UN Special Rapporteur's report on the Maldivian judiciary. "It is also troublesome that some of the Supreme Court's interventions are perceived as arbitrary and as serving the judges' own personal interests," Gabriela Knaul had written in her report six months earlier in May.[18] Waheed, however, called "on foreign governments, the UN, and the Commonwealth to show responsibility and to refrain from issuing statements commenting on, and speculating about, the on-going court case": "Local and international observers did a commendable job in observing the elections. Yet, they do not decide on the cases filed by one or more candidates in an election. It is never done anywhere in the world."

The Maldivian Foreign Minister, Gayoom's daughter Dunya Maumoon, likewise urged the international community to respect the "independent" institutions of the Maldives: "The Maldives, as a young democracy, continues to face a number of challenges in its journey towards consolidating democracy and strengthening its independent institutions. For this journey to continue the constitutional framework set up in the Maldives through a democratic process should be respected and the authority of the independent institutions should be upheld," read her statement.[19]

The injunction, coupled with the government's far from evidence-based confidence in the sanity of the Supreme Court, put the Elections Commission in a difficult position. Far from the supporting the Commission, Attorney General Azima Shukoor—Gayoom's former lawyer—had intervened in the case to dispute the integrity of the voter registry.[20]

The greater challenge was logistical. Preparing for a national election took time, especially in such a geographically spread-out country with poor transport links. Ballot papers had to be printed, thousands of people employed. But the 28 September constitutional deadline for polls approached, and the Supreme Court showed no sign of issuing a verdict. Hearings were being held at strange hours, with little sign of activity beyond light emanating from court building as early as 4am.

Shutdown

On the evening of 27 September, Thowfeek announced that the Elections Commission would hold the run-off poll the following day as demanded by the constitution. This prompted a flurry of activity inside the Supreme Court building.

Suddenly, Special Operations police—members of Gayoom's former "Star Force"—surrounded the Elections Commission's building in Malé. They claimed to have orders from Police Commissioner Abdulla Riyaz to storm the building and confiscate the ballot papers should the Commission proceed with the election. It was a troubling stand-off; if police were to enter the building, arrest Thowfeek and tamper with the ballots, prospects for a legitimate election were non-existent.

Predicting something like this would happen, we had preemptively installed one of *Minivan*'s foreign reporters, Leah Malone, inside the Commission's waiting room before the police sealed off the surrounding streets. Her instructions were to stick to Thowfeek like glue and to immediately relay information should the police step into the building.

The situation was tense. Police were trying to seal off the building. Diplomats were trying to breach the cordon and meet Thowfeek, but found the police uncooperative. The Maldivian media waited outside the building, furious at *Minivan* for having somebody inside.

Officers approached the glass doors, but found themselves face-to-face with Leah. They looked at her expression, and reconsidered their options.

"I think the work *Minivan* did was very useful," said Thowfeek, months later. "There were instances I would have been taken by the police if you were not there. One of your journalists heard they were coming to arrest me. She arrived first, and sat in our waiting room. That was one reason why they didn't take me."

Thowfeek's stand was symbolic. It was obvious that the election could not be held if the entirety of the police force intended to obstruct it. "The Supreme Court has ordered security services to prevent any effort to hold the election tomorrow," the Commission announced in a statement.[21]

"It is the responsibility of this commission to conduct, manage and facilitate all elections and public referendums and ensure that all elections and public referendums are conducted freely and fairly, without intimidation, aggression, undue influence or corruption and ensure that citizens are able to fully exercise the right to vote.

"The commission does not believe that such an atmosphere presently exists in the Maldives."

Thowfeek left the Elections Commission shortly after midnight.

"I feel disappointed after working so hard, to have to drop the second round. It is a big loss to the country," he said.

Strings Attached

The Supreme Court ordered the Elections Commission to cancel all its meetings with foreign delegates. These were a source of nervous paranoia for the government, which relied on controlling access to information. The Foreign Ministry even summoned Indian High Commissioner for interrogation over his efforts to breach the police cordon and meet with Thowfeek. "We are perfectly capable of handling our own problems," announced the Ministry's spokesperson, Ibrahim Muaz.[22]

A week later, on 8 October, the Supreme Court declared the first round of the election annulled.[23]

The verdict was passed by four of the seven Supreme Court judges, the same four who had voted to legitimize the Hulhumale court during the trial to criminalize Nasheed and prevent him from contesting elections. We had Mohamed Naahii watching proceedings in the courtroom. I had him write up his observations and biographies of the four judges for the benefit of the gallery.[24]

A pattern emerged. Justice Ali Hameed, alleged star in the series of leaked sex videos featuring prostitutes in a hotel room looking very much like Colombo's Cinnamon Grand, was also the subject of a July 2013 corruption case involving abuse of state funds.[25] Justice Dr. Ahmed Abdulla Didi was a former member and parliamentary election candidate of the DQP,[26] whose leader Dr. Hassan Saeed had represented the Jumhoree Party in the case. Judge Didi's appointment to the Supreme Court had been contested on the grounds that he lacked the required seven years' experience practising law. Justice Adam Mohamed was also Chair of the Judicial Services Commission (JSC) and the subject of a great deal of attention from Velezinee. He had, in one instance, outright refused to table a no-confidence motion levelled at himself.[27] Justice Abdulla Saeed had meanwhile been recorded pronouncing that Nasheed and his supporters suffered from "yellow fever", and that "by no means should Nasheed be allowed to become president".

The decision of these venerable men to annul the election rested on the contents of a "secret" police report supposedly contending that 5,600 votes were ineligible.[28]

The report was not shown to the Elections Commission, and its lawyers— those still permitted to enter the courtroom—were never given a chance to defend the allegations.

A repeat of the first round was to be held before 20 October, with a potential second round on 3 November, the court declared.

Moreover, the Elections Commission was to abide by a laundry list of restrictive, contradictory and extra-constitutional "guidelines", such as giving police a substantial role in the logistics of the election. Candidates would also be required to sign off each page of the voter registry—effectively giving Yameen and Gasim the power to veto polls until they were ready.

The court's guidelines also demanded the involvement of other government agencies in the election, such as the National Centre for Information Technology, and ordered the Commission to hand over information about its computer systems. Almost immediately these came under attack, with the Commission unable to do anything but watch as its databases were altered and compromised.[29]

Thowfeek and his team doubted that it was even possible for the Commission to follow the court's guidelines and hold an election in the timeframe given—almost certainly the court's intention. They got to work anyway.

Meanwhile, voters identified as deceased by the Supreme Court began coming forward to prove they were indeed very much alive. The report's list of 32 "underage" voters[30] included a 58-year-old woman, a 42-year-old, a 27-year-old, two 24-year-olds and many others eligible to vote. The wife of a 48-year-old man in Malé, who had been removed from the voter registry after the Supreme Court falsely declared her husband to be dead, wrote to the Chief Justice requesting that her "widowhood" be reversed.

The secret police report was finally leaked.[31] Police had scoured the voting records seeking every minor discrepancy, using extensive voter information extracted from the Commission by the court during the hearings, and cross referencing these against voting records.

Thowfeek was unimpressed with their effort. "For example," he observed,[32] "a person called Mohamed Waheed Hassan may have his name on his ID card as Mohamed Waheed. When we gave him the right to vote, [the police report] counted it as a fraudulent vote. But the ID card number, address, date of birth and photo is the same."

"About 1,900 of these cases were identified. A person called Mariyam Waheeda, may have her name spelled as Maryam on one list and Mariyam on the other. We know it is Mariyam Waheeda. We know it is the same person, the date of birth is exact, the ID card number is the same, the photo shows it is the right person. When we give these people the right to vote, the Supreme Court has said that is giving the right to vote to a person who doesn't have the right to vote.

"Similarly, the problem of address, it is quite weird. I could have been issued my ID card when the registry listed me as living in [the house] Haajaraage, but when I changed my address to Thalhamathuge [house], the ID I have is the still the previous ID [with a different address]. Even though I am now registered at Thalhamathuge, I still have the same ID card number, the same date of birth, the same photo. It is very clear I am the same person. We gave the right to vote to these people. And when we did that, [the election] has been annulled. A person can vote with their passport, which doesn't have their address. But there are over 2,800 cases of address mismatches [in the report]. They invalidated the election based on such evidence."

A UN team conducted an expert review of all the issues noted in the document, releasing its findings a month after the annulment of the result. "We feel confident in asserting that the election was all inclusive, there was no disenfranchisement and the quality of the voter register met international standards," declared Assistant Secretary-General for Political Affairs, Oscar Fernandez-Taranco.[33]

Usefully, he took his findings to the UN Security Council. Democracy was threatened in the Maldives and there was, he advised, "potential for trouble".[34]

He could have just asked Velezinee two years ago.

First Round, Take Two

The second attempt at the first round was scheduled for 19 October, a Saturday. Thowfeek hardly left the Elections Commission building except to appear on television, desperately trying to comply with the Supreme Court's exhaustive list of demands. Staff in the Commission said that he appeared to need little sleep himself, focusing instead on keeping up morale. Given the stress of the situation and polarized political loyalties, this was a masterclass in management. "I kept very personal contact with all the staff, especially the permanent staff," he explained, later, when I asked how he kept things together.

"I kept visiting every section and tell them very frankly what was happening, what we were trying to do, what the Supreme Court was doing. I kept sharing information. I asked them to give their 100 per cent support, admiring them and appreciating them. I talked to them and shook their hands one by one. Even if I could not remember them all by name, I wanted them to get a feeling that they were part of the bigger picture."

Although almost nobody had come forward to complain about the voter list after the first round, the Supreme Court demanded that the Commission use an old list held by the Department of National Registration. This was, said Thowfeek, specifically demanded of the court by the PPM and Jumhoree Party. "We worked closely with the Department of National Registration, showing them who was missing, who had been duplicated, and requested they make corrections. But still there were many errors," he said.

There was a week left before the 19 October date set by the Supreme Court. The judges quietly observed as the Elections Commission worked round-the-clock shifts to revise the voter registry and comply with its extensive demands. Miraculously, it appeared as if the election would indeed be held as scheduled.

When this became obvious, the PPM went back to the Supreme Court alleging that the Elections Commission was not following its guidelines. The court obligingly opened at midnight to demand that the Commission repeat the entire re-registration process with fingerprint-verified forms.[35]

The Commission was demoralized. Staff members began receiving anonymous death threats, and one of its five heads, Ogaru Ibrahim Waheed, suddenly resigned.

Buoyed by yet another ruling in its favour, the PPM went back to the court seeking an order barring Nasheed from contesting the election on the grounds of criticizing the judiciary and being "irreligious".

This was a tactical error, given the intense international scrutiny. Gayoom's daughter Dunya Maumoon cooled the fury by declaring it was "not the right time".

The Elections Commission meanwhile launched a panicked voter re-registration drive, and the process repeated as demanded by the court. The election was still on.

Shortly after midnight on 18 October, the day before the election, the PPM and JP announced that they would not sign the new voter register unless the new fingerprinted forms were individually verified.[36]

The Elections Commission pointed out that no institution in the country had the capacity to verify the 60,000 forms in the time required. The police said that the verification process would take at least six months, and announced they would not allow the polls to proceed without signatures from Yameen and Gasim. "Without their signatures, the Maldives Police Service is not willing to support us. They will not give protection to conduct the election and if we hold polls they will be invalidated by the Supreme Court," said Thowfeek.

The MDP quickly signed the lists. But, remarkably, neither Yameen nor Gasim could be found on 18 October. Their phones rang out, text messages were ignored and officials sent to the candidates' houses reported no answer to their knocks.

Two of the three parties contesting the election were actively hiding. The Supreme Court was silent. Thowfeek predicted that the court was planning to prosecute the Elections Commission for failing to hold an election it had itself heartily sabotaged. While his staff scoured Malé for Yameen and Gasim, he managed to contact Chief Justice, Ahmed Faiz. "He told me to keep trying. Send people to their homes and keep trying. He did not say what else we should do," Thowfeek said.

The morning of the vote arrived. At 3.30am, hours before the polls were due to open, the Elections Commission announced that the vote would go ahead as scheduled, without Yameen and Gasim's signatures. "The PPM and JP failed to [sign the lists]. I believe their failure to do what they should do must not stop the entire system," Thowfeek declared. "Just because one person fails to do their duties, refuses to do what they must do, it does not mean everyone else must stop their work, and deprive the Maldivian citizens of their right to vote."

The police reacted predictably. At 5.30am, they issued a statement declaring that they would "not support an election held in contravention of the Supreme Court verdict and guidelines".[37]

The Elections Commission was again surrounded by riot police. Democracy, Thowfeek announced, had "become a plaything". "The Elections Commission has spent MVR70 million [US$4.53 million] on the presidential election. We have worked 15-hour days throughout the holiday period. We are very disappointed, very much frustrated. Police have overstepped their authority and impinged on the EC's constitutional duties. This does not sap our determination. It makes it stronger. Resignation is not a choice."[38]

First Round: Take Three

The end of October approached. The pink and yellow party flags strung above the streets of Malé had begun to fade, colours running in the rain. What had once been a carnival atmosphere had likewise washed into Male's gutters, leaving the city heavy with a sense of tired resignation and thwarted expectations.

By now it was looking increasingly apparent that the Maldives would not have a new president before the end of the presidential term on 11 November. The Police Chief Superintendent, Abdulla Nawaz, had claimed that the decision not to cooperate with the election was based on advice from an assortment of sources, including President Dr. Mohamed Waheed, Attorney General Azima Shukoor and an elections security expert attached to them by the Commonwealth.

Noticing this comment in *Minivan*, the Commonwealth group hastily rang up to distance itself from any involvement. The police looked sheepish.

11 November was a red line for international observers. Foreign opinion finally began to turn against the government in a productive fashion. "Maldives now finds itself at a crucial crossroads. Through weeks of political bickering and questionable delaying tactics, Maldives democracy is now in peril," announced US Ambassador Michelle Sison.[39]

The UN High Commissioner for Human Rights, Navi Pillay, observing that she was "normally the first to defend the independence of [a] judiciary," accused the Maldivian Supreme Court of "subverting the democratic process and violating the right of Maldivians to freely elect their representatives".[40] "The Supreme Court appears set on undermining other independent institutions, stifling criticism and public debate, and depriving litigants of the legal representation of their choice," Pillay said.

The Chief Justice responded indignantly.[41] "The Maldives is a free and independent state. A state that is sovereign and governs itself. False allegations by any party on the Supreme Court's work does not aid strengthening democracy, administration of justice in the Maldives or uphold the rule of law. It does not encourage the promotion of democracy, rule of law or protection of human rights," said Judge Faiz. He announced that henceforth, "legal action will be taken against media organizations or journalists who disseminate false or inauthentic information concerning the judiciary".[42] "Citizens need valid information. Freedom of expression means expressing valid or authentic information. Whether it is information relating to individuals or state institutions, the information conveyed should be valid, there should be no error or deceit in the information."

Courtrooms were not the only weapon. The MDP-inclined television state Raajje TV had become the country's largest broadcaster by virtue of its "deceitful" content. It was stormed by a group of masked men in balaclavas. They took a security guard hostage and destroyed the studios in an impressive petrol-fuelled bonfire, the explosion and subsequent conflagration captured by a surprisingly durable CCTV camera.[43] The security guard was stabbed twice with a machete and hospitalized.

Somehow Raajje TV managed to overcome the total destruction of its studio and equipment and to get back on air later that day, operating with donated cameras.[44] It turned out that the station had received specific threats, passing these on to police that very evening. The police spokesperson, Chief Inspector Hassan Haneef, confirmed to *Minivan* that the police had received this information and "took action by patrolling the area".

A Minivaner suggested that this order had been misunderstood by the officers sent to carry it out. "'Patrolling', not 'petrolling'," he quipped.

The MDP was livid following the disruption of the 19 October poll, its supporters pouring into the streets of Malé and blocking the main road in an "occupy"-style protest. The police responded with urges to the public "not to impede the rights of others while attempting to exercise one's own constitutional rights".

It was a chaotic few weeks. The MDP set its sights on the Attorney General Azima Shukoor as an architect of the crisis. They managed to file a no-confidence motion against her for her role in the annulment of the election.

She called in sick and the no-confidence vote was delayed.[45] The following day somebody put laxative pills in the parliamentary coffee machine, and the vote was further delayed.[46] The vote was eventually held and she was thrown out of office, defiant to the last. She accused Nasheed of selling the Maldives to another country—we took this to mean GMR—and of attempting to include Jewish cultural education in the national curriculum. "I do not accept defying Islam and the Prophet. I believe the country has maintained its sovereignty because Maldivians have maintained the Islamic faith. I do not believe any other religion but Islam should exist in this country. This is my belief," she declared.[47]

The DRP withdrew from the government coalition, their first move of significance since their split with the PPM. Somebody smashed up the Indian High Commissioner's car. The World Economic Forum declared that the Maldives was failing to close the gender gap.

The fourth attempt at the first round of polls was agreed for 9 November with a possible run-off election to be held the following day, just a day before the expiry of the presidential term. The strain was taking its toll, however, and Thowfeek was admitted to hospital complaining of chest pains.[48] Luckily he was alright, but several foreign election observers later confessed that they came close to heart attacks themselves after hearing he had been admitted.

The Elections Commissioner's hospitalization inspired outpourings of public sympathy. The hashtag '#InFuadWeTrust' suddenly began trending on Twitter as hundreds of Maldivians went online to express their appreciation of his persistence. A group of young Maldivians, among them many first-time voters, put together a mosaic of photos of several hundred citizens expressing support, and presented it to him.[49] Thowfeek accepted it graciously, but deflected their thanks to the rest of his team.

First Round: Take Four

The first round finally went ahead that Saturday. It was the fourth attempt.

The results mirrored those of the annulled election almost identically. President Waheed had withdrawn, perhaps wishing to avoid a worse result than first time around. His supporters seemed to respond to his public endorsement of Yameen, taking the PPM to 29.72 per cent of the vote and a decisive lead over Gasim's 23.34 per cent. The MDP increased its share slightly to 46.93 per cent, still not enough to avoid a run-off and in spite of the pro-democracy election campaign run for it by the Supreme Court.

Voter turnout decreased slightly to 87.2 per cent, 208,504 votes out of 239,105 eligible voters.[50]

The outcome was accepted. It had two significant implications. Firstly, it set the stage for a decisive battle between Gayoom and Nasheed. Nobody, even on the PPM side, seriously credited Yameen with achieving the result; Gayoom's endorsement meant everything, and a substantial element of the party's 30 per cent reflected the genuine support and admiration among the population for the man who had ruled them for thirty years. This was a conservative vote for stability, for an omniscient father figure who would strip life of responsibility and thought while ruthlessly cutting down those who dared to rock the boat, disrupting "social harmony" and "our national unity".

Nasheed represented the opposite. His was a disruptive agenda of reform and modernization, but he also came with the chance to vote him out after five years. Few people voting for the PPM would have had serious expectation of ever needing to vote again.

The upcoming vote was therefore one that would finally transcend party politics. It was a referendum on the future vision for the country. Democracy or dictatorship?

The second implication concerned the constitutional crisis of the presidential term. International pressure was strongly against Waheed remaining in office past 11 November, and yet this meant holding the run-off vote in just a day's time. Yameen was adamant that this was not going to happen. "No, the election is not going to happen tomorrow. The simple reason being that the Elections Commission is not prepared for that," declared the PPM candidate at a press conference, once it was clear his party had trumped Gasim in the run-off.[51] "The Elections Commission does not have a list that has been pre-signed by the candidates. What they have is a fresh list," he rambled.

> For verification we need at least 48 hours. So the list they have we are not sure whether that is the list they had for today's voting. So until and unless we are able

to ascertain that this is the same list, we are unable to sign that. So the Elections Commission is not prepared. What they are claiming is that they have the same list but unfortunately if it were the same list our signatures or our representatives' signatures would have been on the list. But unfortunately these are fresh sheets. So we are not sure whether this is the same list we used for voting today. So primarily it is a shortcoming on the part of the Elections Commission. It's nothing to do with PPM or any other party.

What Yameen really needed was time to win over Gasim's support base, and he was prepared to plunge the Maldives into constitutional crisis to do so. President Waheed was expendable and could deal with the international political fallout. The pressure on him to resign and hand power to a transitional arrangement under the speaker of parliament was enormous. "It is unreasonable and unacceptable for parties to continue to demand changes to an agreed election date," said the US State Department. "Voters deserve a greater degree of predictability over something as serious as a presidential election. Changing the goalposts is unfair to Maldivian voters; we believe Maldivians deserve better. To delay second round voting beyond the constitutional requirements for a new government by November 11 will create uncertainties that may destabilize the Maldives."

The constitution required the Speaker, Abdulla Shahid, to take over government. However, Shahid had switched sides to the MDP and was therefore an unpalatable option to Gayoom's camp. Waheed had earlier voiced his opposition to remaining in office—"I do not want to stay in this position even a day beyond November 11"—and had promised to respect the country's best interests. But as outside pressure built he grew belligerent. "The people of our country are not any less capable or less educated than those in other countries, even the Western countries. They cannot come and tell us what to do," he said.[52]

Constitutional Crisis

Parliament moved to appoint the Speaker as head of government from 11 November. The PPM in turn went to the Supreme Court, requesting that Waheed's rule be extended past constitutional limits. To nobody's surprise, the Supreme Court agreed with the PPM.[53] "I am certain that President Waheed will stay with the Maldivian people at this most difficult time we are facing. I have no doubt about that," Yameen told a press gathering.[54]

The foreign election observers, who had spent months extending and cancelling their trips as the court prevaricated, began to mutter darkly about the country's future. "In any other country this would be called treason," remarked one.

Discontent had begun to spread to the military. An appeal had been circulated by senior officers stating their refusal to obey "unlawful" orders issued by an illegitimate presidency. In response, 300 officers were suddenly promoted and new regulation was introduced banning others from inciting "upheaval and chaos [through] speech, writing, action or gesture amongst members of the military".[55]

At 10.30pm, with just an hour and a half before his term was due to expire, President Waheed called a press conference. The vice president, Waheed Deen, had already resigned that morning.

"Today, as the head of state, my responsibility is to protect the country's highest interests. Many Maldivians, international organizations and countries are pressuring me to resign and temporarily hand over the government to the People's Majlis Speaker. On the other hand, even more citizens want me to stay on, to continue with administration of the country, to carry out my duty," he said, announcing his intention to remain in office until the run-off election was held on 16 November.

Parliament disagreed; the Speaker advised state institutions that Waheed was no longer President of the Maldives. Waheed, following his press conference, retreated to the nearby presidential retreat on Aarah.

The international response was vociferous, but misplaced in its direction of attack towards Waheed rather than towards the PPM or courts that had orchestrated the situation. The US Embassy warned that Waheed's action had "endangered the Maldivian people's right to elect a leader of their choice".[56] Sir Don McKinnon, the Commonwealth's Special Envoy, expressed "dismay" but declared that Waheed's decision was "regrettably, not unexpected despite best efforts of the Commonwealth and the United Nations to encourage the President to stay within the constitution".[57]

PPM cabinet ministers claimed that Waheed had arrived at the press conference with a resignation letter, but had been prevailed upon to stay in power in the interest of the Maldivian people. It was, gushed the PPM's corpulent Tourism Minister Ahmed Adheeb, one of "the strongest, most courageous decisions taken in the history of this country".[58]

Two days before the election, Waheed left the Maldives on his $34,000 state visit to Singapore,[59] leaving behind a confused power vacuum and a tape containing his farewell address.[60] In it, he defended his government's record, highlighting the reimbursement of civil servant salaries withheld under the former government's austerity measures, and the "rescue" of the international airport from foreign investors.

He railed against Nasheed's failure to involve his vice president in the affairs of state, and accused him of challenging "the long-standing non-aligned, independent and Islamic character of our foreign policy. Foreigners must not be invited to influence the Maldivian state's powers."

It was an ignominious end.

Showdown

Gasim found himself a man much in demand in the lead-up to the run-off. He may have felt cast aside after the 7 September vote, betrayed by those he believed were obliged to vote for him, but now, just over two months later, both Yameen and Nasheed were begging his favour.

At a rally earlier in November, Nasheed had somewhat awkwardly attempted to sway the Islamic vote with a rally promising that "there will be no room for another religion in this country under an MDP government. This is very clear."[61] It came in response to a pamphlet released the previous week by a group calling itself The Maldives Society of Islamic Research, demanding that the former president "repent" and "return to the true path". That the Maldives was, and would remain, Islamic "is not something we should doubt", Nasheed told the rally, but he acknowledged that "Something that does not exist will exist when you continually talk about it. A lie becomes the truth when you keep repeating it. It enters our hearts as the truth."

Now, with the final round imminent and the prospect of a deal on the table, Gasim suddenly found himself in a conciliatory mood towards Nasheed's religious credentials. Despite Gasim's earlier calls for "jihad"[62] against the former president, Nasheed had now dispelled "doubts and suspicions concerning Islam". "[Nasheed] has said that Islamic norms and principles will be followed in his government. That was something that people had been talking about repeatedly. He has cleared up something that we had misconceived," said the resort tycoon.

Yellow flags began to spring up outside the tycoon's campaign offices. It seemed that the MDP was swaying him.

Gayoom quietly paid Gasim a visit. Exactly what was debated was unclear, although *Haveeru* reported that 33 per cent of the government was offered. Foreign diplomats who met Gasim said that the tycoon was complaining about threats to his businesses and livelihood.

Gayoom met the press, announcing that Saturday's choice was "between the holy religion of Islam and the beloved Maldivian nation on the one hand, and its opposite ways on the other". The introduction of other religions and threats to national sovereignty would, he declared, lead to "loss of peace and security, bloodshed, division and discord".

Gasim then proceeded to endorse Yameen "for the safety of the Ummah [Islamic community] and its future".[63]

I doubted the effect this endorsement would have, attributing much of Gasim's first round performance to the commercial incentives of his campaign. Faced with the choice between Nasheed and the legacy of thirty years of autocracy, these more pragmatic voters would, I felt, be more inclined to vote for the MDP—if they bothered to vote at all. The MDP had a comfortable lead and apathy would only benefit Nasheed. He had only to convince 13 per cent—just 6,180 members of Gasim's support base—to vote for him in order to win.

Nasheed, for his part, expressed relief over having avoided another coalition. He pointed out that the PPM would never have signed the voter lists and permitted the election to go ahead unless the JP backed his candidacy.

He was right. The polls opened as scheduled and the final round unfolded smoothly. *Minivan* did notice a sharp increase in the number of people attempting to photograph their ballot papers, however. Witnesses also reported instances of last-minute vote buying.[64] "At around noon, I saw a guy carrying a zipped money bag, handing out notes to people who came out [of the polls]," said a 26-year-old voter Ali Nasheed. "This is disgraceful on both ends, both those who are selling and buying votes. This is no way to contest in a democratic election. I cast a void vote. There is just no point in a place like this."

Twenty-six-year old Ahmed Thoha claimed that people were selling their ID cards for US$35–65. "They are asking us to give them our National Identification cards in return for money. I heard they were giving sums ranging from MVR500 to MVR1,000," he said. This fee, we learned from a group of young men hanging around one of the polling stations, could be significantly boosted if one waited until the final hours of polling, especially if things were looking close.

Nonetheless, the majority of people we spoke to were hopeful and optimistic, pleased to finally have the opportunity to cast their vote and bring the saga to a close. "I'm so happy to be part of the 50 per cent-plus-one that is about to re-establish democracy," said Rauha Waheed, a first time voter.

Result

Provisional results from the Elections Commission show Maldivians have voted to return to power the family of the Maldives' former 30 year autocracy, giving a democratic mandate to Progressive Party of the Maldives (PPM) candidate Abdulla Yameen.

Yameen, the brother of former autocratic President Maumoon Gayoom who ruled the Maldives for 30 years before being ousted in 2008 by Mohamed Nasheed in the country's first multi-party elections, received 51.39 per cent of the vote (111,203). Nasheed polled 48.61 per cent (105,181)—a difference of just 6022 votes.

Total voter turnout was 91.41 per cent (218,621), the highest since 2008, up five per cent from the first round.

The election was hailed by Transparency Maldives as "credible, transparent and extremely well-administered, as were the two previous rounds."

Yameen's election brings to an end a chapter of controversy and uncertainty over the government's democratic legitimacy, following the ousting of Nasheed in February 2012 amid a police mutiny.

I sat up late into the night writing the story.[65] Many of *Minivan*'s Maldivian staff were broken by the result, and had gone home. For the first time, I had sensed real fear in the air. Zaheena worried about what would happen to her family. Naish was plunged into deep, subterranean introspection. Nazeer wondered how *Minivan* could continue to publish under Yameen, whether he would still have a job. Leah had gone native, as the occasional expat was wont to do. She had disappeared to ruminate with her Maldivian friends, deeply affected.

The PPM victory party in the Nasandhura Palace Hotel appeared a hastily organized affair. Several hundred supporters quietly milled around outside. For such a close victory, I was surprised at the general lack of merriment. In any other country, the reaction of supporters to such a close margin would have been ballistic.

Inside the hotel, former president Maumoon Abdul Gayoom was hogging the microphone. Yameen looked as surprised and confused as any member of the Maldivian public, even slightly uncomfortable in the spotlight. "The most important thing we must do is thank Allah," said Gayoom. "He has given us victory. He has given his religion victory."

Pizza Hut, Six Months Later

"I have been getting a lot of phone calls, SMS messages from unknown people saying they will attack me, kill me and so on," said Thowfeek, in the detached manner of a statistician.

It was nearing the middle of 2014, six months into Yameen's rule. The Supreme Court had sentenced the four remaining election officials to six months imprisonment for the crime of "disobeying orders", suspended for three years on condition of "good behaviour". Thowfeek and his deputy had also been sacked from their jobs by the court, although the validity of this move was doubtful as parliament constitutionally had sole authority over their appointments. Yameen's government had nonetheless used its control of the Finance Ministry to cut off the commissioner's wages, so the issue was moot.

Thowfeek was, he said, urgently looking for work, but had already been turned down from one international role on the grounds of being too qualified. "I would be very happy to work anywhere in the world—Africa, Asia, Europe. I hope I will get an opportunity," he said. "Africa—I could do quite a lot of work there."

I asked Thowfeek if, based on his experience with the 2013 election, the new government was legitimate. He answered carefully. "I think it was done against the constitution. The constitution clearly stated certain dates and timeframes for each and every activity. The first round was held according to the constitution, and the Supreme Court did not have the power to cancel it. But the Attorney General Azima sided with them. The whole procedure became mixed up."

Repeated elections, stops and starts, disappointments and shattered expectations had jaded the electorate, he explained. "People got fed up. There was so much bribery in between the voting. The Supreme Court took the voters list from us and we learned they shared it with the police and some other people. These are things that cannot be done. The validity of the election," he said, "is very much in doubt."

His wife returned from her shopping trip, and we wrapped up the interview. He kindly thanked *Minivan* for its role in the saga. I shook his hand, and asked his wife how she felt about their returning to Malé.

"I don't think he will be safe in Maldives," she said.

"But we have to go back. We have no other option."

EPILOGUE

"The scrupulous and the just, the noble, humane, and devoted natures; the unselfish and the intelligent may begin a movement - but it passes away from them. They are not the leaders of a revolution. They are its victims."

Joseph Conrad

Minivan News journalist Ahmed Rilwan walked through the terminal to catch the ferry home to Hulhumale. Two men followed him. CCTV footage, taken during the early hours of 8 August 2014, was the last time anybody saw him. Multiple witnesses later reported a man being forced into a red vehicle at knifepoint, right outside Rilwan's home. The knife was recovered. Rilwan was not.

The journalist had been receiving threats from several Islamist groups for his outspokenness on social media. Radicalized vigilante gangs had already begun to abduct and interrogate others they decided were guilty of "promoting secularism", holding them at knifepoint, extracting passwords and shutting down Facebook and other social media accounts.[1] The attacks took place quite openly; one victim was even held and interrogated in a café full of people. The police, and government, failed to react, despite the culprits being clearly identified.

Instead, it was left to Rilwan's family, the *Minivan* team and other supporters to conduct a thorough search of Hulhumale. They found no trace of him. Family members reported receiving threats during the search.

The *Minivan* office was attacked, a machete buried in the door. High definition CCTV footage, transmitted by the camera before it was destroyed, clearly identified the leader of one of Malé's radicalized gangs.

"You will be killed or disappeared next, be careful," read a message sent to Zaheena, afterwards. She was now *Minivan*'s deputy editor, and took to finding Rilwan with singular purpose.

"We've chased a hundred leads, obtained and analyzed Rilwan's phone records, and hacked into his social media accounts for clues. We've kept watch at potential sites he may be held, organized petitions, lobbied politicians, held marches, read Rilwan's poetry on the streets. We've papered the city with missing-person posters. When the posters faded in the sun and rain, we put up new ones," she wrote, in an article for *Middlebury Magazine* in the US.[2] "I realized why funeral rites are elevated in all of the world's cultures. We'll never be able to mourn Rilwan properly until we find out what happened to him, until we see his remains. The uncertainty will always keep the pain alive."

The police took statements, promised to find the missing journalist, and then did nothing. The case hardly called for Sherlock Holmes; the suspects were already known to police, and there were only two red cars on Hulhumale. A private investigation found that one of these cars was registered to a member of a notorious crime family implicated in the 2012 murder of MP Afrasheem Ali. The car had been illegally imported to Hulhumale on 4 August—just before Rilwan's abduction—and returned to Malé on 13–15 August, shortly afterwards.

"Not all crimes in the world are solvable," declared Umar Naseer, who had been promoted to Home Minister under Yameen's government.[3] "Americans still have not solved the case of who shot and killed President John F. Kennedy," he explained.

Soon afterwards, several of the suspects in Rilwan's case left to join a growing number of Maldivians fighting in Syria. Reports filtering back to the Maldives suggested that they joined more than 200 active and aspiring Maldivian militants fighting abroad. The government grunted its broad disapproval but failed to take any action to stem the flow. A group of Maldivian jihadists abroad, calling themselves Bilad Al Sham, began tweeting threats and reporting the deaths of those killed fighting.

Whatever the Gayoom clan's feelings on the fundamentalism they had exploited for political benefit, religious extremism was now well out of their control. Young Maldivians attending a music festival in April 2014 were stunned when police stormed the island, searching 200 party-goers and arresting 79.[4] The event was shut down and attendees handcuffed for hours. In October, Yameen yielded to pressure from radicals and made music and dance optional subjects in the schooling system. Many schools, already under pressure, had already taken them off the curriculum.[5]

The concessions to fundamentalism had already begun to affect the country's economy and relationship with the outside world. The fishing sector was crippled when the largest and most profitable export market, Europe, declined to renew the Maldives' duty-free status. This was a result of its continued refusal to conform to international human rights standards—specifically those regarding religious freedom and women's rights.

Fishermen began exporting tuna to Europe at a loss of US$1.66 per kilo. Yameen's government hit on a solution, certifying the fish as "halal" and selling it to the Middle East instead.[6] There was no further information as to whether this had been successful.

Business as Usual

The end of the Maldivian democracy experiment had come not with the manipulated and drawn out deck-stacking of the 2013 presidential election. If anything, the Elections Commission's success at ensuring a fair count while besieged by both the executive and judiciary was an against-the-odds triumph in democratic process.

But the old regime was back in charge. Not only were they engorged with confidence after winning a legitimate term of government, but they had tested the loyalty of the security services and purged the troublemakers.

The puppet courts that had protected the regime from the constitution's new organs of justice had been exposed and subjected to much public mirth. But the MDP and its supporters had shown a lethargic unwillingness to ultimately challenge and reject the courts' authority. Instead, they had followed rules written by those who paid no heed to these themselves. Every attempt by the MDP to compromise with the regime—the Supreme Court appointments, the all-party talks, the Commission of National Inquiry—had seen the party burned.

The writing was on the wall. The parliamentary elections were scheduled for 22 March 2014, and given the legislature's power to evict ministers and reform courts and institutions, there was no way that President Yameen would contest them with the Elections Commission in an honourable state.

Two weeks before the March poll, Thowfeek and the Commission's other outspoken senior officials were convicted and forced out by the Supreme Court on charges of unspecified "contempt". This turned out to be precautionary, as Yameen need not have worried about the vote. What was the point casting your ballot if any result other than a PPM victory was thrown out by the country's highest court?

Apathy, exhaustion and low turnout saw the PPM and its allies sweep the polls, gaining a 54-seat majority. The Gayoom family regime had not only finally regained control of all three arms of state, but destroyed all hope for free and fair elections in the future.

The Maldives was back to business as usual.

Game Over

As predictably as any such regime, Yameen's government grew increasingly paranoid. One by one he turned on his former allies, evicting Gasim from government, calling in the tycoon's loans and freezing his assets. Then he went after the Defence Minister, Mohamed Nazim, the man responsible for taking over the military in the 2012 coup. The police searched Nazim's home, claiming to have discovered a pistol and an improvised explosive device. Nazim was arrested, and perhaps somewhat belatedly, charged with attempting to overthrow the government.

The Vice President, Dr Mohamed Jameel, was next, impeached by pro-government MPs accusing him of disloyalty and plotting to depose the President, as well as "failure to make progress" in improving the health and education portfolios with which he had been entrusted.[7] Jameel, echoing a gripe familiar to the office, complained of being "sidelined". He fled to London and endured his fall from grace in absentia. Yameen replaced him with the 33 year-old tourism minister Ahmed Adeeb, the rotund and favoured scion of PPM. Adeeb was best known for his rumored links to Male's more unpleasant gangs, and a series of photos depicting him entertaining a pair of notorious Armenian gangsters. They were the Artur brothers, linked to drug trafficking, money laundering, raids on media outlets, and other serious crimes in Kenya, including pulling a gun on customs officials.[8] Youth proved no obstacle to installing Adeeb as Vice President, with Yameen forcing a constitutional amendment through parliament lowering the minimum age of the second highest office from 35 to 30. At the same time he brought the maximum down to 65—forever forcing Gasim out of the race. A second constitutional amendment would soon allow for the sale Maldivian territory to foreign parties.

"The natural beauty of the islands has been to Maldives what diamonds were to Sierra Leone: a disaster for the ordinary men and women; an impediment to democracy; an obstacle to human development; and a pathway to massive corruption ... Life as Maldivians have known it for centuries is coming to an end," wrote Azra Naseem, following the announcement.[9]

The regime finally came for Nasheed in February 2015. He was dragged through the street and presented to the court, glasses broken, shirt torn and buttons missing. One arm was in a makeshift sling—his yellow tie. Charged with terrorism, denied a lawyer and deemed a flight risk, he was remanded in custody pending trial. The trial was farcical even by Maldivian judicial standards, with two of the three judges on the panel submitting witness statements to the prosecution. The court refused to hear any defence witnesses on the grounds they "would not be able to refute the evidence" and on 13 March 2015, Nasheed was found guilty and sentenced to 13 years in prison.[10]

The sentencing led to the single largest protest in Maldivian history, with 20,000 people filling the entire length of Malé's main road. Two hundred demonstrators were arrested, the largest number in a decade, together with all opposition leaders. Courts issued blanket 15-day remand periods to those detained. Amnesty issued a press release. Amal Clooney - human rights lawyer and wife of the famous actor George Clooney - announced she was representing Nasheed pro bono and called for targeted sanctions against the regime. The regime, spearheaded by Gayoom's daughter Dunya, hired Cherie Blair for an undisclosed sum to defend itself from Clooney and uphold Nasheed's sentencing, joining the ranks of Blair's other clients such as Kazakhstan and Gambia. Several months later it took on the prominent Washington lobbyists the Podesta Group to unravel the predictably terrible press this generated, at a further cost of US$300,000[11]. Life in the Maldives went on.

I had last seen Nasheed in June 2014, during a visit to Malé for follow-up interviews. We had met in the conference room of the MDP office on Sosun Magu. The building would be set on fire a few months later in September.

"When the first round of the presidential elections were nullified and the international community and others decide to accept it, I realized it would be impossible to win," he said. "Of course, losing it was sad and we wished it hadn't happened. But I saw it coming. It was just not possible and we had the odds stacked against us.

"I don't think I would have done anything differently. Anything else would have gone against the grain of what we think is right and we are trying to do. In terms of campaigning we could have said this, that or the other, less controversy over religion. But I think if that was the case we would have lost somewhere else. I don't think there was much wrong in the strategy."

The MDP had played by rules set, enforced and ignored by the other team. Nasheed was insisting that he would not have done anything differently—but the party's position was hardly enviable. Why didn't they boycott the election after the Supreme Court's annulment, when the international community was finally on their side? "Our team was so cocksure that they were going to win. I was fairly sure myself. There's no stopping it once it's rolling," he said, cheerfully.

Would a boycott have changed the outcome?

"It would have. There were discussions. I think the PPM and the judiciary would have lost control of the election process. The judiciary took over control of the elections process from the elections commissioner. The situation could have been pushed back to where it should have been.

"But the idea was to follow the rules even if you get beaten by them. Exhaust the rules. This is not the end. You can't conclude anything now. This, as you would say in the press, is a developing story."

Departure

But no longer my story.

I left *Minivan* and the Maldives in December 2013. Dan stepped into the editorship with the unenviable task of maintaining morale under Yameen's increasingly oppressive administration.

Neil Merrett had vowed that I would leave before him. In fact, he left two months before I did, eventually taking up a magazine job in London. I opted to stay and see the election through to its bitter end. The delays were personally frustrating. The triumphant ending was within reach. Maldivians would suddenly wake up to the modern, hopeful and progressive future Nasheed represented. The country would become a beacon for the Islamic world, a beacon in which we had played a part: a proof-of-concept that Islam, democracy and human rights could live in harmony. If he didn't work out they could vote him out in five years. Dictatorship had been dodged, toppled and staked once and for all. Meanwhile, the Maldives would become a symbol in the fight against climate change, exciting renewable energy projects powering the tiny islands as great creative and scientific minds, drawn by Nasheed's charisma and political will, flocked to the country.

It was not my place to say this, though. Instead, *Minivan News* fought for there to be an election at all. An election where whatever the surrounding corruption and vote buying, your vote counted on the day's final tally. That was as much as Thowfeek, Velezinee, *Minivan* or any canny diplomat could provide; the final choice was up to Maldivians, and it was stark: democracy or dictatorship. There turned out to be no prison better than the one you build yourself.

A film or novel may have a tragic ending and still be satisfying. But my departure still felt bittersweet. My concern as I boarded the plane was for the lives and livelihoods of friends who stayed behind, those for whom this was not a novel, a real life *Game of Thrones* in the Indian Ocean.

I flew to Sri Lanka and a Dutch woman of extraordinary patience who had waited many months with growing exasperation. She had booked a hotel in the jungle near Negombo. We travelled up into the cool mountains of Ella, stayed a week in a guesthouse overlooking the misty valleys and waterfalls, took the train to the fortress town of Galle, lay on the tourist beaches of Hikkaduwa.

She saw life as something to be enjoyed, work as a means to attain life's pleasures rather than an end in itself. After four years consumed by *Minivan* and the Maldives, it was like trying to learn a new language. I struggled, and failed, and stared into space where purpose had once been. I returned to Sydney and family and finally, far too late, did the honourable thing.

The sudden silence was stressful. At the end of a day of idleness I would find my jaw clenched tight, muscles aching. My younger brother had visited Malé in my final month, arriving on the day of the final election. Crossing the channel on the airport ferry, he joked about Marlow going up the river to retrieve Colonel Kurtz. We relayed it back at the *Minivan* office. That day, nobody laughed.

The hardest feeling to reconcile was the sense from those in power, and those who had been, that the Maldives was a chess game, a population played for amusement as much as for government. I still do not know what to think.

On the way home I missed my connecting flight to Singapore and the airline put everybody up in a hotel. In what may have been a sign of good things to come, the lunch buffet consist almost solely of pork.

The next day I flew into Sydney's Kingsford Smith airport. A customs and quarantine inspector walked up and down interviewing the passengers waiting at the baggage carousel.

"Where've you travelled from?" he asked.

"The Maldives? You lucky bastard."

NOTES

1. CHAINS AND COCONUTS

1. 'Guide to Maldives', Conde Nast Traveller, http://www.cntraveller.com/guides/asia/maldives/maldives/where-to-stay, last accessed 7 Jul. 2015.
2. 'Mohamed Nasheed', Hottest Heads of State, http://hottestheadsofstate.com/2010/05/10/mohamed-nasheed/, last accessed 7 Jul. 2015.
3. 'Doubling salary spend in 2007–09 crippled economy: World Bank', Minivan News, http://minivannewsarchive.com/politics/doubling-salary-spend-in-2007–09-crippled-economy-world-bank-7529, last accessed 29 Jul. 2015.
4. 'Supreme Court backs down from issuing ruling on legality of selling pork and alcohol', Minivan News, http://minivannews.com/politics/supreme-court-backs-down-from-issuing-ruling-on-legality-of-selling-pork-and-alcohol-30334, last accessed 29 Jul. 2015.

2. "CONTROVERSIAL TRANSFER OF POWER"

1. 'Maldives government changes in dramatic scenes after police elements join opposition protest', Minivan News, http://minivannewsarchive.com/politics/live-police-join-opposition-protests-attack-military-headquarters-31592, last accessed 29 Jul. 2015.
2. 'Police fired gun in takeover of MNBC, video reveals', Minivan News, http://minivannewsarchive.com/politics/police-fired-gun-in-takeover-of-mnbc-video-reveals-32053, last accessed 29 Jul. 2015.
3. Photo of police and military officers celebrating outside the state broadcaster on 7 Feb. 2012 http://minivannews.com/files/2012/02/mnbc_maldives.jpg.
4. 'Mutiny in the Maldives', SBS Dateline, http://www.youtube.com/watch?v=akxK-jS9_is, last accessed 29 July 2015.
5. '"In victory be magnanimous": President of Timor-Leste visits Maldives', Minivan News, http://minivannewsarchive.com/politics/in-victory-be-magnanimous-president-of-timor-leste-visits-maldives-3434, last accessed 29 Jul. 2015.

6. 'President of Timor Leste condemns "obvious" coup d'état, "unsettling silence of big powers"', Minivan News, http://minivannewsarchive.com/politics/president-of-timor-leste-condemns-obvious-coup-detat-unsettling-silence-of-big-powers-3239, last accessed 29 Jul. 2015.

7. 'Mob storms National Museum, destroys Buddhist statues: "A significant part of our heritage is lost now"', Minivan News http://minivannewsarchive.com/society/mob-storms-national-museum-destroys-buddhist-statues-a-significant-part-of-our-heritage-is-lost-now-31813, last accessed 29 Jul. 2015.

8. 'Police crackdown sparks riots across the Maldives—"acts of terrorism" say police', Minivan News, http://minivannewsarchive.com/politics/live-mohamed-nasheed-reported-injured-as-mdp-supporters-clash-with-security-forces-31688, last accessed 29 Jul. 2015.

9. 'How To Plan The Perfect Coup: Lessons From Fiji And The Maldives', Huffington Post, http://www.huffingtonpost.com/mohamed-nasheed/plan-the-perfect-coup-maldives_b_1871171.html, last accessed 29 Jul. 2015.

3. MINIVAN NEWS

1. 'Maldives blacklists foreign nationals for suspected terrorist links', Leaked US Embassy cable 05Colombo837, http://cables.mrkva.eu/cable.php?id=32026, last accessed 29 Jul. 2015.

2. 'Police patrols now pedal powered', Minivan News, http://minivannewsarchive.com/politics/police-patrols-now-pedal-powered-5346, last accessed 29 Jul. 2015.

3. '100 information heroes', Reporters Without Borders, http://heroes.rsf.org/en/mariyath-mohammed/ last accessed 29 Jul. 2015.

4. 'DhivehiSitee: Life and times of radicalization and regression in the Maldives', http://www.DhivehiSitee.com, last accessed 29 Jul. 2015.

5. Those who visited a site at least once a day.

6. 'Jameel and Dunya to defend Maldives' human rights record at UNHRC', Minivan News, http://minivannewsarchive.com/politics/jameel-and-dunya-to-defend-maldives-to-defend-human-rights-record-at-unhrc-40411, last accessed 30 Jul. 2015.

7. 'President grants clemency to self-exiled 'Sandhaanu' Luthfy', Minivan News, http://minivannewsarchive.com/politics/president-grants-clemency-to-self-exiled-sandhaanu-luthfy-5796, last accessed 30 Jul 2015.

4. RISE OF THE MDP

1. 'Q&A: Former UK MP for Salisbury Robert Key talks democracy in the Maldives', Minivan News, http://minivannewsarchive.com/politics/qa-former-mp-for-salisbury-robert-key-and-the-democracy-in-the-maldives-16431, last accessed 30 Jul. 2015.

2. 'Letter suggests links between Christian evangelists and Mohamed "Anni" Nasheed',

News Oracle, http://newsoracle-p1.blogspot.com/2008/10/letter-suggests-links-between-christian.html, last accessed 30 Jul. 2015.

3. Forged letter from 'Salisbury Cathedral' to Mohamed Nasheed, http://1.bp.blogspot.com/-8nctkxn2cfQ/TwgXkHNrjRI/AAAAAAAAANQ/zxPPbn-lAJFo/s1600/3004454547_e86c4959fa+%2528Large%2529+%2528Custom%2529.jpg, last accessed 30 Jul. 2015.

4. 'Q&A: Dr Ahmed Shaheed', Minivan News, http://minivannewsarchive.com/politics/qa-dr-ahmed-shaheed-21783, last accessed 30 Jul. 2015.

5. More on this in later chapters. For the impatient: "Yameen implicated in STO blackmarket oil trade with Burmese junta, alleges The Week", Minivan News, http://minivannewsarchive.com/politics/yameen-implicated-in-sto-blackmar-ket-oil-trade-with-burmese-junta-alleges-the-week-16046, last accessed 30 Jul 2015.

6. 'Resort tycoon unveils "Religion and Nationalism Policy", promises to strengthen Islamic faith', Minivan News, http://minivannewsarchive.com/politics/resort-tycoon-unveils-%e2%80%9creligion-and-nationalism-policy%e2%80%9d-prom-ises-to-strengthen-islamic-faith-62015, last accessed 30 Jul. 2015.

7. 'Total import of selected items 2009–2011', Maldives Customs Service, https://docs.google.com/file/d/0B2lSZUo5Pid9cmVLN25PMi1YSExfQlVhQTMt ZWFGWFUxS3hj/, last accessed 30 Jul. 2015.

8. 'A question of Trust: the many promises of Mohamed Nasheed', Haveeru, http://www.haveeru.com.mv/opinion/43662, last accessed 30 July 2015.

9. 'DRP MP Rozaina leaks invoices exposing extravagant spending of former President Gayoom's family', Minivan News, http://minivannewsarchive.com/pol-itics/drp-mp-rozaina-leaks-invoices-exposing-extravagant-spending-of-former-president-gayooms-family-45720, last accessed 30 July 2015.

10. 'Going After Government Looters', New York Times, http://www.nytimes.com/2010/06/12/business/global/12iht-assets12.html?pagewanted=all&_r=1, last accessed 30 July 2015.

11. 'Extreme makeunder in the Maldives', BBC News, http://news.bbc.co.uk/2/hi/south_asia/7895953.stm, last accessed 30 July 2015.

12. 'Doubling salary spend in 2007–09 crippled economy: World Bank', Minivan News, http://minivannewsarchive.com/politics/doubling-salary-spend-in-2007–09-crippled-economy-world-bank-7529, last accessed 30 July 2015.

13 'Cabinet resigns in protest over opposition MPs "scorched earth" politics', Minivan News, http://minivannewsarchive.com/politics/cabinet-resigns-in-protest-over-opposition-mps-scorched-earth-politics-8736, last accessed 30 July 2015.

14. 'Decentralisation bill passed as MDP MPs walk out', Minvan News, http://min-ivannewsarchive.com/politics/decentralisation-bill-passed-as-mdp-mps-walk-out-6444, last accessed 30 July 2015.

15. 'Maldives among only three countries to ever graduate from least-developed sta-tus: UN report', Minivan News, http://minivannewsarchive.com/society/mal-

dives-among-only-three-countries-to-ever-graduate-from-least-developed-status-un-report-18040, last accessed 30 July 2015.

16. 'Economy's pigeons come home to roost', Minivan News, http://minivannewsar-chive.com/politics/economys-pigeons-come-home-to-roost-19668, last accessed 30 July 2015.

17 'Double salary spend in 2007-09 crippled economy: World Bank', Minivan News, http://minivannewsarchive.com/politics/doubling-salary-spend-in-2007-09-crip-pled-economy-world-bank-7529, last accessed 22 Sept 2015.

5. TOURISM, ENVIRONMENT, ECONOMY

1. 'When two cowrie shells could buy a woman', The East African, http://www.thee-astafrican.co.ke/magazine/-/434746/530264/-/15l3r28/-/index.html, last acces-sed 30 July 2015.

2. 'The history of tourism in the Maldives', The Telegraph, http://www.telegraph.co.uk/luxury/travel/3049/the-history-of-tourism-in-the-maldives.html, last acces-sed 30 July 2015.

3. 'Tourism Yearbook 2013', Ministry of Tourism, Arts and Culture Republic of Maldives, http://www.tourism.gov.mv/pubs/Yearbook_2013.pdf, last accessed 30 July 2015.

4. A Maldivian friend tells a story of how the arrival of the portable flashlight greatly traumatized women of her grandmother's generation. Women would sneak off to the beach at night time to do their business, but torches meant that the island's boys would often be waiting in the bushes to surprise and humiliate them. Her grand-mother insisted this was responsible for an epidemic of constipation and greatly hastened the arrival of the flush toilet.

5. 'Times Atlas To Print New World Map Without Tuvalu, Maldives, Manhattan etc', The Telegraph, http://blogs.telegraph.co.uk/news/jamesdelingpole/1001 05854/times-atlas-to-print-new-world-map-without-tuvalu-maldives-manhattan-etc/#disqus_thread, last accessed 30 July 2015.

6. 'Satirical news blog dupes Maldives media', Minivan News, http://minivannews-archive.com/politics/satirical-news-blog-dupes-maldives-media-25886, last acces-sed 30 July 2015.

7. 'HarperCollins confirms Maldives not being erased from Times Atlas as global warming statement', Minivan News, http://minivannewsarchive.com/politics/harpercollins-confirms-maldives-not-being-erased-from-time-atlas-as-global-warm-ing-statement-25948, last accessed 30 July 2015.

8. Image: Swedish geographer Nils-Axel Mörner's experimental tree, http://2.bp.blogspot.com/-FLrEZtjFeUg/TWS0rMZftkI/AAAAAAAAAb0/ty7aTjX-8YGA/s1600/Morner+Tree.jpg, last accessed 30 July 2015.

9. 'Maldives suffering worst coral bleaching since 1998', Minivan News, http://min-ivannewsarchive.com/environment/maldives-suffering-worst-coral-bleaching-since-1998–8132, last accessed 30 July 2015.

10. 'Lithuanian company reveals plans to open island of blondes in the Maldives', Minivan News, http://minivannewsarchive.com/business/lithuanian-company-reveals-plans-to-open-island-of-blondes-in-the-maldives-11103, last accessed 30 July 2015.

11. 'Visiting Danish Ministers announce climate mitigation assistance', Minivan News, http://minivannewsarchive.com/politics/visiting-danish-ministers-announce-climate-mitigation-assistance-13467, last accessed 30 July 2015.

12. 'Maldives democracy must prove it can guarantee liberty: European Commission report', Minivan News, http://minivannewsarchive.com/politics/maldives-democracy-must-prove-it-can-guarantee-liberty-european-commission-report-12202, last accessed 30 July 2015.

13. 'Marine biologist discovers turtle, shark slaughter in Maldives' UNESCO biosphere reserve', Minivan News, http://minivannewsarchive.com/environment/marine-biologist-discovers-turtle-shark-slaughter-in-maldives%e2%80%99-unesco-biosphere-reserve-43986, last accessed 30 July 2015.

14. 'Widespread 'secret' slaughter of endangered sea turtles despite ban; "very tasty" say killers', Minivan News, http://minivannewsarchive.com/politics/widespread-secret-slaughter-of-endangered-sea-turtles-despite-ban-very-tasty-say-killers-55463, last accessed 30 July 2015.

15. 'Tourism business worth US$2.5–3 billion, not US$700 million as thought, says President', Minivan News, http://minivannewsarchive.com/politics/tourism-business-worth-us2-5-3-billion-not-us700-million-as-thought-says-president-20966, last accessed 30 July 2015.

16. 'Surge in Chinese arrivals just a passing fad, cautions MATI', Minivan News, http://minivannewsarchive.com/business/surge-in-chinese-arrivals-just-a-passing-fad-cautions-mati-11692, last accessed 30 July 2015.

17. 'European decline could stall tourism in 2013: MATI', Minivan News, http://minivannewsarchive.com/business/european-decline-could-stall-tourism-in-2013-mati-30597, last accessed 30 July 2015.

18. 'MEGA Maldives Airlines plans rapid expansion as it starts to diversify outside China-Maldives market', Centre for Aviation, http://centreforaviation.com/analysis/mega-maldives-plans-rapid-expansion-as-it-starts-to-diversify-outside-china-maldives-market-162014, last accessed 30 July 2015.

19. 'Maldives rebranded as "always natural"', Minivan News, http://minivannewsarchive.com/society/maldives-rebranded-as-always-natural-27499, last accessed 30 July 2015.

20. Edwards-Jones, Imogen, *Beach Babylon*. Bantam 2007.

21. Romero-Frias, Xavier, *The Maldive Islanders*. Nova Ethnographica Indica, 2003.

22. 'Pyrard—Maldives 1602–1607', Maldives Culture, http://www.maldivesculture.com/index.php?option=com_content&task=category&sectionid=7&id=56&Itemid=75, last accessed 30 July 2015.

23. 'The Maldive Islands, Dhibat-ul-Mahal', Maldives Culture, http://www.maldives-culture.com/index.php?option=com_content&task=view&id=198&Itemid=74, last accessed 30 July 2015.

24. 'A brief analysis on tourism indicators end December 2013', Ministry of Tourism, http://www.tourism.gov.mv/downloads/reports/1statistical_Analysis_End_December_2013.pdf, last accessed 30 July 2015.

25. 'Civil Court injunction prevents government takeover of Alidhoo, Kudarah resorts', Minivan News, http://minivannewsarchive.com/society/civil-court-injunction-prevents-government-takeover-of-alidhoo-kudarah-resorts-59060, last accessed 30 July 2015.

26. 'Leaked Grant Thorton report reveals beneficiaries of BML's risky pre-2008 lending', Minivan News, http://minivannewsarchive.com/politics/leaked-grant-thorton-report-reveals-beneficiaries-of-bml-risky-pre-2008-lending-62676, last accessed 30 July 2015.

27. 'Social stigma limiting employment of local women in resort industry, report finds', Minivan News, http://minivannewsarchive.com/society/social-stigma-limiting-employment-of-local-women-in-resort-industry-report-finds-25467, last accessed 30 July 2015.

28. 'Kurumba management evacuates guests as strike talks deadlock', Minivan News, http://minivannewsarchive.com/society/kurumba-management-evacuates-guests-as-strike-talks-deadlock-10556, last accessed 30 July 2015.

29. 'Comment: New regulation on strikes lacks legality and would wipe out resort workers' constitutional rights', Minivan News, http://minivannewsarchive.com/politics/comment-new-regulation-on-strikes-lacks-legality-and-would-wipe-out-resort-workers%e2%80%99-constitutional-rights-11776, last accessed 30 July 2015.

30. 'Staff threw stones at intruder and left him in the water to drown, alleges Baros staff member', Minivan News, http://minivannewsarchive.com/society/staff-threw-stones-at-intruder-and-left-him-in-the-water-to-drown-alleges-baros-staff-member-17826, last accessed 30 July 2015.

31. 'British woman who died at Kuredhoo "a strong swimmer", say parents', Minivan News, http://minivannewsarchive.com/society/british-woman-who-died-at-kuredhoo-a-strong-swimmer-say-parents-11877, last accessed 30 July 2015.

32. 'Honeymoon bride drowned after wading into sea to cool off sunburn', Daily Mail, http://www.dailymail.co.uk/news/article-1371625/Honeymoon-bride-Sharon-Duval-drowned-wading-sea-cool-sunburn.html, last accessed 30 July 2015.

33. 'Death of tourist at Kuredhoo Island Resort last year was accidental, finds UK inquest', Minivan News, http://minivannewsarchive.com/society/death-of-tourist-at-kuredhoo-island-resort-last-year-was-accidental-finds-uk-inquest-18124, last accessed 30 July 2015.

34. 'Police charge driver in 2011 Kuredu quad-bike crash that killed British newly-

weds', Minivan News, http://minivannewsarchive.com/society/police-charge-driver-in-2011-kuredu-quad-bike-crash-that-killed-british-newlyweds-34009, last accessed 30 July 2015.

35 'Statement from Mr. Lars Petre', Minivan News, http://minivannews.com/files/2011/08/Larspetrestatement.pdf, last accessed 30 July 2015.

36. 'Uncertainty over 2011 case of British couple killed in resort quad bike accident', Minivan News, http://minivannewsarchive.com/society/uncertainty-over-2011-case-of-british-couple-killed-in-resort-quad-bike-accident-54127, last accessed 30 July 2015.

37. 'Mum of tragic Maldives honeymoon groom speaks out after man is charged over deaths of him and his bride', Halifax Courier, http://www.halifaxcourier.co.uk/news/crime/updated-mum-of-tragic-maldives-honeymoon-groom-speaks-out-after-man-is-charged-over-deaths-of-him-and-his-bride-1-4370279, last accessed 30 July 2015.

38. 'Foreigner acquitted of resort crash deaths flees Maldives after prosecutors seek to withhold passport', Minivan News, http://minivannewsarchive.com/politics/foreigner-acquitted-of-resort-crash-deaths-flees-maldives-after-prosecutors-seek-to-withhold-passport-65734, last accessed 30 July 2015.

39. 'Party Island: Sun Island resort employees allege purge of MDP staff', Minivan News, http://minivannewsarchive.com/politics/party-island-sun-island-resort-employees-allege-purge-of-mdp-staff-67997, last accessed 30 July 2015.

40. 'Politics in paradise: Irufushi resort staff complain of political "firing spree"', Minivan News, http://minivannewsarchive.com/politics/politics-in-paradise-irufushi-resort-staff-complain-of-political-firing-spree-67082, last accessed 22 Sept 2015.

41. 'Alidhoo Resort sacks 12 staff members following strike over unpaid salaries', Minivan News, http://minivannewsarchive.com/society/alidhoo-resort-sacks-12-staff-members-following-strike-over-unpaid-salaries-23328, last accessed 30 July 2015.

42. 'Alidhoo Resort staff allegedly still owed wages: "If they don't like it, they can leave," says resort owner Jabir', Minivan News, http://minivannewsarchive.com/politics/alidhoo-resort-staff-allegedly-still-owed-wages-if-they-dont-like-it-they-can-leave-says-resort-owner-jabir-49035, last accessed 30 July 2015.

43. 'Foreign couple mocked as "infidels" and "swine" throughout resort's 'wedding ceremony"', Minivan News, http://minivannewsarchive.com/society/resort-%e2%80%98wedding-ceremony%e2%80%99-in-dhivehi-degrades-tourist-couple-as-infidel-swine-mocks-islam-12671, last accessed 30 July 2015.

44. 'The exploited Maldives 'celebrants' are the victims here, not the Swiss couple', The Guardian, http://www.theguardian.com/commentisfree/2010/oct/29/maldives-resort-swiss-couple, last accessed 30 July 2015.

45. 'President apologises to Vilu Reef couple, invites back to Maldives', Minivan News,

http://minivannewsarchive.com/politics/president-apologises-to-vilu-reef-couple-asks-media-to-respect-their-privacy-12901, last accessed 30 July 2015.

46. 'Post mortem of the wedding saga', Maldives Resort Workers, https://maldivesresortworkers.wordpress.com/2010/10/29/post-mortem-of-the-wedding-saga-headline/, last accessed 30 July 2015.

47. 'Government withdraws controversial new liquor regulations', Minivan News, http://minivannewsarchive.com/politics/government-withdraws-controversial-new-liquor-regulations-3981, last accessed 30 July 2015.

48. 'Importers concerned about dollar shortage', Minivan News, http://minivannewsarchive.com/politics/importers-concerned-about-dollar-shortage-12011, last accessed 30 July 2015.

49. 'Exploitation of Bangladeshi workers worth hundreds of millions, says former High Commissioner', Minivan News, http://minivannewsarchive.com/society/exploitation-of-bangladeshi-workers-worth-hundreds-of-millions-says-former-high-commissioner-10365, last accessed 30 July 2015.

50. 'Human trafficking worth US$123 million, authorities estimate', Minivan News, http://minivannewsarchive.com/politics/human-trafficking-worth-us123-million-authorities-estimate-23342, last accessed 30 July 2015.

51. 'IMF delegation surprised by resilience of Maldivian economy', Minivan News, http://minivannewsarchive.com/politics/imf-delegation-surprised-by-resilience-of-maldivian-economy-77846, last accessed 30 July 2015.

52. 'Comment: Guest house business—my journey', Minivan News, http://minivannewsarchive.com/society/comment-guest-house-business-my-journey-75147, last accessed 30 July 2015.

53. 'Blackmarket dollar crackdown won't address demand, warn businesses, financial experts', Minivan News, http://minivannewsarchive.com/politics/blackmarket-dollar-crackdown-wont-address-demand-warn-businesses-financial-experts-18017, last accessed 30 July 2015.

54. 'Leaked footage from police HQ suggests opposition was prepared to use "military force" on Feb 7', Minivan News, http://minivannewsarchive.com/politics/leaked-footage-from-police-hq-suggests-opposition-was-prepared-to-use-military-force-on-feb-7-33187, last accessed 30 July 2015.

6. RELIGION AND THE "MOSQUERADE"

1. Romero-Frias, Xavier, *The Maldive Islanders*. Nova Ethnographica Indica, 2003.

2. 'Airport traffic controller in suspected suicide', Minivan News, http://minivannewsarchive.com/society/airport-traffic-controller-in-suspected-suicide-9343#sthash.srdhkPYm.dpbs, last accessed 31 July 2015.

3. 'Hanged air traffic controller sought asylum for fear of religious persecution', Minivan News, http://minivannewsarchive.com/society/hanged-air-traffic-controller-sought-asylum-for-fear-of-religious-persecution-9381, last accessed 2 August 2015.

4. 'Maldives a 99.41 per cent Muslim country, claims RISSC report', Minivan News,

http://minivannewsarchive.com/society/maldives-a-99–41-percent-muslim-country-claims-rissc-report-10838, last accessed 2 August 2015.

5. He would later become Islamic Minister. He pops up a lot.

6. 'International Covenant on Civil and Political Rights', United Nations Office on Human Rights, http://www.ohchr.org/en/professionalinterest/pages/ccpr.aspx, last accessed 2 August 2015.

7. 'UNHRC panel grills Maldives delegation on human rights commitments', Minivan News, http://minivannewsarchive.com/politics/unhrc-panel-grills-maldives-delegation-on-human-rights-commitments-40663, last accessed 2 August 2015.

8. 'Constitution of the Maldives', Maldives President's Office, http://www.presidencymaldives.gov.mv/Documents/ConstitutionOfMaldives.pdf, last accessed 2 August 2015.

9. 'Dr. Zakir Naik's response for Maldivian publicly renouncing Islam, who repented 3 days later', Youtube, https://www.youtube.com/watch?v=_sN3u_SLZ9E#t=18 last accessed 2 August 2015.

10. 'Islamic Foundation calls for death sentence if apostate fails to repent', Minivan News, http://minivannewsarchive.com/politics/islamic-foundation-calls-for-death-sentence-if-apostate-fails-to-repent7606, last accessed 2 August 2015.

11. 'Revelations of a former apostate: Mohamed Nazim speaks to Minivan', Minivan News, http://minivannewsarchive.com/society/revelations-of-a-former-apostate-mohamed-nazim-speaks-to-minivan-11617, last accessed 2 August 2015.

12. 'Constitution of the Maldives', Maldives President's Office, http://www.presidencymaldives.gov.mv/Documents/ConstitutionOfMaldives.pdf, last accessed 2 August.

13. Quran 2:256 (Al-Baqarah), Sahih Internationl, http://quran.com/2/256, last accessed 2 August 2015.

14. Throughout this chapter I am particularly indebted to the work of Xavier Romero-Frias, Michael and Fareesha O'Shea's Maldivesculture.com, and Dr Azra Naseem and Mushfique Mohamed's excellent history of Maldivian Islamism,.

15. 'Comment: The inappropriate history of early Maldives', Minivan News, http://minivannewsarchive.com/society/comment-the-inappropriate-history-of-early-maldives-27861, last accessed 2 August 2015.

16. 'The discovery and destruction of the big statue of Thoddu in 1959—Statue smashed a second time at Mulee-aage', Maldives Culture, http://www.maldivesculture.com/index.php?option=com_content&task=view&id=166&Itemid=42, last accessed 2 August 2015.

17. 'Mob storms National Museum, destroys Buddhist statues: "A significant part of our heritage is lost now"', Minivan News, http://minivannewsarchive.com/society/mob-storms-national-museum-destroys-buddhist-statues-a-significant-part-of-our-heritage-is-lost-now-31813, last accessed 2 August 2015.

18. 'Footage leaked of museum vandals destroying pre-Islamic artifacts', Minivan News,—http://minivannewsarchive.com/politics/footage-leaked-of-museum-vandals-destroying-pre-islamic-artifacts-51117, last accessed 2 August 2015.

19. Dr Husain, Mahdi. 'The Rehla of Ibn Battuta—India, Maldive Islands and Ceylon—translation and commentary' Oriental Institute, Baroda, India 1976.

20. 'Islamic Foundation launches certificate course in use of incantations to cure black magic', Minivan News, http://minivannewsarchive.com/society/islamic-foundation-launches-certificate-course-in-use-of-incantations-to-cure-black-magic-24372, last accessed 2 August 2015.

21. 'Masked men break into school to cut down cursed 'Jinn tree'', Minivan News, http://minivannewsarchive.com/politics/masked-men-break-into-school-to-cut-down-cursed-jinn-tree-81926, last accessed 2 August 2015.

22. 'Albino turtle stolen from Sri Lanka was to be used for "black magic on a Maldivian politician"', Minivan News, http://minivannewsarchive.com/politics/albino-turtle-stolen-from-sri-lanka-was-to-be-used-for-black-magic-on-a-maldivian-politician-73806, last accessed 2 August 2015.

23. 'Police conduct witch hunt on Thakandhoo after children allegedly possessed by evil spirits', Minivan News, http://minivannewsarchive.com/politics/police-conduct-witch-hunt-on-thakandhoo-65383, last accessed 2 August 2015.

24. 'Comment: The inappropriate history of early Maldives', Minivan News, http://minivannewsarchive.com/politics/busting-black-magic-in-guraidhoo-66428, last accessed 2 August 2015.

25. 'The rise and fall of the Maldivian shipping fleet', Minivan News, http://minivannewsarchive.com/business/the-rise-and-fall-of-the-maldivian-shipping-fleet-2260, last accessed 2 August 2015.

26. 'Suvadive Republic 1959–1963', Maldives Culture, http://www.maldivesculture.com/index.php?option=com_content&task=category&sectionid=7&id=51&Itemid=76, last accessed 2 August 2015.

27. Ellis, Royston. *A Man For All Islands: A biography of Maumoon Abdul Gayoom, President of the Maldives* (1998) Times Editions.

28. Colton, Elizabeth: The Elite of the Maldives, Sociopolitical Organisation and Change (1995).

29. Colton, Elizabeth: The Elite of the Maldives, Sociopolitical Organisation and Change (1995).

30. Colton, Elizabeth: The Elite of the Maldives, Sociopolitical Organisation and Change (1995).

31. 'The Long Road from Islam to Islamism: A Short History', Dhivehi Sitee, http://www.dhivehisitee.com/religion/islamism-maldives/, last accessed 2 August 2015.

32. 'The Long Road from Islam to Islamism: A Short History', Dhivehi Sitee, http://www.dhivehisitee.com/religion/islamism-maldives/, last accessed 2 August 2015.

33. 'Indian teacher tied up after islanders mistake compass for crucifix', Minivan News,

http://minivannewsarchive.com/news-in-brief/indian-teacher-rescued-after-islanders-mistake-compass-for-crucifix-11756, last accessed 2 August 2015.

34. 'Teacher preaches Christianity "to leave country" in lieu of vacation', Minivan News, http://minivannewsarchive.com/society/teacher-preaches-christianity-to-leave-country-in-lieu-of-vacation-3760, last accessed 2 August 2015.

35. 'Islamic Ministry claims Christians, Freemasons secretly working to "eradicate" Islam in the Maldives', Minivan News, http://minivannewsarchive.com/politics/islamic-ministry-claims-christians-freemasons-secretly-working-to-eradicate-islam-in-the-maldives-52751, last accessed 2 August 2015.

36. 'Israeli flag burnings and 'sit-together' marks tale of two protests on International Human Rights Day', Minivan News, http://minivannewsarchive.com/society/israeli-flag-burnings-and-sit-together-marks-tale-of-two-protests-on-international-human-rights-day-14277, last accessed 2 August 2015.

37. 'Israeli eye surgeons visiting Maldives to "illegally harvest organs", claims Islamic Foundation', Minivan News, http://minivannewsarchive.com/politics/israeli-eye-surgeons-visiting-maldives-to-illegally-harvest-organs-claims-islamic-foundation-13872, last accessed 2 August 2015.

38. 'Salaf calls on government to offer military training to citizens "before Jews take over the country"', Minivan News, http://minivannewsarchive.com/society/salaf-calls-on-government-to-offer-military-training-to-citizens-before-jews-take-over-the-country%e2%80%9d-14063, last accessed 2 August 2015.

39. 'RISSC report ranks State Islamic Minister among top 500 most influential Muslims', Minivan News, http://minivannewsarchive.com/news-in-brief/rissc-report-ranks-state-islamic-minister-among-top-500-most-influential-muslims-10751, last accessed 2 August 2015.

40. 'L'Arabia dei Tropici', Vanity Fair Italy, http://iosonoqui.vanityfair.it/category/maldive/, last accessed 2 August 2015.

41. 'The culture of flogging in the Maldives: a systematic abuse of human rights', Minivan News, http://minivannewsarchive.com/politics/the-culture-of-flogging-in-the-maldives-a-systematic-abuse-of-human-rights-55092, last accessed 2 August 2015.

42. '100 Information Heroes: Mariyath Mohamed', Reporters Without Borders, http://heroes.rsf.org/en/mariyath-mohammed/, last accessed 2 August 2015.

43. 'Save the Maldives from fundamentalists', The Guardian, http://www.theguardian.com/commentisfree/belief/2009/sep/28/maldives-wahhabi-islam, last accessed 3 August 2015.

44. 'Maldivian Islamic groups call for arrest of UN High Commissioner on Human Rights', Minivan News, http://minivannewsarchive.com/politics/maldivian-islamic-groups-call-for-arrest-of-un-high-commissioner-on-human-rights-28676, last accessed 3 August 2015.

45. 'Islamic Minister, MPs, PPM and religious groups condemn UN Human Rights

Commissioner', Minivan News, http://minivannewsarchive.com/society/islamic-minister-mps-ppm-and-and-religious-groups-condemn-human-rights-commissioner-28687, last accessed 3 August 2015.

46. 'Banished to Paradise', Middlebury Magazine, http://sites.middlebury.edu/middmag/2011/08/02/banished-to-paradise/, last accessed 3 August 2015.

47. 'Discovery of dead baby in outdoor shower a distressing reminder of the Maldives' failure to address unwanted pregnancies', Minivan News, http://minivannewsarchive.com/society/discovery-of-dead-baby-in-outdoor-shower-a-distressing-reminder-of-the-maldives-failure-to-address-unwanted-pregnancies-39815, last accessed 3 August 2015.

48. 'Negative campaigns will not only damage Maldives tourism, but the country as a whole: Maleeh', Sun Online, http://www.sun.mv/english/10890, last accessed 3 August 2015.

49. 'Maldives minister slams "dubious" motives behind Avaaz boycott campaign', Minivan News, http://minivannewsarchive.com/politics/maldives-minister-slams-%e2%80%9cdubious%e2%80%9d-motives-behind-avaaz-boycott-campaign-55511, last accessed 3 August 2015.

50. 'One million people sign petition calling for end to flogging of women and children in the Maldives', Minivan News, http://minivannews.com/politics/one-million-people-sign-petition-calling-for-end-to-flogging-of-women-and-children-in-the-maldives-55045, last accessed 3 August 2015.

51. '15 year-old rape victim deserves flogging for separate crime of fornication: Adhaalath Party', Minivan News, http://minivannewsarchive.com/politics/15-year-old-rape-victim-deserves-flogging-for-crime-of-fornication-adhaalath-party-53861, last accessed 3 August 2015.

52. 'Maldives failed "at every level" to protect minor charged with fornication from years of abuse', Minivan News, http://minivannews.com/politics/maldives-failed-%E2%80%9Cat-every-level%E2%80%9D-to-protect-minor-charged-with-fornication-from-years-of-abuse-54984, last accessed 3 August 2015.

53. 'Maldives High Court overturns flogging sentence for 15 year-old charged with fornication', Minivan News, http://minivannewsarchive.com/politics/maldives-high-court-overturns-flogging-sentence-for-15-year-old-charged-with-fornication-63028, last accessed 3 August 2015.

54. 'Highest divorce rate', Guinness World Records, http://www.guinnessworldrecords.com/world-records/highest-divorce-rate/, last accessed 3 August 2015.

55. Dr. Husain, Mahdi. 'The Rehla of Ibn Battuta—India, Maldive Islands and Ceylon' Oriental Institute, Baroda, India 1976.

56. 'Police take 16 year-old girl into custody for "dressing inappropriately"', Minivan News, http://minivannewsarchive.com/society/police-take-16-year-old-girl-into-custody-for-dressing-inappropriately-57429, last accessed 3 Aug 2015.

57. '"G-Spot" doesn't exist, contends shop owner in ongoing case against Economic

Development Ministry', Minivan News, http://minivannewsarchive.com/society/g-spot-doesnt-exist-contends-shop-owner-in-ongoing-case-against-economic-ministry-17298, last accessed 3 Aug 2015.

58. Hilath.com, archived on the Wayback Machine: https://web.archive.org/web/20141219231149/http://www.hilath.com/, last accessed 3 Aug 2015.

59. 'Imam among seven men arrested for homosexual activity', Minivan News, http://minivannewsarchive.com/society/six-men-and-an-imam-arrested-for-homosexual-activity-956, last accessed 3 Aug 2015.

60. 'Four Maldivians questioned for allegedly committing bestiality with a goat', Minivan News, http://minivannewsarchive.com/society/four-maldivians-questioned-for-allegedly-committing-bestiality-with-a-goat-18289, last accessed 3 Aug 2015.

61. 'Tea shop closed by MFDA after live goat found in toilet', Minivan News, http://minivannewsarchive.com/society/tea-shop-closed-by-mfda-after-live-goat-found-in-toilet-21246, last accessed 3 Aug 2015.

62. 'Reproductive Health Knowledge and Behaviour of Young Unmarried Women in Maldives', United Nations Population Fund, http://countryoffice.unfpa.org/maldives/drive/UNFPARHReport_reduced.pdf, last accessed 3 Aug 2015.

63. 'Abortion in the Maldives: the untold story', Minivan News, http://minivannewsarchive.com/society/abortion-in-the-maldives-the-untold-story-2191, last accessed 3 Aug 2015.

64. 'Adhaalath Party calls for execution of mothers who abort children', Minivan News, http://minivannewsarchive.com/politics/adhaalath-party-calls-for-execution-of-mothers-who-abort-children-21775, last accessed 3 Aug 2015.

65. 'Mother of abandoned milk can infant sentenced to one year imprisonment', Minivan News, http://minivannewsarchive.com/society/mother-of-abandoned-milk-can-infant-sentenced-to-one-year-imprisonment-27209, last accessed 3 Aug 2015.

66. 'Comment: Rehendhi a Minivan News plot to promote "national sissyness" and "lesbian relations"', Minivan News, http://minivannewsarchive.com/society/comment-rehendhi-a-minivan-news-plot-to-promote-national-sissyness-and-lesbian-relations-among-women-7651, last accessed 3 Aug 2015.

67. 'New religious unity regulations crack down on extremist preaching in Maldives', Minivan News, http://minivannewsarchive.com/society/new-religious-unity-regulations-crack-down-on-extremist-preaching-in-maldives-25734, last accessed 3 Aug 2015.

68. 'Criminal court grants police warrant to obtain IP address of Minivan News commentator accused of "violating Islamic principles"', Minivan News, http://minivannewsarchive.com/society/criminal-court-grants-police-warrant-to-obtain-ip-address-of-minivan-news-commentator-accused-of-%e2%80%9cviolating-islamic-rinciples%e2%80%9d-48406, last accessed 3 Aug 2015.

7. EXTREMISM: SUN, SAND AND SHARIA

1. Khaldun, Ibn. 'The Muqaddimah—An Introduction to History' (1377) translated from Arabic to English 1958.

2. 'Slashed journalist claims attack was targeted assassination by Islamic radicals', Minivan News, http://minivannewsarchive.com/society/slashed-journalist-claims-attack-was-targeted-assassination-by-islamic-radicals-40078, last accessed 3 Aug 2015.

3. 'Slashed journalist claims attack was targeted assassination by Islamic radicals', Minivan News, http://minivannewsarchive.com/society/slashed-journalist-claims-attack-was-targeted-assassination-by-islamic-radicals-40078, last accessed 3 Aug 2015.

4. 'PPM MP Dr Afrasheem found brutally murdered', Minivan News, http://minivannewsarchive.com/politics/ppm-mp-dr-afrasheem-found-brutally-murdered-44721, last accessed 3 Aug 2015.

5. 'Humam sentenced to death for murder of Dr Afrasheem', Minivan News, http://minivannewsarchive.com/politics/human-sentenced-to-death-for-murder-of-dr-afrasheem-75319, last accessed 3 Aug 2015.

6. 'Father of main suspect in Afrasheem murder case accuses police of coercion', http://minivannewsarchive.com/politics/father-of-main-suspect-in-mp-afrasheem-murder-case-accuses-police-of-coercion-59142, last accessed 3 Aug 2015.

7. 'Tsunami watch alert cancelled after 8.6 earthquake and aftershock off Indonesia', Minivan News, http://minivannewsarchive.com/politics/live-tsunami-warning-issued-for-indian-ocean-35115, last accessed 3 Aug 2015.

8. 'Islamic Extremism in the Maldives', Dhivehi Sitee, http://www.dhivehisitee.com/parliament/islamic-extremism-maldives-alive-killing/, last accessed 3 Aug 2015.

9. 'The Maldives: From Charybdis to Scylla?', Dhivehi Observer, http://web.archive.org/web/20120218075509/http://www.dhivehiobserver.com/maldivesroyalfamily/maldives_romero_open_letter.htm, last accessed 3 Aug 2015.

10. 'Bomb—IED (Maldives) Mobile phone video', Youtube, https://www.youtube.com/watch?v=Yhpfq66i7kg, last accessed 3 Aug 2015.

11. "Maldives bomb blast CCTV footage', Youtube, https://www.youtube.com/watch?v=jxbJyUeucZ4, last accessed 3 Aug 2015.

12. 'Maldives: Bombing Investigation Yielding Results' US Embassy cable #07COLOMBO1400, Wikileaks, https://cablegatesearch.wikileaks.org/cable.php?id=07COLOMBO1400&q=bombing%20maldives, last accessed 3 Aug 2015.

13. 'Diplomatic Security Daily', US Embassy cable 08STATE116943, Wikileaks, https://cablegatesearch.wikileaks.org/cable.php?id=08STATE116943&q=bombing%20maldives, last accessed 3 Aug 2015.

14. 'US citizen arrested for funding Maldivian terrorist in Lahore bombing', Minivan News, http://minivannewsarchive.com/politics/us-citizen-arrested-for-funding-maldivian-terrorist-in-lahore-bombing-54230, last accessed 3 Aug 2015.

15. 'Maldivian detainees repatriated from Pakistan, Minivan News, http://minivan-newsarchive.com/politics/maldivian-detainees-repatriated-from-pakistan-3296, last accessed 3 Aug 2015.

16. The Guantanamo Files: Ibrahim Fauzee, Wikileaks, https://wikileaks.org/gitmo/prisoner/730.html, last accessed 3 Aug 2015.

17. 'Government decreases sentences of Sultan Park bombers under Clemency Act', Minivan News, http://minivannewsarchive.com/society/government-decreases-sentences-of-sultan-park-bombers-under-clemency-act-10440, last accessed 3 Aug 2015.

18. Maldives hosts secret Taliban talks, Minivan News, http://minivannewsarchive.com/politics/maldives-hosts-secret-taliban-talks-2948, last accessed 3 Aug 2015.

19. 'Afghans talk peace in the Maldives', Al-Jazeera English, https://www.youtube.com/watch?v=kDeWfEa_C68, last accessed 3 Aug 2015.

20. 'President's dancing shames nation: Adhaalath Party', Minivan News, http://min-ivannewsarchive.com/politics/presidents-dancing-shames-nation-adhaalath-party-21312/comment-page-1, last accessed 3 Aug 2015.

21. 'Waheed: Master or Puppet?', Dhivehi Sitee, http://www.dhivehisitee.com/exec-utive/waheed-master-puppet/, last accessed 3 Aug 2015.

22. 'Media Monitoring Maldives', Transparency Maldives, http://minivannews.com/files/2011/12/media_monitoring_PRINT.pdf, last accessed 3 Aug 2015.

8. VELEZINEE, THE JUDICIARY AND THE SILENT COUP

1. 'Runaway judiciary leaves the Maldives "at a dangerous junction", says Velezinee', Minivan News, http://minivannewsarchive.com/politics/runaway-judiciary-leaves-the-maldives-at-a-dangerous-junction-says-velezinee-16544, last accessed 3 Aug 2015.

2. 'JSC forged documents for Supreme Court case, alleges Velezinee', Minivan News, http://minivannewsarchive.com/politics/jsc-forged-documents-for-supreme-court-case-alleges-velezinee-16021, last accessed 3 Aug 2015.

3. 'Runaway judiciary leaves the Maldives "at a dangerous junction", says Velezinee', Minivan News, http://minivannewsarchive.com/politics/runaway-judiciary-leaves-the-maldives-at-a-dangerous-junction-says-velezinee-16544, last accessed 3 Aug 2015.

4. '"Sunlight is the best antiseptic": the case for an independent judiciary', Minivan News, http://minivannewsarchive.com/politics/sunlight-is-the-best-antiseptic-the-case-for-an-independent-judiciary-17732, last accessed 3 Aug 2015.

5. 'JSC decision could "rob nation of an honest judiciary", warns member', Minivan News, http://minivannewsarchive.com/politics/jsc-decision-could-rob-nation-of-an-honest-judiciary-warns-member-6959, last accessed 3 Aug 2015.

6. 'Judge frees Nazim from all corruption charges: "acts not enough to criminalise"', Minivan News, http://minivannewsarchive.com/politics/judge-frees-nazim-from-

all-corruption-charges-acts-not-enough-to-criminalise-32494, last accessed 3 Aug 2015.

7. 'Criminal Court again orders release of high profile drug case suspect, despite High Court overruling decision', Minivan News, http://minivannewsarchive. com/society/criminal-court-again-orders-release-of-high-profile-drug-case-suspect-despite-high-court-overruling-decision-20696, last accessed 3 Aug 2015.

8. 'Chief Judge Abdulla Mohamed takes over 'Sun' Shiyam's case', Minivan News, http://minivannewsarchive.com/politics/chief-judge-abdulla-mohamed-takes-over-sun-shiyams-case-85290, last accessed 3 Aug 2015.

9. 'Rapid Situation Assessment of Gangs in Male', Asia Foundation, http://minivannews.com/files/2012/10/gangs.pdf, last accessed 3 Aug 2015.

10. Video of Velezinee's Aug 2010 attempt to stop the JSC reappointing the old judiciary, Youtube, https://www.youtube.com/watch?v=RcHvdLtOBeg, last accessed 3 Aug 2015.

11. 'JSC reappoints 59 judges in ceremony, evicts Velezinee', Minivan News, http:// minivannewsarchive.com/society/jsc-reappoints-59-judges-in-ceremony-evicts-velezinee-10084, last accessed 3 Aug 2015.

12. 'Judges legitimised JSC's actions with their silence', Minivan News, http://minivannewsarchive.com/society/judges-legitimised-jscs-actions-with-their-silence-17901, last accessed 3 Aug 2015.

13. 'Supreme Court judges' appointments not temporary: Chief Justice Abdulla Saeed', Minivan News, http://minivannewsarchive.com/news-in-brief/supreme-court-judges-appointments-not-temporary-chief-justice-abdulla-saeed-8610, last accessed 3 Aug 2015.

14. 'Constitutional disaster averted as Parliament approves Supreme Court', Minivan News, http://minivannewsarchive.com/politics/constitutional-disaster-averted-as-parliament-approves-supreme-court-10233, last accessed 3 Aug 2015.

15. '"If I keep silent, I have become a traitor": Velezinee vows to continue campaign against "silent coup"', Minivan News, http://minivannewsarchive.com/society/if-i-keep-silent-i-have-become-a-traitor-velezinee-vows-to-continue-campaign-against-silent-coup-14963, last accessed 3 Aug 2015.

16. 'Velezinee proposes motion to 'confirm sanity' of JSC Chairman', Minivan News, http://minivannewsarchive.com/politics/velezinee-proposes-motion-to-confirm-sanity-of-jsc-chairman-13677, last accessed 3 Aug 2015.

17. '"Courageous and exemplary work": President dismisses JSC Velezinee', Minivan News, http://minivannewsarchive.com/politics/courageous-and-exemplary-work-president-dismisses-jsc-velezinee-20551, last accessed 3 Aug 2015.

18. 'Translation: "President Nasheed's devious plot to destroy the Islamic faith of Maldivians"', Minivan News, http://minivannewsarchive.com/politics/translation-president-nasheed%e2%80%99s-devious-plot-to-destroy-the-islamic-faith-of-maldivians-30991, last accessed 3 Aug 2015.

19. Police arrest 14 in massive Facebook nude photo blackmail ring', Minivan News, http://minivannewsarchive.com/society/police-arrest-14-in-massive-facebook-nude-photo-blackmail-ring-16396, last accessed 3 Aug 2015.

20. 'False allegations against government "a criminal offence": President's Office', Minivan News, http://minivannewsarchive.com/politics/false-allegations-against-government-a-criminal-offence-presidents-office-30661, last accessed 3 Aug 2015.

21. 'Journalists banned from Deputy Speaker corruption trial', Minivan News, http://minivannewsarchive.com/politics/journalists-banned-from-deputy-speaker-corruption-trial-24668, last accessed 3 Aug 2015.

22. 'Court releases murder suspect citing lack of cooperation from Health Ministry', Minivan News, http://minivannewsarchive.com/society/court-releases-murder-suspect-citing-lack-of-cooperation-from-health-ministry-16225, last accessed 3 Aug 2015.

23. 'Gang murders 21 year-old man near Alikileygefaanu Magu in Galolhu', Minivan News, http://minivannewsarchive.com/society/gang-murders-21-year-old-man-near-alikileygefaanu-magu-in-galolhu-17277, last accessed 3 Aug 2015.

24. 'Criminal Court obstructing corruption investigation, police allege', Minivan News, http://minivannewsarchive.com/politics/criminal-court obstructing-corruption-investigation-police-allege-9510, last accessed 3 Aug 2015.

25. 'High Court overturns Criminal Court suspension of MP Imthiyaz', Minivan News, http://minivannewsarchive.com/politics/high-court-overturns-criminal-court-suspension-of-mp-imthiyaz-30268, last accessed 3 Aug 2015.

26. 'Chief Judge "took entire criminal justice system in his fist": Afeef', Minivan News, http://minivannewsarchive.com/politics/chief-judge-took-entire-criminal-justice-system-in-his-fist-afeef-30926, last accessed 3 Aug 2015.

27. 'Q&A: Silent coup has cost Maldives a judiciary, says Aishath Velezinee', http://minivannewsarchive.com/politics/qa-we-talking-about-not-having-a-judiciary-says-aishath-velezinee-31158, last accessed 3 Aug 2015.

28. Velezinee, Aishath. 'The Failed Silent Coup: In Defeat They Reached for the Gun'(2012), http://www.maldivesculture.com/pdf_files/Velezinee-A_The-Failed-Silent-Coup_Maldives-2012.pdf, last accessed 3 Aug. 2015.

29. 'Failure of judiciary, JSC and parliament justified detention of Abdulla Mohamed, contends Velezinee in new book', Minivan News, http://minivannewsarchive.com/society/failure-of-judiciary-jsc-and-parliament-justified-detention-of-abdulla-mohamed-contends-velezinee-in-new-book-43728, last accessed 3 Aug 2015.

30. 'Chief Judge "took entire criminal justice system in his fist": Afeef', Minivan News, http://minivannewsarchive.com/politics/chief-judge-took-entire-criminal-justice-system-in-his-fist-afeef-30926, last accessed 3 Aug 2015.

31. 'SAARC Secretary General's resignation first in regional body's history', Minivan News, http://minivannewsarchive.com/society/saarc-secretary-generals-resignation-first-in-regional-bodys-history-31063, last accessed 3 Aug 2015.

32. 'SAARC Secretary General attacks government over detention of Chief Judge',

Minivan News, http://minivannewsarchive.com/politics/saarc-secretary-general-attacks-government-over-detention-of-chief-judge-30944, last accessed 3 Aug 2015.

33. 'Maldives faces judicial crisis', ABC Radio Australia, http://www.radioaustralia.net.au/international/radio/onairhighlights/maldives-faces-judicial-crisis, last accessed 3 Aug 2015.

34. 'Allegations against Chief Judge first sent to Gayoom in 2005', Minivan News, http://minivannewsarchive.com/politics/allegations-against-chief-judge-first-sent-to-gayoom-in-2005–31241, last accessed 3 Aug. 2015.

35. 'Q&A: President Dr Mohamed Waheed Hassan', Minivan News, http://minivannewsarchive.com/politics/qa-president-dr-mohamed-waheed-hassan-32268, last accessed 3 Aug. 2015.

36. 'Commonwealth to provide technical assistance to help resolve Maldives' judicial crisis', Minivan News, http://minivannewsarchive.com/politics/commonwealth-to-provide-technical-assistance-to-resolve-maldives-judicial-crisis-31479, last accessed 3 Aug. 2015.

37. 'Nasheed calls for Dr Waheed to step down, hold elections in two months', Minivan News, http://minivannewsarchive.com/politics/live-arrest-warrant-issued-for-nasheed-31781, last accessed 3 Aug. 2015.

38. 'PG files charges against former President Nasheed over Judge Abdulla's detention', Minivan News, http://minivannewsarchive.com/politics/pg-files-charges-against-former-president-nasheed-over-judge-abdulla%e2%80%99s-deten-tion-40711, last accessed 3 Aug. 2015.

39. 'Documents from JSC show Gasim is lobbying Hulhumale' court bench: MDP', Minivan News, http://minivannewsarchive.com/politics/documents-from-jsc-show-gasim-is-lobbying-hulhumale-court-bench-mdp-54484, last accessed 3 Aug. 2015.

40. 'Report on Bar Human Rights Committee Hearing Observation: The Maldives', UK Bar Human Rights Committee, http://www.barhumanrights.org.uk/node/363, last accessed 3 Aug. 2015.

41. 'Tension surges in Male' as police arrest former President Mohamed Nasheed', Minivan News, http://minivannewsarchive.com/politics/live-tension-surges-in-male-as-police-arrest-former-president-mohamed-nasheed-53994, last accessed 3 Aug. 2015.

42. 'Government asks India to hand over Nasheed, as MDP slam arrest warrant from "kangaroo court"', Minivan News, http://minivannewsarchive.com/politics/government-asks-india-to-hand-over-nasheed-as-mdp-slam-arrest-warrant-from-kangaroo-court-53232, last accessed 3 Aug. 2015.

43. 'US, UK, UN call for restraint, "inclusive" presidential elections', Minivan News, http://minivannewsarchive.com/politics/us-uk-un-call-for-inclusive-presidential-elections-52986, last accessed 3 Aug. 2015.

44. 'Banished to Paradise', Middlebury Magazine, http://sites.middlebury.edu/middmag/2011/08/02/banished-to-paradise/3/, last accessed 3 Aug. 2015.

45. 'Report of the Special Rapporteur on the independence of judges and lawyers, Gabriela Knaul', UN Human Rights Council, http://www.ohchr.org/Documents/HRBodies/HRCouncil/RegularSession/Session23/A   HRC-23–43-Add3_en.pdf, last accessed 3 Aug. 2015.

46. 'A justice system in crisis: UN Special Rapporteur's report', http://minivannews-archive.com/politics/a-justice-system-in-crisis-un-special-rapporteurs-report-585 41', last accessed 3 Aug. 2015.

47. 'Statement at the interactive Dialogue with the Special Rapporteur on the Independence of Judges and Lawyers', Maldives Government, http://minivan-news.com/files/2013/06/Maldives_Concerned_08.pdf, last accessed 3 Aug. 2015.

48. '"International actors should not undermine governments": Maldives responds to UN Special Rapporteur', Minivan News, http://minivannewsarchive.com/politics/international-actors-should-not-undermine-governments-maldives-responds-to-un-special-rapporteur-58897, last accessed 3 Aug. 2015.

49. 'JSC member/presidential candidate Gasim Ibrahim accuses UN Special Rapporteur of lying, joking', Minivan News, http://minivannewsarchive.com/politics/jsc-memberpresidential-candidate-gasim-ibrahim-accuses-un-special-rap-porteur-of-lying-joking-53790, last accessed 3 Aug. 2015.

50. '"JSC politicised, trying to eliminate Nasheed and MDP from elections"', Minivan News, http://minivannewsarchive.com/politics/jsc-politicised-trying-to-elimi-nate-nasheed-and-mdp-from-elections-jsc-member-shuaib-54149, last accessed 3 Aug. 2015.

9. PRESIDENT WAHEED AND THE ART OF 'LEGITIMACY'

1. '"Be courageous; Today you are all mujaheddin": President Dr Waheed', Minivan News, http://minivannewsarchive.com/society/be-courageous-today-you-are-all-mujaheddin-president-dr-waheed-32597, last accessed 3 Aug. 2015.

2. 'Nasheed announces former university chancellor Musthafa Luthfy as running mate', Minivan News, http://minivannewsarchive.com/politics/nasheed-announces-for-mer-university-chancellor-musthafa-luthfy-as-running-mate-61168, last accessed 3 Aug. 2015.

3. 'Umar Naseer alleges PPM primaries rigged, declares "war within the party"', Minivan News, http://minivannewsarchive.com/politics/umar-naseer-alleges-ppm-primaries-rigged-declares-%e2%80%9cwar-within-the-party%e2%80%9d-55590, last accessed 3 Aug. 2015.

4. 'Government is still "one man show", says Vice President Dr Waheed', Minivan News, http://minivannewsarchive.com/politics/government-is-still-one-man-show-says-vice-president-dr-waheed-5898, last accessed 3 Aug. 2015.

5. '"I'm too old to sit around. We genuinely want to improve the way things work": Dr Waheed', Minivan News, http://minivannewsarchive.com/politics/i%e2%80%99m-too-old-to-sit-around-we-genuinely-want-to-improve-the-way-things-work-dr-waheed-6407, last accessed 3 Aug. 2015.

6. 'Waheed come and waheed go,' Youtube, https://www.youtube.com/watch?v=
i5t6MvEkPAY, last accessed 3 Aug. 2015.

7. 'Freedom from fear: are we about to lose it?', Dr Waheed's website, http://www.
drwaheed.com/blog/freedom-from-fear-are-we-about-to-lose-it, last accessed
3 Aug. 2015.

8. "We call on the police and the army to pledge allegiance to the Vice President":
Umar Naseer', Minivan News, http://minivannewsarchive.com/politics/we-call-
on-the-police-and-the-army-to-pledge-allegiance-to-the-vice-president-umar-nas-
eer-jan-31–31948, last accessed 3 Aug. 2015.

9. '"Nasheed never phoned me": Waheed on 7/2', Dhivehi Sitee, http://www.dhi-
vehisitee.com/executive/waheed-coni/, last accessed 3 Aug. 2015.

10. 'Supreme Court Judge Ali Hameed & Saeed', Youtube, https://www.youtube.
com/watch?v=ZEKk8lgMH8o, last accessed 3 Aug. 2015.

11. 'Transcript: Leaked audio of Deputy CEO of Maldives Ports Limited, Ahmed
Faiz', Minivan News, http://minivannewsarchive.com/politics/transcript-leaked-
audio-of-deputy-ceo-of-maldives-ports-ahmed-faiz-42284, last accessed 3 Aug.
2015.

12. 'Translation: Leaked "coup agreement"', Minivan News, http://minivannewsar-
chive.com/politics/government-is-still-one-man-show-says-vice-president-dr-wa-
heed-5898, last accessed 3 Aug. 2015.

13. 'Mulay failed to pass information on coup to Indian government: Open Magazine',
Minivan News, http://minivannewsarchive.com/politics/mulay-failed-to-pass-
information-on-coup-to-indian-government-open-magazine-36772, last accessed
3 Aug. 2015.

14. 'Daily Press Briefing, 7 Feb. 2012', US Department of State, http://www.state.
gov/r/pa/prs/dpb/2012/02/183489.htm, last accessed 3 Aug. 2015.

15. 'Daily Press Briefing, 8 Feb. 2012', US Department of State, http://www.state.
gov/r/pa/prs/dpb/2012/02/183574.htm#MALDIVES, last accessed 3 Aug.
2015.

16. 'Daily Press Briefing, 9 Feb. 2012', US Department of State, http://www.state.
gov/r/pa/prs/dpb/2012/02/183639.htm#MALDIVES, last accessed 3 Aug.
2015.

17. 'President Waheed appoints seven state ministers, including Gayoom's son',
Minivan News, http://minivannewsarchive.com/politics/president-waheed-
appoints-seven-state-ministers-includes-gayoom%e2%80%99s-son-32972, last
accessed 3 Aug. 2015.

18. 'Recording of Dr. Hassan Saeed mocking President Waheed', Youtube, https://
www.youtube.com/watch?x-yt-cl=84838260&x-yt-
ts=1422327029&v=jnzoNDFjEx8, last accessed 3 Aug. 2015.

19. 'Dr Waheed "politically the weakest person in the Maldives": political advisor,
Hassan Saeed', Minivan News, http://minivannewsarchive.com/politics/dr-
waheed-politically-the-weakest-person-in-the-maldives-political-advisor-hassan-
saeed-32569, last accessed 3 Aug. 2015.

20. 'Q&A: President Dr Mohamed Waheed Hassan', Minivan News, http://minivan-newsarchive.com/politics/qa-president-dr-mohamed-waheed-hassan-32268, last accessed 3 Aug. 2015.

21. '"President Waheed says no elections until 2013": Malaysian consultant Dr Ananda Kumarasiri', Minivan News, http://minivannewsarchive.com/politics/%e2%80%9cpresident-waheed-says-no-elections-until-2013%e2%80%9d-malaysian-consultant-dr-ananda-kumarasiri-32580, last accessed 3 Aug. 2015.

22. 'Maldives ready with roadmap towards a full-fledged democracy', Sunday Observer (Sri Lanka), http://www.sundayobserver.lk/2012/02/26/fea03.asp, last accessed 3 Aug. 2015.

23. '"You are my brother and I will always love you": Dr Waheed's brother resigns from UK post, calls for President to follow', Minivan News, http://minivannewsarchive.com/politics/%e2%80%9cyou-are-my-brother-and-i-will-always-love-you%e2%80%9d-dr-waheed%e2%80%99s-brother-resigns-from-uk-post-calls-for-president-to-follow-32202, last accessed 3 Aug. 2015.

24. '"I told them to surrender; otherwise Nasheed might lose his life", Umar Naseer tells PPM rally', Minivan News, http://minivannewsarchive.com/politics/i-told-them-to-surrender-otherwise-he-might-lose-life-umar-naseer-tells-ppm-rally-32062, last accessed 3 Aug. 2015.

25. 'Commonwealth suspends Maldives from CMAG, calls for "formal" investigation with "international participation"', Minivan News, http://minivannewsarchive.com/politics/commonwealth-suspends-maldives-from-cmag-calls-for-formal-investigation-with-international-participation-32470, last accessed 3 Aug. 2015.

26. 'Fiji: a case study in the realities of Commonwealth suspension', Minivan News, http://minivannewsarchive.com/politics/fiji-a-case-study-in-the-realities-of-commonwealth-suspension-36068, last accessed 3 Aug. 2015.

27. 'EU backs early Presidential Elections', Minivan News, http://minivannewsarchive.com/politics/eu-backs-early-presidential-elections-32447, last accessed 3 Aug. 2015.

28. 'Concluding statement, Extraordinary Meeting of the Commonwealth Ministerial Action Group 22 Feb. 2012', Commonwealth, http://thecommonwealth.org/media/press-release/extraordinary-meeting-commonwealth-ministerial-action-group-cmag#sthash.H9iZEM2J.dpuf, last accessed 3 Aug. 2015.

29. 'Committee of National Inquiry cannot wait for international assistance: Shafeeu', Minivan News, http://minivannewsarchive.com/politics/committee-of-national-inquiry-cannot-wait-for-international-assistance-shafeeu-35269, last accessed 3 Aug. 2015.

30. 'Maldivian NGOs call for "immediate changes" to inquiry commission', Minivan News, http://minivannewsarchive.com/politics/maldivian-ngos-call-for-immediate-changes-to-inquiry-commission-35914, last accessed 3 Aug. 2015.

31. 'CMAG warns of "stronger measures" against government unless CNI is reformed,

Minivan News, http://minivannewsarchive.com/politics/cmag-warns-of-stronger-measures-against-government-unless-cni-is-reformed-35618, last accessed 3 Aug. 2015.

32. 'Government dismisses Commonwealth's "biased" early election calls, fears "civil war"', Minivan News, http://minivannewsarchive.com/politics/government-dismisses-commonwealths-biased-early-election-calls-fears-civil-war-33454, last accessed 3 Aug. 2015.

33. 'Gayoom urges "rethink" of Maldives Commonwealth membership'. Minivan News, http://minivannewsarchive.com/news-in-brief/gayoom-urges-%e2%80%9crethink%e2%80%9d-of-maldives-commonwealth-membership-36343, last accessed 3 Aug. 2015.

34. 'Commonwealth "intimidating", "punishing" Maldives without mandate, Waheed tells diplomats', Minivan News, http://minivannewsarchive.com/politics/commonwealth-intimidating-punishing-maldives-without-mandate-waheed-tells-diplomats-37378, last accessed 3 Aug. 2015.

35. 'Former Commission of National Inquiry panel releases timeline "for public opinion"', Minivan News, http://minivannewsarchive.com/politics/former-commission-of-national-inquiry-panel-releases-timeline-for-public-opinion-38627, last accessed 3 Aug. 2015.

36. 'CONI "Timeline": For You Opinion Only', Dhivehi Sitee, http://www.dhivehisitee.com/executive/coni-timeline-for-your-opinion-only/, last accessed 3 Aug. 2015.

37. 'Singapore. Another of Lee Kuan Yew's disgraceful judges, G.P. Selvam', Singapore Dissident, http://singaporedissident.blogspot.com/2010/01/singapore-another-of-lee-kuan-yews.html, last accessed 3 Aug. 2015.

38. 'Singapore's Lee Ruling Family's attack dog, former Judge GP Selvam travels to the Maldives for more dirty work', Singapore Dissident, http://singaporedissident.blogspot.com/2012/06/singapores-lee-ruling-familys-attack.html, last accessed 3 Aug. 2015.

39. 'No matter what the CNI conclusion maybe, won't accept that it was a coup: Gayoom', Haveeru News, http://www.haveeru.com.mv/news/43732, last accessed 3 Aug. 2015.

40. 'If I had no role in coup, I don't have to resign, Waheed tells BBC', Minivan News, http://minivannewsarchive.com/politics/if-i-had-no-role-in-coup-i-dont-have-to-resign-waheed-tells-bbc-38730, last accessed 3 Aug. 2015.

41. 'Maldives president rejects call for elections', Financial Times, http://www.ft.com/cms/s/0/a2b3bdd8-b188–11e1-bbf9–00144feabdc0.html#axzz1xHmdLnyD, last accessed 3 Aug. 2015.

42. 'President Waheed meets coalition members ahead of CNI report release', Minivan News, http://minivannewsarchive.com/politics/president-waheed-meets-coalition-members-ahead-of-cni-report-release-42996, last accessed 3 Aug. 2015.

43. 'MDP gears up for "direct action" protest as Gahaa Saeed resigns from CNI',

Minivan News, http://minivannewsarchive.com/politics/mdp-gears-up-for-direct-action-protest-as-gahaa-saeed-resigns-from-cni-43007, last accessed 3 Aug. 2015.

44. 'Report of the Commission of National Inquiry', President's Office, http://minivannews.com/files/2013/08/CoNI-Report.pdf, last accessed 3 Aug. 2015.

45. 'No coup, no duress, no mutiny: CNI report', Minivan News, http://minivannewsarchive.com/politics/no-coup-no-duress-no-mutiny-cni-report-43074, last accessed 3 Aug. 2015.

46. 'Overview and Observations of the International Advisers', President's Office, https://web.archive.org/web/20120906232702/http://www.coni.org.mv/coni/wp-content/uploads/AppendicesXVI.pdf, last accessed 3 Aug. 2015.

47. '"I realised it was all going wrong": member Saeed on CNI's final days', Minivan News, http://minivannewsarchive.com/politics/%e2%80%9ci-realised-it-was-all-going-wrong-member-saeed-on-cnis-final-days-43143, last accessed 3 Aug. 2015.

48. 'CNI report "selective", "flawed", "exceeded mandate": Sri Lankan legal experts', Minivan News, http://minivannewsarchive.com/politics/cni-report-selective-flawed-exceeded-mandate-sri-lankan-legal-experts-43589, last accessed 3 Aug. 2015.

49. '"I realised it was all going wrong": member Saeed on CNI's final days', Minivan News, http://minivannewsarchive.com/politics/%e2%80%9ci-realised-it-was-all-going-wrong-member-saeed-on-cnis-final-days-43143, last accessed 3 Aug. 2015.

50. 'CNI report "based on false premise that Abdulla Mohamed is a constitutionally appointed judge": Velezinee', Minivan News, http://minivannewsarchive.com/politics/cni-report-based-on-false-premise-that-abdulla-mohamed-is-a-constitutionally-appointed-judge-velezinee-43411, last accessed 3 Aug. 2015.

51. 'CNI report leaves Maldives with "awkward", "comical" precedent: Nasheed', Minivan News, http://minivannewsarchive.com/politics/cni-report-leaves-maldives-with-awkward-comical-precedent-nasheed-43178, last accessed 3 Aug. 2015.

52. 'Canadian Foreign Minister "glad that Maldives remains on CMAG agenda"', Minivan News, http://minivannewsarchive.com/politics/canadian-foreign-minister-glad-that-maldives-remains-on-cmag-agenda-44543, last accessed 3 Aug. 2015.

53. 'Canada Deeply Troubled by Democratic Deficit in Maldives', Government of Canada, http://news.gc.ca/web/article-en.do?nid=697389, last accessed 3 Aug. 2015.

54. Signed agreement between government of the Maldives and Baroness Patricia Scotland, https://dl.dropboxusercontent.com/u/58139472/letter135–1.pdf, last accessed 3 Aug. 2015.

55. 'Government employs Baroness Scotland to challenge legality of "unfair", "biased" Commonwealth intervention', Minivan News, http://minivannewsarchive.com/

politics/government-employs-baroness-scotland-to-challenge-legality-of-unfair-biased-commonwealth-intervention-41554, last accessed 3 Aug. 2015.

56. 'Baroness Scotland paid £7,500 A DAY to advise Maldives 'coup leader' accused of torture', Daily Mail, http://www.dailymail.co.uk/news/article-2183394/Baroness-Scotland-paid-7–500-A-DAY-advise-Maldives-coup-leader-accused-torture.html, last accessed 3 Aug. 2015.

57. 'Government paid Baroness Scotland £50,000 in excess of agreed consultancy fee', Minivan News, http://minivannewsarchive.com/politics/government-paid-baroness-scotland-50000-in-excess-of-agreed-consultancy-fee-59362, last accessed 3 Aug. 2015.

58. 'Ruder Finn picks up controversial Maldives brief', PR Week, http://www.prweek.com/article/1128604/ruder-finn-picks-controversial-maldives-brief, last accessed 3 Aug. 2015.

59. 'Request for proposals', Maldives Marketing and PR Corporation, http://minivannews.com/files/2012/04/maldives-rfp.pdf, last accessed 3 Aug. 2015.

60. 'Criminal court frees 2007 Sultan Park bombing suspect', Minivan News, http://minivannewsarchive.com/politics/criminal-court-frees-2007-sultan-park-bombing-suspect-37242, last accessed 3 Aug. 2015.

61. 'MPs ban Israel flights, but withdraw resolutions against Pillay, GMR, SAARC ', Minivan News, http://minivannewsarchive.com/politics/mps-ban-israel-flights-but-withdraw-resolutions-against-pillay-gmr-saarc-monuments-36293, last accessed 3 Aug. 2015.

62. 'Government's contract with Ruder Finn PR firm expires', Minivan News, http://minivannewsarchive.com/politics/governments-contract-with-ruder-finn-pr-firm-expires-47393, last accessed 3 Aug. 2015.

63. '"Administrative issue" behind delayed civil service wage payments: Finance Minister', Minivan News, http://minivannewsarchive.com/society/administrative-issue-behind-delayed-civil-service-wage-payments-finance-minister-41464, last accessed 3 Aug. 2015.

64. 'Government's changes to resort lease payments will cost Maldives US$135 million: MDP', Minivan News, http://minivannewsarchive.com/politics/governments-changes-to-resort-lease-payments-will-lose-maldives-us135-million-mdp-32895, last accessed 3 Aug. 2015.

65. '"Dire economic outlook" as budget deficit estimated to reach 27 per cent of GDP', Minivan News, http://minivannewsarchive.com/politics/dire-economic-outlook-as-budget-deficit-estimated-to-reach-27-percent-of-gdp-36808, last accessed 3 Aug. 2015.

66. 'Rising oil price forces STELCO to call in US$10 million in unpaid government bills', Minivan News, http://minivannewsarchive.com/society/rising-oil-price-forces-stelco-to-call-in-us10-million-in-unpaid-government-bills-45951, last accessed 3 Aug. 2015.

67. 'Government cannot pay state salaries without Indian cash: Finance Minister', Minivan News, http://minivannewsarchive.com/politics/government-cannot-pay-state-salaries-without-indian-cash-finance-minister-46305, last accessed 3 Aug. 2015.

68. 'Government signs Male International Airport to GMR-Malaysia Airports consortium', Minivan News, http://minivannewsarchive.com/politics/government-signs-male-international-airport-to-gmr-malaysia-airports-consortium-8720, last accessed 3 Aug. 2015.

69. 'Government signs Male International Airport to GMR-Malaysia Airports consortium', Minivan News, http://minivannewsarchive.com/politics/government-signs-male-international-airport-to-gmr-malaysia-airports-consortium-8720, last accessed 3 Aug. 2015.

70. 'GMR not worried about airport politicking, will invest US$373 million', Minivan News, http://minivannewsarchive.com/politics/gmr-not-worried-about-airport-politicking-will-invest-us373-million-9300, last accessed 3 Aug. 2015.

71. 'Bidding party urges to re-evaluate airport bids,' Haveeru News, http://www.haveeru.com.mv/english/details/30766/Kuwait_posts_28_billion_dollars_provisional_surplus__, last accessed 3 Aug. 2015.

72. 'Airport deal "will allow Israeli flights to stop over after bombing Arab countries": Umar Naseer', Minivan News, http://minivannewsarchive.com/politics/privatisation-of-airport-ridiculous-says-umar-naseer-8686, last accessed 3 Aug. 2015.

73. 'GMR dismantles Alpha duty-free', Minivan News, http://minivannewsarchive.com/society/gmr-dismantles-alpha-duty-free-29038, last accessed 3 Aug. 2015.

74. 'GMR could colonise economy: DQP', Minivan News, http://minivannewsarchive.com/politics/gmr-could-colonise-economy-dqp-29593, last accessed 3 Aug. 2015.

75. 'Giving the Airport to GMR: Beginning of Enslavement', Dhivehi Qaumee Party (translated by Minivan News), http://minivannews.com/files/2012/03/DQP-GMR-booklet-translation.docx, last accessed 3 Aug. 2015.

76. 'Civil Court rules airport development charge invalid as GMR opens airline office complex', Minivan News, http://minivannewsarchive.com/politics/civil-court-rules-airport-development-charge-invalid-as-gmr-opens-airline-office-complex-29198, last accessed 3 Aug. 2015.

77. 'President's Special Advisor appeals to Indian PM to terminate GMR contract, warns of "rising extremism"', Minivan News, http://minivannewsarchive.com/politics/presidents-special-advisor-appeals-to-indian-pm-to-terminate-gmr-contract-warns-of-rising-extremism-47273, last accessed 3 Aug. 2015.

78. 'GMR offers to exempt Maldivian nationals from airport development charge', Minivan News, http://minivannewsarchive.com/politics/gmr-offers-to-exempt-maldivian-nationals-from-airport-development-charge-37033, last accessed 3 Aug. 2015.

79. 'Televised allegations by President spokeperson against Indian High Commissioner

spark diplomatic incident', Minivan News, http://minivannewsarchive.com/politics/televised-allegations-by-president-spokeperson-against-indian-high-commissioner-spark-diplomatic-incident-47174, last accessed 3 Aug. 2015.

80. 'President's Office Spokesperson "stands by" comments against GMR, Indian High Commissioner', Minivan News, http://minivannewsarchive.com/politics/presidents-office-spokesperson-stands-by-comments-against-gmr-indian-high-commissioner-47534, last accessed 3 Aug. 2015.

81. 'Cabinet voids US$511 million GMR contract, gives airport developer seven day ultimatum to leave', Minivan News, http://minivannewsarchive.com/politics/cabinet-voids-us511-million-gmr-contract-gives-investor-seven-day-ultimatum-to-leave-48023, last accessed 3 Aug. 2015.

82. 'Government continues bid to seize airport despite injunction from High Court of Singapore', Minivan News, http://minivannewsarchive.com/politics/government-continues-bid-to-seize-airport-despite-injunction-from-high-court-of-singapore-48312, last accessed 3 Aug. 2015.

83. 'Government continues bid to seize airport despite injunction from High Court of Singapore', Minivan News, http://minivannewsarchive.com/politics/government-continues-bid-to-seize-airport-despite-injunction-from-high-court-of-singapore-48312, last accessed 3 Aug. 2015.

84. 'Government takes over airport, evicts GMR', Minivan News, http://minivannewsarchive.com/politics/government-takes-over-airport-evicts-gmr-48477, last accessed 3 Aug. 2015.

85. 'GMR compensation claim of US$1.4 billion eclipses annual state budget', Minivan News, http://minivannewsarchive.com/politics/gmr-compensation-claim-of-us1-4-billion-eclipses-annual-state-budget-60008, last accessed 3 Aug. 2015.

86. 'International airports body urges caution over foreign investment in Ibrahim Nasir International Airport', Minivan News, http://minivannewsarchive.com/politics/international-airports-body-urges-caution-over-foreign-investment-in-ibrahim-nasir-international-airport-58021, last accessed 3 Aug. 2015.

87. 'GMR wins arbitration case, tribunal deems airport deal was "valid and binding"', Minivan News, http://minivannewsarchive.com/politics/gmr-wins-arbitration-case-tribunal-deems-airport-deal-was-valid-and-binding-87209, last accessed 3 Aug. 2015.

88. 'Ruling coalition demand MDP "stop use of black magic, sexual and erotic tools", "not walk in groups of more than 10"', Minivan News, http://minivannewsarchive.com/politics/ruling-coalition-demand-mdp-stop-use-of-black-magic-sexual-and-erotic-tools-not-walk-in-groups-of-more-than-10-38514, last accessed 3 Aug. 2015.

89. 'Cabinet confirms decision to take over second MDP protest site at Usfasgandu', Minivan News, http://minivannewsarchive.com/politics/cabinet-confirms-decision-to-take-over-second-mdp-protest-site-at-usfasgandu-37066, last accessed 3 Aug. 2015.

90. 'Security forces clear MDP protest camp area', Minivan News, http://minivan-newsarchive.com/politics/live-update-security-forces-clear-mdp-protest-camp-area-33723,last accessed 3 Aug. 2015.

91. 'Condoms and black magic: police raid Usfasgandu', Minivan News, http://min-ivannewsarchive.com/politics/condoms-and-black-magic-police-raid-usfas-gandu-38178, last accessed 3 Aug. 2015.

92. 'Who turned out the light: Maldives' solar ambitions plunged into darkness', Minivan News, http://minivannewsarchive.com/politics/who-turned-out-the-light-maldives%e2%80%99-solar-ambitions-plunged-into-darkness-39667, last accessed 3 Aug. 2015.

93. '"Maldives cannot afford to be an inward looking, xenophobic country": former President Nasheed', Minivan News, http://minivannewsarchive.com/politics/maldives-cannot-afford-to-be-an-inward-looking-xenophobic-country-former-president-nasheed-61638, last accessed 3 Aug. 2015.

94. '"A country does not have to be invaded to lose its sovereignty": President Waheed', Minivan News, http://minivannewsarchive.com/politics/a-country-does-not-have-to-be-invaded-to-lose-its-sovereignty-president-waheed-61640, last accessed 3 Aug. 2015.

95. 'President Waheed met with angry protests during "bittersweet" campaign trip to Thinadhoo', Minivan News, http://minivannewsarchive.com/politics/presi-dent-waheed-met-with-angry-protests-during-bittersweet-campaign-trip-tothi-nadhoo-59422, last accessed 3 Aug. 2015.

96. 'Maldives June 2013 crisis', purported GCHQ tap of conversation between President Waheed, daughter and son-in-law, http://i.imgur.com/bJ4ycTq.jpg,%20http://i.imgur.com/nmYvZHy.jpg, last accessed 3 Aug. 2015.

97. 'Supposed GCHQ tap of President, daughter, son-in-law discusses martial law, foreign worker voting, "smear campaigns"', Minivan News, http://minivannews-archive.com/politics/supposed-gchq-tap-of-president-daughter-son-in-law-dis-cusses-martial-law-foreign-worker-voting-smear-campaigns-61288, last accessed 3 Aug. 2015.

98. 'DQP, Dr Hassan Saeed quit President Waheed's coalition: "too much family, expatriate influence"', Minivan News, http://minivannewsarchive.com/politics/dqp-dr-hassan-saeed-quit-president-waheed%e2%80%99s-coalition-%e2%80%9ctoo-much-family-expatriate-influence%e2%80%9d-61253, last accessed 3 Aug. 2015.

99. 'President Waheed commutes sentences of 35 convicts, approves lump sum pay-ment for ministers', Minivan News, http://minivannewsarchive.com/politics/president-waheed-commutes-sentences-of-35-convicts-approves-lump-sum-pay-ment-for-ministers-71080, last accessed 3 Aug. 2015.

100. 'Government paying Grant Thornton £4.6 million to halt STO oil trade inves-tigation', Minivan News, http://minivannewsarchive.com/politics/government-paying-grant-thornton-4–6-million-to-halt-sto-oil-trade-investigation-65581, last accessed 3 Aug. 2015.

101. 'Yameen implicated in STO blackmarket oil trade with Burmese junta, alleges The Week', Minivan News, http://minivannewsarchive.com/politics/yameen-implicated-in-sto-blackmarket-oil-trade-with-burmese-junta-alleges-the-week-16046, last accessed 3 Aug. 2015.

102. 'Speaker advises state institutions that Waheed no longer in power', Minivan News, http://minivannewsarchive.com/politics/speaker-advises-state-institutions-that-waheed-no-longer-in-power-71384, last accessed 3 Aug. 2015.

103. 'President says he is "unconcerned" as Maldives back on CMAG formal agenda', Minivan News, http://minivannewsarchive.com/politics/maldives-back-on-cmag-formal-agenda-president-says-he-is-unconcerned-71572, last accessed 3 Aug. 2015.

104. 'President Waheed to leave Maldives indefinitely two days before elections', Minivan News, http://minivannewsarchive.com/politics/president-waheed-to-leave-maldives-indefinitely-two-days-before-elections-71569, last accessed 3 Aug. 2015.

105. 'President Waheed to back PPM in second round, stepping down as GIP head', Minivan News, http://minivannewsarchive.com/politics/president-waheed-to-back-ppm-in-second-round-stepping-down-as-gip-head-65464, last accessed 3 Aug. 2015.

106. 'Issues in Democratic Transition: Recent Experiences from Maldives and some Arab States', Lee Kuan Yew School of Public Policy, Youtube, https://www.youtube.com/watch?v=YLhY9Q5Zf14, last accessed 3 Aug. 2015.

10. ELECTION

1. 'Former President Nasheed submits candidacy for 2013 Presidential Elections', Minivan News, http://minivannewsarchive.com/politics/former-president-nasheed-submits-candidacy-for-2013-presidential-elections-61227, last accessed 3 Aug. 2015.

2. '"Costed and Budgeted 2013–2018': MDP manifesto launched", Minivan News, http://minivannewsarchive.com/politics/costed-and-budgeted-2013–2018-mdp-manifesto-launched-63365, last accessed 3 Aug. 2015.

3. 'PPM manifesto released to criticism over economic plans', Minivan News, http://minivannewsarchive.com/politics/ppm-manifesto-released-to-criticism-over-economic-plans-64552, last accessed 3 Aug. 2015.

4. 'Q&A: Former President Mohamed Nasheed', Minivan News, http://minivannewsarchive.com/politics/qa-former-president-mohamed-nasheed-64583, last accessed 3 Aug. 2015.

5. 'Vote-buying, political polarisation, credibility critical challenges for 2013 elections: Transparency Maldives report', Minivan News, http://minivannewsarchive.com/politics/vote-buying-political-polarisation-credibility-critical-challenges-for-2013-elections-transparency-maldives-report-55352, last accessed 3 Aug. 2015.

6. 'Covering Kaashidhoo's 'buy-election', *Minivan News*, http://minivannewsarchive.com/politics/covering-kaashidhoos-buy-election-35954, last accessed 3 Aug. 2015.

7. 'Loyalty, support, money: The motivation behind Male's political decoration', *Minivan News*, http://minivannewsarchive.com/politics/loyalty-support-money-the-motivation-behind-males-political-decoration-64518, last accessed 3 Aug. 2015.

8. 'Police summon white magic practitioner to investigate possible cursed coconut', *Minivan News*, http://minivannewsarchive.com/politics/police-summon-white-magic-practitioner-to-investigate-possible-cursed-coconut-64483, last accessed 3 Aug. 2015.

9. 'Parents object to ballot box in Guraidhoo School over allegations of black magic', *Minivan News*, http://minivannewsarchive.com/politics/parents-object-to-ballot-box-in-guraidhoo-school-over-allegations-of-black-magic-61404, last accessed 3 Aug. 2015.

10. 'Cursed coconuts on Fuvahmulah allegedly used to disrupt elections', *Minivan News*, http://minivannewsarchive.com/politics/cursed-coconuts-on-fuvahmulah-allegedly-used-to-disrupt-elections-64726, last accessed 3 Aug. 2015.

11. 'Maldives vote-rigging row after 'black magic coconut' is found near polling booth', *The Independent*, http://www.independent.co.uk/news/world/asia/maldives-voterigging-row-after-black-magic-coconut-is-found-near-polling-booth-8800993.html, last accessed 3 Aug. 2015.

12. 'Commonwealth, Indian election observers praise conduct of polls', *Minivan News*, http://minivannewsarchive.com/politics/commonwealth-indian-election-observers-praise-conduct-of-polls-65167, last accessed 3 Aug. 2015.

13. '"God Willing, Gasim will be President on November 11": Gasim', *Minivan News*, http://minivannewsarchive.com/politics/god-willing-gasim-will-be-president-on-november-11-gasim-65748, last accessed 3 Aug. 2015.

14. 'Pronounced dead: 'Deceased' voters found to be alive', *Minivan News*, http://minivannewsarchive.com/politics/pronounced-dead-deceased-voters-found-to-be-alive-70355, last accessed 3 Aug. 2015.

15. 'Supreme Court ejects lawyer defending Elections Commission', *Minivan News*, http://minivannewsarchive.com/politics/supreme-court-ejects-lawyers-defending-elections-commission-66524, last accessed 3 Aug. 2015.

16. 'Elections Commission announces final first round election results', *Minivan News*, http://minivannewsarchive.com/politics/elections-commission-announces-final-first-round-election-results-65539, last accessed 3 Aug. 2015.

17. 'Supreme Court issues injunction indefinitely delaying election run-off', *Minivan News*, http://minivannewsarchive.com/politics/supreme-court-issues-injunction-indefinitely-delaying-election-run-off-66448, last accessed 3 Aug. 2015.

18. 'Global concern as Maldivian court suspends presidential election', *Minivan News*, http://minivannewsarchive.com/politics/global-condemnation-as-maldivian-court-suspends-presidential-election-66642, last accessed 3 Aug. 2015.

19. 'International observers should "help, not hinder" state institutions: Foreign Ministry', Minivan News, http://minivannewsarchive.com/politics/international-observers-should-%e2%80%9chelp-not-hinder-state-institutions-foreign-minis-try-66180, last accessed 3 Aug. 2015.

20. 'AG's election intervention constitutional, yet morally questionable: senior legal source', Minivan News, http://minivannewsarchive.com/politics/ags-election-intervention-constitutional-yet-%e2%80%9cmoral-grounds%e2%80%9d-ques-tionable-senior-legal-source-66335, last accessed 3 Aug. 2015.

21. 'Elections Commission declares unable to conduct "free and fair vote" on Sept 28, as police surround building', Minivan News, http://minivannewsarchive.com/politics/elections-commission-says-unable-to-conduct-free-and-fair-vote-on-sept-28-as-police-surround-building-66965, last accessed 3 Aug. 2015.

22. "Indian High Commissioner summoned to foreign ministry over 'interference'", Haveeeru News, http://www.haveeru.com.mv/news/51427, last accessed 3 Aug. 2015.

23. 'Supreme Court annuls first round of presidential elections', Minivan News, http://minivannewsarchive.com/politics/supreme-court-annuls-first-round-of-presiden-tial-elections-67952, last accessed 3 Aug. 2015.

24. 'Observing the Supreme Court in action', Minivan News, http://minivannewsar-chive.com/politics/observing-the-supreme-court-in-action-68113, last accessed 3 Aug. 2015.

25. 'ACC forwards phone bill corruption case against Supreme Court Judge', http://minivannewsarchive.com/politics/acc-forwards-phone-bill-corruption-case-against-supreme-court-judge-61696, last accessed 3 Aug. 2015.

26. 'Dr Ahmed Abdulla Didi—Video Profile', Youtube, https://www.youtube.com/watch?v=wFqXa-U0xUQ, last accessed 3 Aug. 2015.

27. 'JSC rejects no-confidence motion against Chair Adam Mohamed', Minivan News, http://minivannewsarchive.com/politics/jsc-rejects-no-confidence-motion-against-chair-adam-mohamed-63416, last accessed 3 Aug. 2015.

28. 'Supreme Court Verdict: Points of Note', Dhivehi Sitee, http://www.dhivehisi-tee.com/election-2013/comment-piece/supreme-court-verdict-points-note/, last accessed 3 Aug. 2015.

29. 'Elections Commissioner slams Supreme Court, police, PPM, JP over annulment of first round', Minivan News, http://minivannewsarchive.com/politics/elections-commissioner-slams-supreme-court-police-ppm-jp-over-annulment-of-first-round-69289, last accessed 3 Aug. 2015.

30. 'Eligible voters listed as underage in secret police report', Minivan News, http://minivannewsarchive.com/news-in-brief/eligible-voters-listed-as-underage-in-secret-police-report-71087, last accessed 3 Aug. 2015.

31. 'Translation: Election annulment's confidential police report', Minivan News, http://minivannewsarchive.com/politics/translation-election-annulments-con-fidential-police-report-70519, last accessed 3 Aug. 2015.

32. 'Elections Commissioner slams Supreme Court, police, PPM, JP over annulment of first round', Minivan News, http://minivannewsarchive.com/politics/elections-commissioner-slams-supreme-court-police-ppm-jp-over-annulment-of-first-round-69289, last accessed 3 Aug. 2015.

33. 'Expert UN review dismisses secret police report used to justify annulment of Sept 7 polls', Minivan News, http://minivannewsarchive.com/politics/expert-un-review-dismisses-secret-police-report-used-to-justify-annulment-of-sept-7-polls-71078, last accessed 3 Aug. 2015.

34. '"Potential for trouble": UN Security Council briefed on Maldives', Minivan News, http://minivannewsarchive.com/politics/%e2%80%9cpotential-for-trouble%e2%80%9d-un-security-council-briefed-on-maldives-67701, last accessed 3 Aug. 2015.

35. 'Supreme Court orders Elections Commission to restart re-registration process', Minivan News, http://minivannewsarchive.com/politics/supreme-court-orders-elections-commission-to-restart-registration-process-68299, last accessed 3 Aug. 2015.

36. 'Elections Commission unable to reach PPM and JP leaders to sign off on electoral register', Minivan News, http://minivannewsarchive.com/politics/elections-commission-unable-to-reach-ppm-and-jp-leaders-to-sign-off-on-electoral-register-68879, last accessed 3 Aug. 2015.

37. 'October 19 election to proceed as planned: Elections Commission', Minivan News, http://minivannewsarchive.com/politics/october-19-election-to-proceed-as-planned-elections-commission-68987, last accessed 3 Aug. 2015.

38. '"We should be angry, not disheartened": Nasheed', Minivan News, http://minivannewsarchive.com/politics/live-police-move-to-halt-election-ec-69017, last accessed 3 Aug. 2015.

39. 'Maldivian Democracy on the Brink', Haveeru News, http://www.haveeru.com.mv/opinion/51993, last accessed 3 Aug. 2015.

40. '"Supreme Court is subverting the democratic process": UN High Commissioner', Minivan News, http://minivannewsarchive.com/politics/%e2%80%9csupreme-court-is-subverting-the-democratic-process%e2%80%9d-un-high-commissioner-for-human-rights-70326, last accessed 3 Aug. 2015.

41. 'Translation of Chief Justice Ahmed Faiz's response to UN High Commissioner for Human Rights', Minivan News, http://minivannews.com/files/2013/10/Chief-Justices-response-to-Navi-Pillay.pdf, last accessed 3 Aug. 2015.

42. 'Chief Justice threatens action against dissemination of "invalid information"', Minivan News, http://minivannewsarchive.com/politics/chief-justice-threatens-action-against-dissemination-of-invalid-information-69989, last accessed 3 Aug. 2015.

43. 'Raajje TV destroyed in arson attack', Minivan News, http://minivannewsarchive.com/politics/raajje-tv-destroyed-in-arson-attack-67833, last accessed 3 Aug. 2015.

44. 'Raajje TV returns to air with donated equipment, after station's firebombing',

Minivan News, http://minivannewsarchive.com/politics/raajje-tv-returns-to-air-with-donated-equipment-after-stations-firebombing-67884, last accessed 3 Aug. 2015.

45. 'No-confidence motion delayed after Attorney General calls in sick', Minivan News, http://minivannewsarchive.com/politics/no-confidence-motion-delayed-after-attorney-general-calls-in-sick-70022, last accessed 3 Aug. 2015.

46. 'Unknown pills discovered inside Majlis coffee machine', Minivan News, http://minivannewsarchive.com/politics/unknown-pills-discovered-inside-majlis-coffee-machine-70107, last accessed 3 Aug. 2015.

47. 'Defiant Attorney General Azima Shakoor voted out of office', Minivan News, http://minivannewsarchive.com/politics/defiant-attorney-general-azima-shakoor-voted-out-of-office-70179, last accessed 3 Aug. 2015.

48. 'Fuwad discharged from hospital, EC prepares for November 10 second round', Minivan News, http://minivannewsarchive.com/politics/fuwad-discharged-from-hospital-ec-prepares-for-november-10-second-round-70983, last accessed 3 Aug. 2015.

49. 'Maldivians convey "1000 Thanks" to the Elections Commission', Minivan News, http://minivannewsarchive.com/politics/maldivians-convey-%e2%80%9c1000-thanks%e2%80%9d-to-the-elections-commission-71033, last accessed 3 Aug. 2015.

50. 'Nasheed to face Yameen in run-off as polls mirror annulled Sept 7 results', Minivan News, http://minivannewsarchive.com/politics/nasheed-to-face-yameen-in-run-off-as-polls-mirror-annulled-sept-7-results-71269, last accessed 3 Aug. 2015.

51. 'Maldives Decides 2013—The re-vote', Minivan News, http://minivannewsarchive.com/politics/maldives-decides-2013-%E2%80%93-live-updates-71138, last accessed 3 Aug. 2015.

52. '"I do not want to stay in this position even a day beyond November 11": President Waheed', Minivan News, http://minivannewsarchive.com/politics/%e2%80%9ci-do-not-want-to-stay-in-this-position-even-a-day-beyond-november-11%e2%80%9d-president-waheed-69388, last accessed 3 Aug. 2015.

53. 'Supreme Court declares current president will remain past November 11', Minivan News, http://minivannewsarchive.com/news-in-brief/supreme-court-declares-current-president-will-remain-past-november-11–71243, last accessed 3 Aug. 2015.

54. 'International community obliged to delegitimise President Waheed: Nasheed', Minivan News, http://minivannewsarchive.com/politics/international-community-obliged-to-delegitimise-president-waheed-nasheed-71355, last accessed 3 Aug. 2015.

55. 'MNDF officers sign appeal not to obey government's orders following expiry of presidential term', Minivan News, http://minivannewsarchive.com/politics/mndf-officers-sign-appeal-not-to-obey-governments-orders-following-expiry-of-presidential-term-71225, last accessed 3 Aug. 2015.

56. 'Waheed's "unprecedented" decision to stay "has endangered the Maldivian people's right to elect a leader of their choice": US', Minivan News, http://minivannewsarchive.com/politics/waheeds-unprecedented-decision-to-stay-has-endangered-the-maldivian-people%e2%80%99s-right-to-elect-a-leader-of-their-choice-us-71469, last accessed 3 Aug. 2015.

57. 'Speaker advises state institutions that Waheed no longer in power', Minivan News, http://minivannewsarchive.com/politics/speaker-advises-state-institutions-that-waheed-no-longer-in-power-71384, last accessed 3 Aug. 2015.

58. 'Waheed arrived at President's Office with resignation statement but we advised him to stay, say ministers', Minivan News, http://minivannewsarchive.com/politics/waheed-arrived-at-presidents-office-with-resignation-statement-but-cabinet-advised-him-to-stay-say-ministers-71420, last accessed 3 Aug. 2015.

59. 'President Waheed to leave Maldives indefinitely two days before elections', Minivan News, http://minivannewsarchive.com/politics/president-waheed-to-leave-maldives-indefinitely-two-days-before-elections-71569, last accessed 3 Aug. 2015.

60. 'President Waheed delivers farewell addesss', Minivan News, http://minivannewsarchive.com/politics/president-waheed-delivers-farewell-address-71724, last accessed 3 Aug. 2015.

61. 'Other religions will not be allowed under MDP government, says Nasheed', Minivan News, http://minivannewsarchive.com/politics/other-religions-will-not-be-allowed-under-mdp-government-says-nasheed-70489, last accessed 3 Aug. 2015.

62. 'Gasim calls for "jihad" against "Nasheed's antics": local media', Minivan News, http://minivannewsarchive.com/politics/gasim-calls-for-%e2%80%9cjihad%e2%80%9d-against-%e2%80%9cnasheeds-antics%e2%80%9d-local-media-41574, last accessed 3 Aug. 2015.

63. 'Vote Yameen for "safety of the Ummah," says Gasim', Minivan News, http://minivannewsarchive.com/politics/vote-yameen-for-safety-of-the-ummah-says-gasim-71640, last accessed 3 Aug. 2015.

64. 'Yameen to become Maldives' 6th president', Minivan News, http://minivannewsarchive.com/politics/live-yameen-ahead-with-52-percent-as-maldives-awaits-provisional-results-71754, last accessed 3 Aug. 2015.

65. 'Abdulla Yameen wins Maldives 2013 presidential election with 51.39 per cent of the vote', Minivan News, http://minivannewsarchive.com/politics/abdulla-yameen-wins-maldives-2013-presidential-election-with-51–39-percent-of-the-vote-71981, last accessed 3 Aug. 2015.

EPILOGUE

1. 'Vigilante mobs abduct young men in push to identify online secular activists', Minivan News, http://minivannewsarchive.com/politics/vigilante-mobs-abduct-young-men-in-push-to-identify-online-secular-activists-86720, last accessed 3 Aug. 2015.

2. 'Run to the Roar', Middlebury Magazine, http://sites.middlebury.edu/middmag/2015/02/06/run-to-the-roar/2/, last accessed 3 Aug. 2015.

3. '"Not all crimes in the world are solvable": Home minister says on Rilwan's disappearance', Minivan News, http://minivannewsarchive.com/politics/%e2%80%9cnot-all-crimes-in-the-world-are-solvable%e2%80%9d-home-minister-says-on-rilwan%e2%80%99s-disappearance-90875, last accessed 3 Aug. 2015.

4. '200 searched and 79 arrested at music festival in Maldives', Minivan News, http://minivannewsarchive.com/society/200-searched-and-60-arrested-at-music-festival-in-maldives-82990, last accessed 3 Aug. 2015.

5. 'President makes creative arts optional after pressure from religious conservatives', Minivan News, http://minivannewsarchive.com/society/president-makes-creative-arts-optional-after-pressure-from-religious-conservatives-90672, last accessed 3 Aug. 2015.

6. 'Government eyes alternative fish export markets, Maldives fish to be labelled 'halal'', Minivan News, http://minivannewsarchive.com/business/government-eyes-alternative-fish-export-markets-maldives-fish-to-be-labelled-%e2%80%98halal%e2%80%99–72479, last accessed 3 Aug. 2015.

7. 'Parliament impeaches Vice President Dr Jameel in absentia', Minivan News, http://minivannewsarchive.com/politics/parliament-impeaches-vice-president-dr-jameel-in-absentia-101143#sthash.eRTQv7T2.dpuf, last accessed 3 Aug. 2015.

8. 'Artur brothers "direct threat to national security": MP Fahmy', Minivan News, http://minivannewsarchive.com/politics/artur-brothers-direct-threat-to-national-security-mp-fahmy-55624, last accessed 3 Aug. 2015.

9. 'What we talk about when we talk about independence', Dhivehi Sitee, http://www.dhivehisitee.com/guest-contributors/what-we-talk-about-when-we-talk-about-independence/, last accessed 3 Aug. 2015.

10. 'Former President Nasheed found guilty of terrorism, sentenced to 13 years in prison', Minivan News, http://minivannewsarchive.com/politics/former-president-nasheed-found-guilty-of-terrorism-sentenced-to-13-years-in-prison-93263', last accessed 3 Aug. 2015.

11. 'Maldives hires US Lobbyist Podesta Group for US$300,000', Minivan News, http://maldivesindependent.com/politics/maldives-hires-us-lobbyist-podesta-group-for-us300000-117660, last accessed 1 October 2015.